When Pigs Fly

Other *Pearls Before Swine* Collections

50,000,000 Pearls Fans Can't Be Wrong
The Saturday Evening Pearls
Macho Macho Animals
The Sopratos
Da Brudderhood of Zeeba Zeeba Eata
The Ratvolution Will Not Be Televised
Nighthogs
This Little Piggy Stayed Home
BLTs Taste So Darn Good

Treasuries

Pearls Sells Out
The Crass Menagerie
Lions and Tigers and Crocs, Oh My!
Sgt. Piggy's Lonely Hearts Club Comic

Gift Book

Da Crockydile Book o' Frendsheep

When Pigs Fly

A *Pearls Before Swine* Collection

by Stephan Pastis

Andrews McMeel
Publishing, LLC
Kansas City • Sydney • London

Pearls Before Swine is distributed internationally by United Feature Syndicate.

When Pigs Fly copyright © 2010 by Stephan Pastis. All rights reserved. Printed in China. No part of this book may be used or reproduced in any manner whatsoever without written permission except in the case of reprints in the context of reviews.

Andrews McMeel Publishing, LLC
an Andrews McMeel Universal company
1130 Walnut Street, Kansas City, Missouri 64106

www.andrewsmcmeel.com

13 14 15 16 17 SDB 10 9 8 7 6 5 4 3 2

ISBN: 978-0-7407-9737-8

Library of Congress Control Number: 2010921944

Pearls Before Swine can be viewed on the Internet at
www.pearlscomic.com.

These strips appeared in newspapers from November 17, 2008, to August 23, 2009.

Introduction

In my junior year of college, I moved out of the dorms and got my first apartment with my friend Raul.

He was bigger than me.

For dinner, Raul would often eat a can of beans straight out of the can.

Every time he ate his can of beans, he would look over at me and say the same thing:

"If the world blew up right now and we were the only survivors around for miles, and all we had left was this one can of beans, the can would be mine because I'm bigger than you, and you would starve."

I'm sure that for most people, light dinner conversation does not include apocalyptic fights to the death, but for me, the "beans" hypothetical had a stark poetic beauty to it.

And in the twenty years since, I have found myself applying the "can of beans" test to almost everyone I meet. Especially cartoonists.

It's easy to do because every year professional cartoonists meet at an annual awards banquet called the Reubens. While most attendees use the event to reconnect and chat with cartoonists they haven't seen for a year, I use it to apply the "can of beans" test to every cartoonist I see.

This up-close-and-personal view of the cartoonists has allowed me to categorize all cartoonists into one of two lists: List "A" and List "B." List "A" contains the cartoonists whose can of beans I could take. List "B" contains the cartoonists who could take *my* can.

Here is List "A":

- Mark Tatulli (*Lio*): Short and feisty, but not feisty enough. Can is mine.
- Rick Kirkman (*Baby Blues*): Big but aging. Can is mine.
- Bill Amend (*FoxTrot*): Rail thin. Could take his can and perhaps his spoon as well.
- Jeff Keane (*Family Circus*): Big but slow. Could take his can and flee.
- Patrick McDonnell (*Mutts*): Too sweet to fight back. Advantage: Mine.

- Dave Coverly (*Speed Bump*): Even thinner than Amend. Could take his can and perhaps even make him cry.
- Jerry Scott (*Zits*/*Baby Blues*): So distracted by having to come up with fourteen gags every week, he'd have no time to protect can. Can mine.
- Brian Crane (*Pickles*): As nice as McDonnell. No beans for him.
- Mike Peters (*Mother Goose and Grimm*): Decent size, but easily distracted. Would forget he even had can.

Here is List "B":

- Darby Conley (*Get Fuzzy*): Big. Played rugby. Can is his.
- Jim Davis (*Garfield*): Not particularly big, but could pay someone to take my can.
- Cathy Guisewite (*Cathy*): Tiny, thin, but ridiculously charming. Would make me *want* to give her my can.
- Tom Richmond (*Mad Magazine*): Huge. Works out. I'd give him the can *and* Amend's spoon.
- Garry Trudeau (*Doonesbury*): Not particularly strong, but I'd hand him my can for a drawing of Uncle Duke.
- Dan Piraro (*Bizarro*): Short, but freakishly smart. Would somehow convince me giving him my can was in my best interest.
- Scott Adams (*Dilbert*): Not big either, but once trained to be hypnotist. Would give him my can and not know why.

As for Raul, the originator of the "beans" test, the last I heard he was living in Idaho. Which is good. Because I live in California. So if the world were to blow up today, it wouldn't be *him* I'd be fighting for the can.

In fact, with any luck, this cataclysmic event will occur while I'm at the Reubens. I say that because the Reubens allows you to pick who you sit next to.

And I'm picking the seat between Bill Amend and Dave Coverly.

Let the bean wars begin.

Stephan Pastis
September 2010

For Raul, the Genius Behind the Beans Test

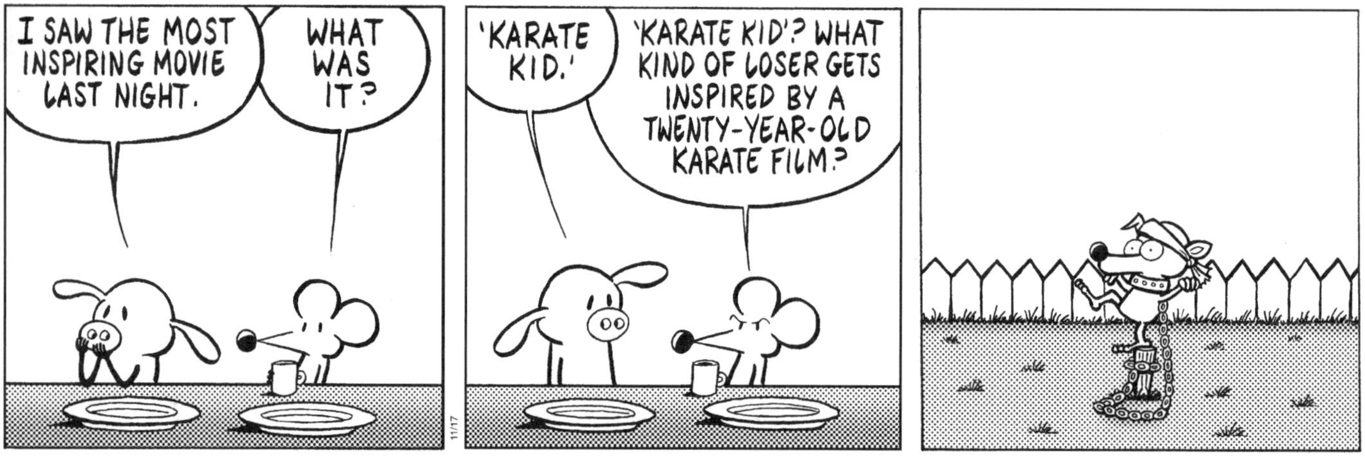
I SAW THE MOST INSPIRING MOVIE LAST NIGHT.
WHAT WAS IT?
'KARATE KID.'
'KARATE KID'? WHAT KIND OF LOSER GETS INSPIRED BY A TWENTY-YEAR-OLD KARATE FILM?

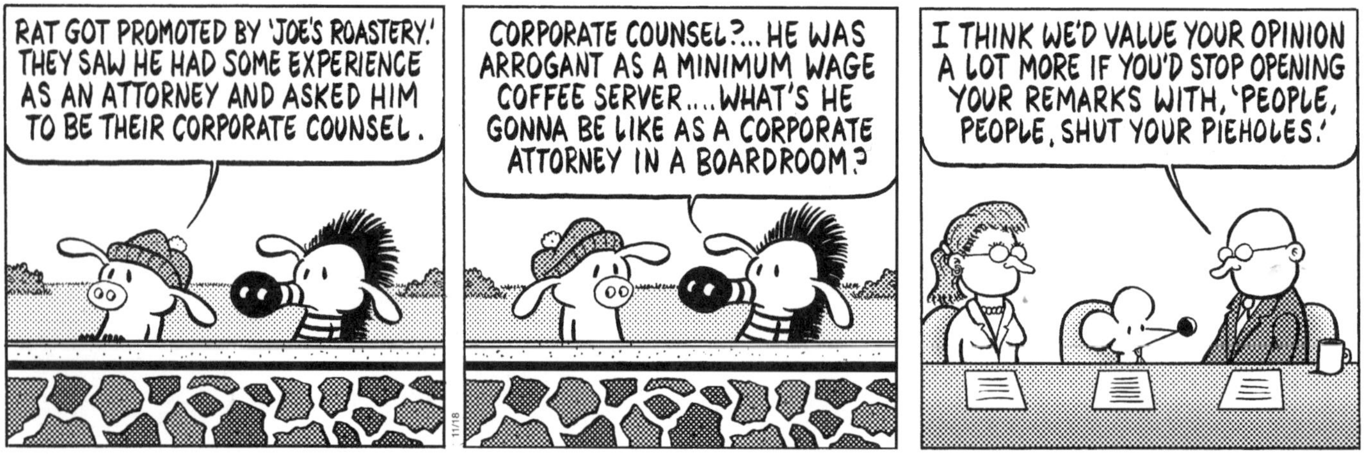
RAT GOT PROMOTED BY 'JOE'S ROASTERY.' THEY SAW HE HAD SOME EXPERIENCE AS AN ATTORNEY AND ASKED HIM TO BE THEIR CORPORATE COUNSEL.
CORPORATE COUNSEL?... HE WAS ARROGANT AS A MINIMUM WAGE COFFEE SERVER.... WHAT'S HE GONNA BE LIKE AS A CORPORATE ATTORNEY IN A BOARDROOM?
I THINK WE'D VALUE YOUR OPINION A LOT MORE IF YOU'D STOP OPENING YOUR REMARKS WITH, 'PEOPLE, PEOPLE, SHUT YOUR PIEHOLES.'

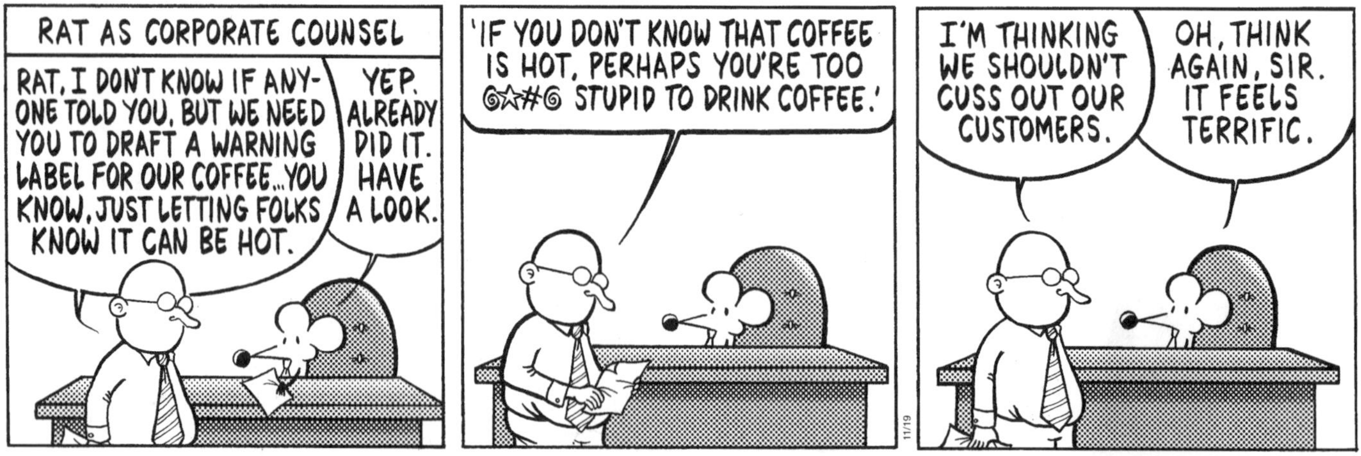
RAT AS CORPORATE COUNSEL
RAT, I DON'T KNOW IF ANYONE TOLD YOU, BUT WE NEED YOU TO DRAFT A WARNING LABEL FOR OUR COFFEE...YOU KNOW, JUST LETTING FOLKS KNOW IT CAN BE HOT.
YEP. ALREADY DID IT. HAVE A LOOK.
'IF YOU DON'T KNOW THAT COFFEE IS HOT, PERHAPS YOU'RE TOO @☆#@ STUPID TO DRINK COFFEE.'
I'M THINKING WE SHOULDN'T CUSS OUT OUR CUSTOMERS.
OH, THINK AGAIN, SIR. IT FEELS TERRIFIC.

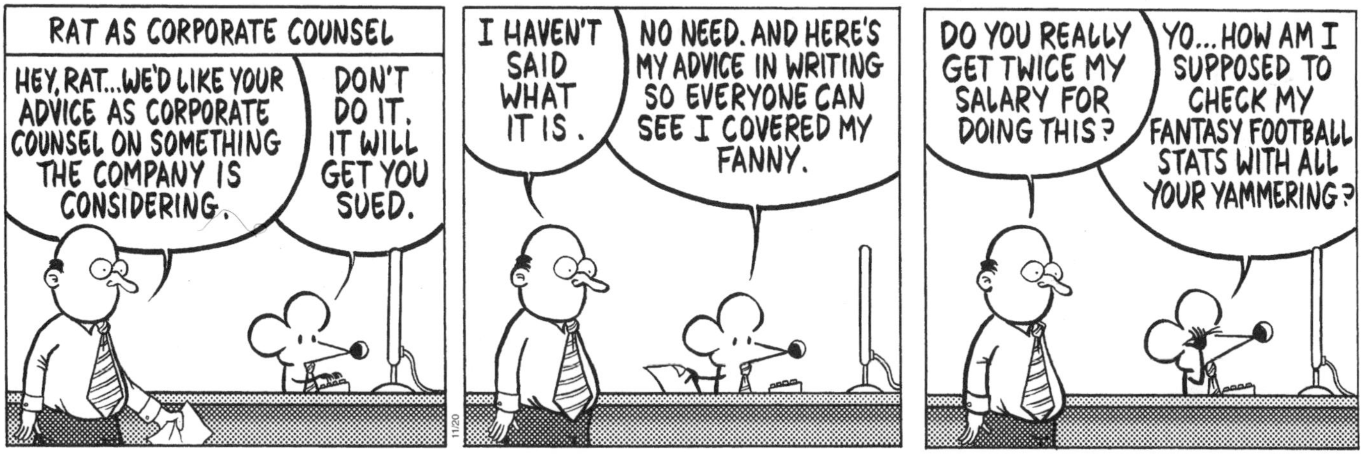
RAT AS CORPORATE COUNSEL
HEY, RAT...WE'D LIKE YOUR ADVICE AS CORPORATE COUNSEL ON SOMETHING THE COMPANY IS CONSIDERING.
DON'T DO IT. IT WILL GET YOU SUED.
I HAVEN'T SAID WHAT IT IS.
NO NEED. AND HERE'S MY ADVICE IN WRITING SO EVERYONE CAN SEE I COVERED MY FANNY.
DO YOU REALLY GET TWICE MY SALARY FOR DOING THIS?
YO...HOW AM I SUPPOSED TO CHECK MY FANTASY FOOTBALL STATS WITH ALL YOUR YAMMERING?

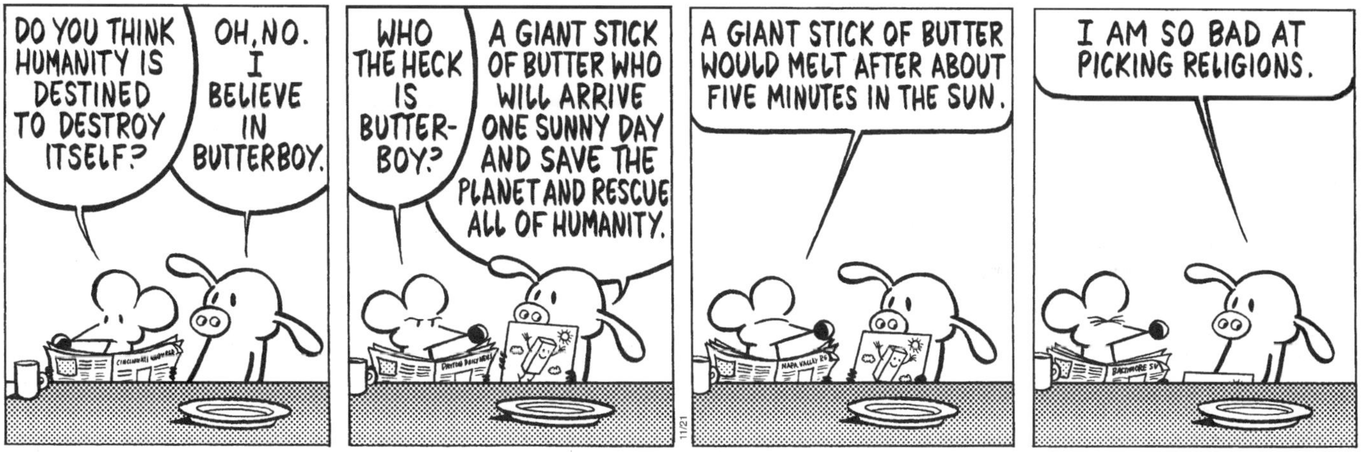
DO YOU THINK HUMANITY IS DESTINED TO DESTROY ITSELF?
OH, NO. I BELIEVE IN BUTTERBOY.
WHO THE HECK IS BUTTER-BOY?
A GIANT STICK OF BUTTER WHO WILL ARRIVE ONE SUNNY DAY AND SAVE THE PLANET AND RESCUE ALL OF HUMANITY.
A GIANT STICK OF BUTTER WOULD MELT AFTER ABOUT FIVE MINUTES IN THE SUN.
I AM SO BAD AT PICKING RELIGIONS.

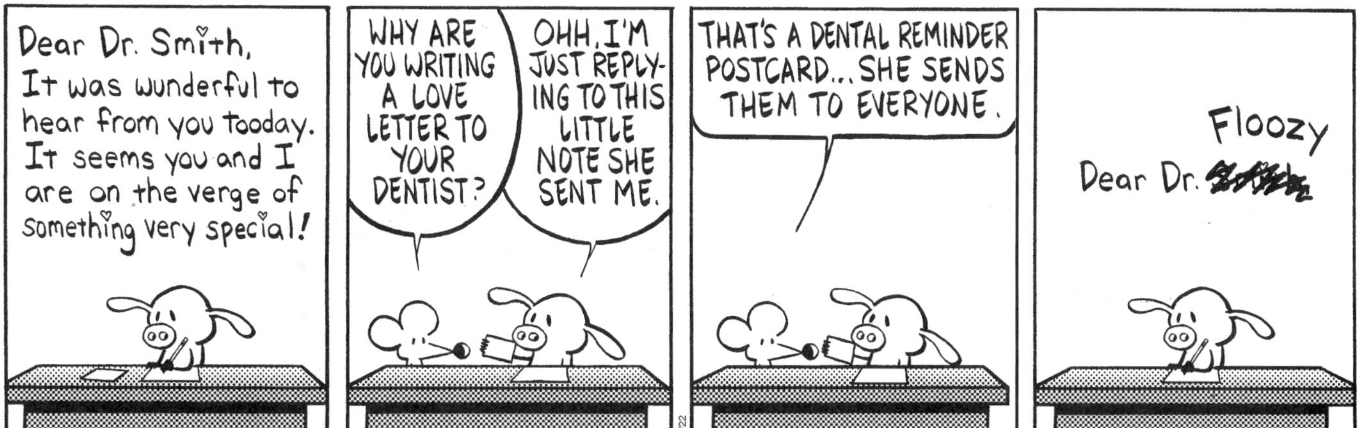
Dear Dr. Smith,
It was wunderful to hear from you tooday. It seems you and I are on the verge of something very special!
WHY ARE YOU WRITING A LOVE LETTER TO YOUR DENTIST?
OHH, I'M JUST REPLY-ING TO THIS LITTLE NOTE SHE SENT ME.
THAT'S A DENTAL REMINDER POSTCARD... SHE SENDS THEM TO EVERYONE.
Floozy
Dear Dr.

HI THERE, RAT... DID YOU MEET MY IMAGINARY FRIENDS? THIS IS BOB AND THIS IS LARRY.

WHATEVER, DUDE. I DON'T HAVE TIME FOR YOUR STUPID GAMES.

SORRY.

FORGET ABOUT IT... LISTEN, CAN I BORROW TEN BUCKS? I DON'T HAVE ANY CASH FOR LUNCH.

I'D LOVE TO HELP, BUT I HAVE TO SAVE MY MONEY. I GOT A $300 TICKET.

TICKET? FOR WHAT?

DRIVING IN THE CARPOOL LANE YESTERDAY.

YOU DUMB PIG... WHY'D YOU DO THAT?

BECAUSE I THOUGHT YOU ONLY NEEDED THREE PEOPLE IN THE CAR TO USE IT.

YOU DO.

WELL, NOW THAT WASN'T *OUR* EXPERIENCE, WAS IT, BOYS?

I THINK I'LL EAT AT HOME.

WHOA WHOA WHOA, BOB... LET'S NOT GO CALLING THE COP A RACIST.

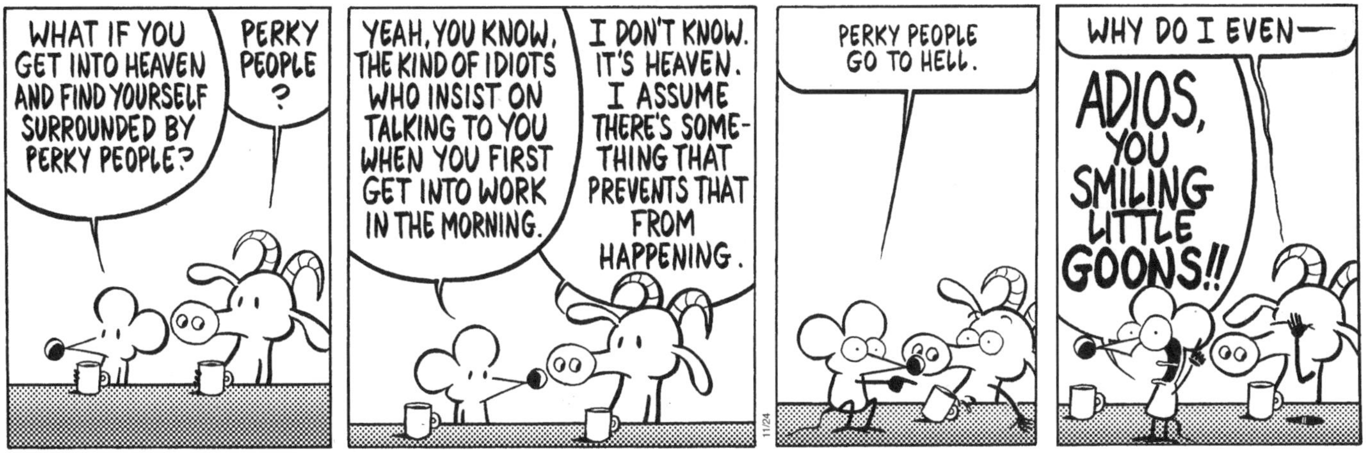
WHAT IF YOU GET INTO HEAVEN AND FIND YOURSELF SURROUNDED BY PERKY PEOPLE?
PERKY PEOPLE ?
YEAH, YOU KNOW, THE KIND OF IDIOTS WHO INSIST ON TALKING TO YOU WHEN YOU FIRST GET INTO WORK IN THE MORNING.
I DON'T KNOW. IT'S HEAVEN. I ASSUME THERE'S SOMETHING THAT PREVENTS THAT FROM HAPPENING.
PERKY PEOPLE GO TO HELL.
WHY DO I EVEN—
ADIOS, YOU SMILING LITTLE GOONS!!

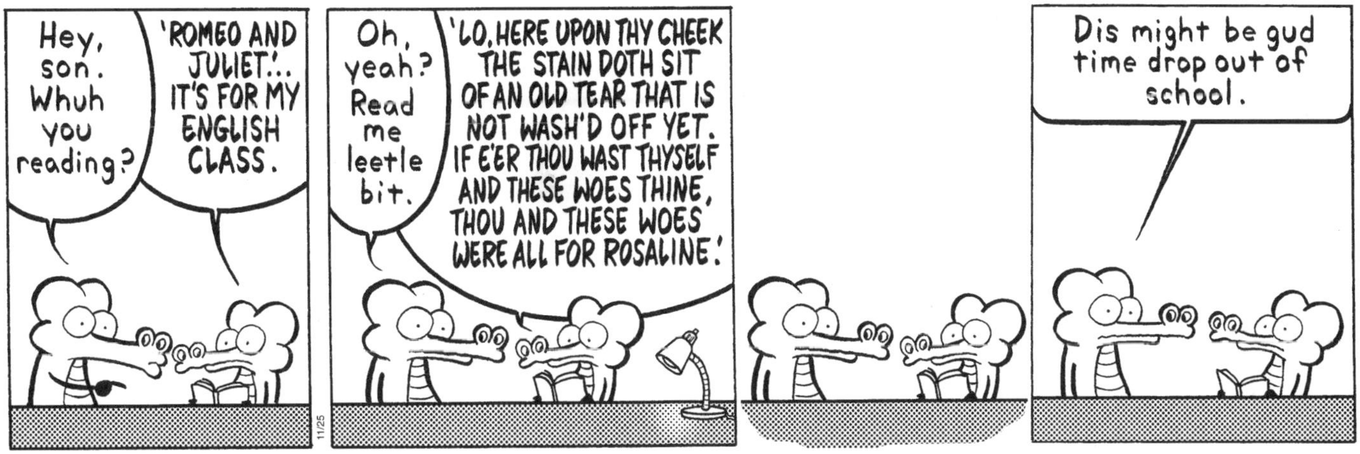
Hey, son. Whuh you reading?
'ROMEO AND JULIET'... IT'S FOR MY ENGLISH CLASS.
Oh, yeah? Read me leetle bit.
'LO, HERE UPON THY CHEEK THE STAIN DOTH SIT OF AN OLD TEAR THAT IS NOT WASH'D OFF YET. IF E'ER THOU WAST THYSELF AND THESE WOES THINE, THOU AND THESE WOES WERE ALL FOR ROSALINE.'
Dis might be gud time drop out of school.

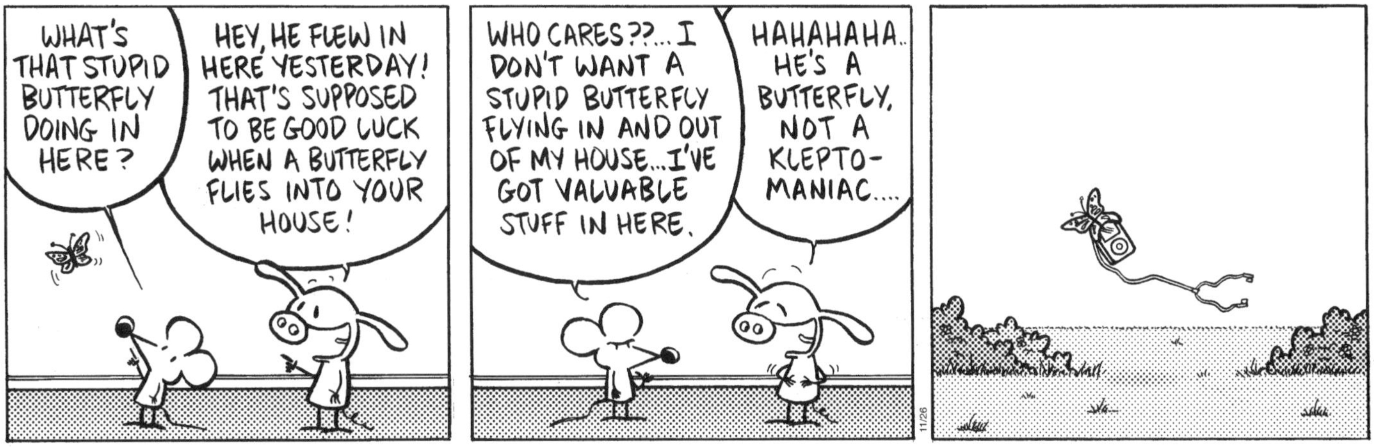
WHAT'S THAT STUPID BUTTERFLY DOING IN HERE?
HEY, HE FLEW IN HERE YESTERDAY! THAT'S SUPPOSED TO BE GOOD LUCK WHEN A BUTTERFLY FLIES INTO YOUR HOUSE!
WHO CARES??... I DON'T WANT A STUPID BUTTERFLY FLYING IN AND OUT OF MY HOUSE... I'VE GOT VALUABLE STUFF IN HERE.
HAHAHAHA.. HE'S A BUTTERFLY, NOT A KLEPTOMANIAC....

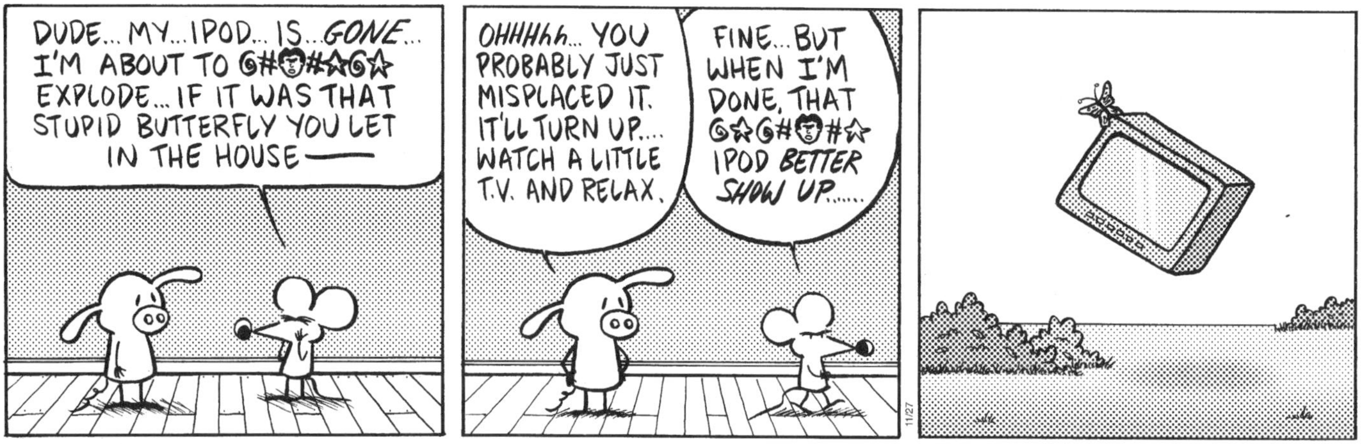
DUDE... MY... IPOD... IS... *GONE*... I'M ABOUT TO @#☺#☆@☆ EXPLODE... IF IT WAS THAT STUPID BUTTERFLY YOU LET IN THE HOUSE—
OHHHhh... YOU PROBABLY JUST MISPLACED IT. IT'LL TURN UP.... WATCH A LITTLE T.V. AND RELAX.
FINE... BUT WHEN I'M DONE, THAT @☆@#☺#☆ IPOD *BETTER SHOW UP*......
11/27

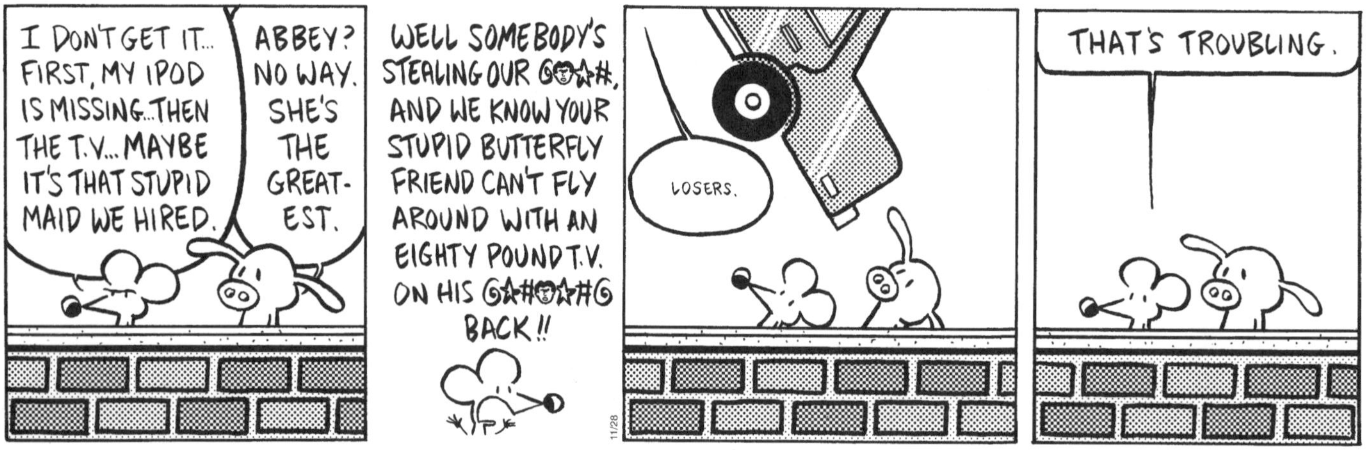
I DON'T GET IT... FIRST, MY IPOD IS MISSING... THEN THE T.V... MAYBE IT'S THAT STUPID MAID WE HIRED.
ABBEY? NO WAY. SHE'S THE GREAT-EST.
WELL SOMEBODY'S STEALING OUR @☺☆#, AND WE KNOW YOUR STUPID BUTTERFLY FRIEND CAN'T FLY AROUND WITH AN EIGHTY POUND T.V. ON HIS @☆#☺☆#@ BACK!!
11/28
LOSERS.
THAT'S TROUBLING.

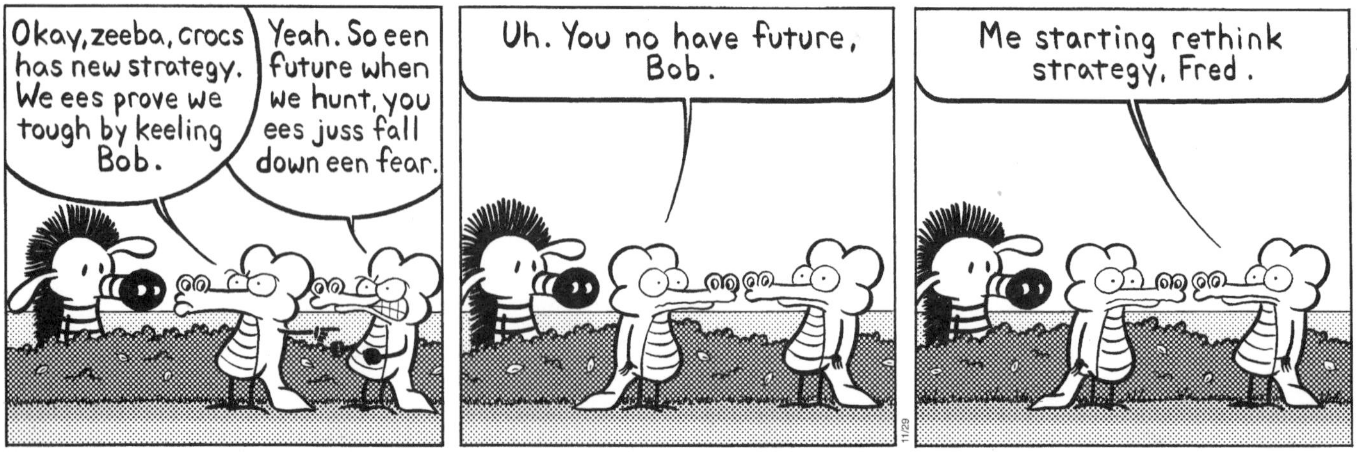
Okay, zeeba, crocs has new strategy. We ees prove we tough by keeling Bob.
Yeah. So een future when we hunt, you ees juss fall down een fear.
Uh. You no have future, Bob.
Me starting rethink strategy, Fred.
11/29

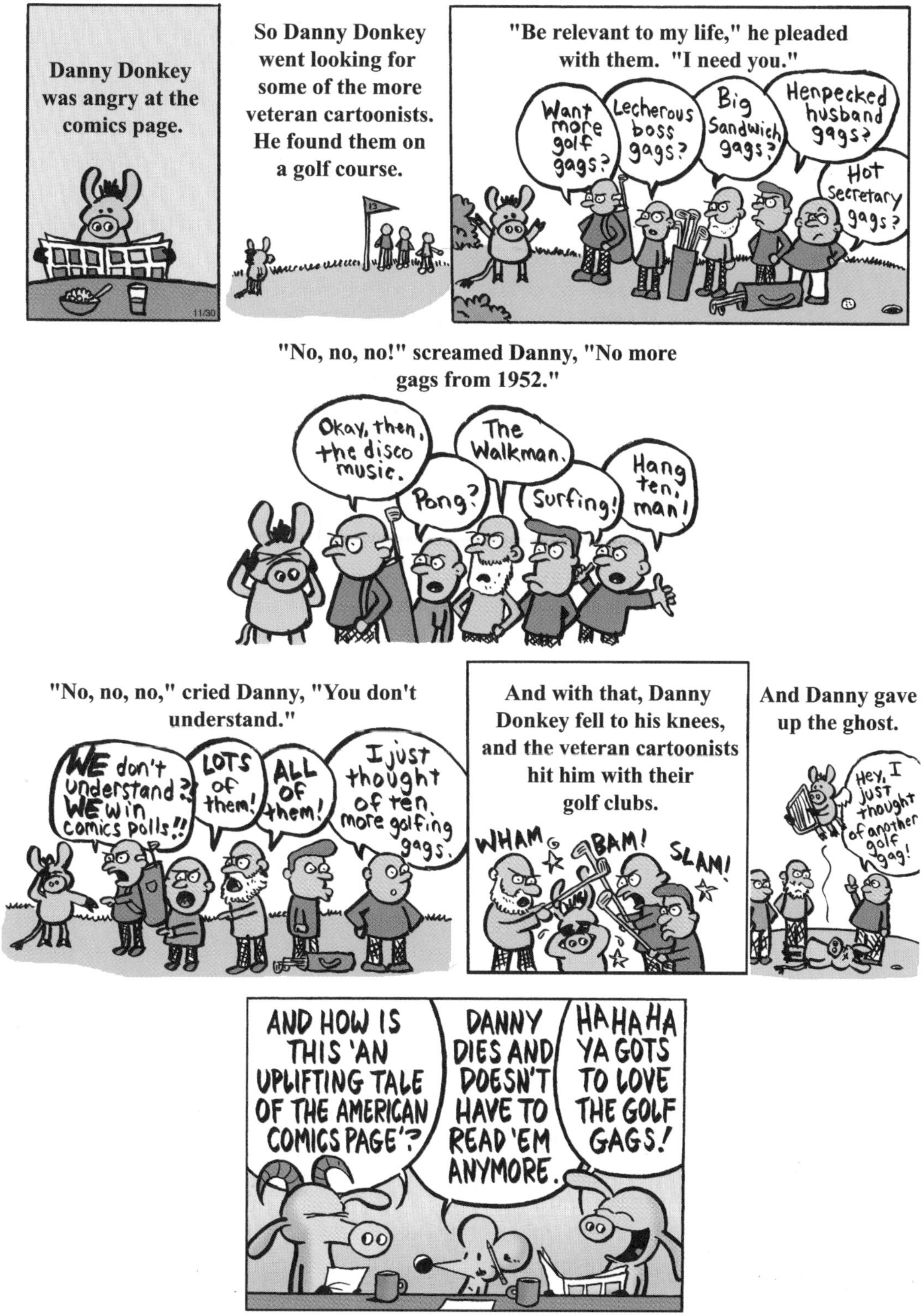
Danny Donkey was angry at the comics page.
11/30
So Danny Donkey went looking for some of the more veteran cartoonists. He found them on a golf course.
"Be relevant to my life," he pleaded with them. "I need you."
Want more golf gags?
Lecherous boss gags?
Big Sandwich gags?
Henpecked husband gags?
Hot secretary gags?
"No, no, no!" screamed Danny, "No more gags from 1952."
Okay, then, the disco music.
Pong?
The Walkman.
Surfing!
Hang ten, man!
"No, no, no," cried Danny, "You don't understand."
WE don't understand?! WE win comics polls!!
LOTS of them!
ALL of them!
I just thought of ten more golfing gags.
And with that, Danny Donkey fell to his knees, and the veteran cartoonists hit him with their golf clubs.
WHAM
BAM!
SLAM!
And Danny gave up the ghost.
Hey, I just thought of another golf gag!
AND HOW IS THIS 'AN UPLIFTING TALE OF THE AMERICAN COMICS PAGE'?
DANNY DIES AND DOESN'T HAVE TO READ 'EM ANYMORE.
HA HA HA YA GOTS TO LOVE THE GOLF GAGS!

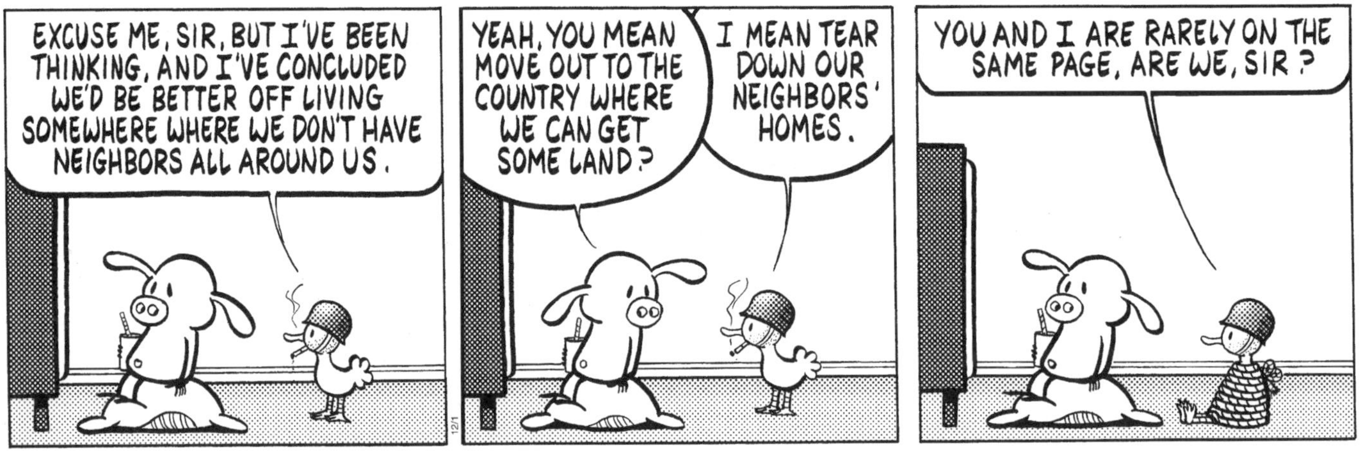
EXCUSE ME, SIR, BUT I'VE BEEN THINKING, AND I'VE CONCLUDED WE'D BE BETTER OFF LIVING SOMEWHERE WHERE WE DON'T HAVE NEIGHBORS ALL AROUND US.
YEAH, YOU MEAN MOVE OUT TO THE COUNTRY WHERE WE CAN GET SOME LAND?
I MEAN TEAR DOWN OUR NEIGHBORS' HOMES.
YOU AND I ARE RARELY ON THE SAME PAGE, ARE WE, SIR?

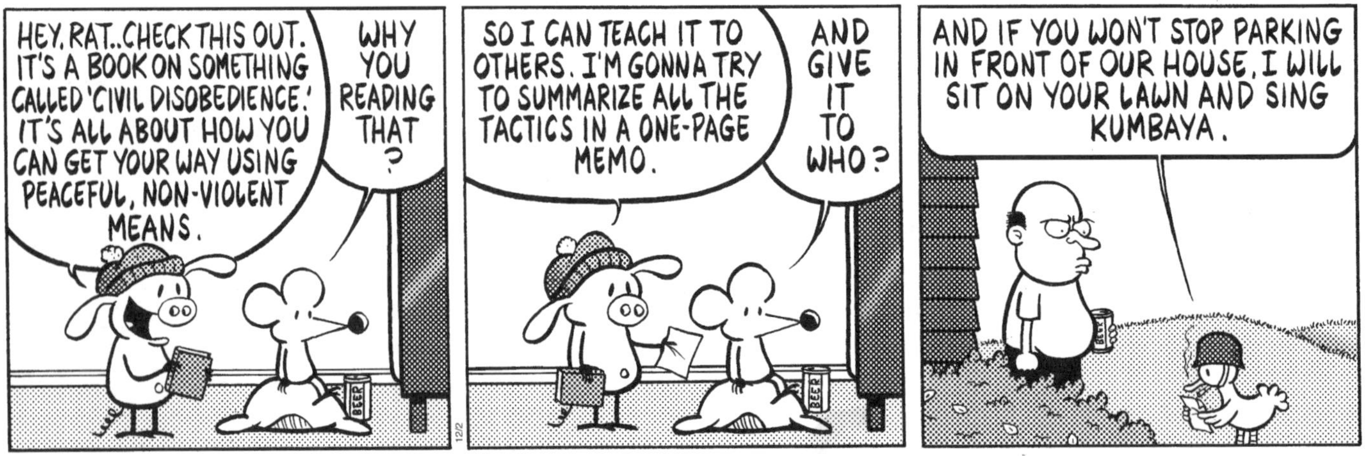
HEY, RAT..CHECK THIS OUT. IT'S A BOOK ON SOMETHING CALLED 'CIVIL DISOBEDIENCE.' IT'S ALL ABOUT HOW YOU CAN GET YOUR WAY USING PEACEFUL, NON-VIOLENT MEANS.
WHY YOU READING THAT?
SO I CAN TEACH IT TO OTHERS. I'M GONNA TRY TO SUMMARIZE ALL THE TACTICS IN A ONE-PAGE MEMO.
AND GIVE IT TO WHO?
AND IF YOU WON'T STOP PARKING IN FRONT OF OUR HOUSE, I WILL SIT ON YOUR LAWN AND SING KUMBAYA.

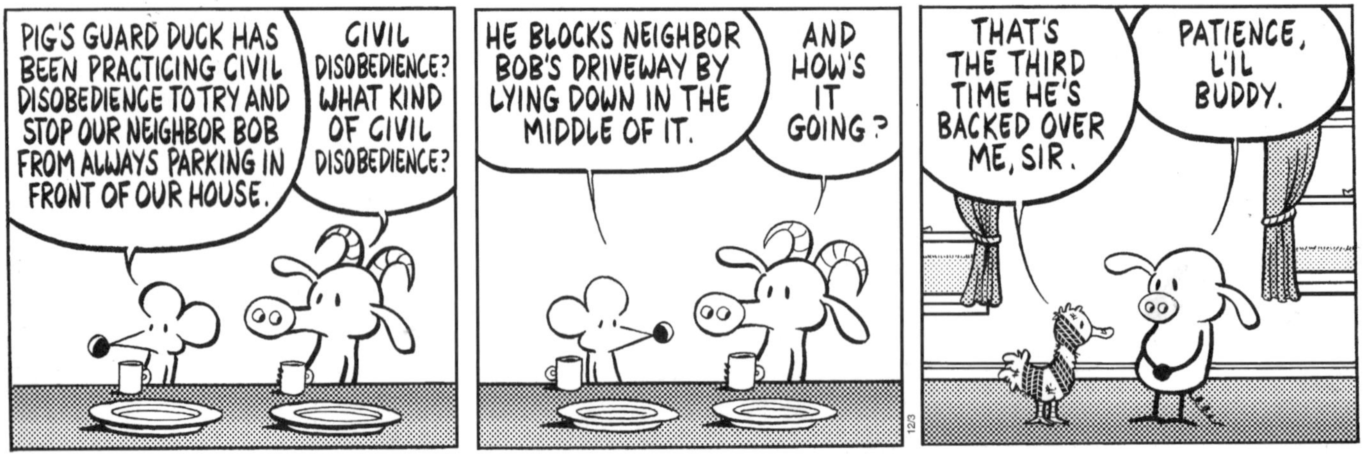
PIG'S GUARD DUCK HAS BEEN PRACTICING CIVIL DISOBEDIENCE TO TRY AND STOP OUR NEIGHBOR BOB FROM ALWAYS PARKING IN FRONT OF OUR HOUSE.
CIVIL DISOBEDIENCE? WHAT KIND OF CIVIL DISOBEDIENCE?
HE BLOCKS NEIGHBOR BOB'S DRIVEWAY BY LYING DOWN IN THE MIDDLE OF IT.
AND HOW'S IT GOING?
THAT'S THE THIRD TIME HE'S BACKED OVER ME, SIR.
PATIENCE, L'IL BUDDY.

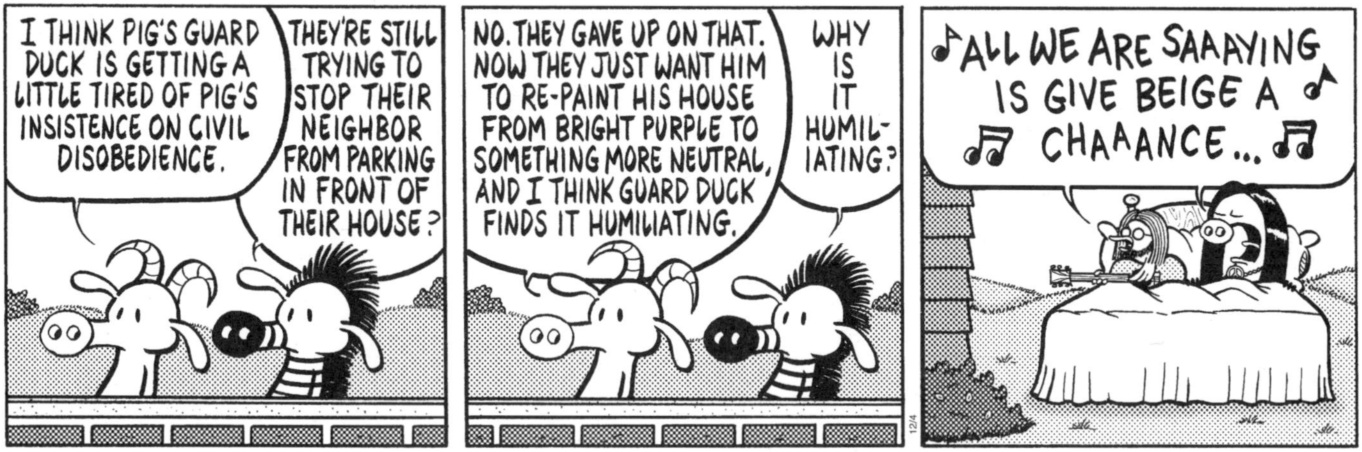
I THINK PIG'S GUARD DUCK IS GETTING A LITTLE TIRED OF PIG'S INSISTENCE ON CIVIL DISOBEDIENCE.
THEY'RE STILL TRYING TO STOP THEIR NEIGHBOR FROM PARKING IN FRONT OF THEIR HOUSE?
NO. THEY GAVE UP ON THAT. NOW THEY JUST WANT HIM TO RE-PAINT HIS HOUSE FROM BRIGHT PURPLE TO SOMETHING MORE NEUTRAL, AND I THINK GUARD DUCK FINDS IT HUMILIATING.
WHY IS IT HUMILIATING?
12/4
ALL WE ARE SAAAYING IS GIVE BEIGE A CHAAANCE...

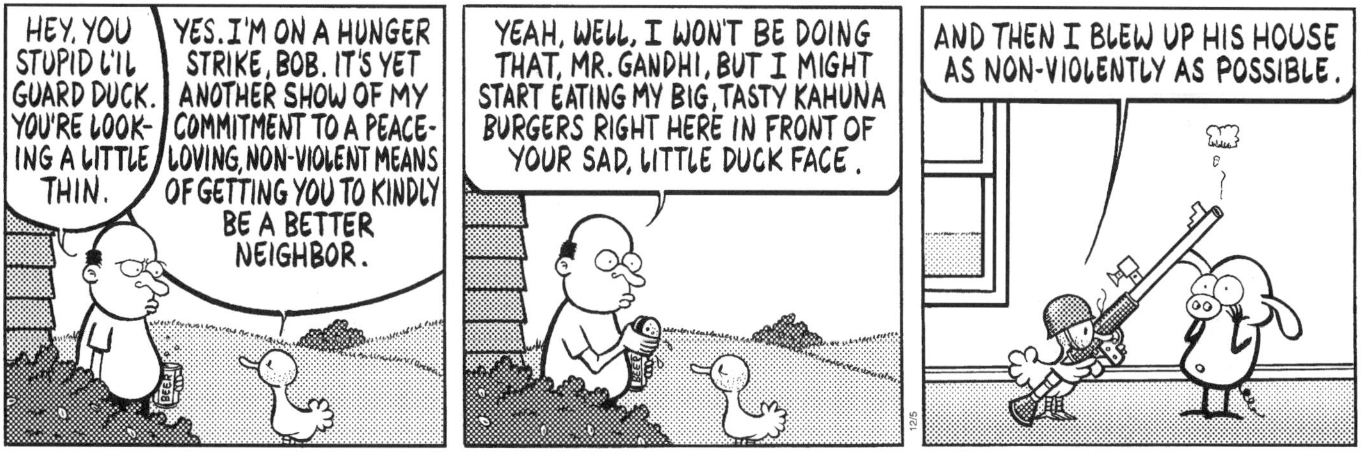
HEY, YOU STUPID L'IL GUARD DUCK. YOU'RE LOOKING A LITTLE THIN.
YES. I'M ON A HUNGER STRIKE, BOB. IT'S YET ANOTHER SHOW OF MY COMMITMENT TO A PEACE-LOVING, NON-VIOLENT MEANS OF GETTING YOU TO KINDLY BE A BETTER NEIGHBOR.
BEER
YEAH, WELL, I WON'T BE DOING THAT, MR. GANDHI, BUT I MIGHT START EATING MY BIG, TASTY KAHUNA BURGERS RIGHT HERE IN FRONT OF YOUR SAD, LITTLE DUCK FACE.
BEER
12/5
AND THEN I BLEW UP HIS HOUSE AS NON-VIOLENTLY AS POSSIBLE.

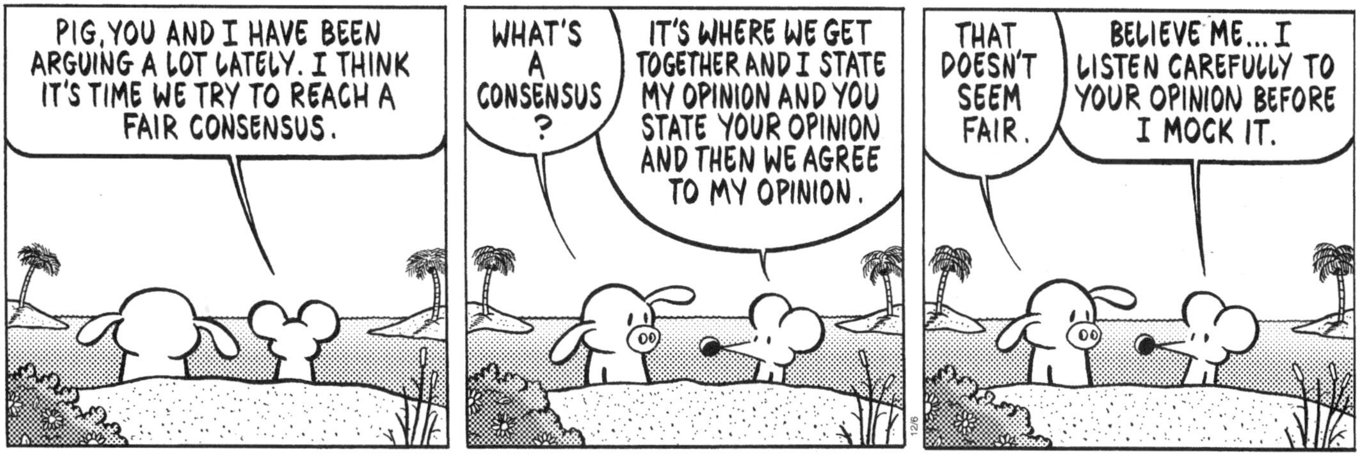
PIG, YOU AND I HAVE BEEN ARGUING A LOT LATELY. I THINK IT'S TIME WE TRY TO REACH A FAIR CONSENSUS.
WHAT'S A CONSENSUS?
IT'S WHERE WE GET TOGETHER AND I STATE MY OPINION AND YOU STATE YOUR OPINION AND THEN WE AGREE TO MY OPINION.
12/6
THAT DOESN'T SEEM FAIR.
BELIEVE ME... I LISTEN CAREFULLY TO YOUR OPINION BEFORE I MOCK IT.

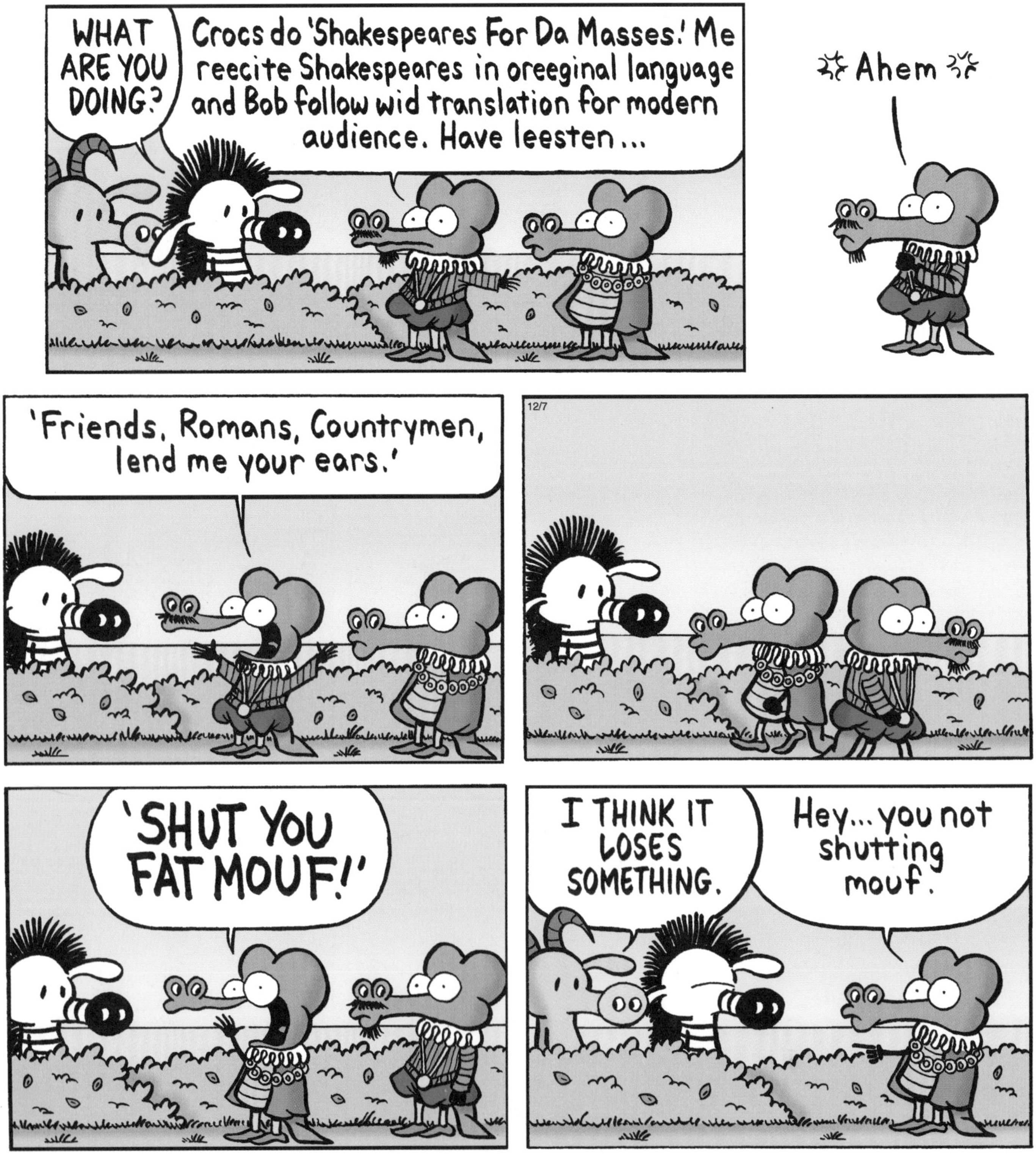
WHAT ARE YOU DOING?
Crocs do 'Shakespeares For Da Masses.' Me reecite Shakespeares in oreeginal language and Bob follow wid translation for modern audience. Have leesten...
Ahem
'Friends, Romans, Countrymen, lend me your ears.'
12/7
'SHUT YOU FAT MOUF!'
I THINK IT LOSES SOMETHING.
Hey... you not shutting mouf.

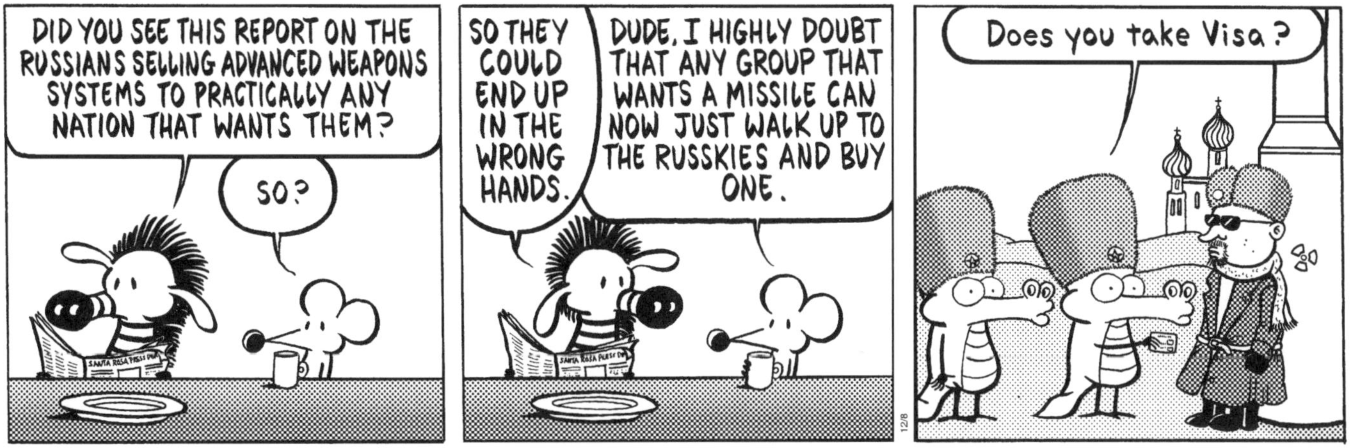
DID YOU SEE THIS REPORT ON THE RUSSIANS SELLING ADVANCED WEAPONS SYSTEMS TO PRACTICALLY ANY NATION THAT WANTS THEM?
SO?
SO THEY COULD END UP IN THE WRONG HANDS.
DUDE, I HIGHLY DOUBT THAT ANY GROUP THAT WANTS A MISSILE CAN NOW JUST WALK UP TO THE RUSSKIES AND BUY ONE.
12/8
Does you take Visa?

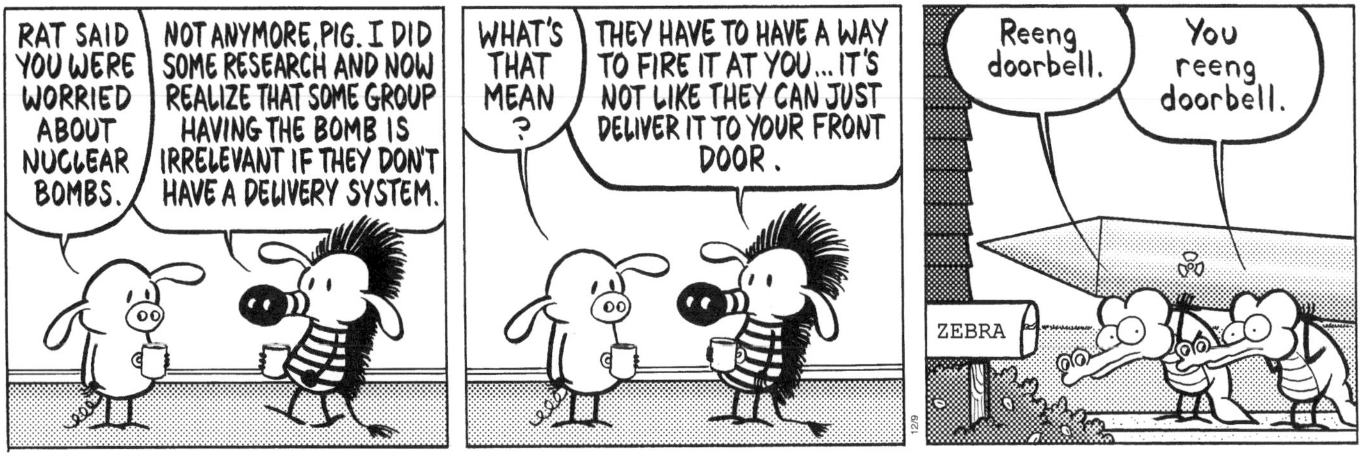
RAT SAID YOU WERE WORRIED ABOUT NUCLEAR BOMBS.
NOT ANYMORE, PIG. I DID SOME RESEARCH AND NOW REALIZE THAT SOME GROUP HAVING THE BOMB IS IRRELEVANT IF THEY DON'T HAVE A DELIVERY SYSTEM.
WHAT'S THAT MEAN?
THEY HAVE TO HAVE A WAY TO FIRE IT AT YOU... IT'S NOT LIKE THEY CAN JUST DELIVER IT TO YOUR FRONT DOOR.
12/9
Reeng doorbell.
You reeng doorbell.
ZEBRA

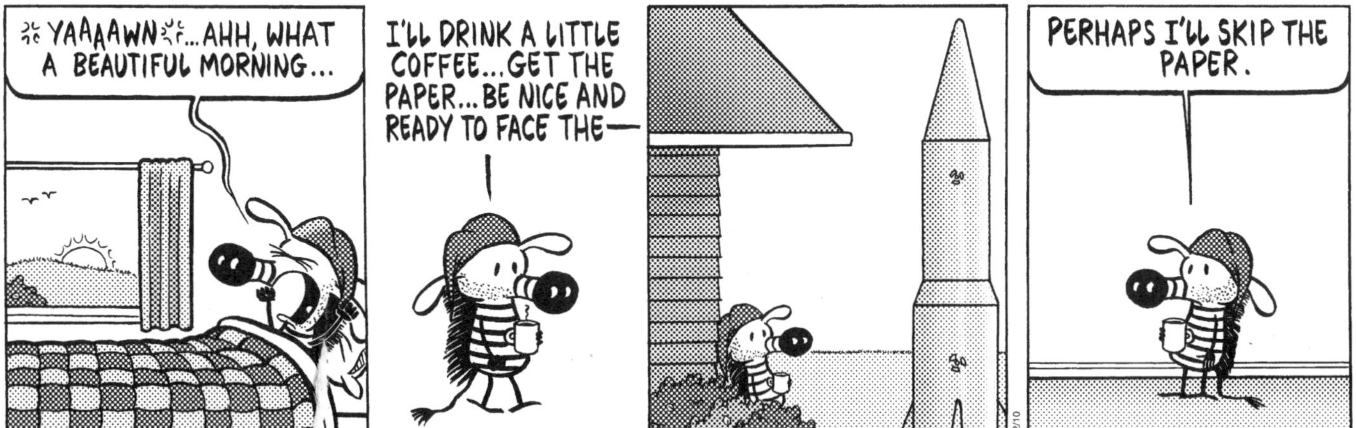
YAAAAWN...AHH, WHAT A BEAUTIFUL MORNING...
I'LL DRINK A LITTLE COFFEE...GET THE PAPER...BE NICE AND READY TO FACE THE—
12/10
PERHAPS I'LL SKIP THE PAPER.

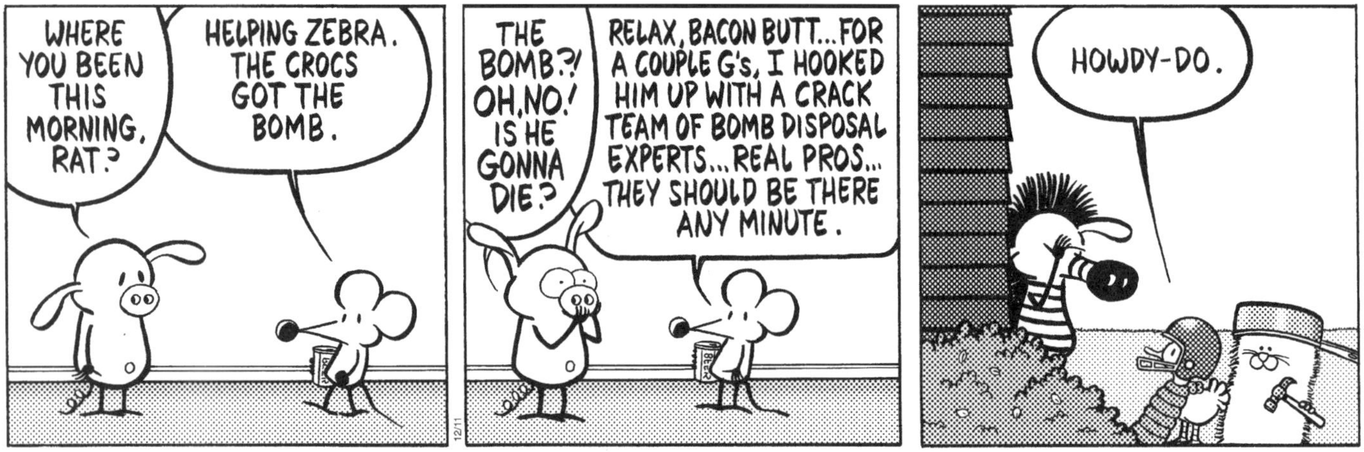
WHERE YOU BEEN THIS MORNING, RAT?
HELPING ZEBRA. THE CROCS GOT THE BOMB.
THE BOMB?! OH, NO! IS HE GONNA DIE?
RELAX, BACON BUTT...FOR A COUPLE G's, I HOOKED HIM UP WITH A CRACK TEAM OF BOMB DISPOSAL EXPERTS...REAL PROS...THEY SHOULD BE THERE ANY MINUTE.
12/11
HOWDY-DO.

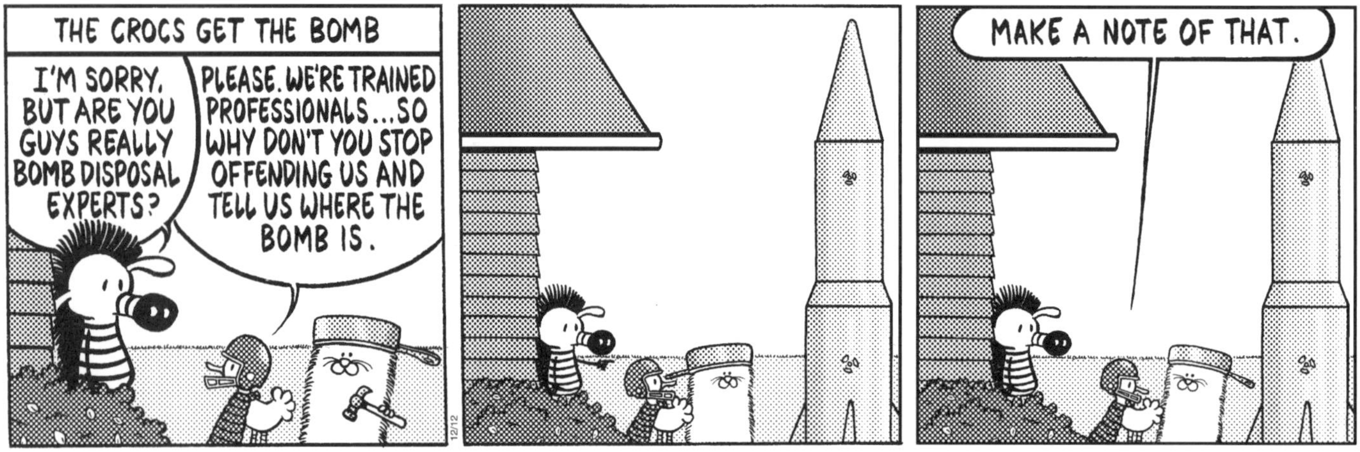
THE CROCS GET THE BOMB
I'M SORRY, BUT ARE YOU GUYS REALLY BOMB DISPOSAL EXPERTS?
PLEASE. WE'RE TRAINED PROFESSIONALS...SO WHY DON'T YOU STOP OFFENDING US AND TELL US WHERE THE BOMB IS.
12/12
MAKE A NOTE OF THAT.

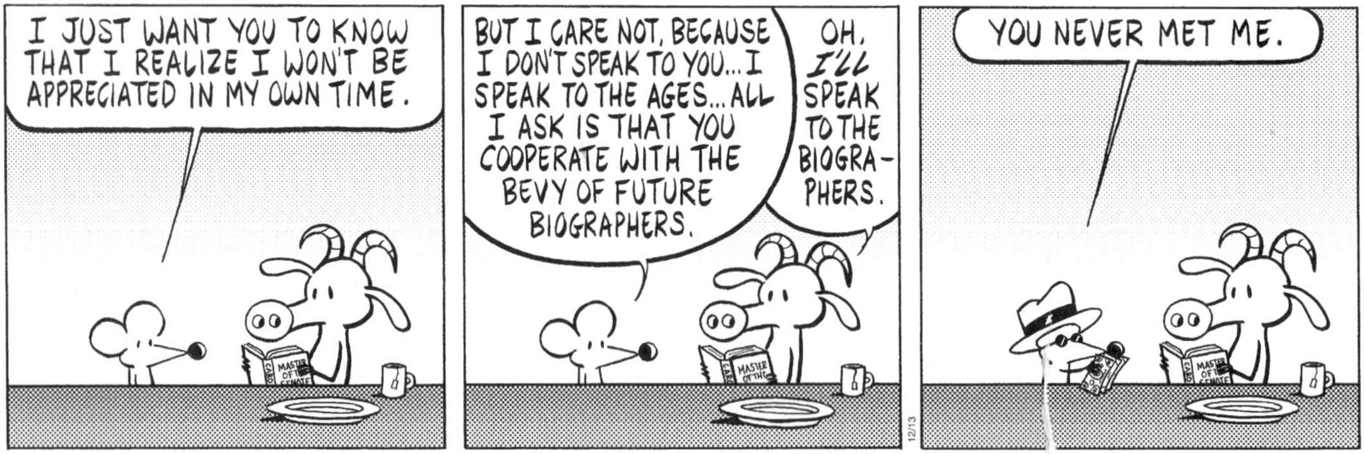
I JUST WANT YOU TO KNOW THAT I REALIZE I WON'T BE APPRECIATED IN MY OWN TIME.
BUT I CARE NOT, BECAUSE I DON'T SPEAK TO YOU...I SPEAK TO THE AGES...ALL I ASK IS THAT YOU COOPERATE WITH THE BEVY OF FUTURE BIOGRAPHERS.
OH, I'LL SPEAK TO THE BIOGRAPHERS.
12/13
YOU NEVER MET ME.

Elly Elephant was the sweetest elephant who ever lived.
12/14
Every day when she awoke, she told herself, "Today I will make someone else's life better."
So Elly Elephant gave money to friends.
I'll give you money.
Thank you, Elly.
She did favors for relatives.
I'll help you move.
Thank you, Elly.
And she helped all of her neighbors.
I'll mow your lawn.
Thank you, Elly.
One day Elly Elephant's house burned down. "It is okay," she said, "because I have friends and relatives and neighbors. They will help me as I have helped them."
But no one came.
So Elly Elephant gathered together all of her friends and relatives and neighbors.
And pounced on their heads.
Pounce Pounce Pounce
THIS IS THE CHILDREN'S BOOK CHARACTER YOU'RE CALLING THE NEW 'WINNIE THE POOH'?!
YEAH, IT'S LIKE WINNIE THE POOH IF HE WEIGHED MORE AND COULD KILL PEOPLE.
CHAPTER TWO... 'ROO IS THROUGH.'

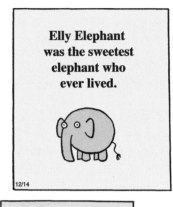

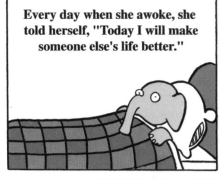

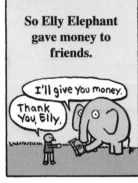

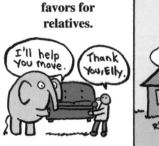

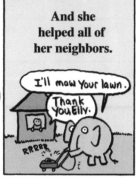

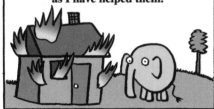

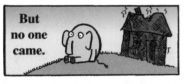

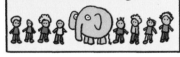

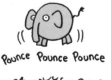

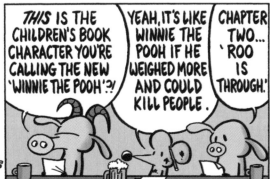

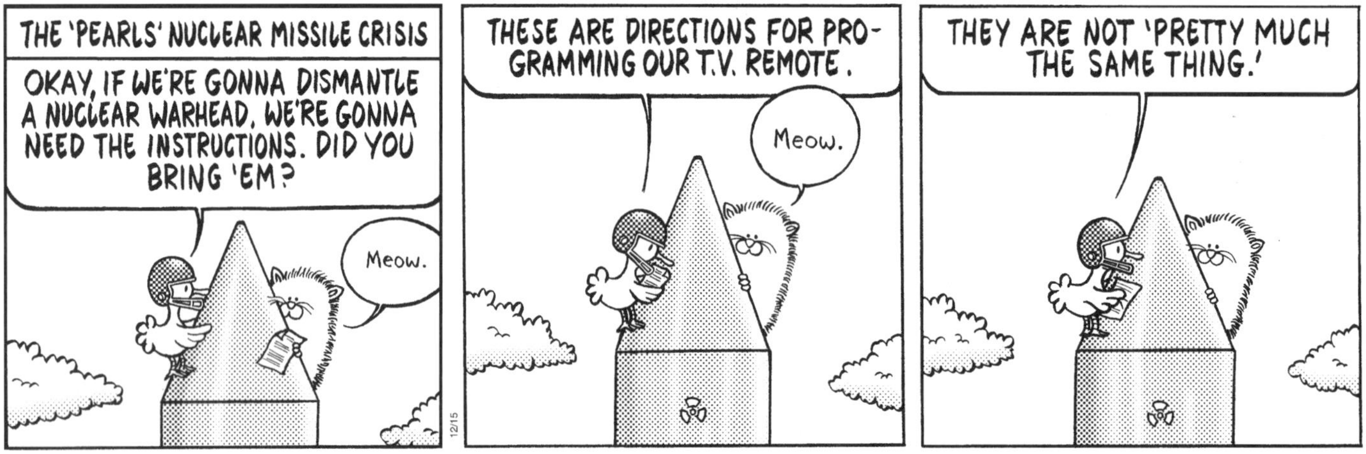
THE 'PEARLS' NUCLEAR MISSILE CRISIS
OKAY, IF WE'RE GONNA DISMANTLE A NUCLEAR WARHEAD, WE'RE GONNA NEED THE INSTRUCTIONS. DID YOU BRING 'EM?
Meow.
12/15
THESE ARE DIRECTIONS FOR PROGRAMMING OUR T.V. REMOTE.
Meow.
THEY ARE NOT 'PRETTY MUCH THE SAME THING.'

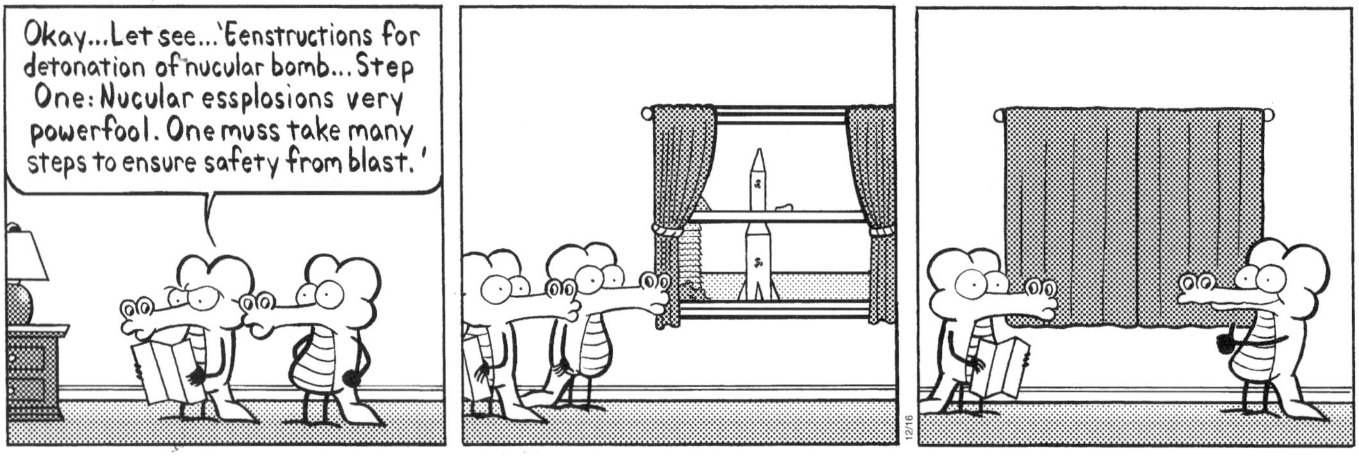
Okay... Let see... 'Eenstructions for detonation of nucular bomb... Step One: Nucular essplosions very powerfool. One muss take many steps to ensure safety from blast.'
12/16

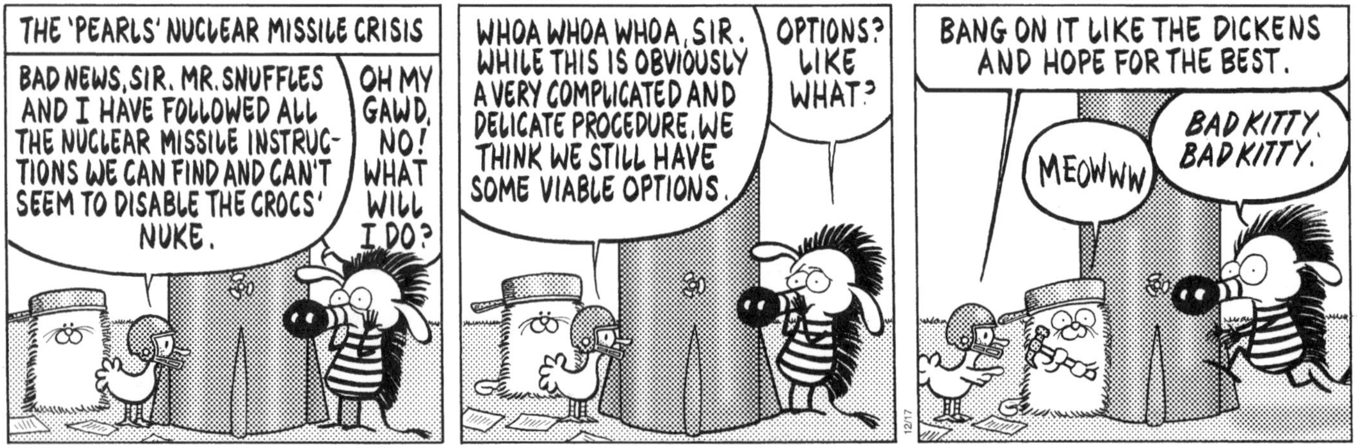
THE 'PEARLS' NUCLEAR MISSILE CRISIS
BAD NEWS, SIR. MR. SNUFFLES AND I HAVE FOLLOWED ALL THE NUCLEAR MISSILE INSTRUCTIONS WE CAN FIND AND CAN'T SEEM TO DISABLE THE CROCS' NUKE.
OH MY GAWD, NO! WHAT WILL I DO?
WHOA WHOA WHOA, SIR. WHILE THIS IS OBVIOUSLY A VERY COMPLICATED AND DELICATE PROCEDURE, WE THINK WE STILL HAVE SOME VIABLE OPTIONS.
OPTIONS? LIKE WHAT?
12/17
BANG ON IT LIKE THE DICKENS AND HOPE FOR THE BEST.
MEOWWW
BAD KITTY. BAD KITTY.

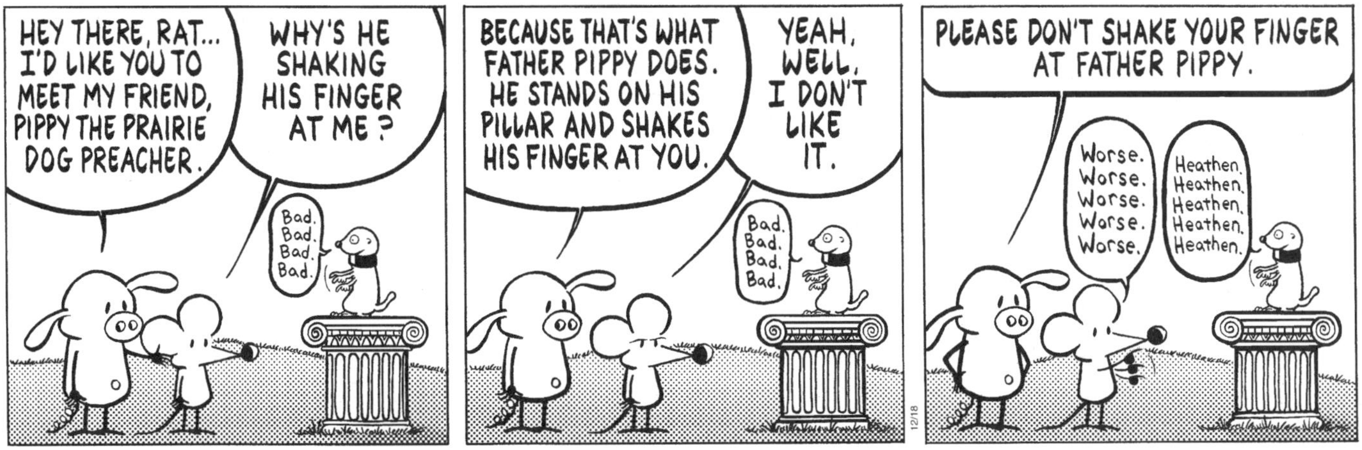
HEY THERE, RAT... I'D LIKE YOU TO MEET MY FRIEND, PIPPY THE PRAIRIE DOG PREACHER.
WHY'S HE SHAKING HIS FINGER AT ME?
Bad. Bad. Bad. Bad.
BECAUSE THAT'S WHAT FATHER PIPPY DOES. HE STANDS ON HIS PILLAR AND SHAKES HIS FINGER AT YOU.
YEAH, WELL, I DON'T LIKE IT.
Bad. Bad. Bad. Bad.
PLEASE DON'T SHAKE YOUR FINGER AT FATHER PIPPY.
Worse. Worse. Worse. Worse. Worse.
Heathen. Heathen. Heathen. Heathen. Heathen.

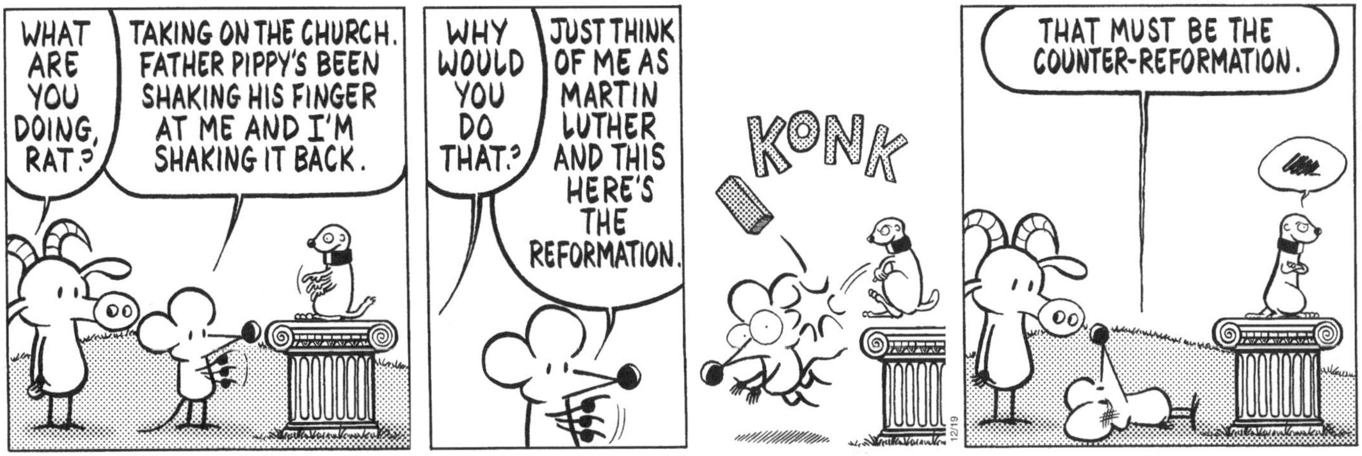
WHAT ARE YOU DOING, RAT?
TAKING ON THE CHURCH. FATHER PIPPY'S BEEN SHAKING HIS FINGER AT ME AND I'M SHAKING IT BACK.
WHY WOULD YOU DO THAT?
JUST THINK OF ME AS MARTIN LUTHER AND THIS HERE'S THE REFORMATION.
KONK
THAT MUST BE THE COUNTER-REFORMATION.

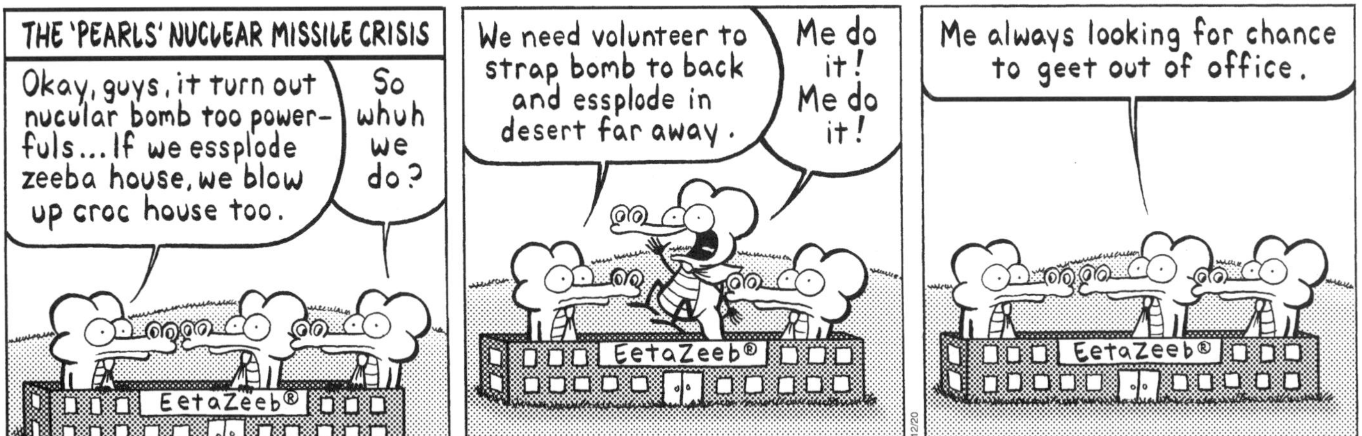
THE 'PEARLS' NUCLEAR MISSILE CRISIS
Okay, guys, it turn out nucular bomb too power-fuls... If we essplode zeeba house, we blow up croc house too.
So whuh we do?
EetaZeeb®
We need volunteer to strap bomb to back and essplode in desert far away.
Me do it! Me do it!
EetaZeeb®
Me always looking for chance to geet out of office.
EetaZeeb®

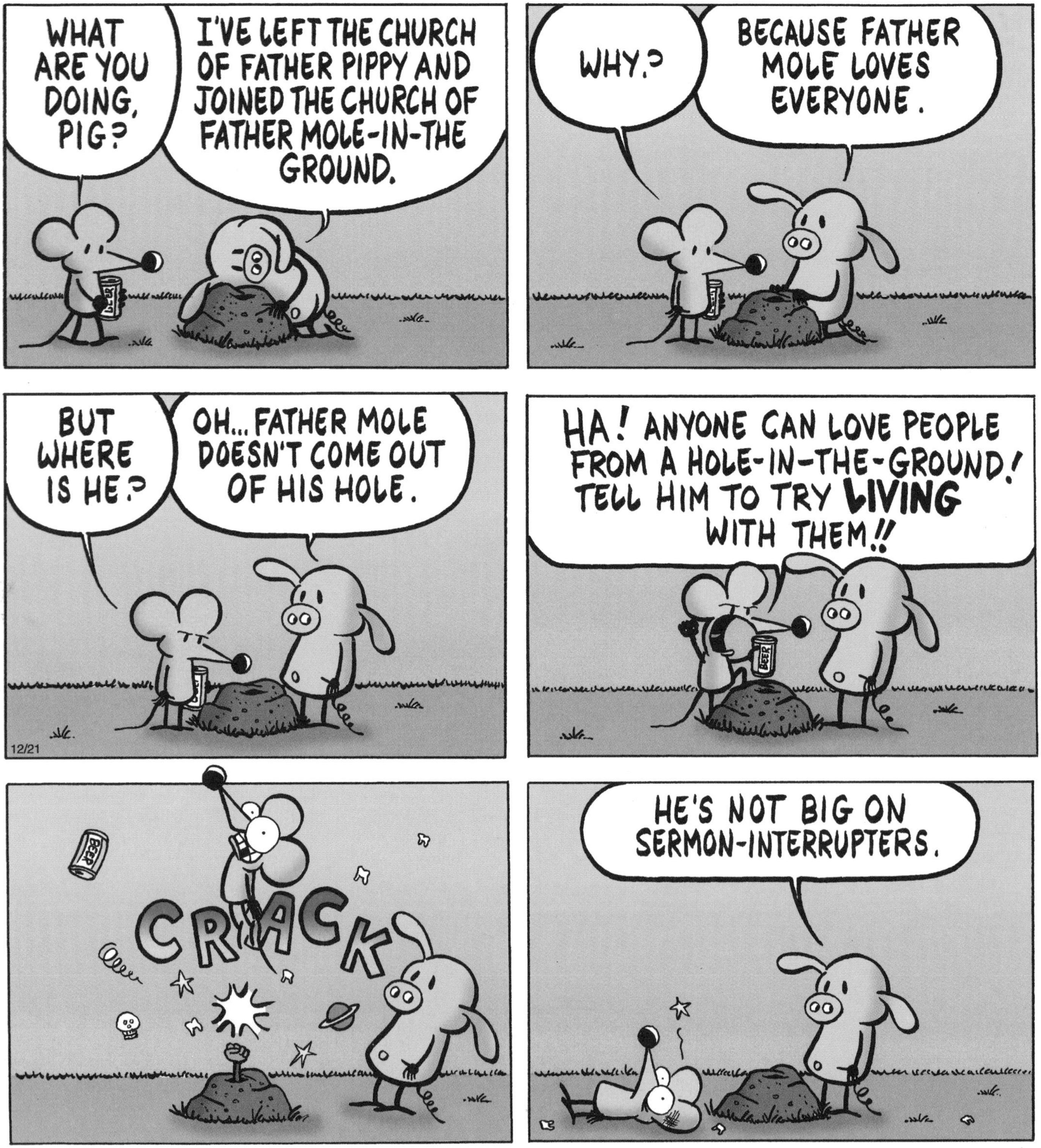
WHAT ARE YOU DOING, PIG?
I'VE LEFT THE CHURCH OF FATHER PIPPY AND JOINED THE CHURCH OF FATHER MOLE-IN-THE GROUND.
WHY?
BECAUSE FATHER MOLE LOVES EVERYONE.
BUT WHERE IS HE?
OH... FATHER MOLE DOESN'T COME OUT OF HIS HOLE.
12/21
HA! ANYONE CAN LOVE PEOPLE FROM A HOLE-IN-THE-GROUND! TELL HIM TO TRY LIVING WITH THEM!!
CRACK
HE'S NOT BIG ON SERMON-INTERRUPTERS.

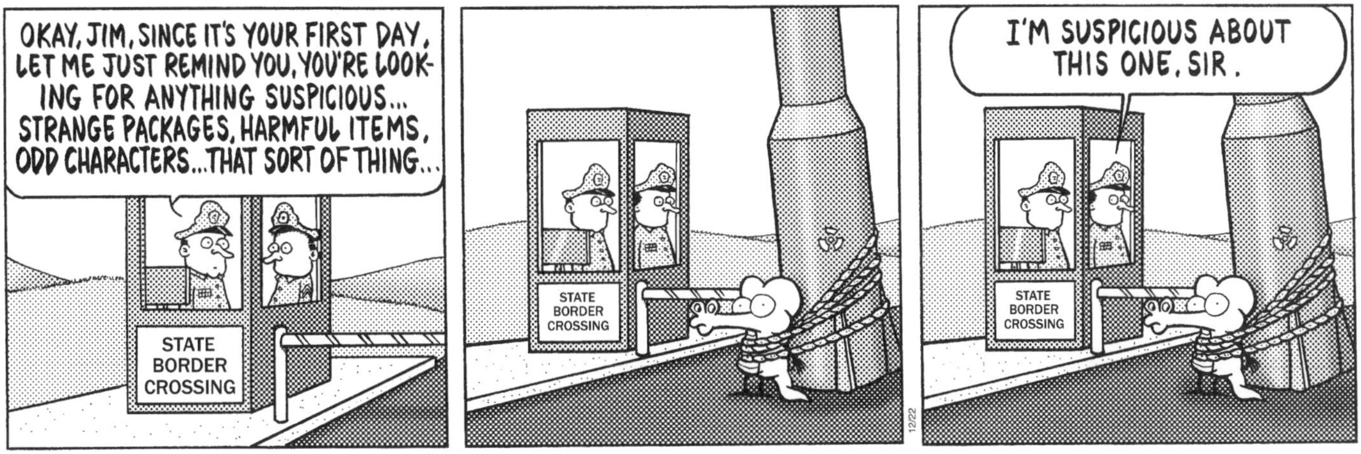
OKAY, JIM, SINCE IT'S YOUR FIRST DAY, LET ME JUST REMIND YOU, YOU'RE LOOKING FOR ANYTHING SUSPICIOUS... STRANGE PACKAGES, HARMFUL ITEMS, ODD CHARACTERS...THAT SORT OF THING...
STATE BORDER CROSSING
STATE BORDER CROSSING
12/22
STATE BORDER CROSSING
I'M SUSPICIOUS ABOUT THIS ONE, SIR.

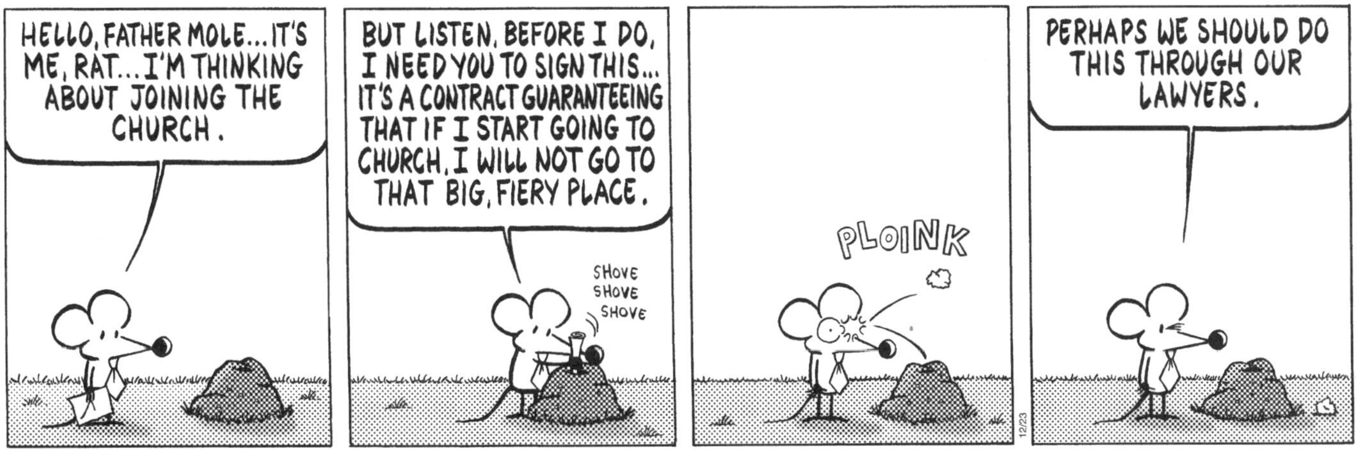
HELLO, FATHER MOLE...IT'S ME, RAT...I'M THINKING ABOUT JOINING THE CHURCH.
BUT LISTEN, BEFORE I DO, I NEED YOU TO SIGN THIS... IT'S A CONTRACT GUARANTEEING THAT IF I START GOING TO CHURCH, I WILL NOT GO TO THAT BIG, FIERY PLACE.
SHOVE SHOVE SHOVE
PLOINK
12/23
PERHAPS WE SHOULD DO THIS THROUGH OUR LAWYERS.

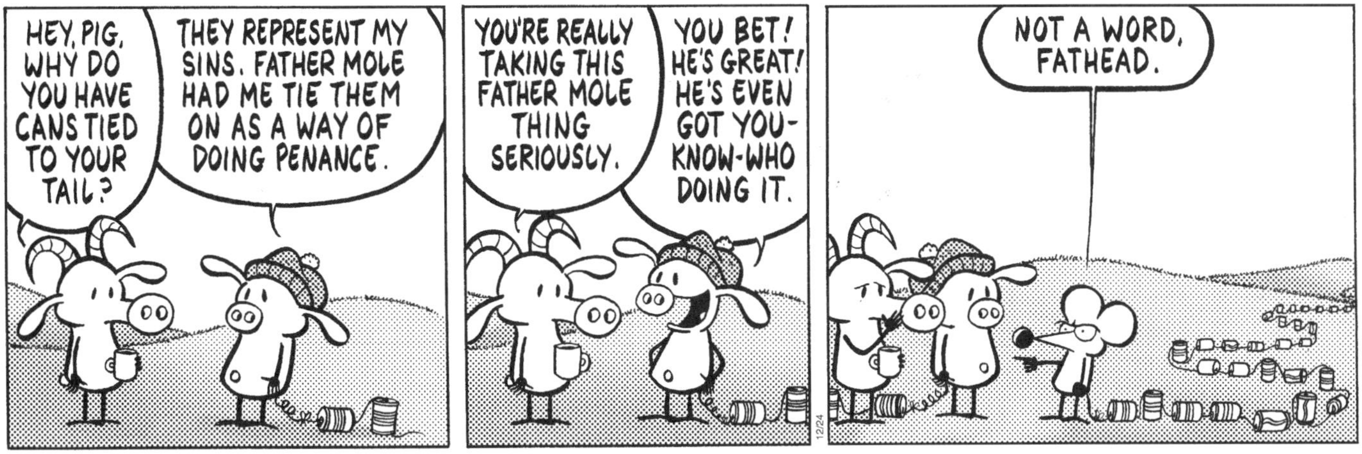
HEY, PIG, WHY DO YOU HAVE CANS TIED TO YOUR TAIL?
THEY REPRESENT MY SINS. FATHER MOLE HAD ME TIE THEM ON AS A WAY OF DOING PENANCE.
YOU'RE REALLY TAKING THIS FATHER MOLE THING SERIOUSLY.
YOU BET! HE'S GREAT! HE'S EVEN GOT YOU-KNOW-WHO DOING IT.
12/24
NOT A WORD, FATHEAD.

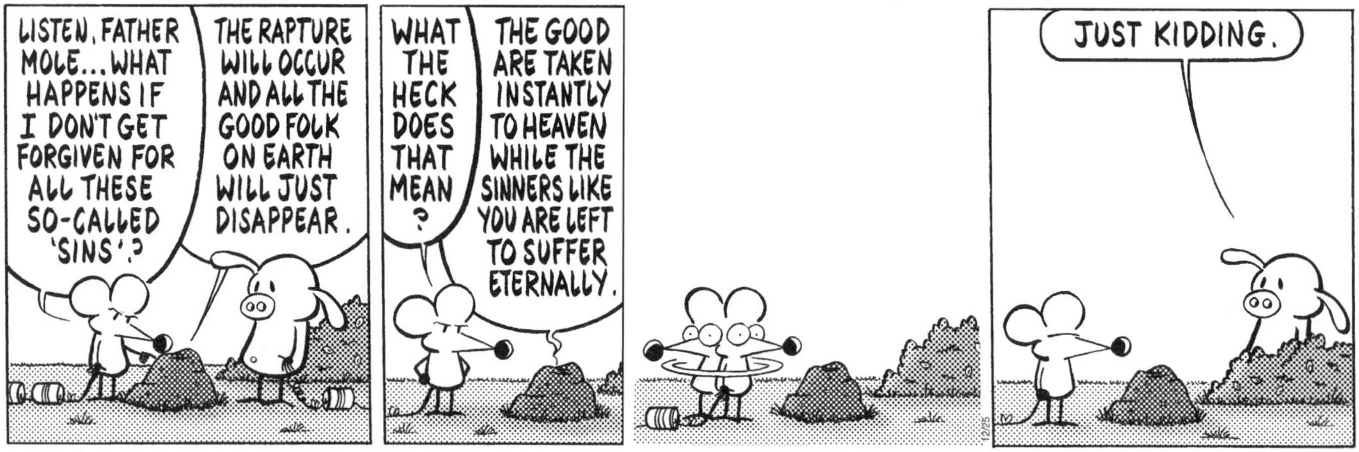
LISTEN, FATHER MOLE... WHAT HAPPENS IF I DON'T GET FORGIVEN FOR ALL THESE SO-CALLED 'SINS'?
THE RAPTURE WILL OCCUR AND ALL THE GOOD FOLK ON EARTH WILL JUST DISAPPEAR.
WHAT THE HECK DOES THAT MEAN?
THE GOOD ARE TAKEN INSTANTLY TO HEAVEN WHILE THE SINNERS LIKE YOU ARE LEFT TO SUFFER ETERNALLY.
JUST KIDDING.

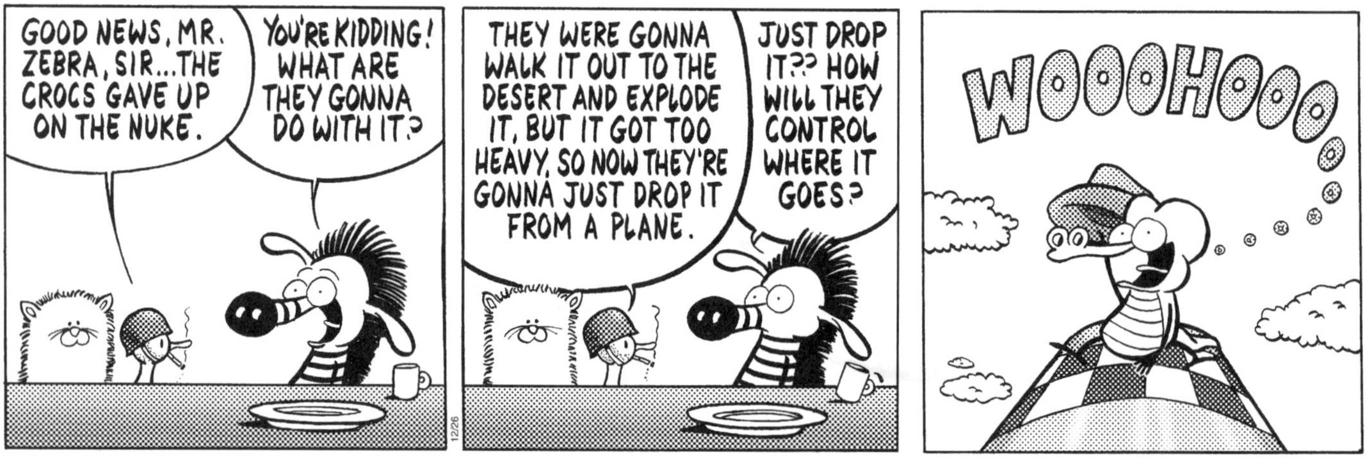
GOOD NEWS, MR. ZEBRA, SIR...THE CROCS GAVE UP ON THE NUKE.
YOU'RE KIDDING! WHAT ARE THEY GONNA DO WITH IT?
THEY WERE GONNA WALK IT OUT TO THE DESERT AND EXPLODE IT, BUT IT GOT TOO HEAVY, SO NOW THEY'RE GONNA JUST DROP IT FROM A PLANE.
JUST DROP IT?? HOW WILL THEY CONTROL WHERE IT GOES?
WOOOHOOO

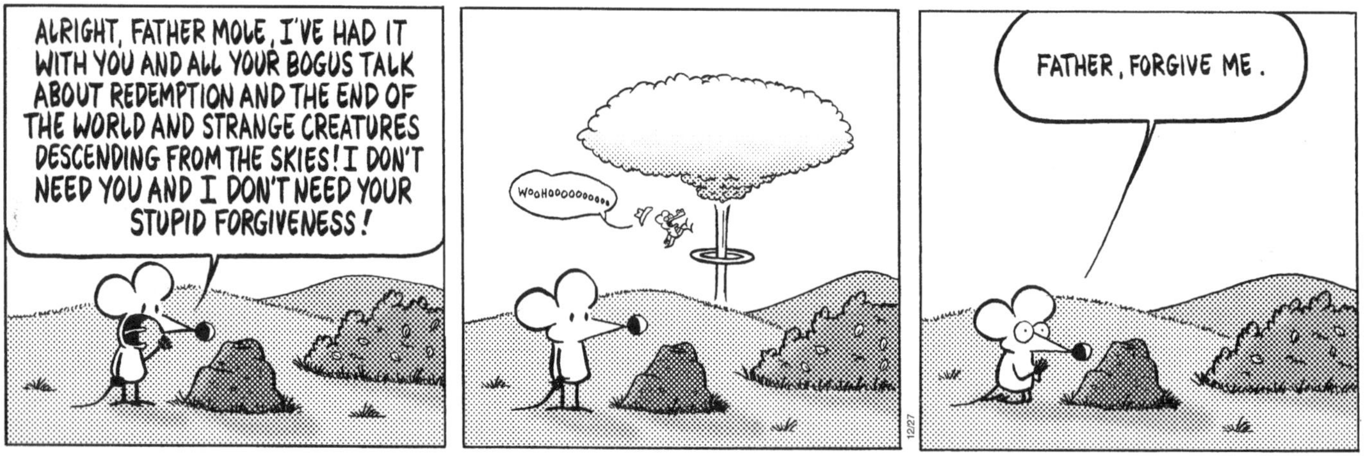
ALRIGHT, FATHER MOLE, I'VE HAD IT WITH YOU AND ALL YOUR BOGUS TALK ABOUT REDEMPTION AND THE END OF THE WORLD AND STRANGE CREATURES DESCENDING FROM THE SKIES! I DON'T NEED YOU AND I DON'T NEED YOUR STUPID FORGIVENESS!
FATHER, FORGIVE ME.

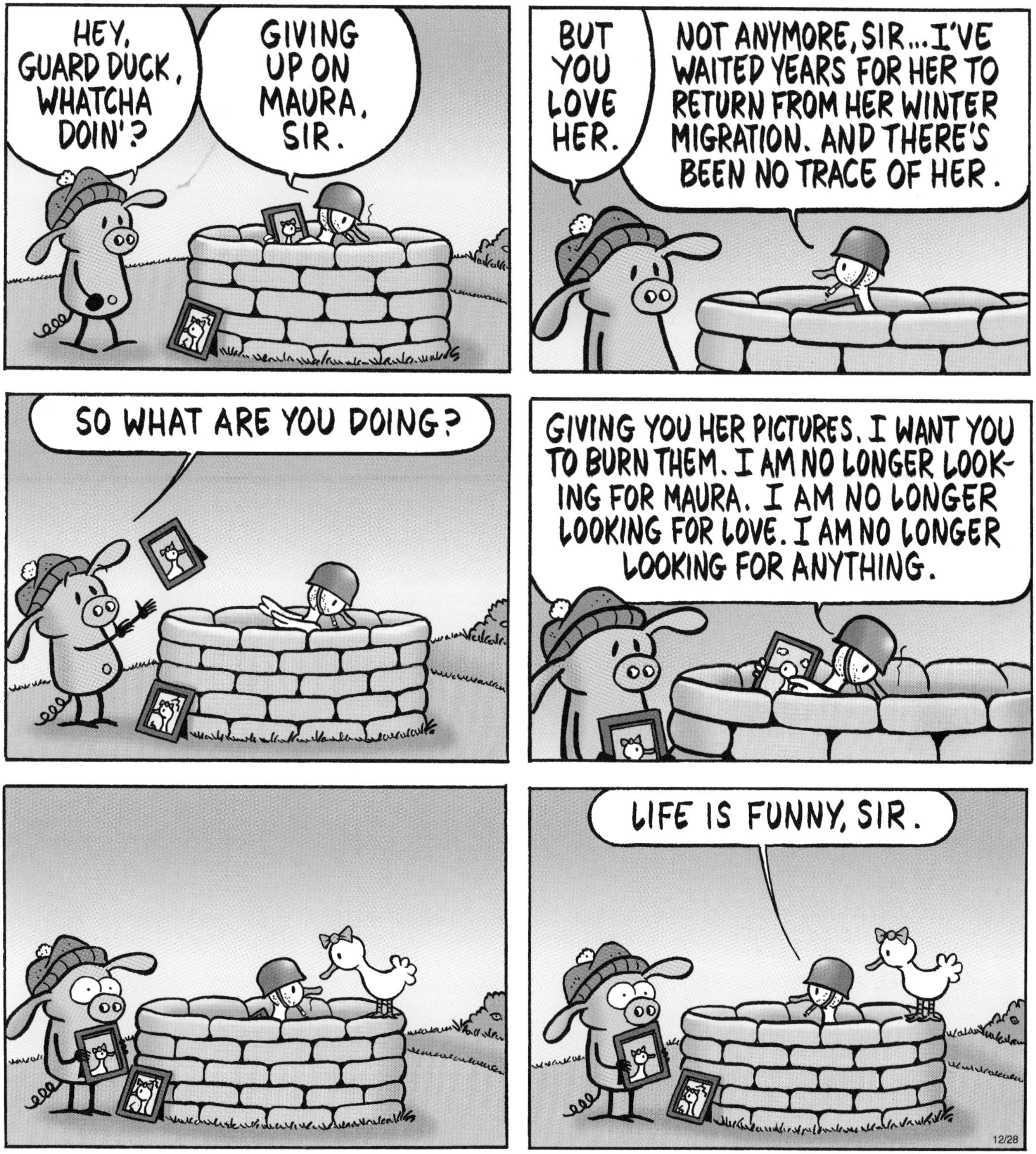
HEY, GUARD DUCK, WHATCHA DOIN'?
GIVING UP ON MAURA, SIR.
BUT YOU LOVE HER.
NOT ANYMORE, SIR...I'VE WAITED YEARS FOR HER TO RETURN FROM HER WINTER MIGRATION. AND THERE'S BEEN NO TRACE OF HER.
SO WHAT ARE YOU DOING?
GIVING YOU HER PICTURES. I WANT YOU TO BURN THEM. I AM NO LONGER LOOKING FOR MAURA. I AM NO LONGER LOOKING FOR LOVE. I AM NO LONGER LOOKING FOR ANYTHING.
LIFE IS FUNNY, SIR.
12/28

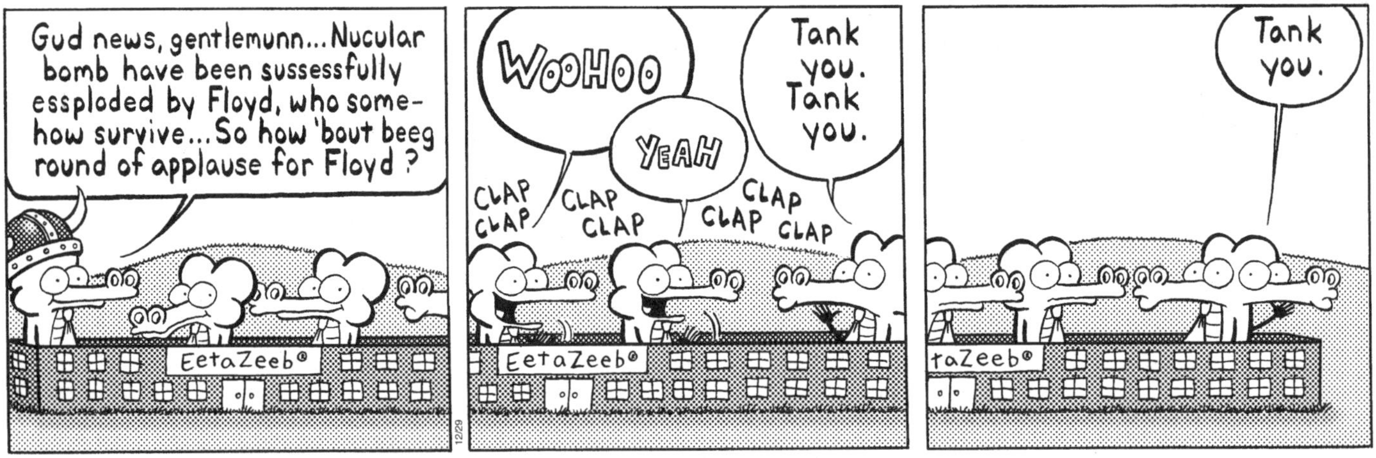
Gud news, gentlemunn... Nucular bomb have been sussessfully essploded by Floyd, who somehow survive... So how 'bout beeg round of applause for Floyd?
EetaZeeb®
WOOHOO
YEAH
Tank you. Tank you.
CLAP CLAP
CLAP CLAP
CLAP CLAP CLAP
EetaZeeb®
Tank you.
taZeeb®

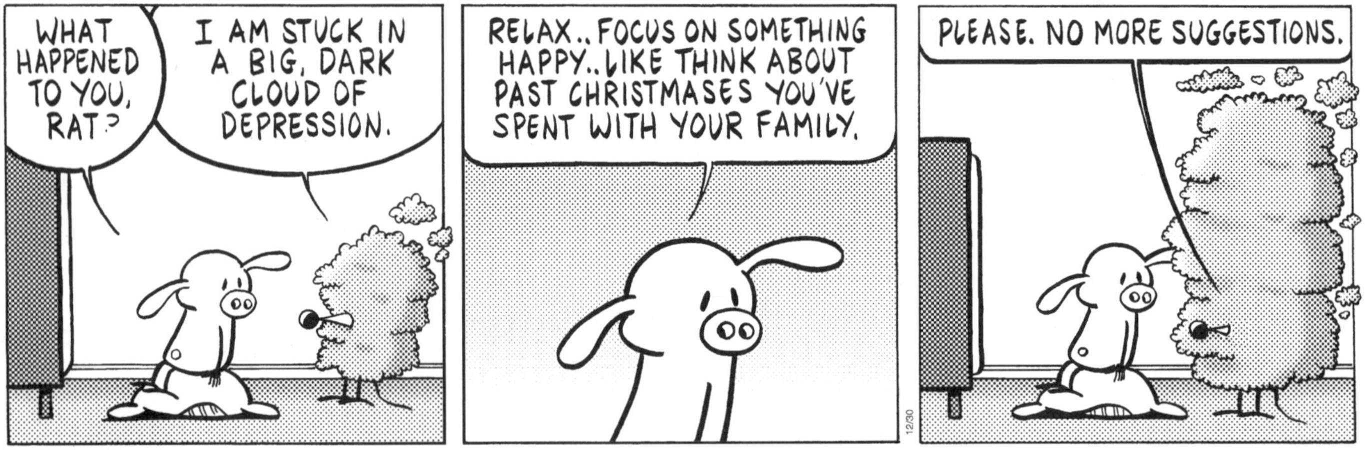
WHAT HAPPENED TO YOU, RAT?
I AM STUCK IN A BIG, DARK CLOUD OF DEPRESSION.
RELAX.. FOCUS ON SOMETHING HAPPY.. LIKE THINK ABOUT PAST CHRISTMASES YOU'VE SPENT WITH YOUR FAMILY.
PLEASE. NO MORE SUGGESTIONS.

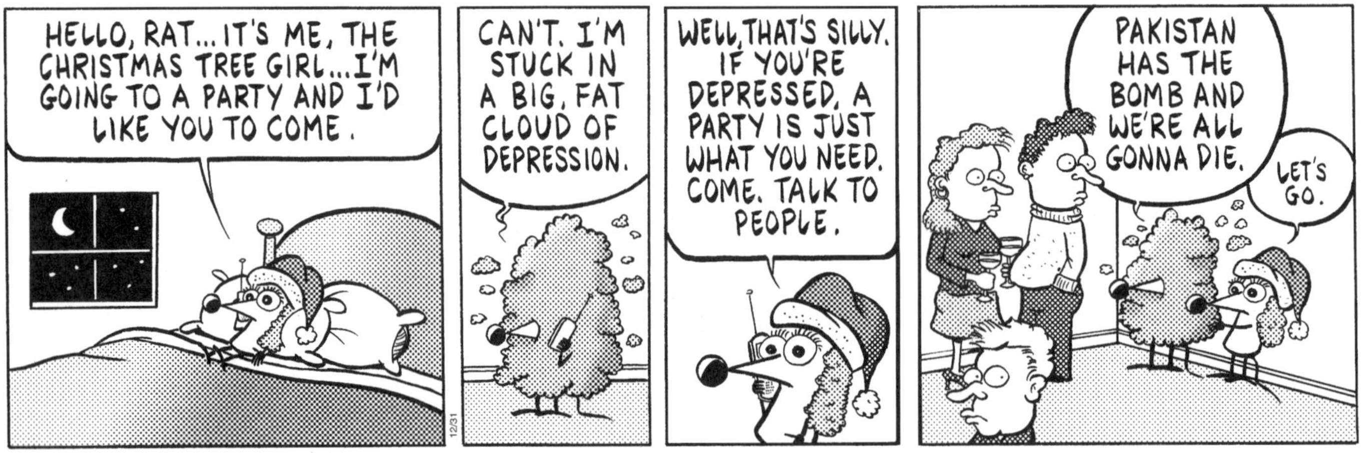
HELLO, RAT... IT'S ME, THE CHRISTMAS TREE GIRL... I'M GOING TO A PARTY AND I'D LIKE YOU TO COME.
CAN'T. I'M STUCK IN A BIG, FAT CLOUD OF DEPRESSION.
WELL, THAT'S SILLY. IF YOU'RE DEPRESSED, A PARTY IS JUST WHAT YOU NEED. COME. TALK TO PEOPLE.
PAKISTAN HAS THE BOMB AND WE'RE ALL GONNA DIE.
LET'S GO.

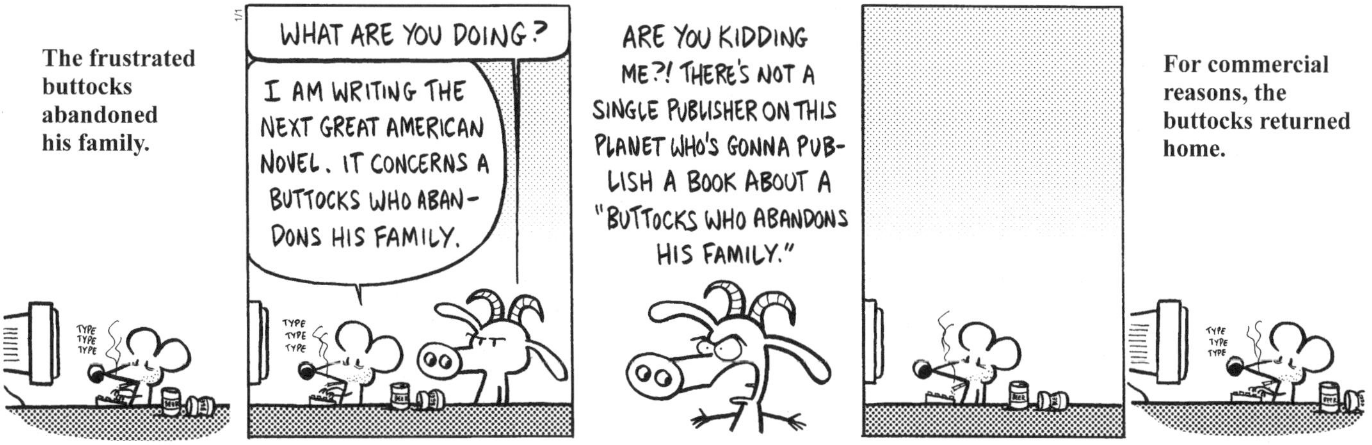
The frustrated buttocks abandoned his family.
TYPE TYPE TYPE
WHAT ARE YOU DOING?
I AM WRITING THE NEXT GREAT AMERICAN NOVEL. IT CONCERNS A BUTTOCKS WHO ABANDONS HIS FAMILY.
ARE YOU KIDDING ME?! THERE'S NOT A SINGLE PUBLISHER ON THIS PLANET WHO'S GONNA PUBLISH A BOOK ABOUT A "BUTTOCKS WHO ABANDONS HIS FAMILY."
For commercial reasons, the buttocks returned home.
TYPE TYPE TYPE

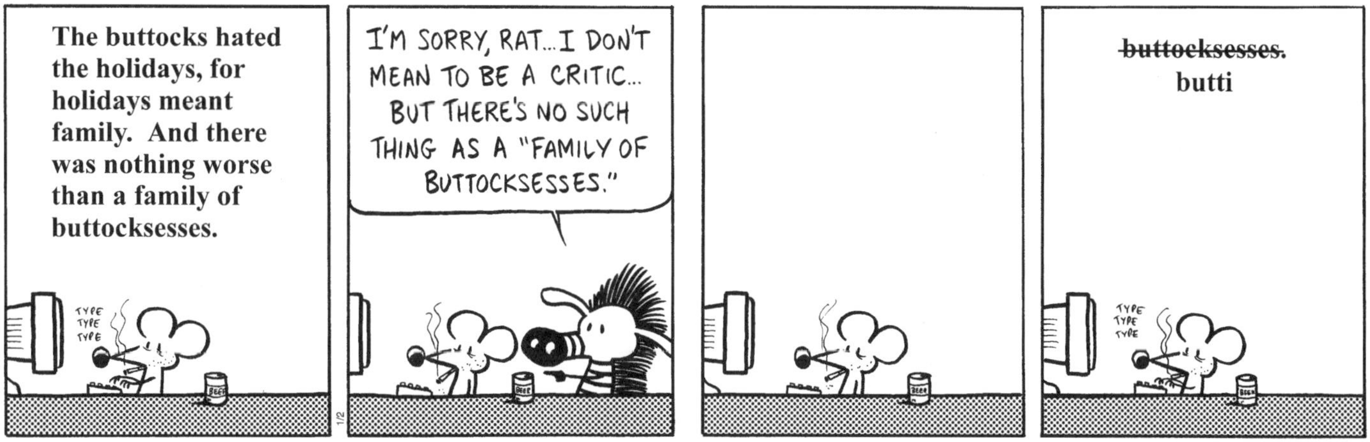
The buttocks hated the holidays, for holidays meant family. And there was nothing worse than a family of buttocksesses.
TYPE TYPE TYPE
I'M SORRY, RAT... I DON'T MEAN TO BE A CRITIC... BUT THERE'S NO SUCH THING AS A "FAMILY OF BUTTOCKSESSES."
~~buttocksesses.~~
butti
TYPE TYPE TYPE

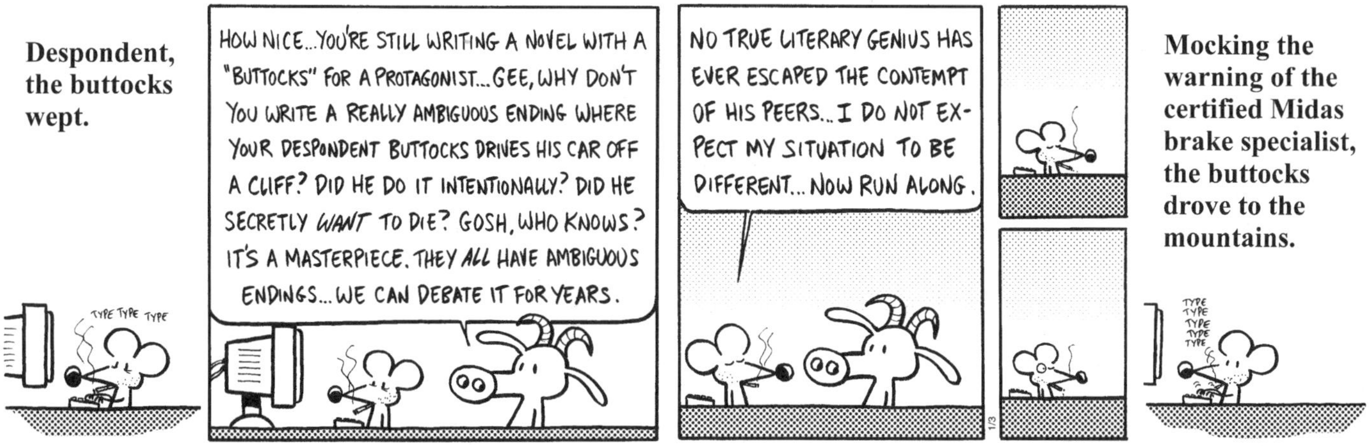
Despondent, the buttocks wept.
TYPE TYPE TYPE
HOW NICE... YOU'RE STILL WRITING A NOVEL WITH A "BUTTOCKS" FOR A PROTAGONIST... GEE, WHY DON'T YOU WRITE A REALLY AMBIGUOUS ENDING WHERE YOUR DESPONDENT BUTTOCKS DRIVES HIS CAR OFF A CLIFF? DID HE DO IT INTENTIONALLY? DID HE SECRETLY *WANT* TO DIE? GOSH, WHO KNOWS? IT'S A MASTERPIECE. THEY *ALL* HAVE AMBIGUOUS ENDINGS... WE CAN DEBATE IT FOR YEARS.
NO TRUE LITERARY GENIUS HAS EVER ESCAPED THE CONTEMPT OF HIS PEERS... I DO NOT EXPECT MY SITUATION TO BE DIFFERENT... NOW RUN ALONG.
Mocking the warning of the certified Midas brake specialist, the buttocks drove to the mountains.
TYPE TYPE TYPE TYPE TYPE

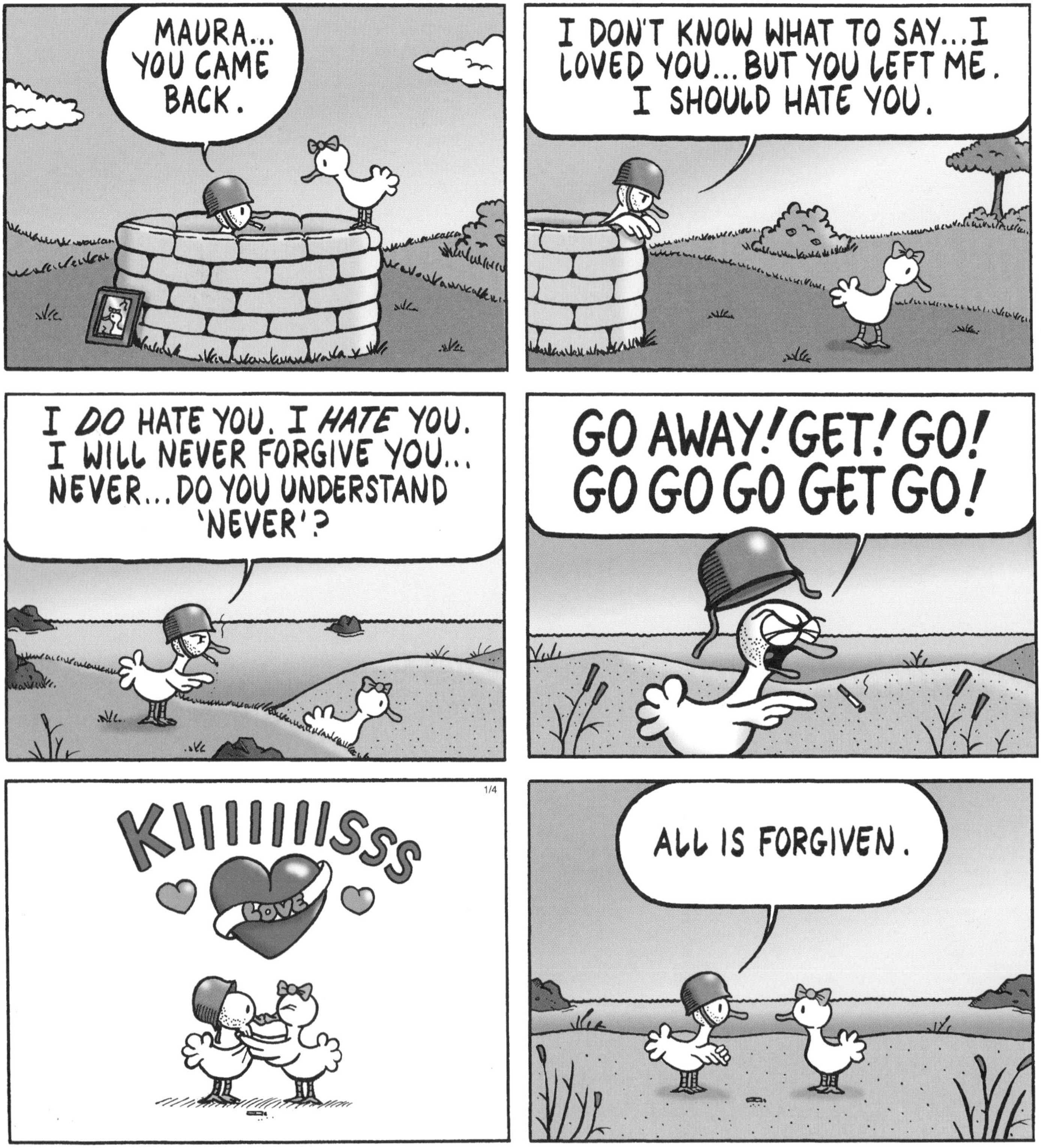
MAURA... YOU CAME BACK.
I DON'T KNOW WHAT TO SAY...I LOVED YOU...BUT YOU LEFT ME. I SHOULD HATE YOU.
I *DO* HATE YOU. I *HATE* YOU. I WILL NEVER FORGIVE YOU... NEVER...DO YOU UNDERSTAND 'NEVER'?
GO AWAY! GET! GO! GO GO GO GET GO!
KIIIIIIIISSS
LOVE
ALL IS FORGIVEN.

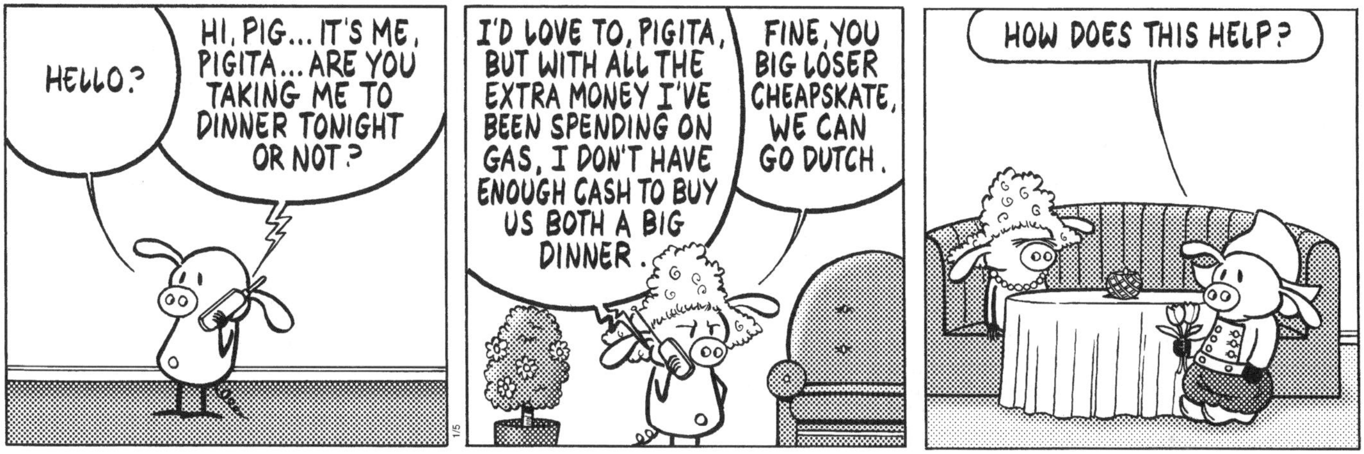
HELLO?
HI, PIG... IT'S ME, PIGITA... ARE YOU TAKING ME TO DINNER TONIGHT OR NOT?
I'D LOVE TO, PIGITA, BUT WITH ALL THE EXTRA MONEY I'VE BEEN SPENDING ON GAS, I DON'T HAVE ENOUGH CASH TO BUY US BOTH A BIG DINNER.
FINE, YOU BIG LOSER CHEAPSKATE, WE CAN GO DUTCH.
HOW DOES THIS HELP?
1/5

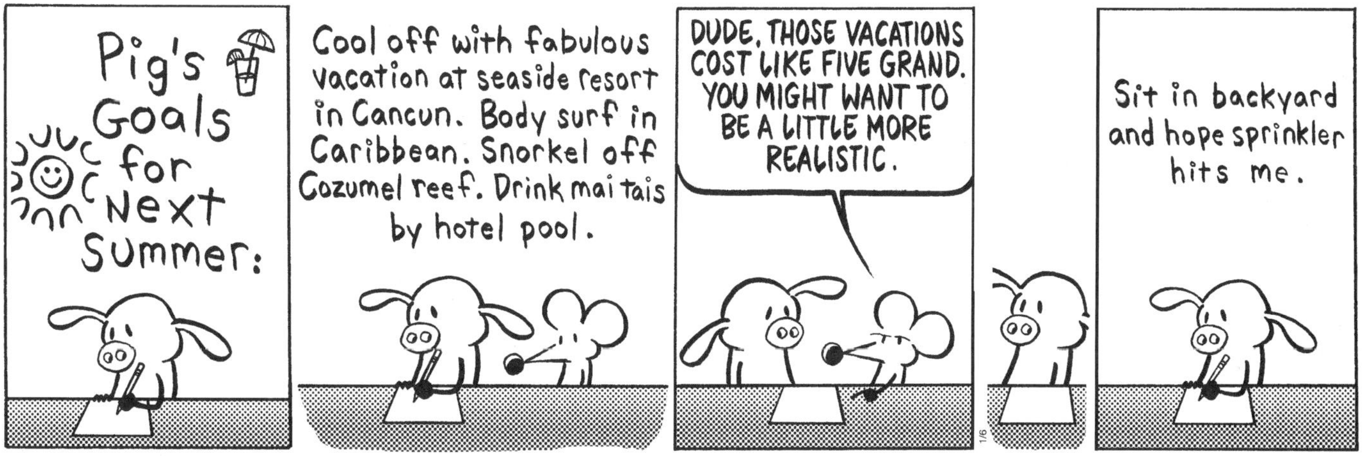
Pig's Goals for Next Summer:
Cool off with fabulous vacation at seaside resort in Cancun. Body surf in Caribbean. Snorkel off Cozumel reef. Drink mai tais by hotel pool.
DUDE, THOSE VACATIONS COST LIKE FIVE GRAND. YOU MIGHT WANT TO BE A LITTLE MORE REALISTIC.
Sit in backyard and hope sprinkler hits me.
1/6

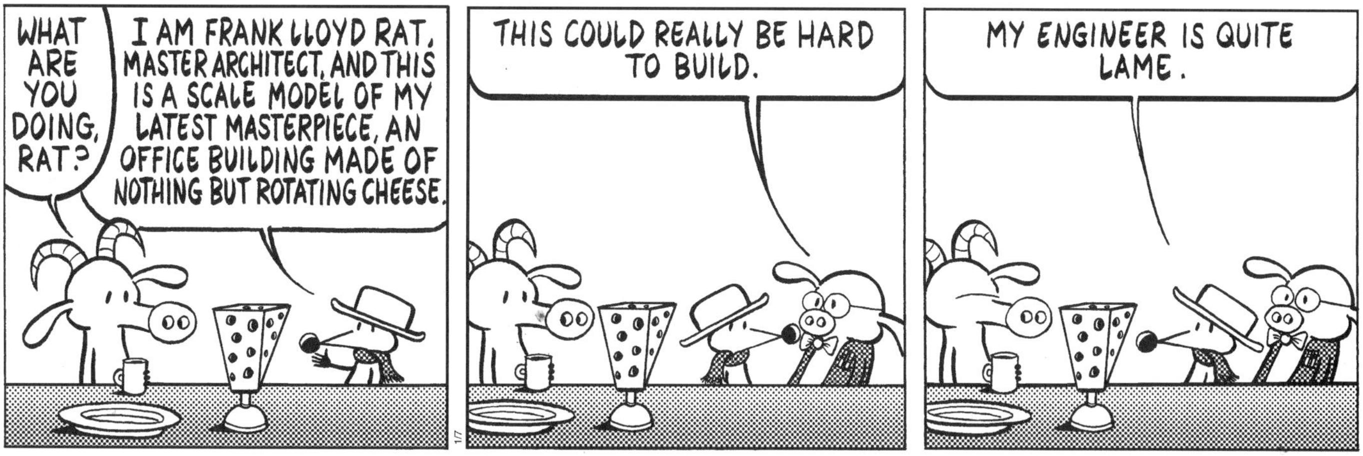
WHAT ARE YOU DOING, RAT?
I AM FRANK LLOYD RAT, MASTER ARCHITECT, AND THIS IS A SCALE MODEL OF MY LATEST MASTERPIECE, AN OFFICE BUILDING MADE OF NOTHING BUT ROTATING CHEESE.
THIS COULD REALLY BE HARD TO BUILD.
MY ENGINEER IS QUITE LAME.
1/7

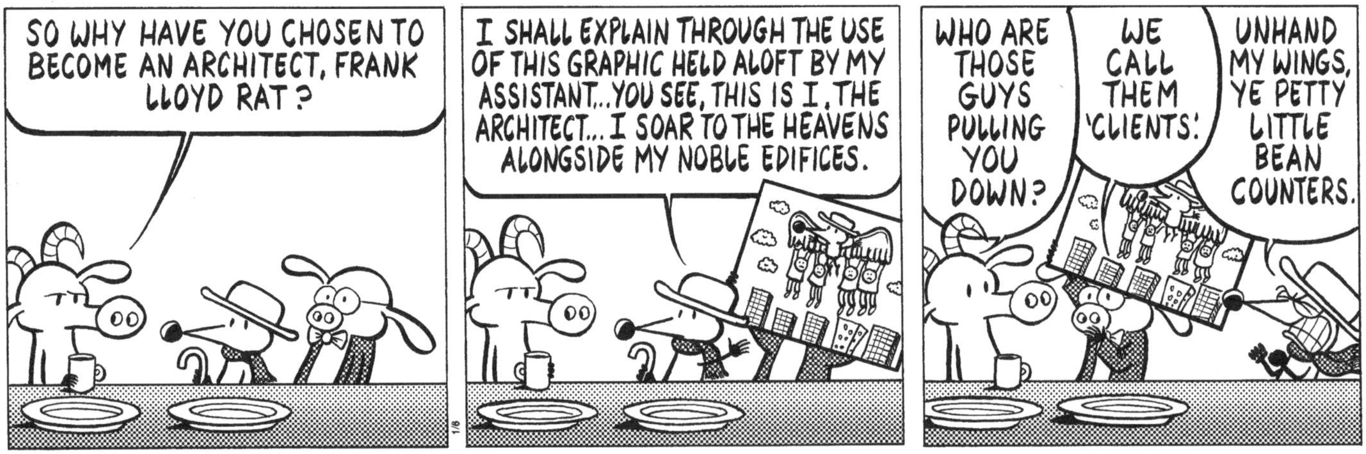
SO WHY HAVE YOU CHOSEN TO BECOME AN ARCHITECT, FRANK LLOYD RAT?
I SHALL EXPLAIN THROUGH THE USE OF THIS GRAPHIC HELD ALOFT BY MY ASSISTANT...YOU SEE, THIS IS I, THE ARCHITECT... I SOAR TO THE HEAVENS ALONGSIDE MY NOBLE EDIFICES.
WHO ARE THOSE GUYS PULLING YOU DOWN?
WE CALL THEM 'CLIENTS.'
UNHAND MY WINGS, YE PETTY LITTLE BEAN COUNTERS.

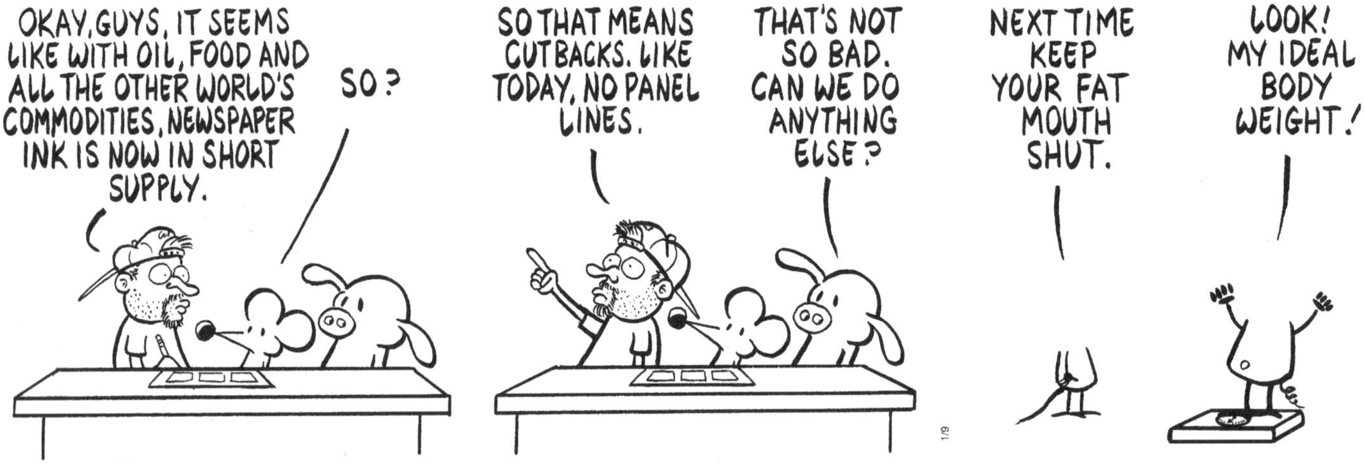
OKAY, GUYS, IT SEEMS LIKE WITH OIL, FOOD AND ALL THE OTHER WORLD'S COMMODITIES, NEWSPAPER INK IS NOW IN SHORT SUPPLY.
SO?
SO THAT MEANS CUTBACKS. LIKE TODAY, NO PANEL LINES.
THAT'S NOT SO BAD. CAN WE DO ANYTHING ELSE?
NEXT TIME KEEP YOUR FAT MOUTH SHUT.
LOOK! MY IDEAL BODY WEIGHT!

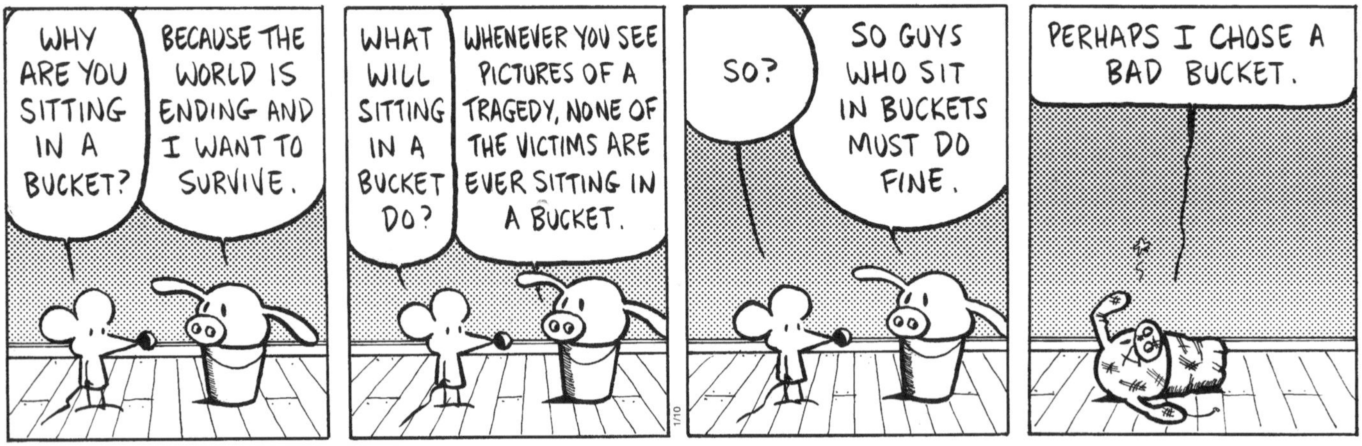
WHY ARE YOU SITTING IN A BUCKET?
BECAUSE THE WORLD IS ENDING AND I WANT TO SURVIVE.
WHAT WILL SITTING IN A BUCKET DO?
WHENEVER YOU SEE PICTURES OF A TRAGEDY, NONE OF THE VICTIMS ARE EVER SITTING IN A BUCKET.
SO?
SO GUYS WHO SIT IN BUCKETS MUST DO FINE.
PERHAPS I CHOSE A BAD BUCKET.

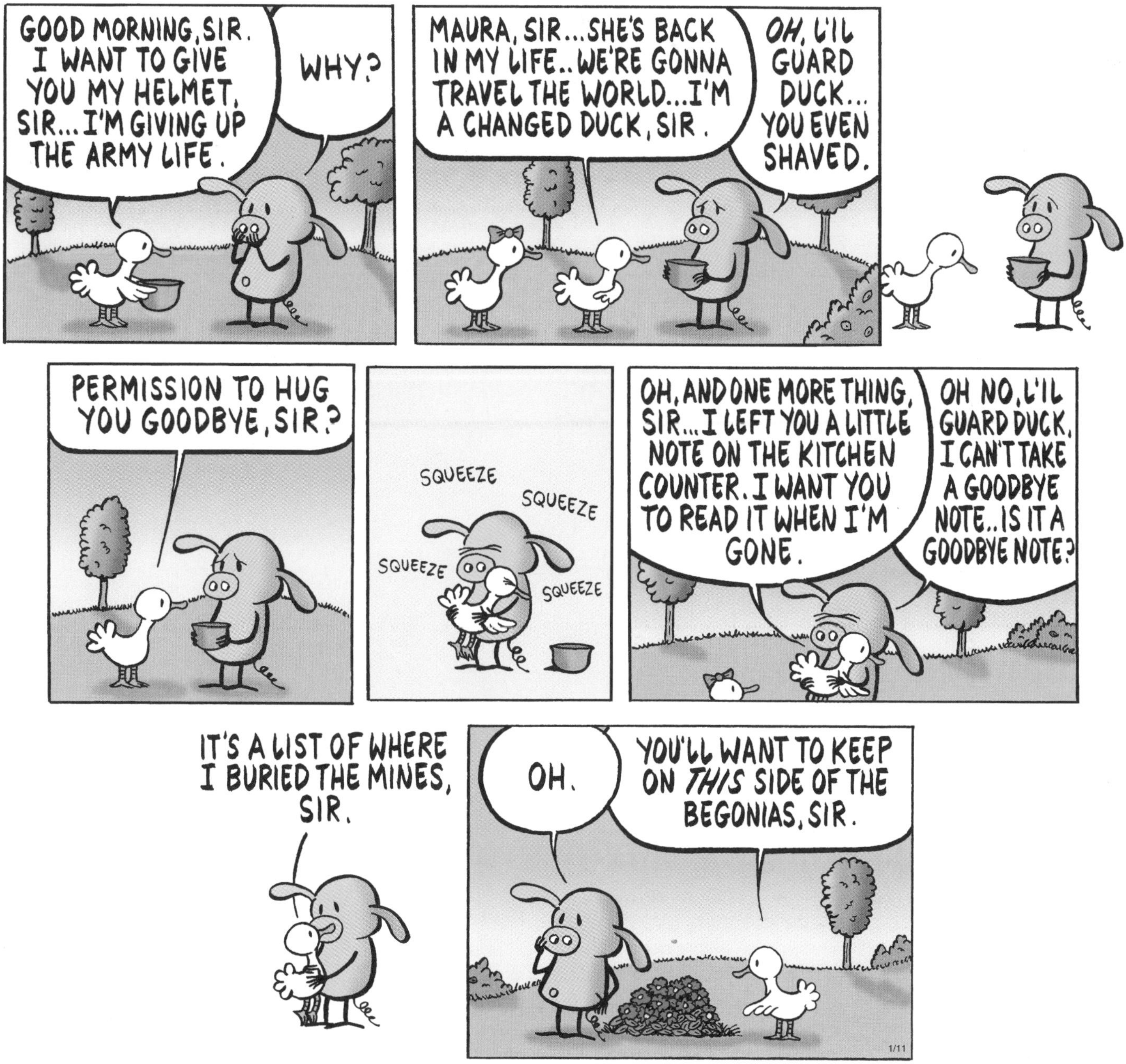
GOOD MORNING, SIR. I WANT TO GIVE YOU MY HELMET, SIR... I'M GIVING UP THE ARMY LIFE.
WHY?
MAURA, SIR... SHE'S BACK IN MY LIFE.. WE'RE GONNA TRAVEL THE WORLD... I'M A CHANGED DUCK, SIR.
OH, L'IL GUARD DUCK... YOU EVEN SHAVED.
PERMISSION TO HUG YOU GOODBYE, SIR?
SQUEEZE
SQUEEZE
SQUEEZE
SQUEEZE
OH, AND ONE MORE THING, SIR... I LEFT YOU A LITTLE NOTE ON THE KITCHEN COUNTER. I WANT YOU TO READ IT WHEN I'M GONE.
OH NO, L'IL GUARD DUCK, I CAN'T TAKE A GOODBYE NOTE.. IS IT A GOODBYE NOTE?
IT'S A LIST OF WHERE I BURIED THE MINES, SIR.
OH.
YOU'LL WANT TO KEEP ON *THIS* SIDE OF THE BEGONIAS, SIR.
1/11

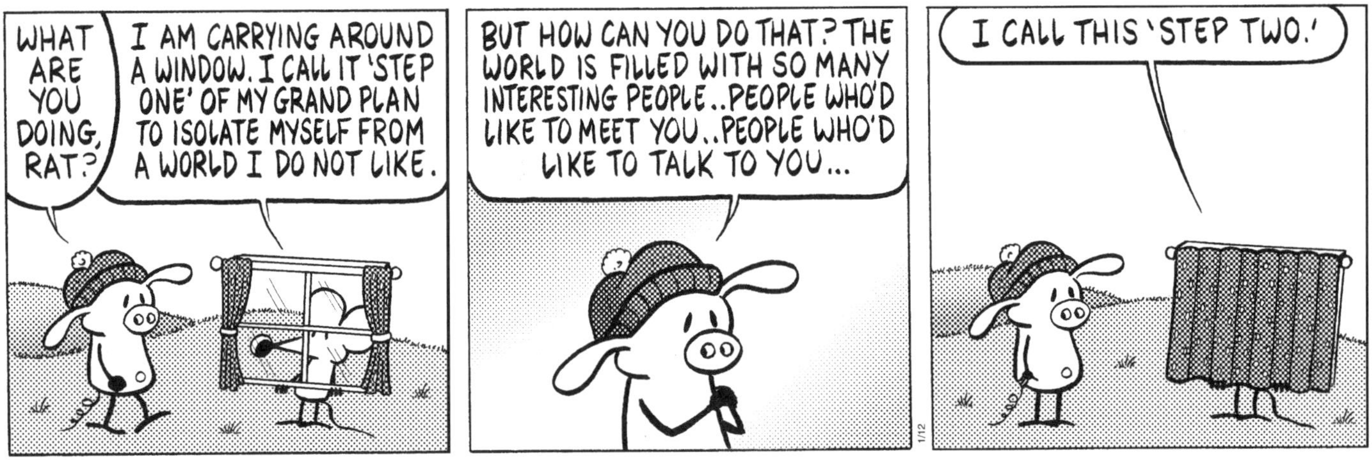
WHAT ARE YOU DOING, RAT?
I AM CARRYING AROUND A WINDOW. I CALL IT 'STEP ONE' OF MY GRAND PLAN TO ISOLATE MYSELF FROM A WORLD I DO NOT LIKE.
BUT HOW CAN YOU DO THAT? THE WORLD IS FILLED WITH SO MANY INTERESTING PEOPLE..PEOPLE WHO'D LIKE TO MEET YOU..PEOPLE WHO'D LIKE TO TALK TO YOU...
1/12
I CALL THIS 'STEP TWO.'

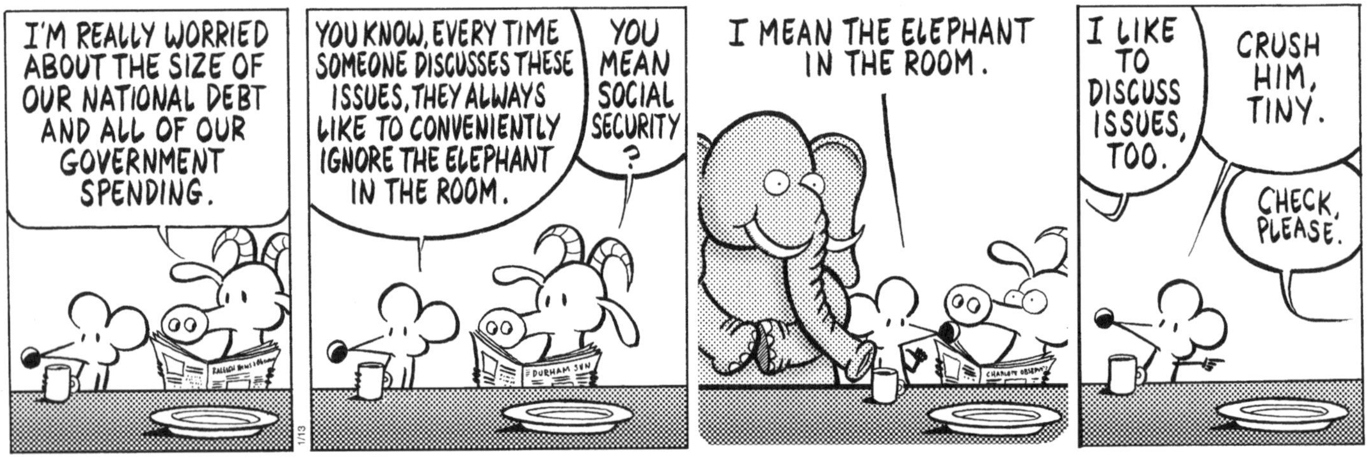
I'M REALLY WORRIED ABOUT THE SIZE OF OUR NATIONAL DEBT AND ALL OF OUR GOVERNMENT SPENDING.
1/13
YOU KNOW, EVERY TIME SOMEONE DISCUSSES THESE ISSUES, THEY ALWAYS LIKE TO CONVENIENTLY IGNORE THE ELEPHANT IN THE ROOM.
YOU MEAN SOCIAL SECURITY?
DURHAM SUN
I MEAN THE ELEPHANT IN THE ROOM.
I LIKE TO DISCUSS ISSUES, TOO.
CRUSH HIM, TINY.
CHECK, PLEASE.

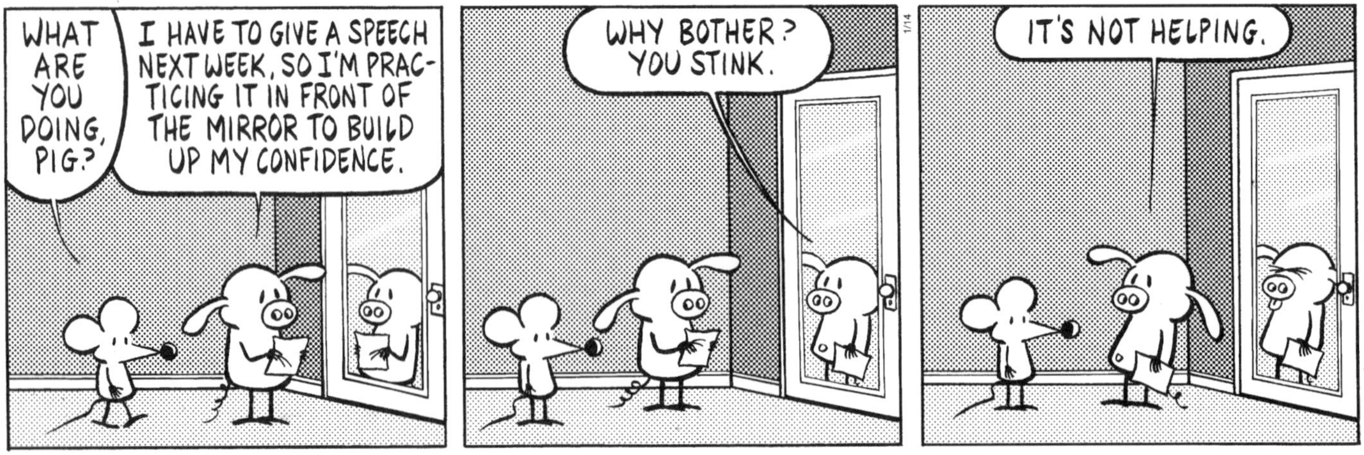
WHAT ARE YOU DOING, PIG?
I HAVE TO GIVE A SPEECH NEXT WEEK, SO I'M PRACTICING IT IN FRONT OF THE MIRROR TO BUILD UP MY CONFIDENCE.
WHY BOTHER? YOU STINK.
1/14
IT'S NOT HELPING.

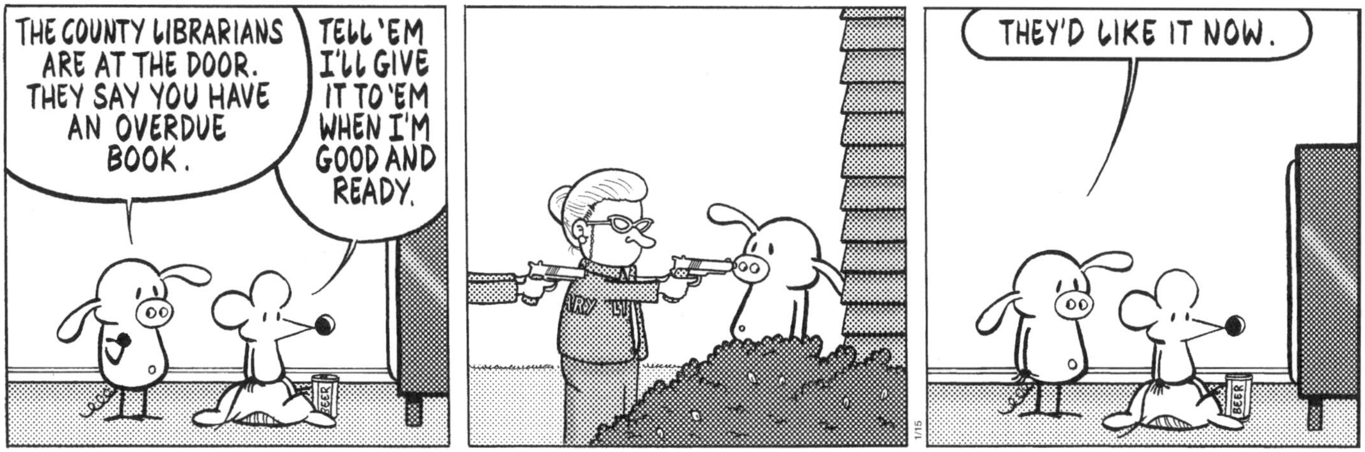
THE COUNTY LIBRARIANS ARE AT THE DOOR. THEY SAY YOU HAVE AN OVERDUE BOOK.
TELL 'EM I'LL GIVE IT TO 'EM WHEN I'M GOOD AND READY.
THEY'D LIKE IT NOW.
1/15

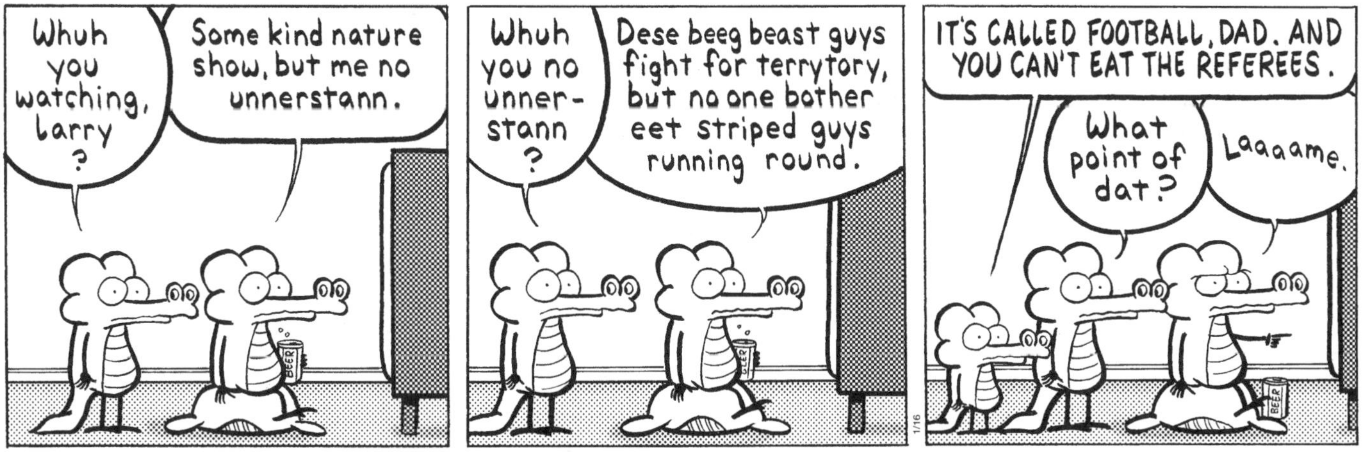
Whuh you watching, Larry?
Some kind nature show, but me no unnerstann.
Whuh you no unner-stann?
Dese beeg beast guys fight for terrytory, but no one bother eet striped guys running round.
IT'S CALLED FOOTBALL, DAD. AND YOU CAN'T EAT THE REFEREES.
What point of dat?
Laaaame.
1/16

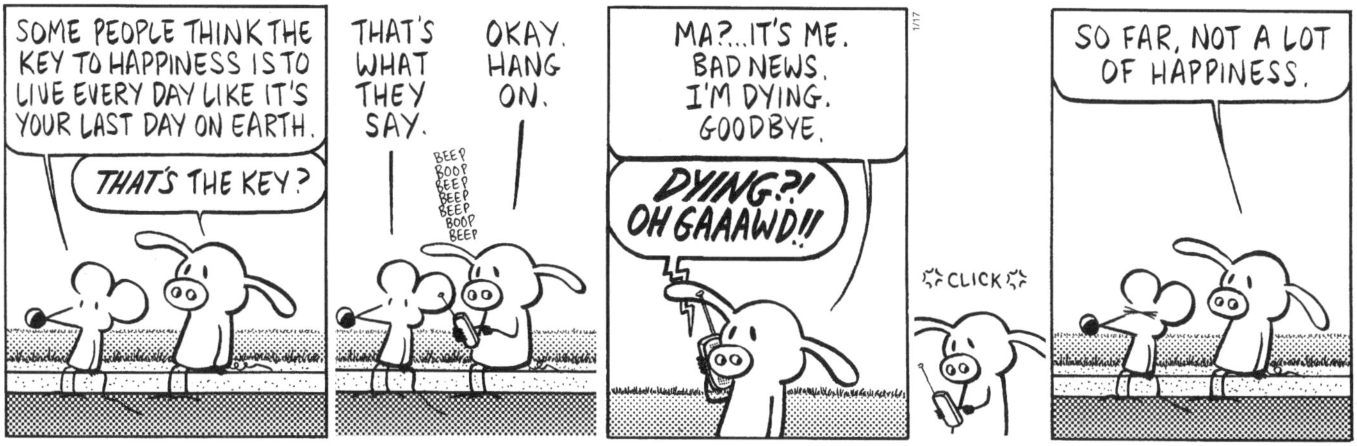
SOME PEOPLE THINK THE KEY TO HAPPINESS IS TO LIVE EVERY DAY LIKE IT'S YOUR LAST DAY ON EARTH.
THAT'S THE KEY?
THAT'S WHAT THEY SAY.
OKAY. HANG ON.
BEEP BOOP BEEP BEEP BEEP BOOP BEEP
MA?...IT'S ME. BAD NEWS. I'M DYING. GOODBYE.
DYING?! OH GAAAWD!!
CLICK
SO FAR, NOT A LOT OF HAPPINESS.
1/17

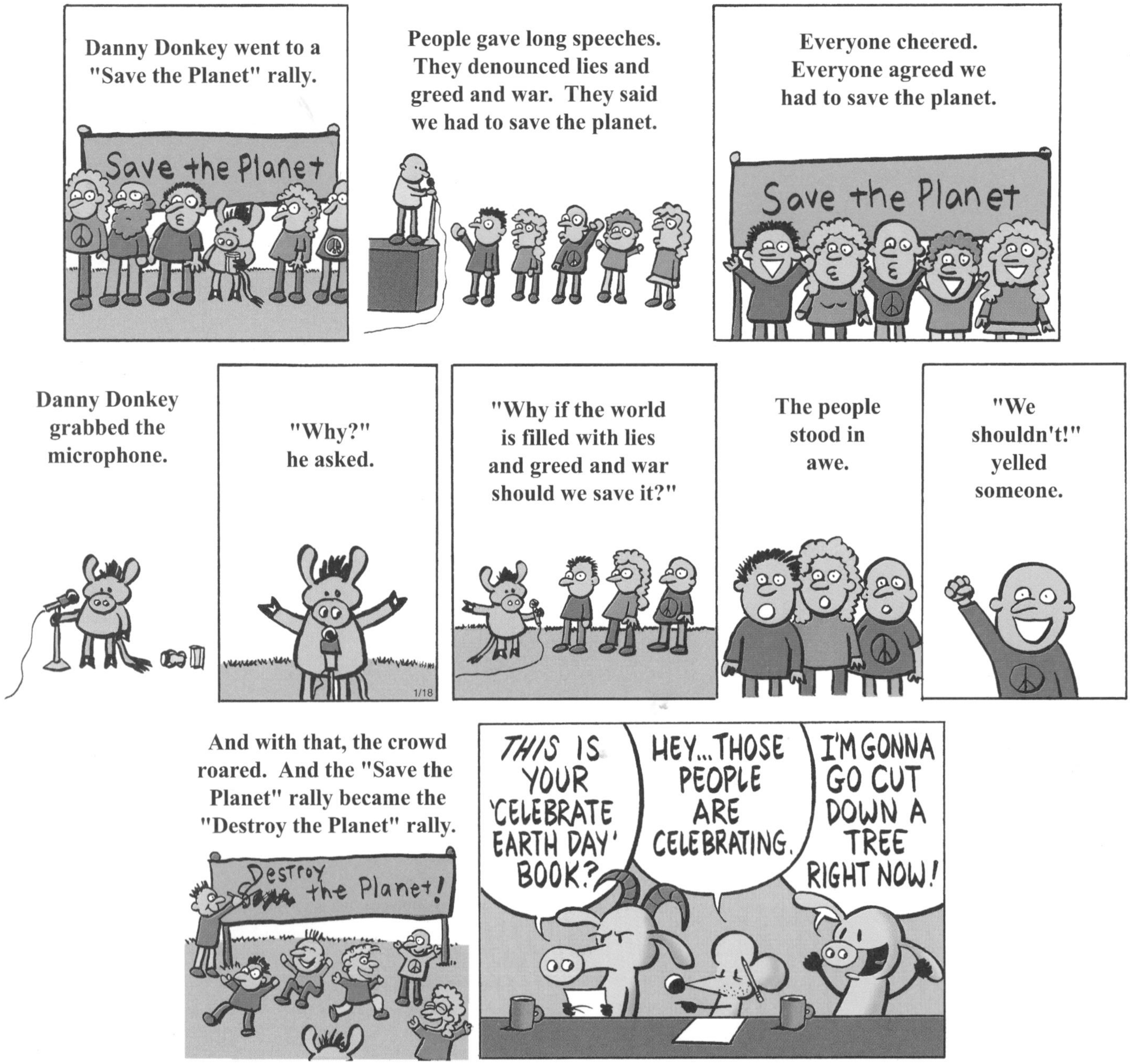
Danny Donkey went to a "Save the Planet" rally.
Save the Planet
People gave long speeches. They denounced lies and greed and war. They said we had to save the planet.
Everyone cheered. Everyone agreed we had to save the planet.
Save the Planet
Danny Donkey grabbed the microphone.
"Why?" he asked.
1/18
"Why if the world is filled with lies and greed and war should we save it?"
The people stood in awe.
"We shouldn't!" yelled someone.
And with that, the crowd roared. And the "Save the Planet" rally became the "Destroy the Planet" rally.
Destroy the Planet!
THIS IS YOUR 'CELEBRATE EARTH DAY' BOOK?
HEY... THOSE PEOPLE ARE CELEBRATING.
I'M GONNA GO CUT DOWN A TREE RIGHT NOW!

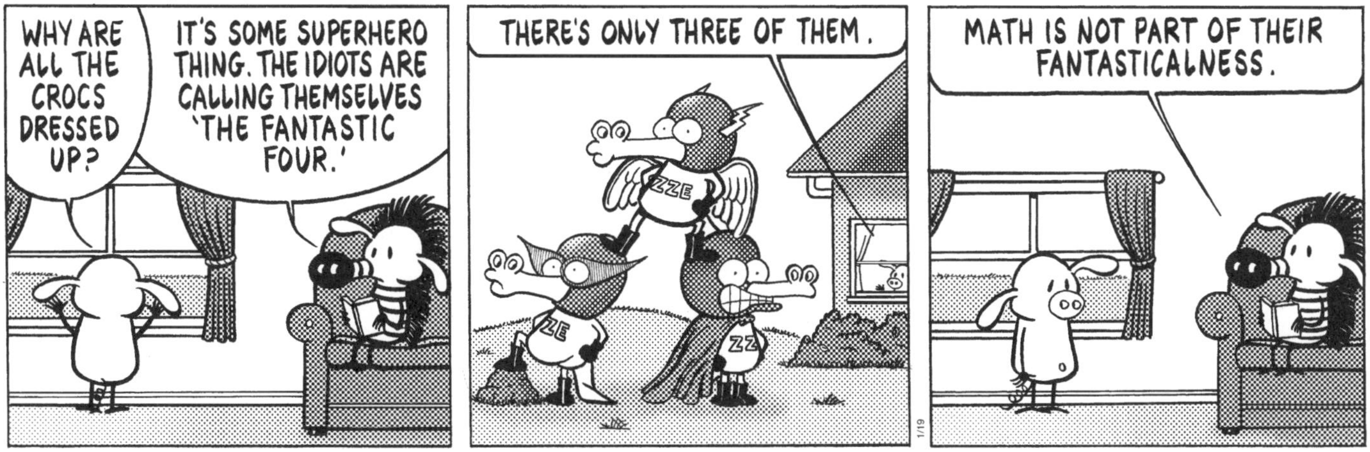
WHY ARE ALL THE CROCS DRESSED UP?
IT'S SOME SUPERHERO THING. THE IDIOTS ARE CALLING THEMSELVES 'THE FANTASTIC FOUR.'
THERE'S ONLY THREE OF THEM.
ZZE
ZE
ZZ
MATH IS NOT PART OF THEIR FANTASTICALNESS.
1/19

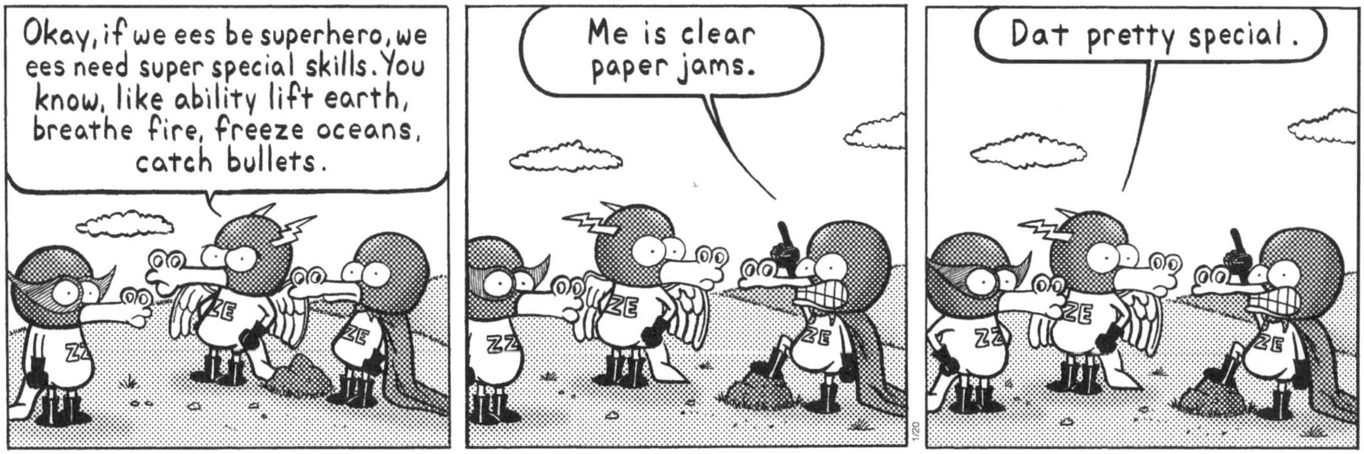
Okay, if we ees be superhero, we ees need super special skills. You know, like ability lift earth, breathe fire, freeze oceans, catch bullets.
Me is clear paper jams.
Dat pretty special.
1/20

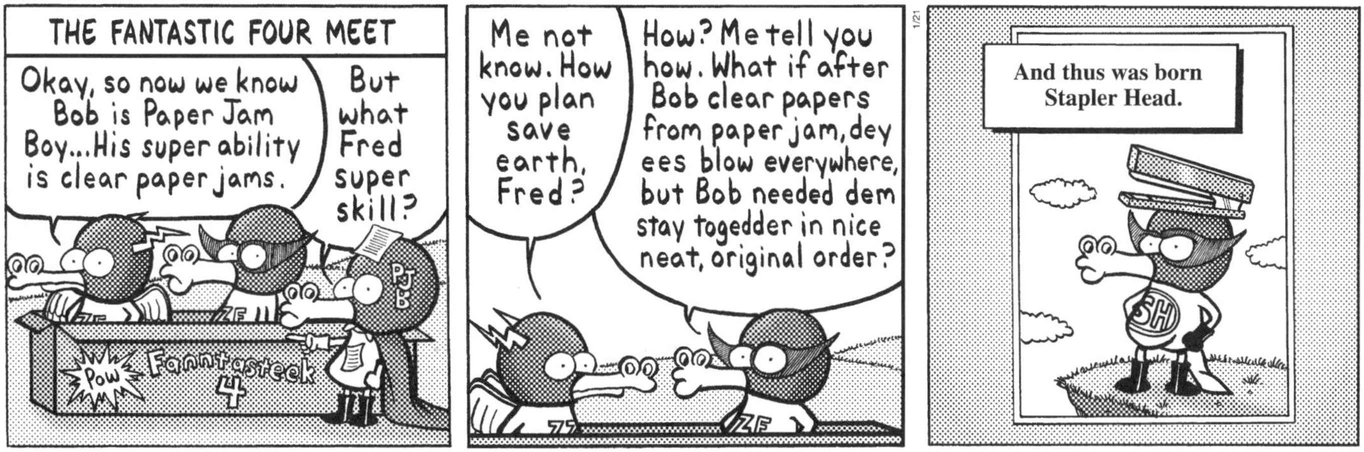
THE FANTASTIC FOUR MEET
Okay, so now we know Bob is Paper Jam Boy...His super ability is clear paper jams.
But what Fred super skill?
PJB
Pow
Fanntasteek 4
Me not know. How you plan save earth, Fred?
How? Me tell you how. What if after Bob clear papers from paper jam, dey ees blow everywhere, but Bob needed dem stay togedder in nice neat, original order?
And thus was born Stapler Head.
SH
1/21

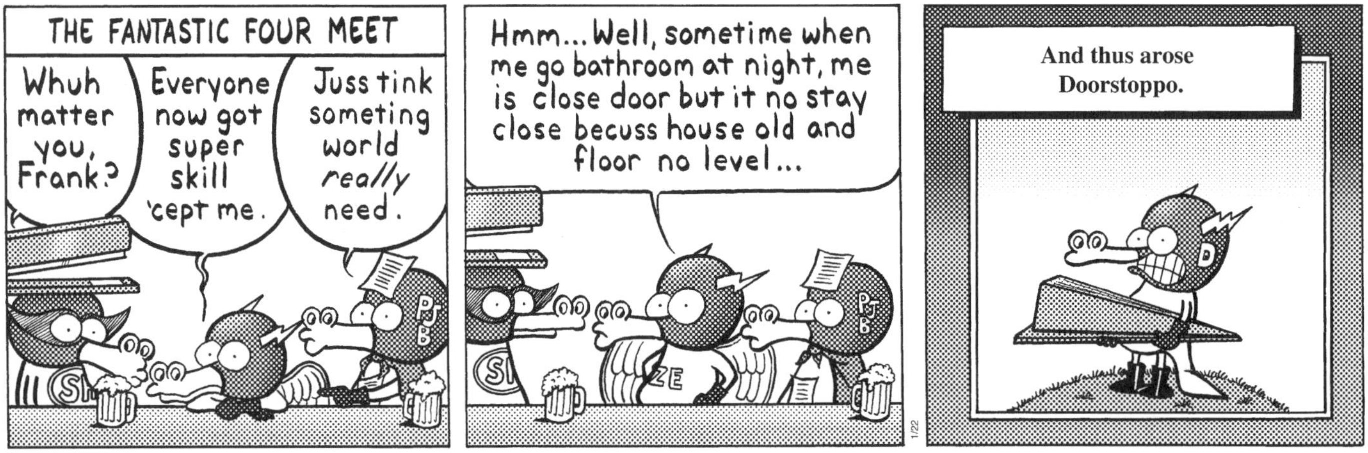
THE FANTASTIC FOUR MEET
Whuh matter you, Frank?
Everyone now got super skill 'cept me.
Juss tink someting world *really* need.
Hmm... Well, sometime when me go bathroom at night, me is close door but it no stay close becuss house old and floor no level...
1/22
And thus arose Doorstoppo.

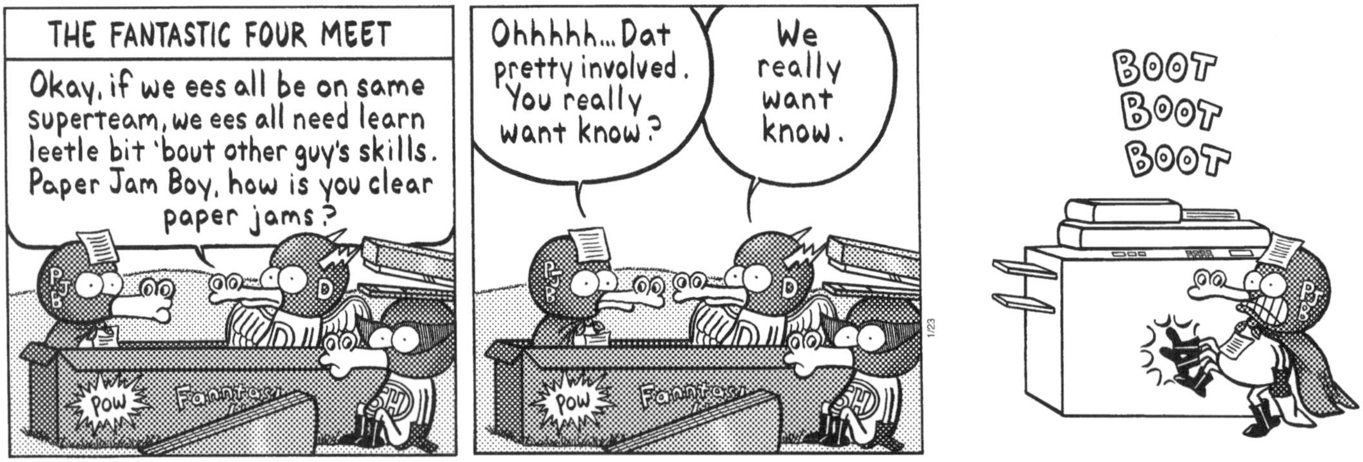
THE FANTASTIC FOUR MEET
Okay, if we ees all be on same superteam, we ees all need learn leetle bit 'bout other guy's skills. Paper Jam Boy, how is you clear paper jams?
Ohhhhh... Dat pretty involved. You really want know?
We really want know.
1/23
BOOT BOOT BOOT

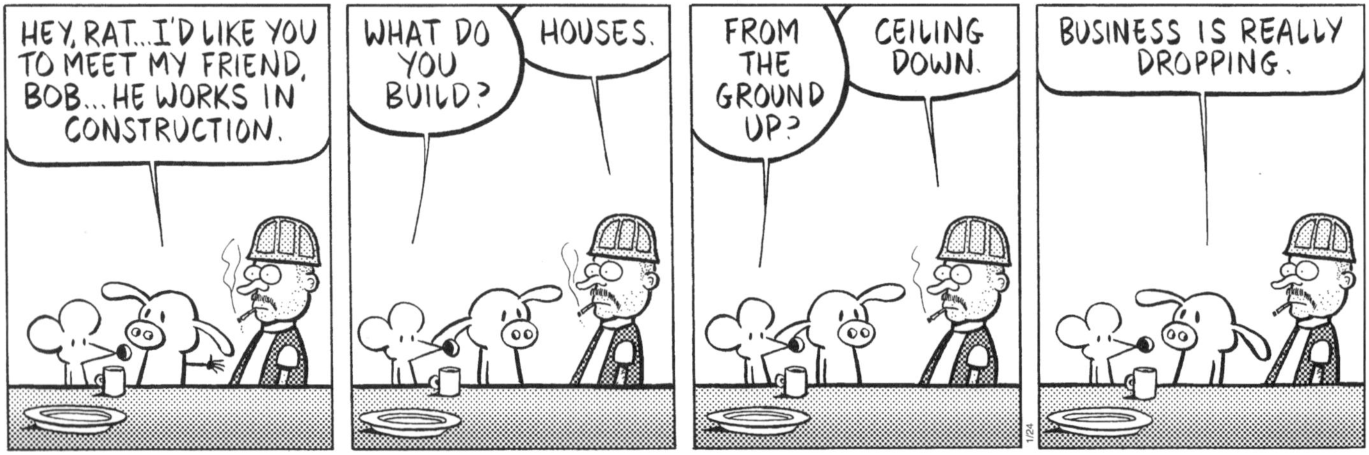
HEY, RAT... I'D LIKE YOU TO MEET MY FRIEND, BOB... HE WORKS IN CONSTRUCTION.
WHAT DO YOU BUILD?
HOUSES.
FROM THE GROUND UP?
CEILING DOWN.
1/24
BUSINESS IS REALLY DROPPING.

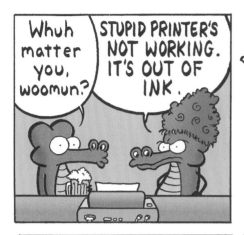

Whuh matter you, woomun?

STUPID PRINTER'S NOT WORKING. IT'S OUT OF INK.

PFOO PFOO PFOO PFOO

PAPER JAM BOY!

It ees me.

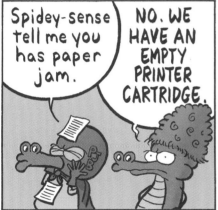

Spidey-sense tell me you has paper jam.

NO. WE HAVE AN EMPTY PRINTER CARTRIDGE.

Preenter cartridge? Dat like sooo esspensive...Such reep-off...And me no has power to feex...Oh, no...Me fading fast...Look...like...evil...preenter......

...defeet me.

THUD!

YOUR SUPERHERO IS SOMETHING LESS THAN SUPER.

CURSE YOU, EVIL HOOLITT PACKURD!!!

1/25

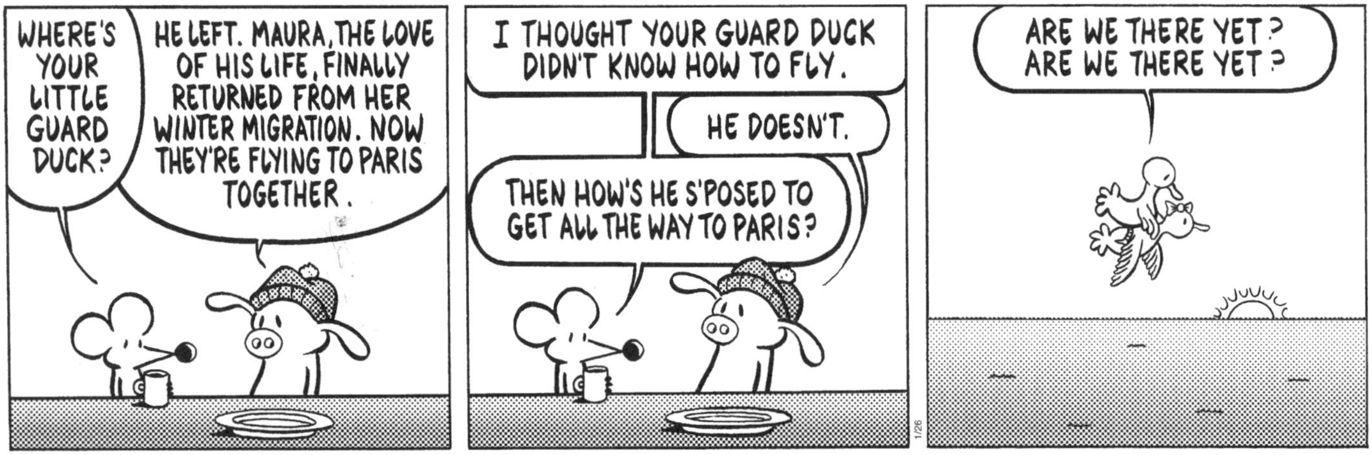
WHERE'S YOUR LITTLE GUARD DUCK?
HE LEFT. MAURA, THE LOVE OF HIS LIFE, FINALLY RETURNED FROM HER WINTER MIGRATION. NOW THEY'RE FLYING TO PARIS TOGETHER.
I THOUGHT YOUR GUARD DUCK DIDN'T KNOW HOW TO FLY.
HE DOESN'T.
THEN HOW'S HE S'POSED TO GET ALL THE WAY TO PARIS?
1/26
ARE WE THERE YET? ARE WE THERE YET?

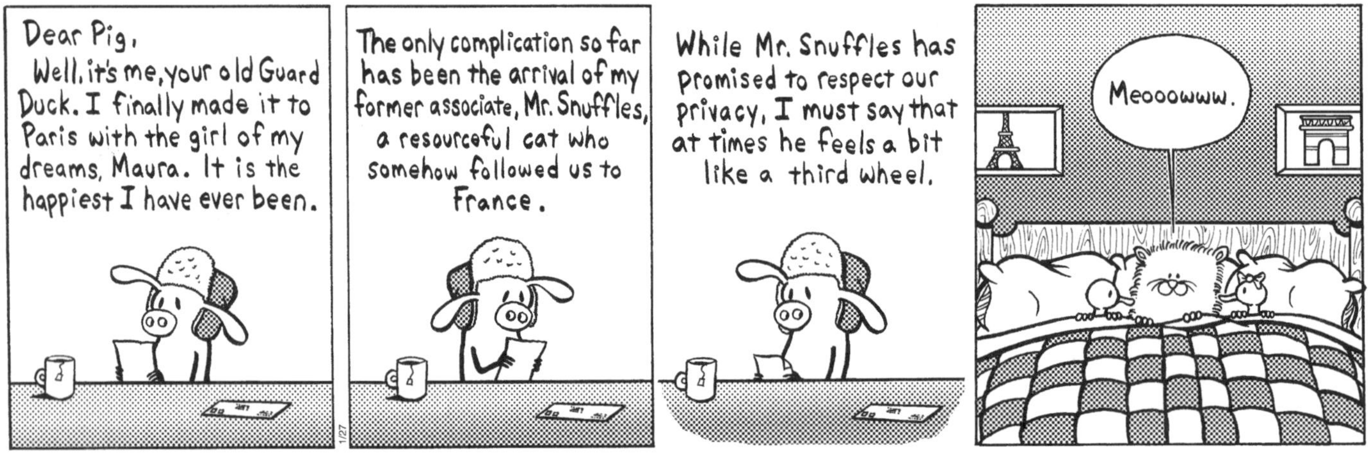
Dear Pig,
Well, it's me, your old Guard Duck. I finally made it to Paris with the girl of my dreams, Maura. It is the happiest I have ever been.
1/27
The only complication so far has been the arrival of my former associate, Mr. Snuffles, a resourceful cat who somehow followed us to France.
While Mr. Snuffles has promised to respect our privacy, I must say that at times he feels a bit like a third wheel.
Meooowww.

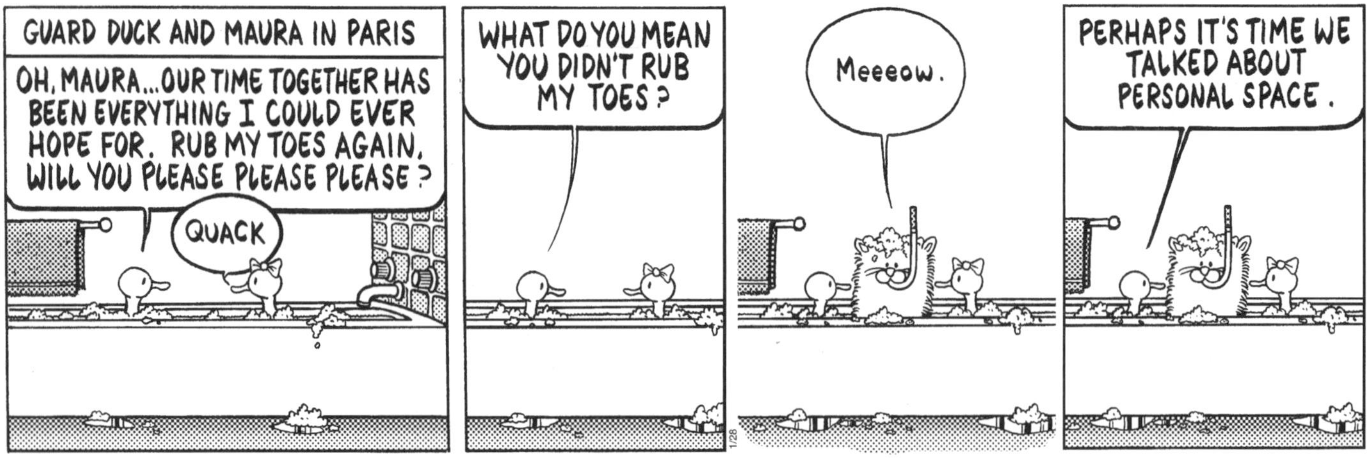
GUARD DUCK AND MAURA IN PARIS
OH, MAURA...OUR TIME TOGETHER HAS BEEN EVERYTHING I COULD EVER HOPE FOR. RUB MY TOES AGAIN, WILL YOU PLEASE PLEASE PLEASE?
QUACK
WHAT DO YOU MEAN YOU DIDN'T RUB MY TOES?
1/28
Meeeow.
PERHAPS IT'S TIME WE TALKED ABOUT PERSONAL SPACE.

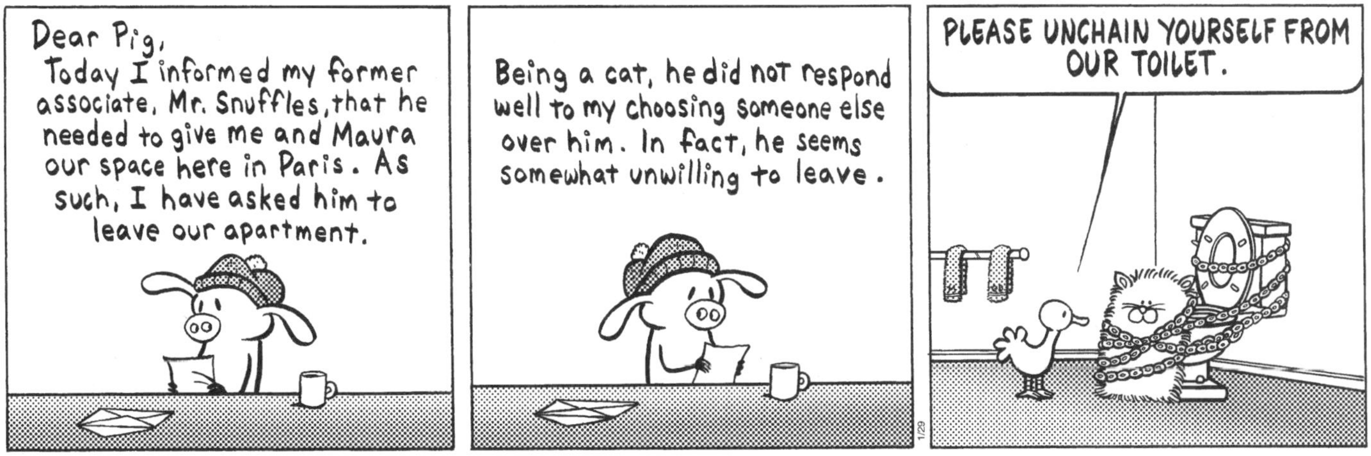
Dear Pig,
Today I informed my former associate, Mr. Snuffles, that he needed to give me and Maura our space here in Paris. As such, I have asked him to leave our apartment.
Being a cat, he did not respond well to my choosing someone else over him. In fact, he seems somewhat unwilling to leave.
1/29
PLEASE UNCHAIN YOURSELF FROM OUR TOILET.

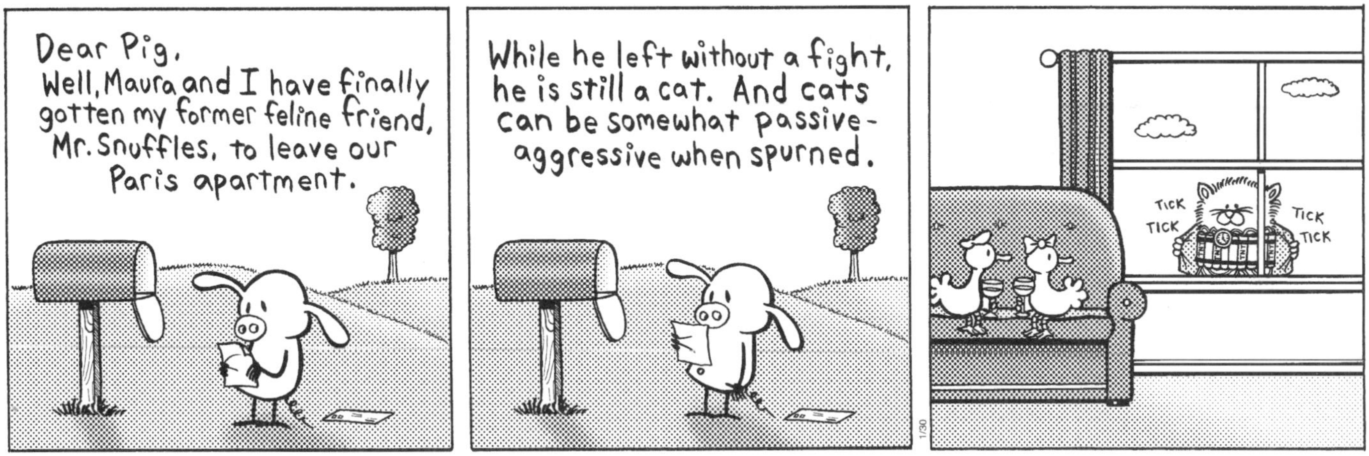
Dear Pig,
Well, Maura and I have finally gotten my former feline friend, Mr. Snuffles, to leave our Paris apartment.
While he left without a fight, he is still a cat. And cats can be somewhat passive-aggressive when spurned.
1/30
TICK TICK
TICK TICK

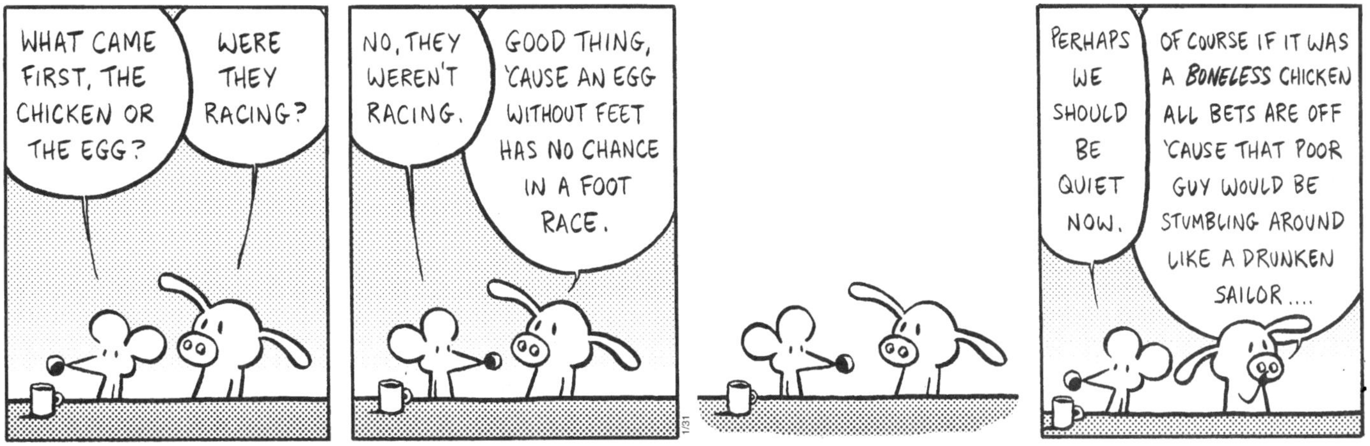
WHAT CAME FIRST, THE CHICKEN OR THE EGG?
WERE THEY RACING?
NO, THEY WEREN'T RACING.
GOOD THING, 'CAUSE AN EGG WITHOUT FEET HAS NO CHANCE IN A FOOT RACE.
1/31
PERHAPS WE SHOULD BE QUIET NOW.
OF COURSE IF IT WAS A BONELESS CHICKEN ALL BETS ARE OFF 'CAUSE THAT POOR GUY WOULD BE STUMBLING AROUND LIKE A DRUNKEN SAILOR....

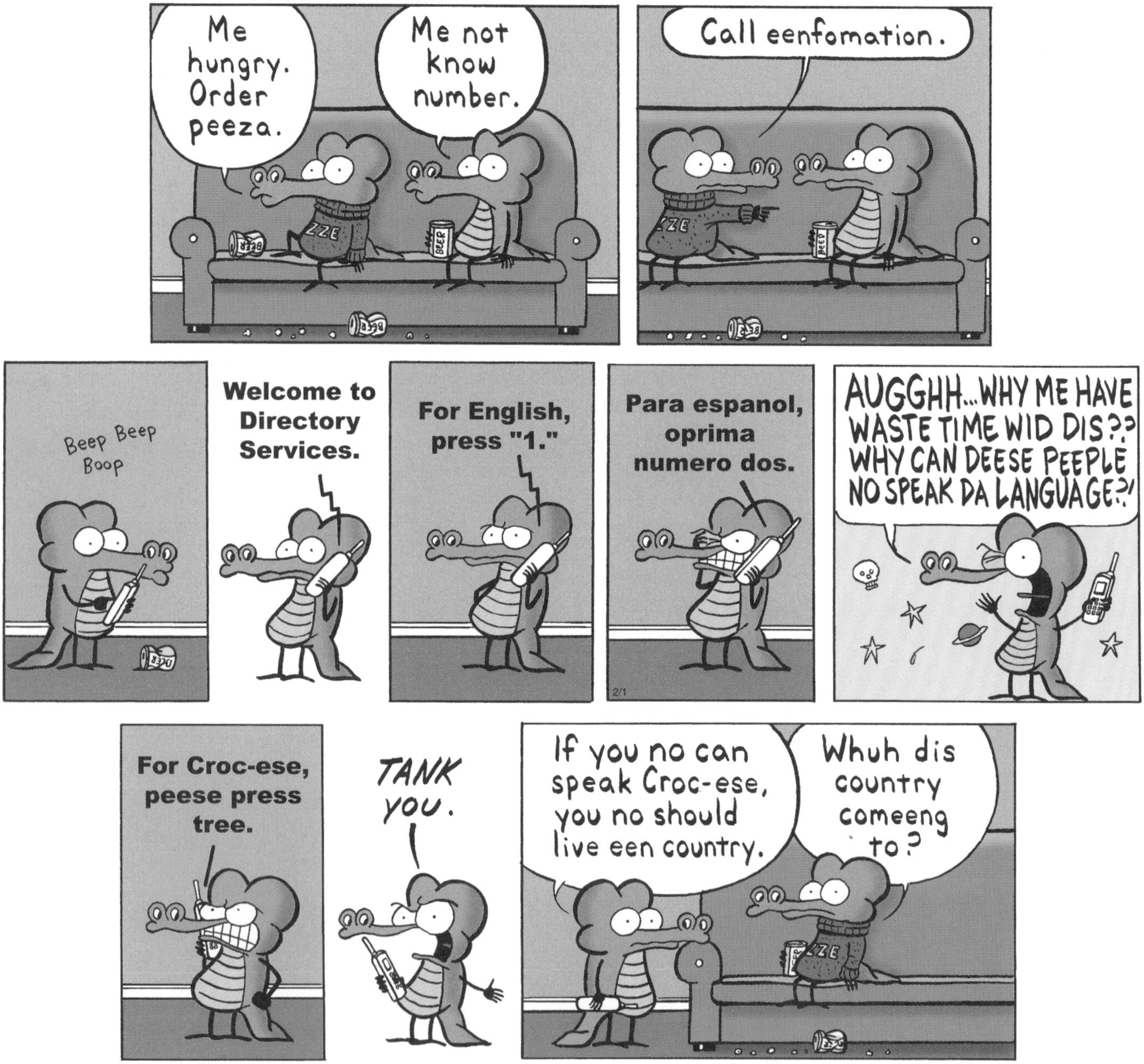
Me hungry. Order peeza.
Me not know number.
Call eenfomation.
Beep Beep Boop
Welcome to Directory Services.
For English, press "1."
Para espanol, oprima numero dos.
AUGGHH...WHY ME HAVE WASTE TIME WID DIS??
WHY CAN DEESE PEEPLE NO SPEAK DA LANGUAGE?!
For Croc-ese, peese press tree.
TANK YOU.
If you no can speak Croc-ese, you no should live een country.
Whuh dis country comeeng to?

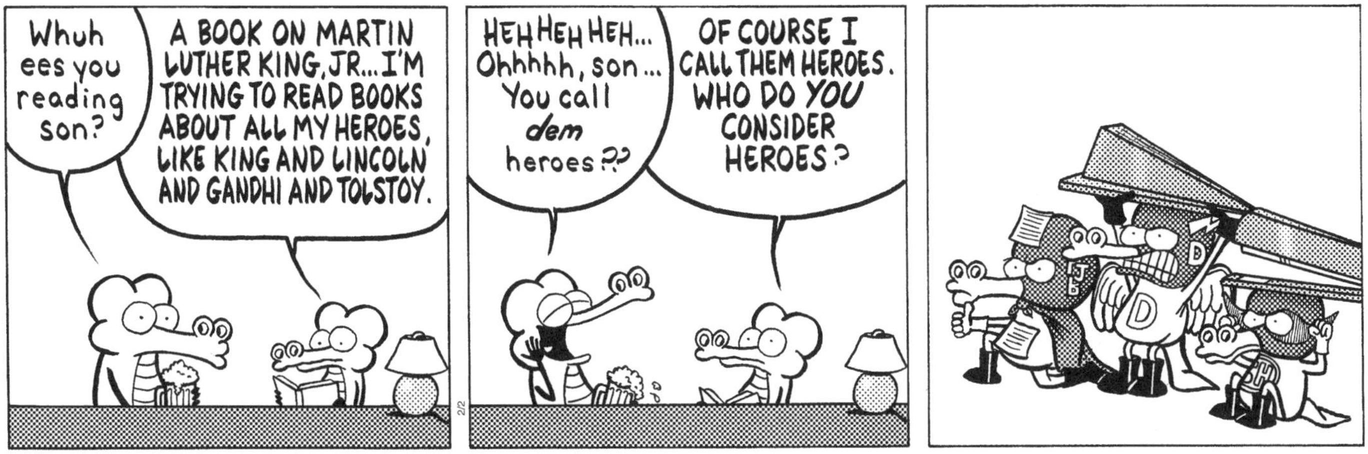
Whuh ees you reading son?
A BOOK ON MARTIN LUTHER KING, JR... I'M TRYING TO READ BOOKS ABOUT ALL MY HEROES, LIKE KING AND LINCOLN AND GANDHI AND TOLSTOY.
HEH HEH HEH... Ohhhhh, son... You call *dem* heroes ??
OF COURSE I CALL THEM HEROES. WHO DO *YOU* CONSIDER HEROES?

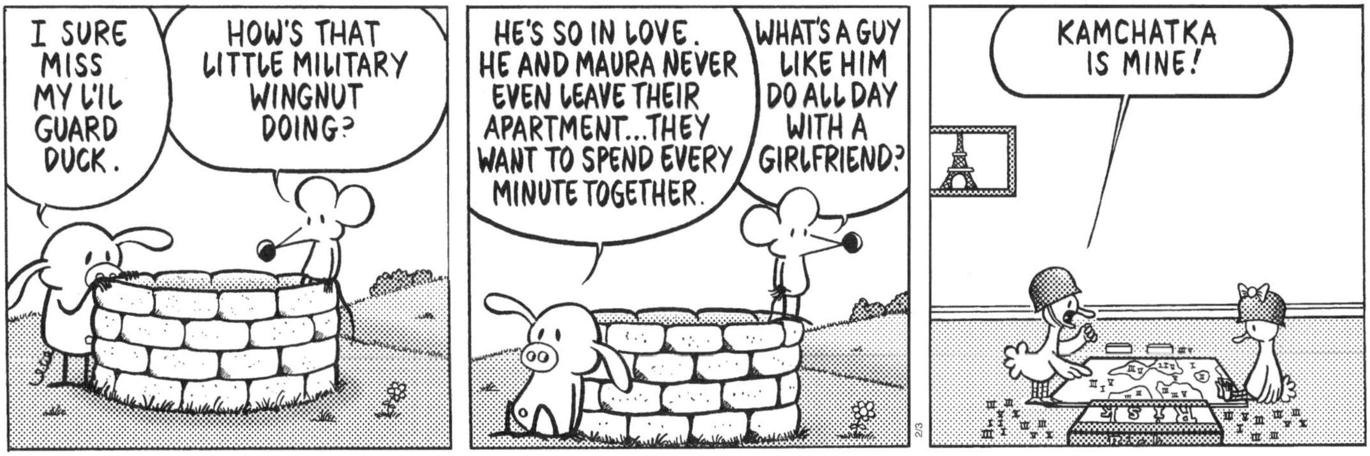
I SURE MISS MY L'IL GUARD DUCK.
HOW'S THAT LITTLE MILITARY WINGNUT DOING?
HE'S SO IN LOVE. HE AND MAURA NEVER EVEN LEAVE THEIR APARTMENT... THEY WANT TO SPEND EVERY MINUTE TOGETHER.
WHAT'S A GUY LIKE HIM DO ALL DAY WITH A GIRLFRIEND?
KAMCHATKA IS MINE!

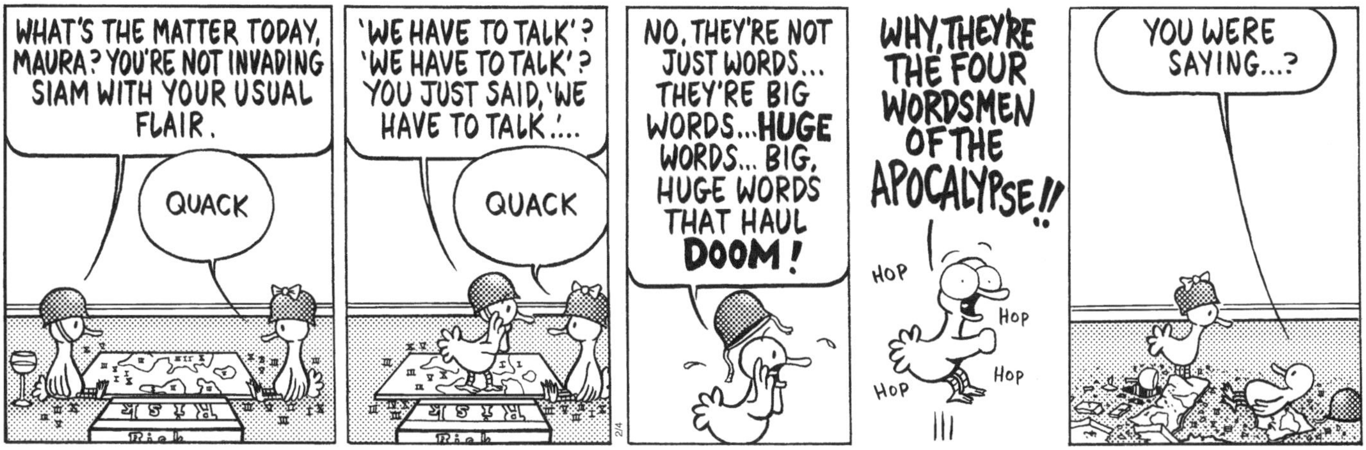
WHAT'S THE MATTER TODAY, MAURA? YOU'RE NOT INVADING SIAM WITH YOUR USUAL FLAIR.
QUACK
'WE HAVE TO TALK'? 'WE HAVE TO TALK'? YOU JUST SAID, 'WE HAVE TO TALK.'...
QUACK
NO, THEY'RE NOT JUST WORDS... THEY'RE BIG WORDS... **HUGE** WORDS... BIG, HUGE WORDS THAT HAUL **DOOM**!
WHY, THEY'RE THE FOUR WORDSMEN OF THE APOCALYPSE!!
HOP
HOP
HOP
HOP
YOU WERE SAYING...?

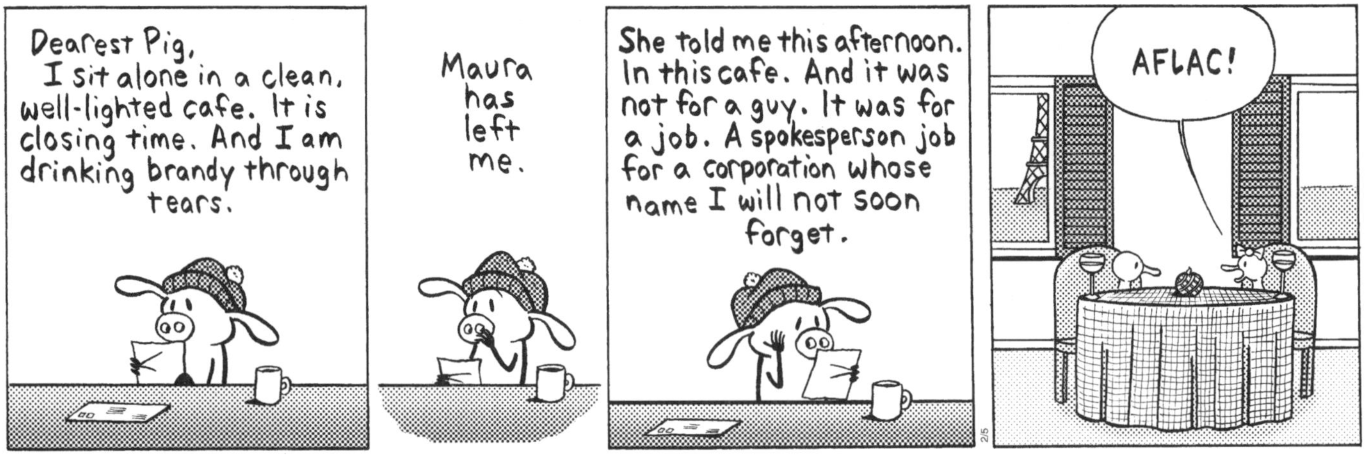
Dearest Pig,
I sit alone in a clean, well-lighted cafe. It is closing time. And I am drinking brandy through tears.
Maura has left me.
She told me this afternoon. In this cafe. And it was not for a guy. It was for a job. A spokesperson job for a corporation whose name I will not soon forget.
2/5
AFLAC!

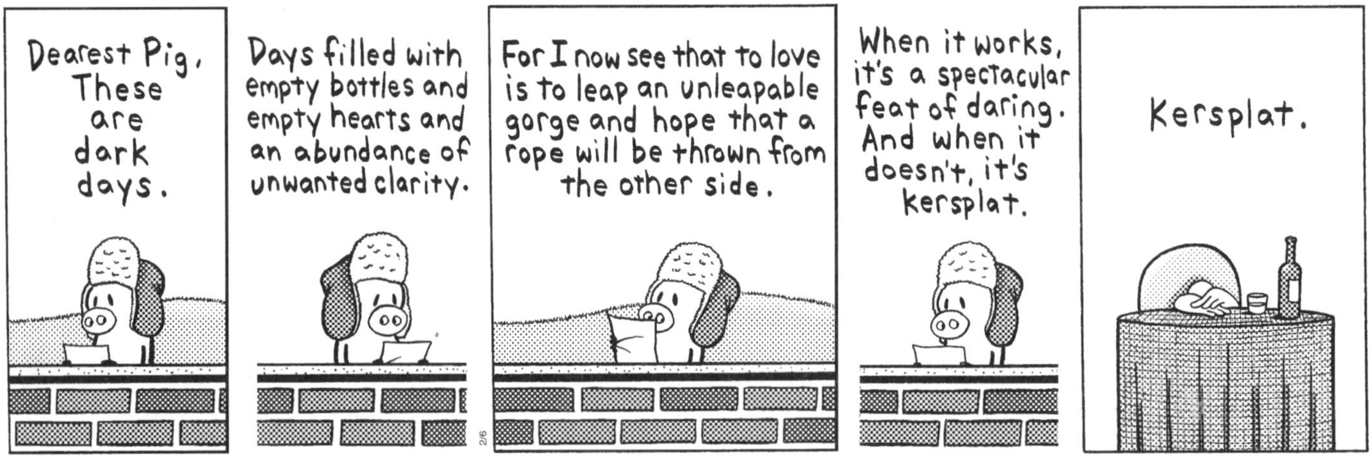
Dearest Pig, These are dark days.
Days filled with empty bottles and empty hearts and an abundance of unwanted clarity.
2/6
For I now see that to love is to leap an unleapable gorge and hope that a rope will be thrown from the other side.
When it works, it's a spectacular feat of daring. And when it doesn't, it's kersplat.
Kersplat.

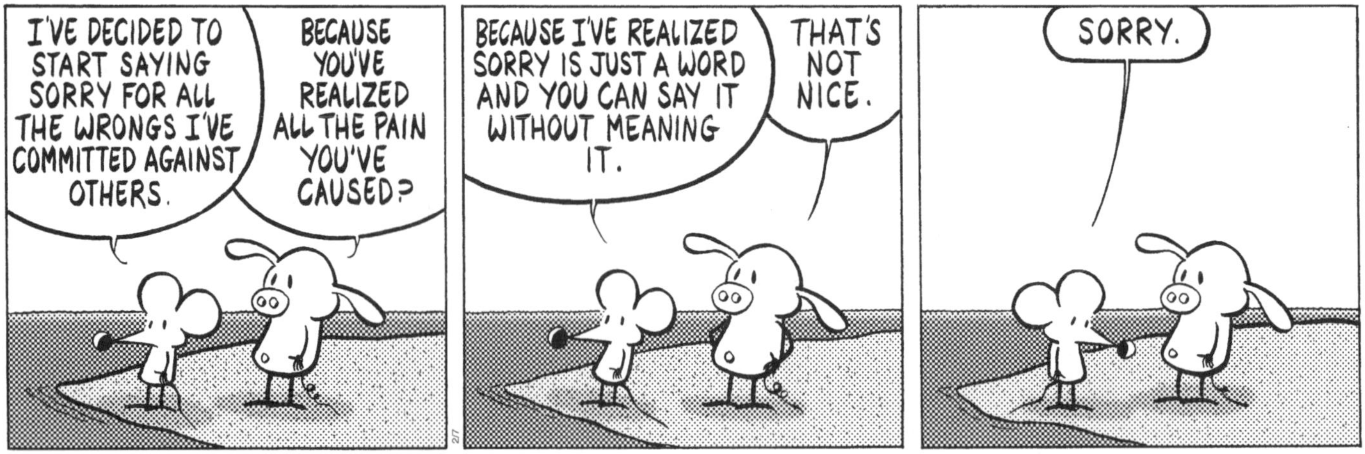
I'VE DECIDED TO START SAYING SORRY FOR ALL THE WRONGS I'VE COMMITTED AGAINST OTHERS.
BECAUSE YOU'VE REALIZED ALL THE PAIN YOU'VE CAUSED?
2/7
BECAUSE I'VE REALIZED SORRY IS JUST A WORD AND YOU CAN SAY IT WITHOUT MEANING IT.
THAT'S NOT NICE.
SORRY.

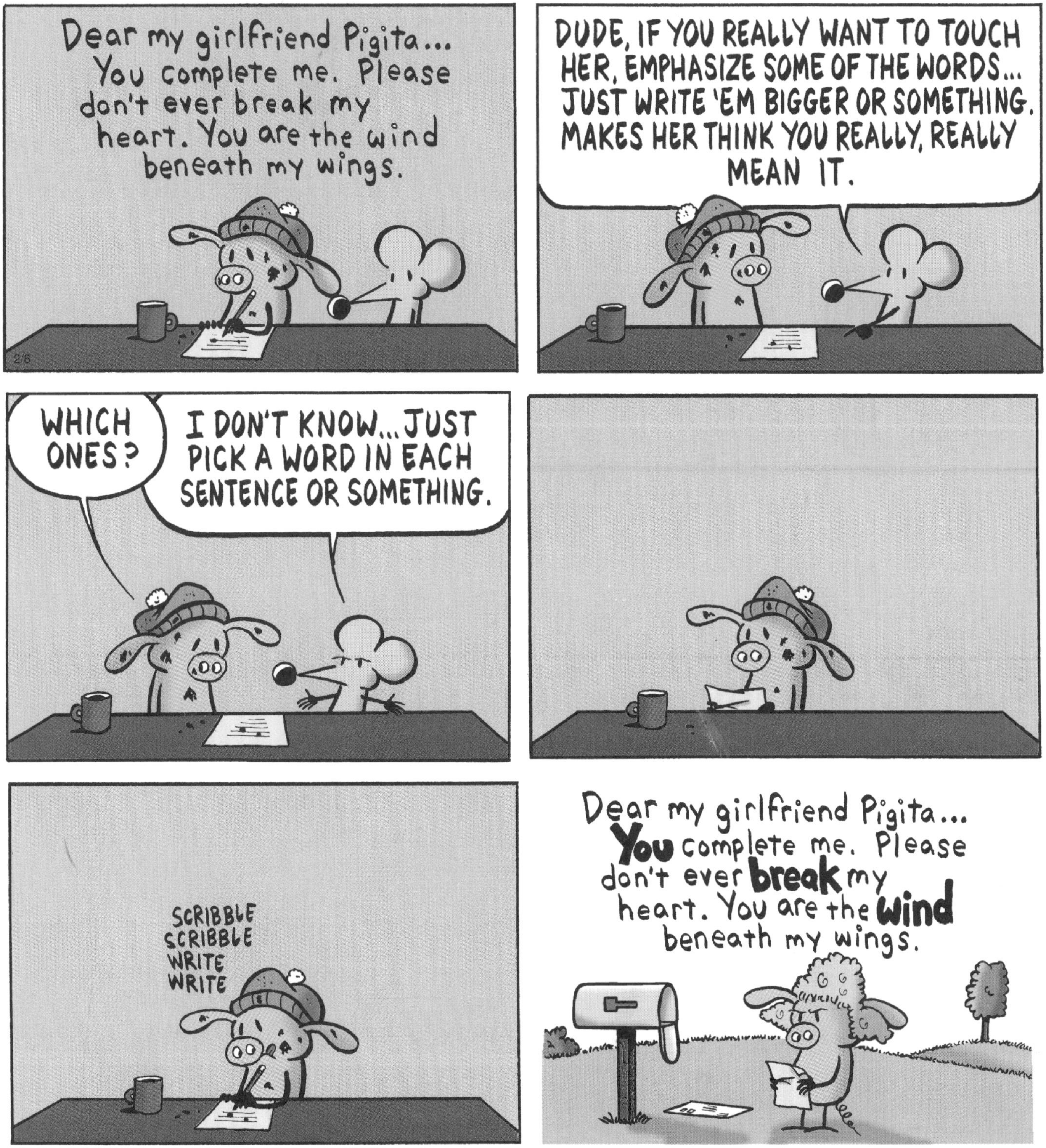
Dear my girlfriend Pigita... You complete me. Please don't ever break my heart. You are the wind beneath my wings.
2/8
DUDE, IF YOU REALLY WANT TO TOUCH HER, EMPHASIZE SOME OF THE WORDS... JUST WRITE 'EM BIGGER OR SOMETHING. MAKES HER THINK YOU REALLY, REALLY MEAN IT.
WHICH ONES?
I DON'T KNOW... JUST PICK A WORD IN EACH SENTENCE OR SOMETHING.
SCRIBBLE SCRIBBLE WRITE WRITE
Dear my girlfriend Pigita... You complete me. Please don't ever break my heart. You are the wind beneath my wings.

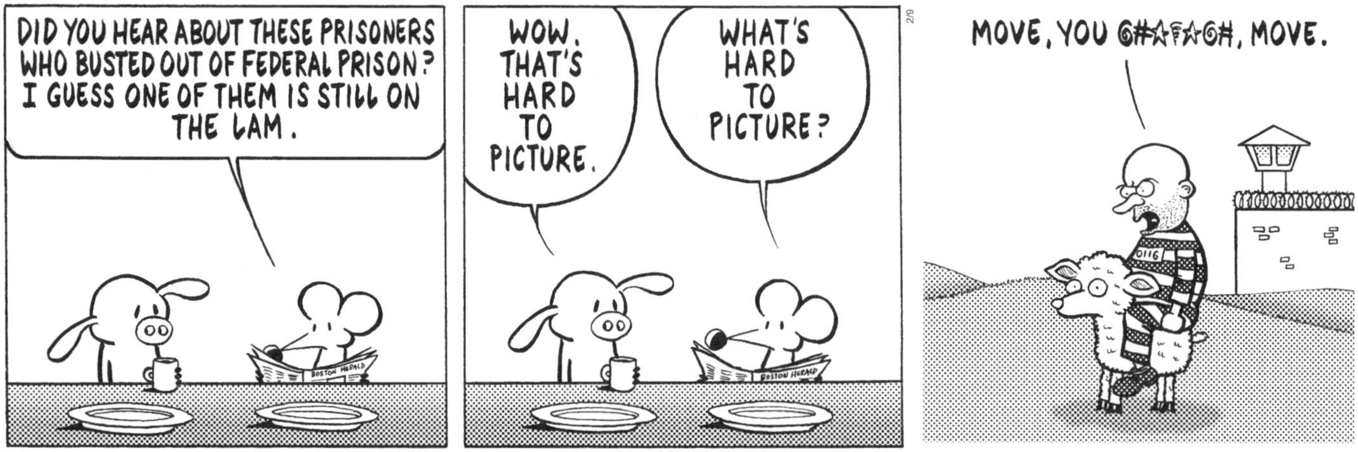
DID YOU HEAR ABOUT THESE PRISONERS WHO BUSTED OUT OF FEDERAL PRISON? I GUESS ONE OF THEM IS STILL ON THE LAM.
WOW. THAT'S HARD TO PICTURE.
WHAT'S HARD TO PICTURE?
2/9
MOVE, YOU @#☆!☆@#, MOVE.

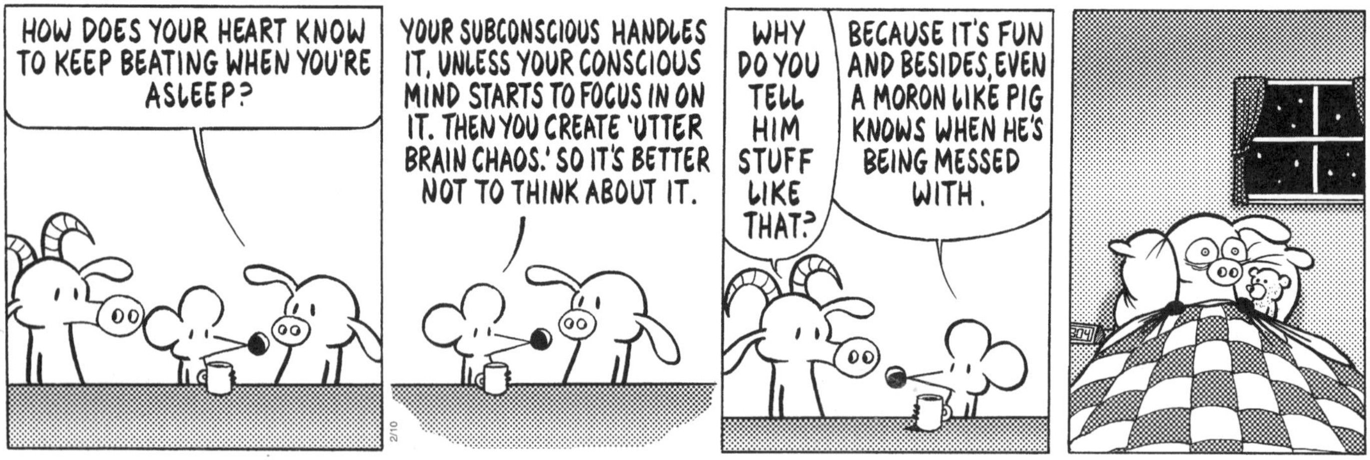
HOW DOES YOUR HEART KNOW TO KEEP BEATING WHEN YOU'RE ASLEEP?
2/10
YOUR SUBCONSCIOUS HANDLES IT, UNLESS YOUR CONSCIOUS MIND STARTS TO FOCUS IN ON IT. THEN YOU CREATE 'UTTER BRAIN CHAOS.' SO IT'S BETTER NOT TO THINK ABOUT IT.
WHY DO YOU TELL HIM STUFF LIKE THAT?
BECAUSE IT'S FUN AND BESIDES, EVEN A MORON LIKE PIG KNOWS WHEN HE'S BEING MESSED WITH.

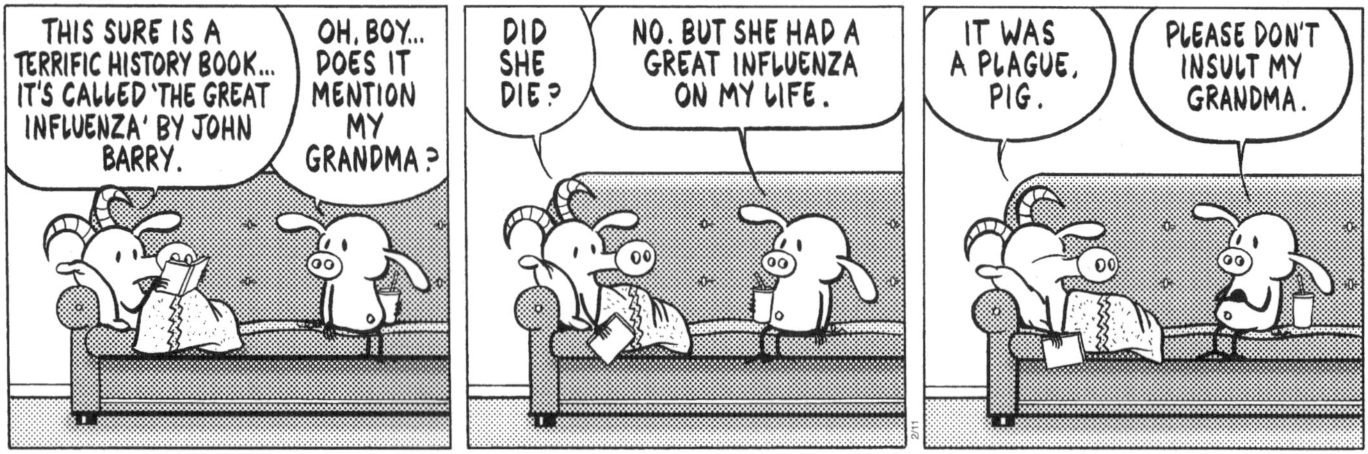
THIS SURE IS A TERRIFIC HISTORY BOOK... IT'S CALLED 'THE GREAT INFLUENZA' BY JOHN BARRY.
OH, BOY... DOES IT MENTION MY GRANDMA?
DID SHE DIE?
NO. BUT SHE HAD A GREAT INFLUENZA ON MY LIFE.
2/11
IT WAS A PLAGUE, PIG.
PLEASE DON'T INSULT MY GRANDMA.

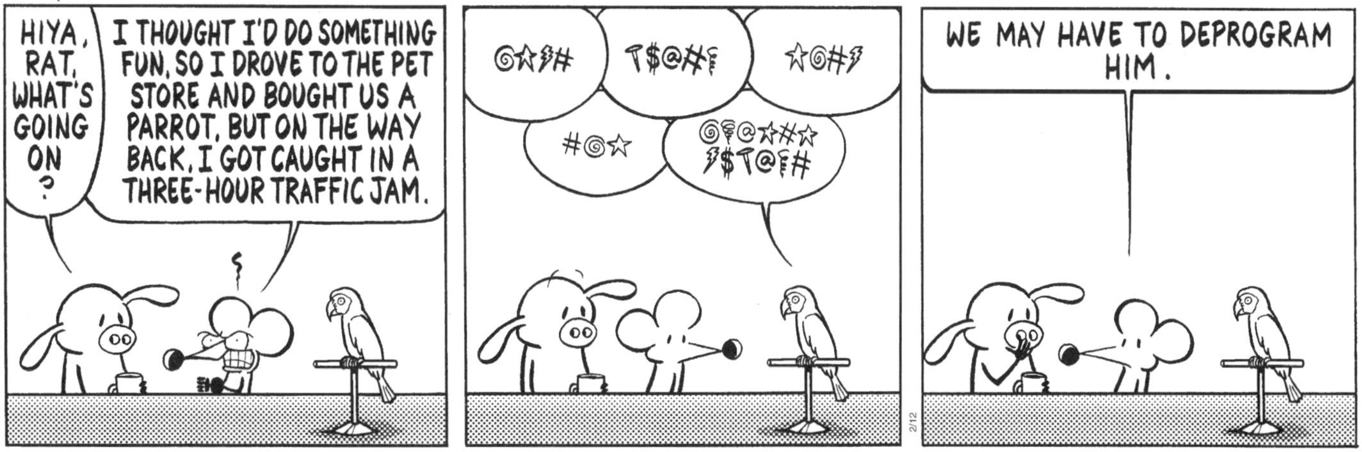
HIYA, RAT, WHAT'S GOING ON ?
I THOUGHT I'D DO SOMETHING FUN, SO I DROVE TO THE PET STORE AND BOUGHT US A PARROT, BUT ON THE WAY BACK, I GOT CAUGHT IN A THREE-HOUR TRAFFIC JAM.
WE MAY HAVE TO DEPROGRAM HIM.

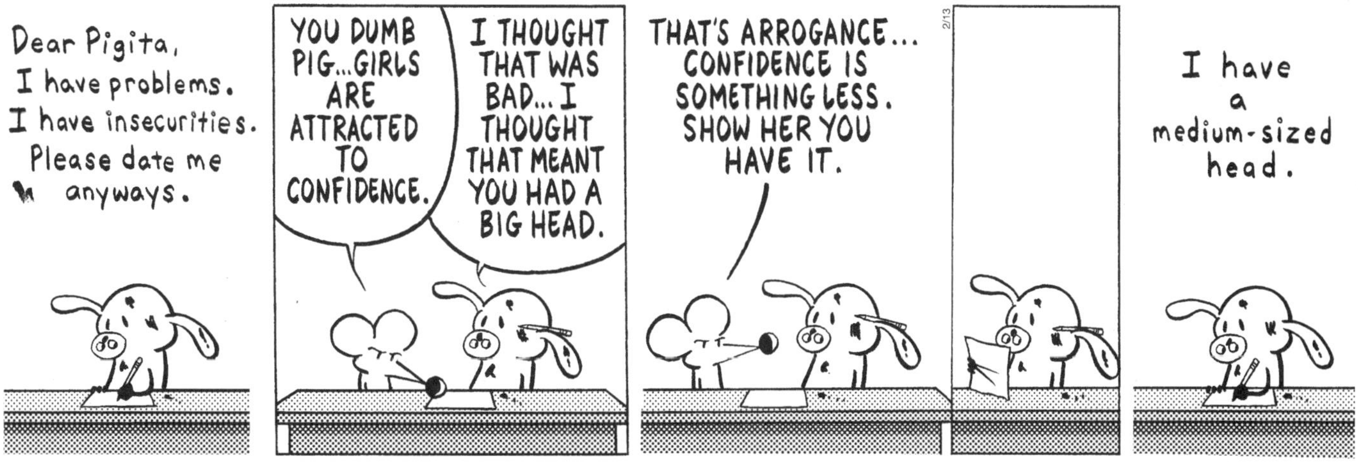
Dear Pigita,
I have problems.
I have insecurities.
Please date me anyways.
YOU DUMB PIG...GIRLS ARE ATTRACTED TO CONFIDENCE.
I THOUGHT THAT WAS BAD... I THOUGHT THAT MEANT YOU HAD A BIG HEAD.
THAT'S ARROGANCE... CONFIDENCE IS SOMETHING LESS. SHOW HER YOU HAVE IT.
I have a medium-sized head.

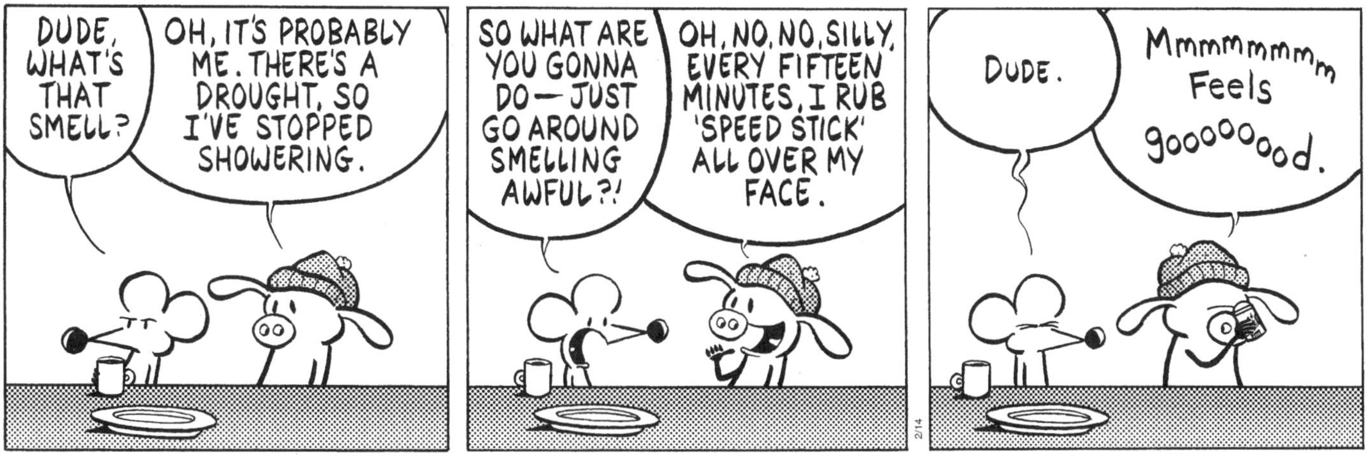
DUDE, WHAT'S THAT SMELL?
OH, IT'S PROBABLY ME. THERE'S A DROUGHT, SO I'VE STOPPED SHOWERING.
SO WHAT ARE YOU GONNA DO— JUST GO AROUND SMELLING AWFUL?!
OH, NO, NO, SILLY, EVERY FIFTEEN MINUTES, I RUB 'SPEED STICK' ALL OVER MY FACE.
DUDE.
Mmmmmmmm Feels goooooood.

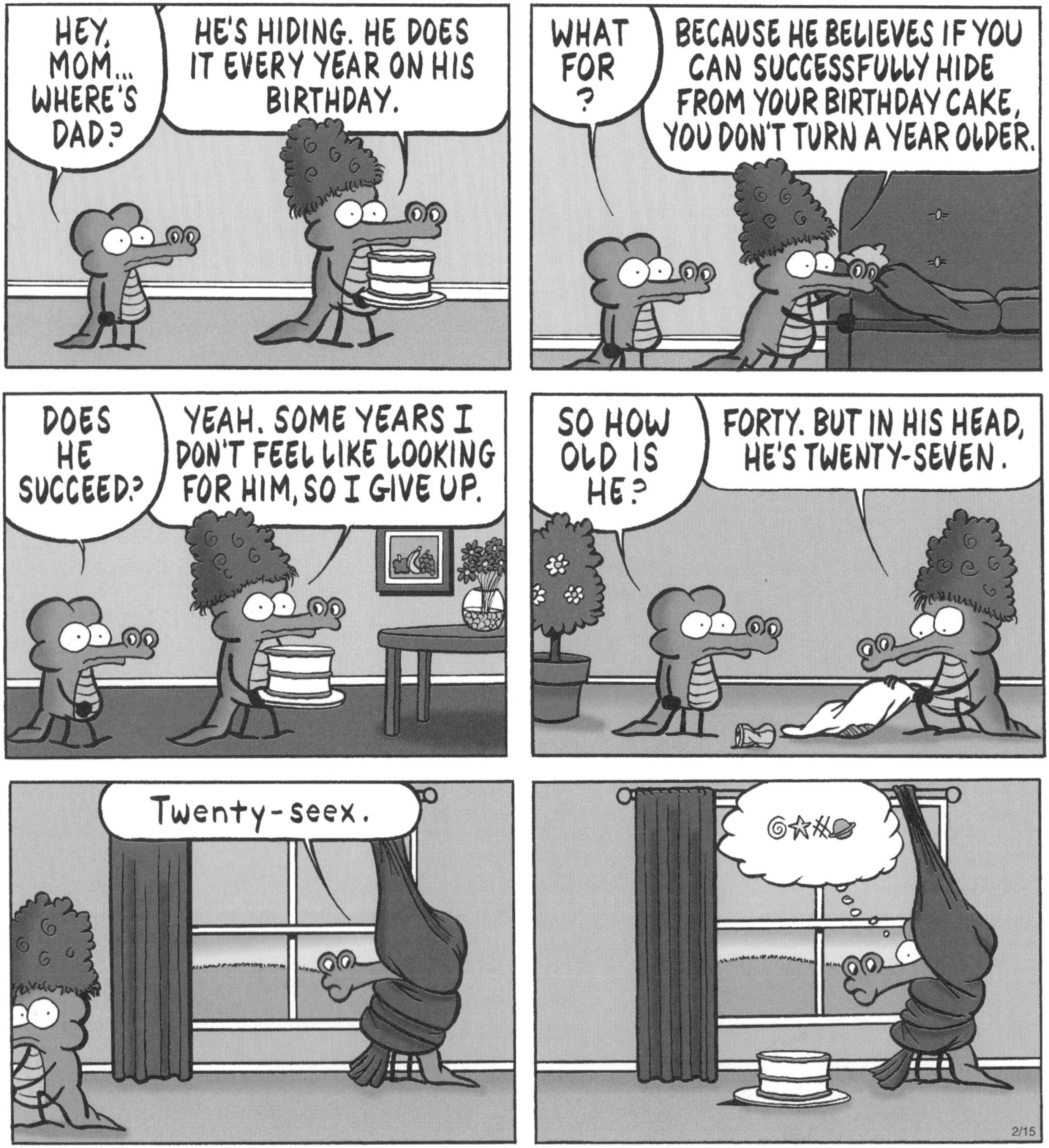
HEY, MOM... WHERE'S DAD?
HE'S HIDING. HE DOES IT EVERY YEAR ON HIS BIRTHDAY.
WHAT FOR?
BECAUSE HE BELIEVES IF YOU CAN SUCCESSFULLY HIDE FROM YOUR BIRTHDAY CAKE, YOU DON'T TURN A YEAR OLDER.
DOES HE SUCCEED?
YEAH. SOME YEARS I DON'T FEEL LIKE LOOKING FOR HIM, SO I GIVE UP.
SO HOW OLD IS HE?
FORTY. BUT IN HIS HEAD, HE'S TWENTY-SEVEN.
Twenty-seex.
2/15

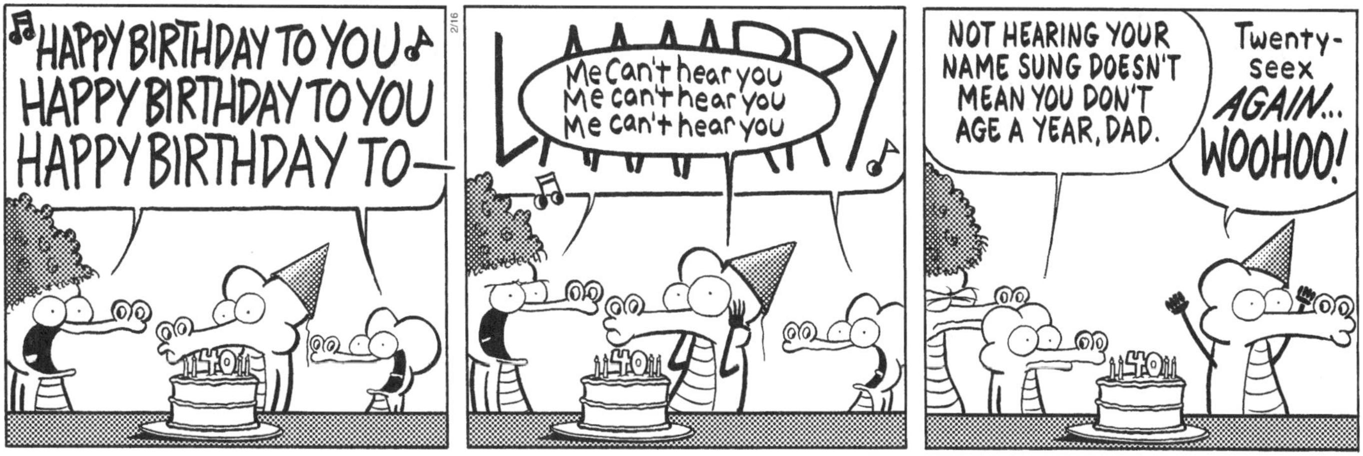
HAPPY BIRTHDAY TO YOU
HAPPY BIRTHDAY TO YOU
HAPPY BIRTHDAY TO—
2/16
Me can't hear you
Me can't hear you
Me can't hear you
NOT HEARING YOUR NAME SUNG DOESN'T MEAN YOU DON'T AGE A YEAR, DAD.
Twenty-seex AGAIN... WOOHOO!

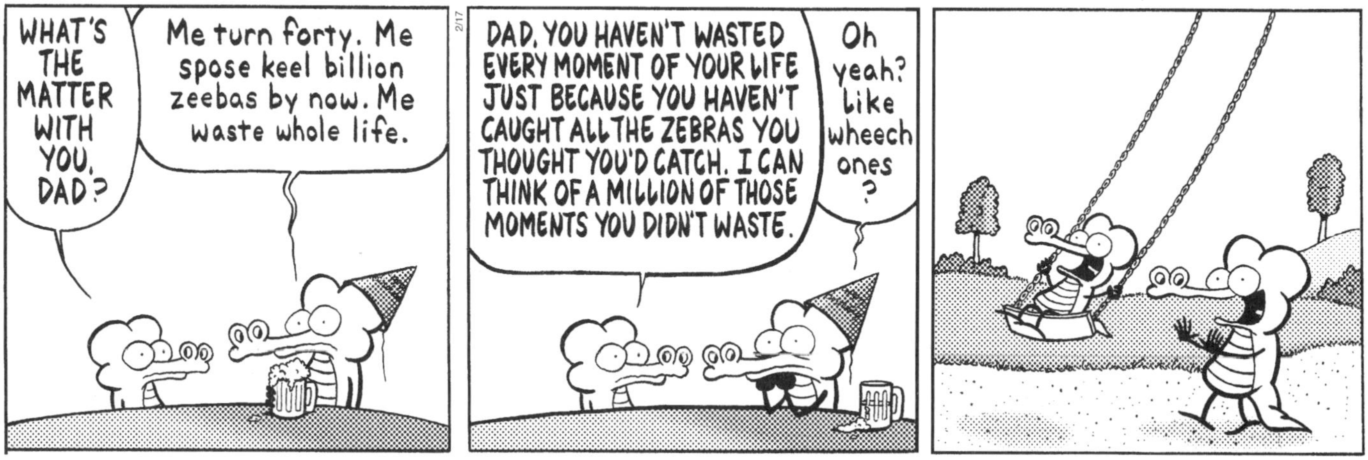
WHAT'S THE MATTER WITH YOU, DAD?
Me turn forty. Me spose keel billion zeebas by now. Me waste whole life.
2/17
DAD, YOU HAVEN'T WASTED EVERY MOMENT OF YOUR LIFE JUST BECAUSE YOU HAVEN'T CAUGHT ALL THE ZEBRAS YOU THOUGHT YOU'D CATCH. I CAN THINK OF A MILLION OF THOSE MOMENTS YOU DIDN'T WASTE.
Oh yeah? Like wheech ones?

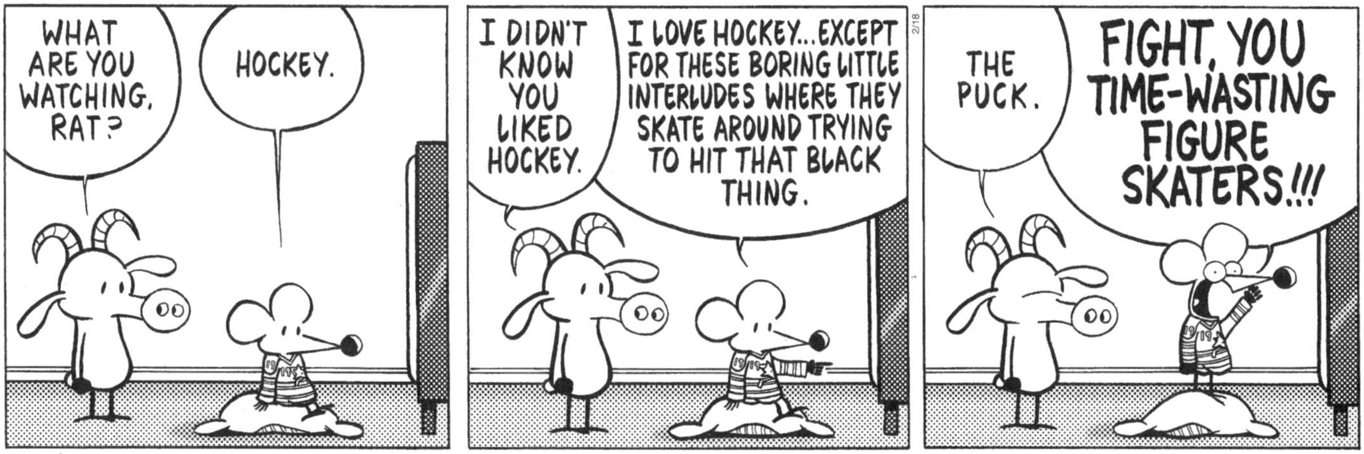
WHAT ARE YOU WATCHING, RAT?
HOCKEY.
I DIDN'T KNOW YOU LIKED HOCKEY.
I LOVE HOCKEY... EXCEPT FOR THESE BORING LITTLE INTERLUDES WHERE THEY SKATE AROUND TRYING TO HIT THAT BLACK THING.
2/18
THE PUCK.
FIGHT, YOU TIME-WASTING FIGURE SKATERS!!!

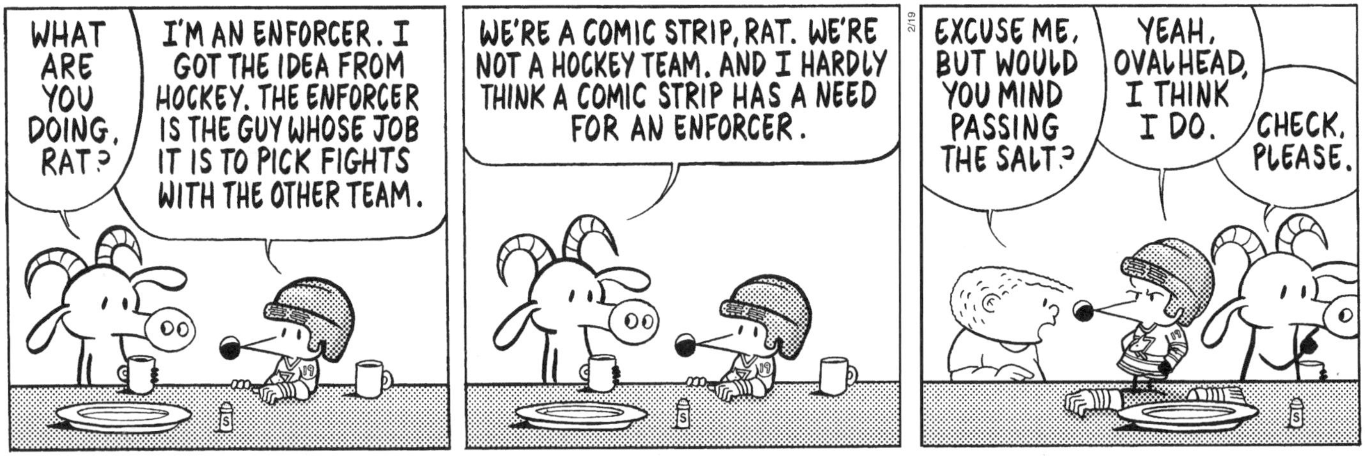
WHAT ARE YOU DOING, RAT?
I'M AN ENFORCER. I GOT THE IDEA FROM HOCKEY. THE ENFORCER IS THE GUY WHOSE JOB IT IS TO PICK FIGHTS WITH THE OTHER TEAM.
WE'RE A COMIC STRIP, RAT. WE'RE NOT A HOCKEY TEAM. AND I HARDLY THINK A COMIC STRIP HAS A NEED FOR AN ENFORCER.
2/19
EXCUSE ME, BUT WOULD YOU MIND PASSING THE SALT?
YEAH, OVALHEAD, I THINK I DO.
CHECK, PLEASE.

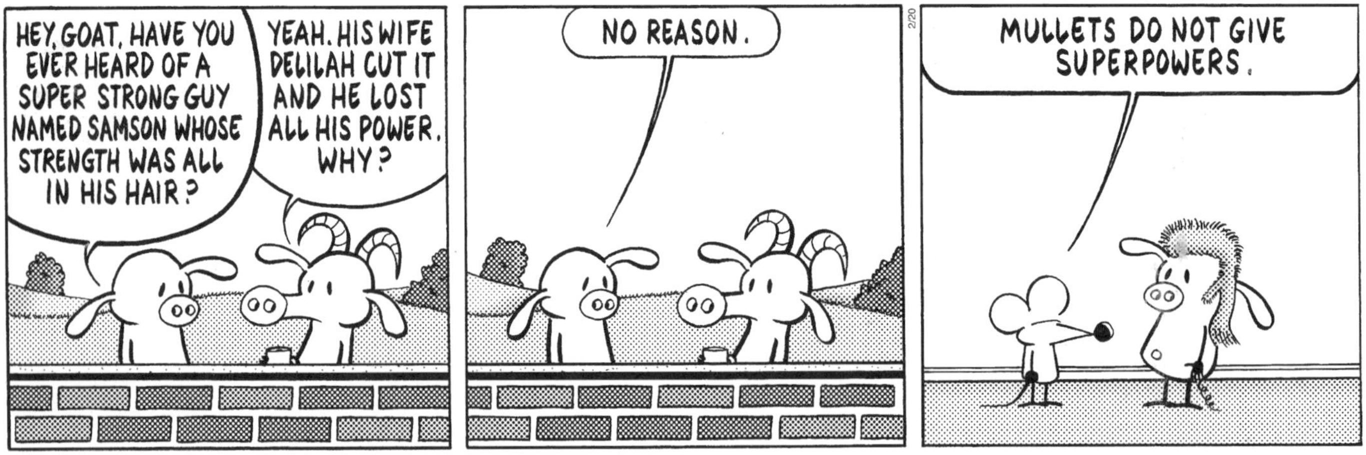
HEY, GOAT, HAVE YOU EVER HEARD OF A SUPER STRONG GUY NAMED SAMSON WHOSE STRENGTH WAS ALL IN HIS HAIR?
YEAH. HIS WIFE DELILAH CUT IT AND HE LOST ALL HIS POWER. WHY?
NO REASON.
2/20
MULLETS DO NOT GIVE SUPERPOWERS.

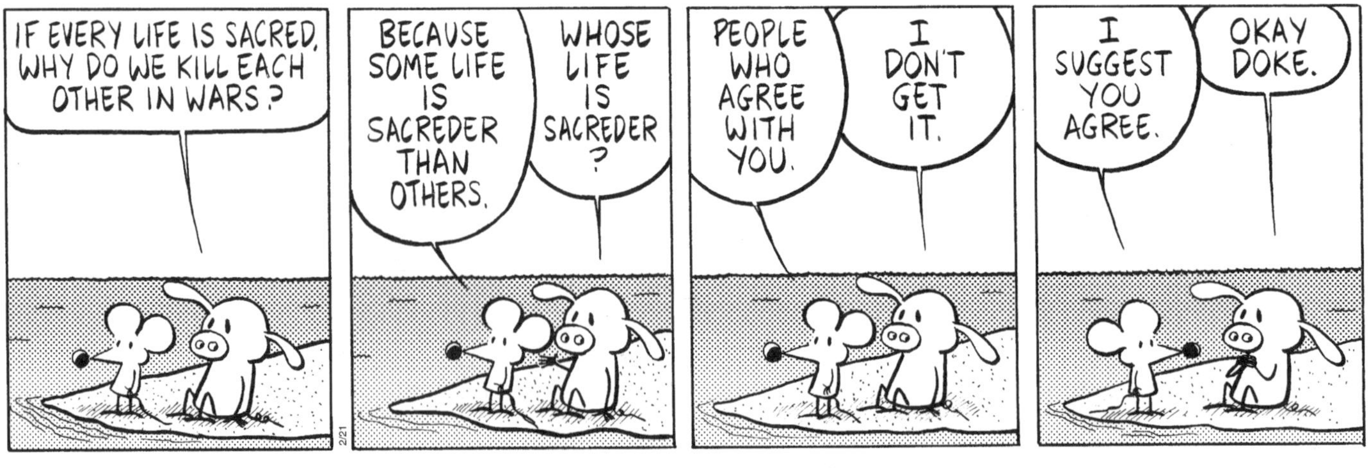
IF EVERY LIFE IS SACRED, WHY DO WE KILL EACH OTHER IN WARS?
2/21
BECAUSE SOME LIFE IS SACREDER THAN OTHERS.
WHOSE LIFE IS SACREDER?
PEOPLE WHO AGREE WITH YOU.
I DON'T GET IT.
I SUGGEST YOU AGREE.
OKAY DOKE.

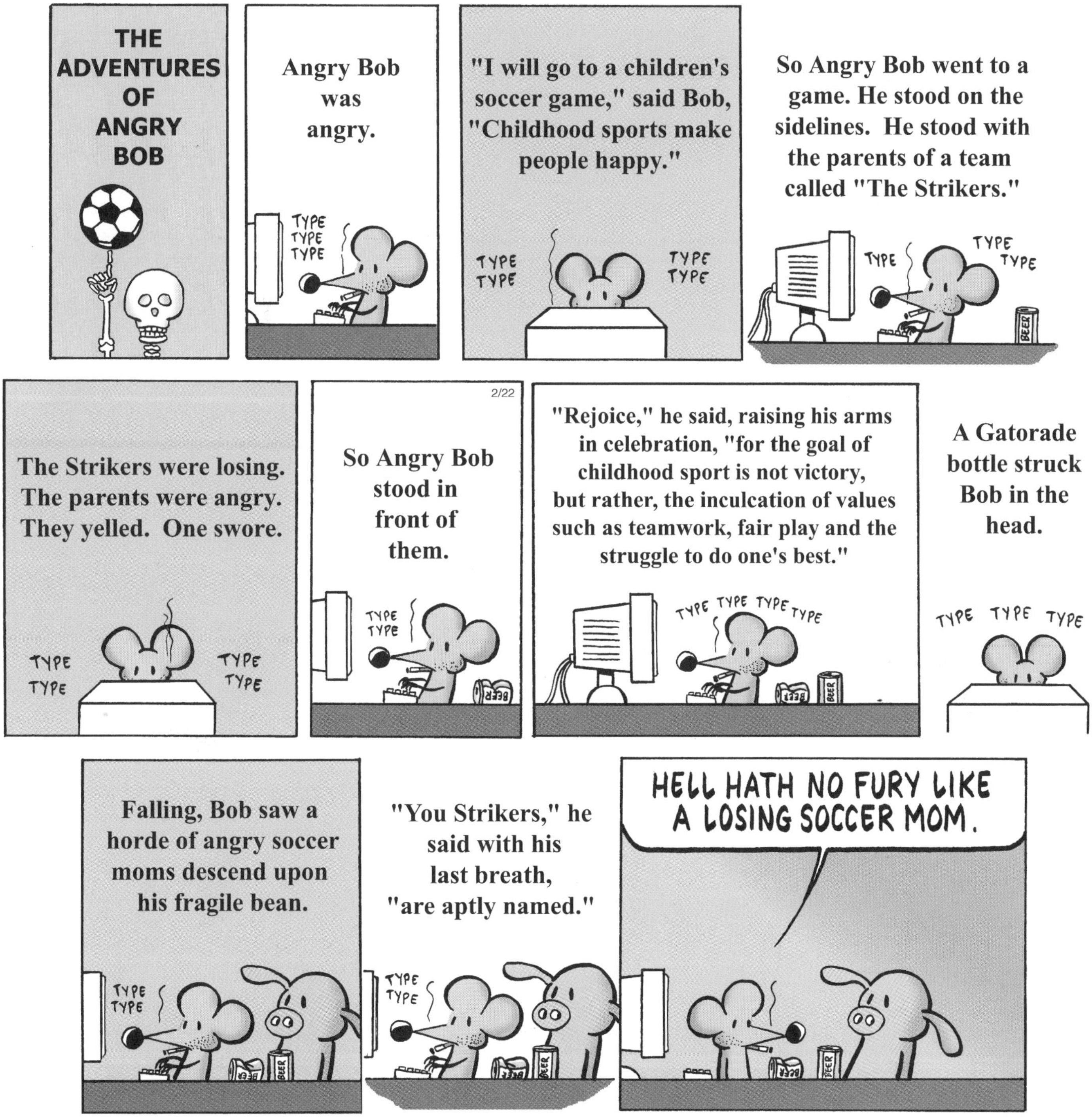
THE ADVENTURES OF ANGRY BOB
Angry Bob was angry.
TYPE TYPE TYPE
"I will go to a children's soccer game," said Bob, "Childhood sports make people happy."
TYPE TYPE
TYPE TYPE
So Angry Bob went to a game. He stood on the sidelines. He stood with the parents of a team called "The Strikers."
TYPE
TYPE TYPE
BEER
The Strikers were losing. The parents were angry. They yelled. One swore.
TYPE TYPE
TYPE TYPE
2/22
So Angry Bob stood in front of them.
TYPE TYPE
BEER
"Rejoice," he said, raising his arms in celebration, "for the goal of childhood sport is not victory, but rather, the inculcation of values such as teamwork, fair play and the struggle to do one's best."
TYPE TYPE TYPE TYPE
BEER
BEER
A Gatorade bottle struck Bob in the head.
TYPE TYPE TYPE
Falling, Bob saw a horde of angry soccer moms descend upon his fragile bean.
TYPE TYPE
BEER
BEER
"You Strikers," he said with his last breath, "are aptly named."
TYPE TYPE
BEER
BEER
HELL HATH NO FURY LIKE A LOSING SOCCER MOM.
BEER
BEER

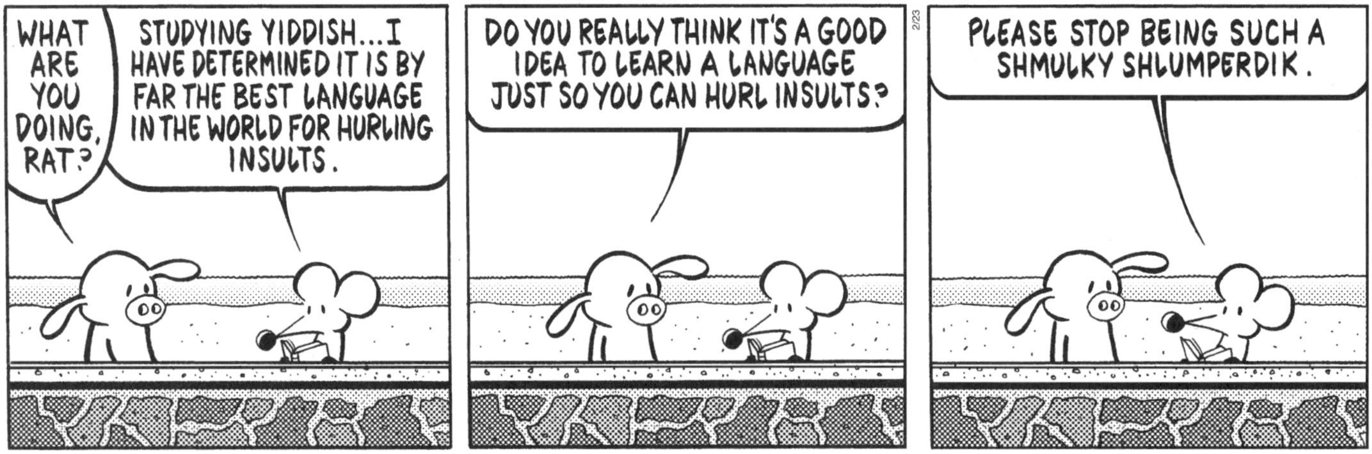
WHAT ARE YOU DOING, RAT?
STUDYING YIDDISH...I HAVE DETERMINED IT IS BY FAR THE BEST LANGUAGE IN THE WORLD FOR HURLING INSULTS.
DO YOU REALLY THINK IT'S A GOOD IDEA TO LEARN A LANGUAGE JUST SO YOU CAN HURL INSULTS?
PLEASE STOP BEING SUCH A SHMULKY SHLUMPERDIK.

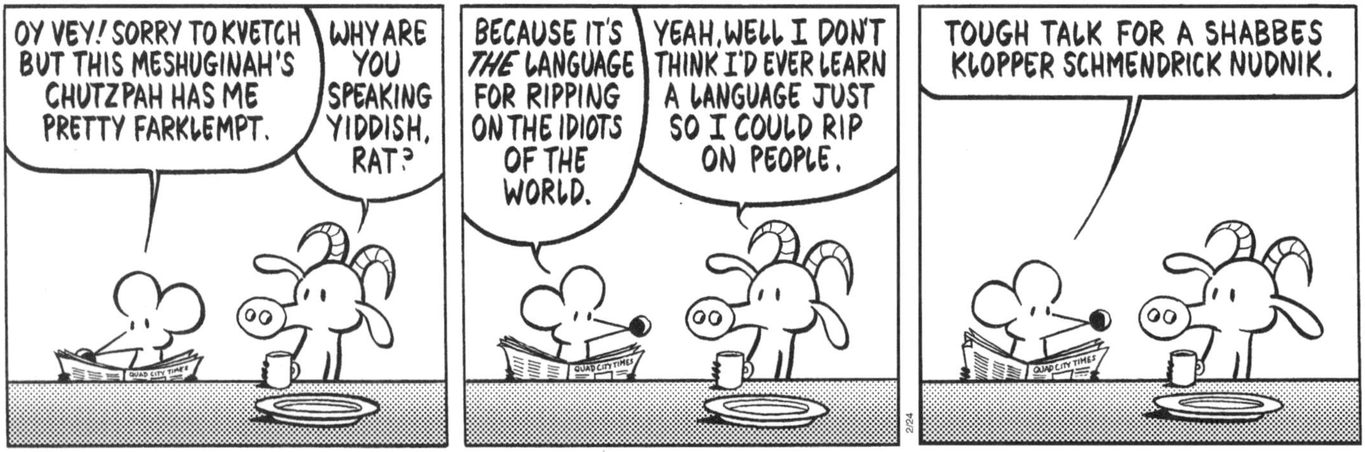
OY VEY! SORRY TO KVETCH BUT THIS MESHUGINAH'S CHUTZPAH HAS ME PRETTY FARKLEMPT.
WHY ARE YOU SPEAKING YIDDISH, RAT?
BECAUSE IT'S THE LANGUAGE FOR RIPPING ON THE IDIOTS OF THE WORLD.
YEAH, WELL I DON'T THINK I'D EVER LEARN A LANGUAGE JUST SO I COULD RIP ON PEOPLE.
TOUGH TALK FOR A SHABBES KLOPPER SCHMENDRICK NUDNIK.

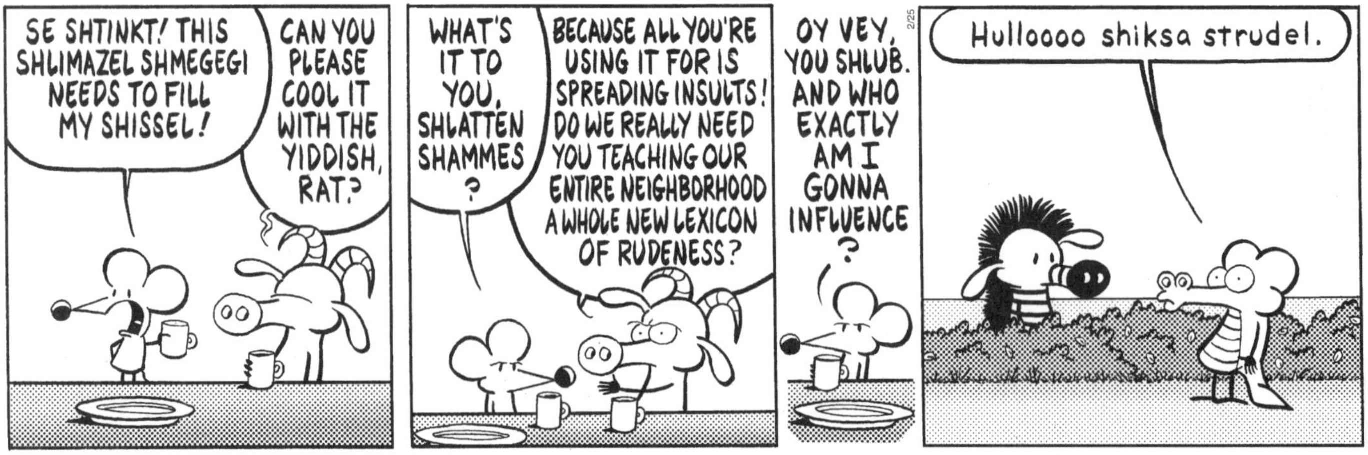
SE SHTINKT! THIS SHLIMAZEL SHMEGEGI NEEDS TO FILL MY SHISSEL!
CAN YOU PLEASE COOL IT WITH THE YIDDISH, RAT?
WHAT'S IT TO YOU, SHLATTEN SHAMMES?
BECAUSE ALL YOU'RE USING IT FOR IS SPREADING INSULTS! DO WE REALLY NEED YOU TEACHING OUR ENTIRE NEIGHBORHOOD A WHOLE NEW LEXICON OF RUDENESS?
OY VEY, YOU SHLUB. AND WHO EXACTLY AM I GONNA INFLUENCE?
Hulloooo shiksa strudel.

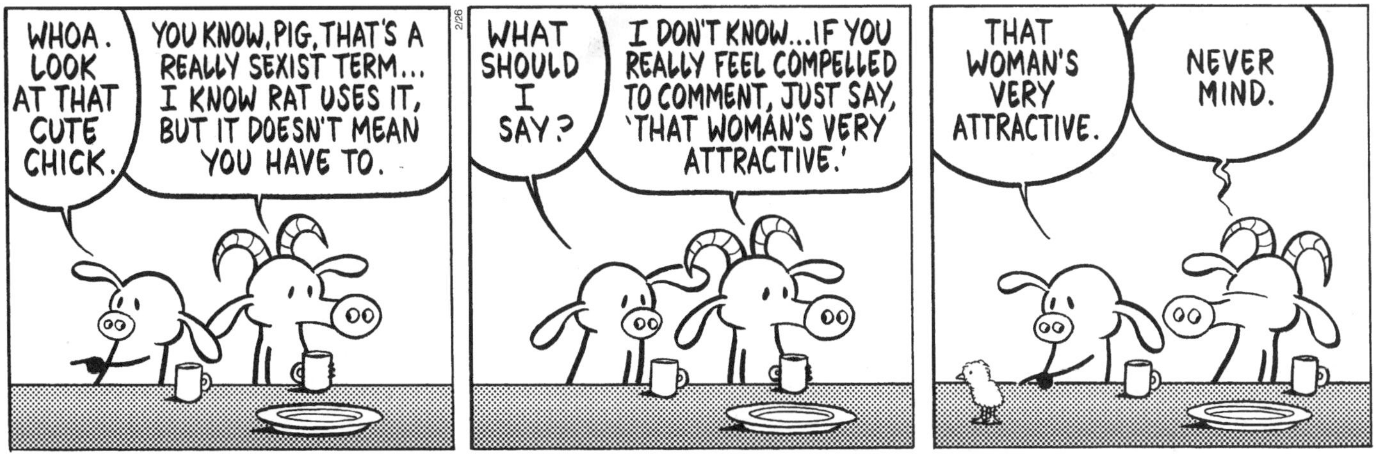
WHOA. LOOK AT THAT CUTE CHICK.
YOU KNOW, PIG, THAT'S A REALLY SEXIST TERM... I KNOW RAT USES IT, BUT IT DOESN'T MEAN YOU HAVE TO.
2/26
WHAT SHOULD I SAY?
I DON'T KNOW...IF YOU REALLY FEEL COMPELLED TO COMMENT, JUST SAY, 'THAT WOMAN'S VERY ATTRACTIVE.'
THAT WOMAN'S VERY ATTRACTIVE.
NEVER MIND.

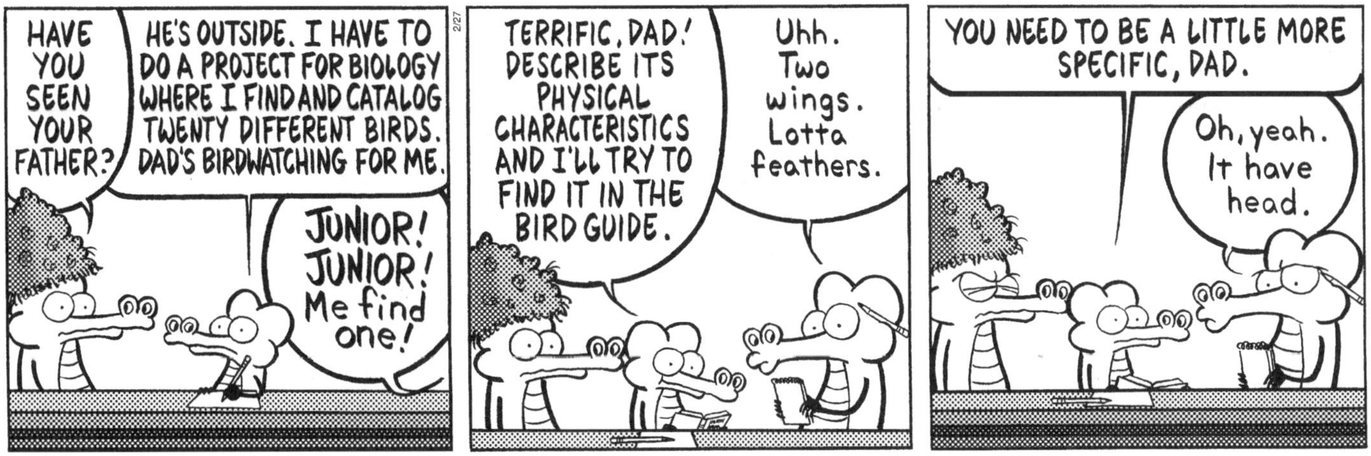
HAVE YOU SEEN YOUR FATHER?
HE'S OUTSIDE. I HAVE TO DO A PROJECT FOR BIOLOGY WHERE I FIND AND CATALOG TWENTY DIFFERENT BIRDS. DAD'S BIRDWATCHING FOR ME.
2/27
JUNIOR! JUNIOR! Me find one!
TERRIFIC, DAD! DESCRIBE ITS PHYSICAL CHARACTERISTICS AND I'LL TRY TO FIND IT IN THE BIRD GUIDE.
Uhh. Two wings. Lotta feathers.
YOU NEED TO BE A LITTLE MORE SPECIFIC, DAD.
Oh, yeah. It have head.

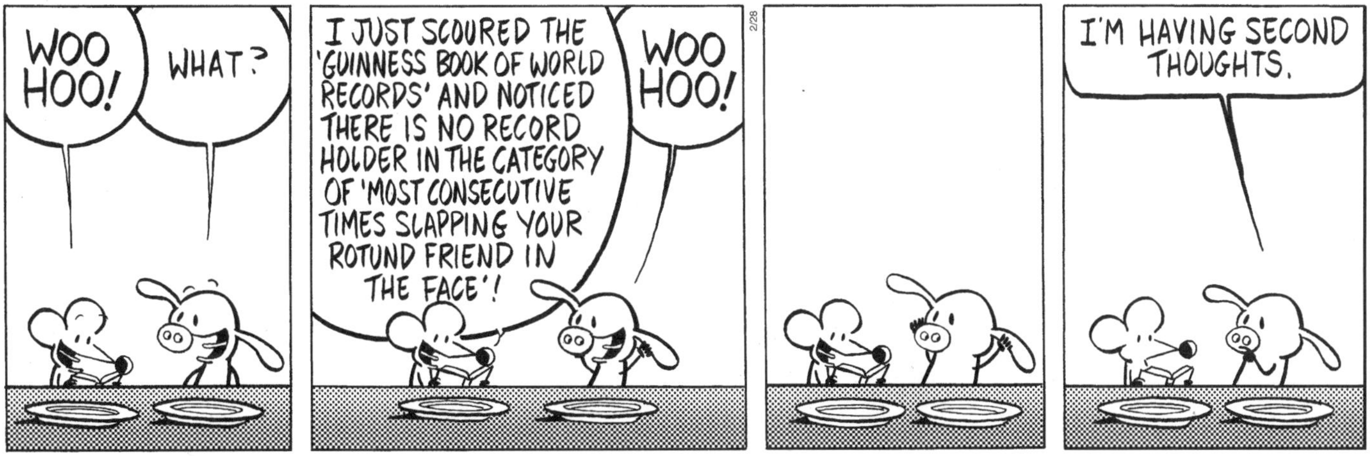
WOO HOO!
WHAT?
I JUST SCOURED THE 'GUINNESS BOOK OF WORLD RECORDS' AND NOTICED THERE IS NO RECORD HOLDER IN THE CATEGORY OF 'MOST CONSECUTIVE TIMES SLAPPING YOUR ROTUND FRIEND IN THE FACE'!
WOO HOO!
2/28
I'M HAVING SECOND THOUGHTS.

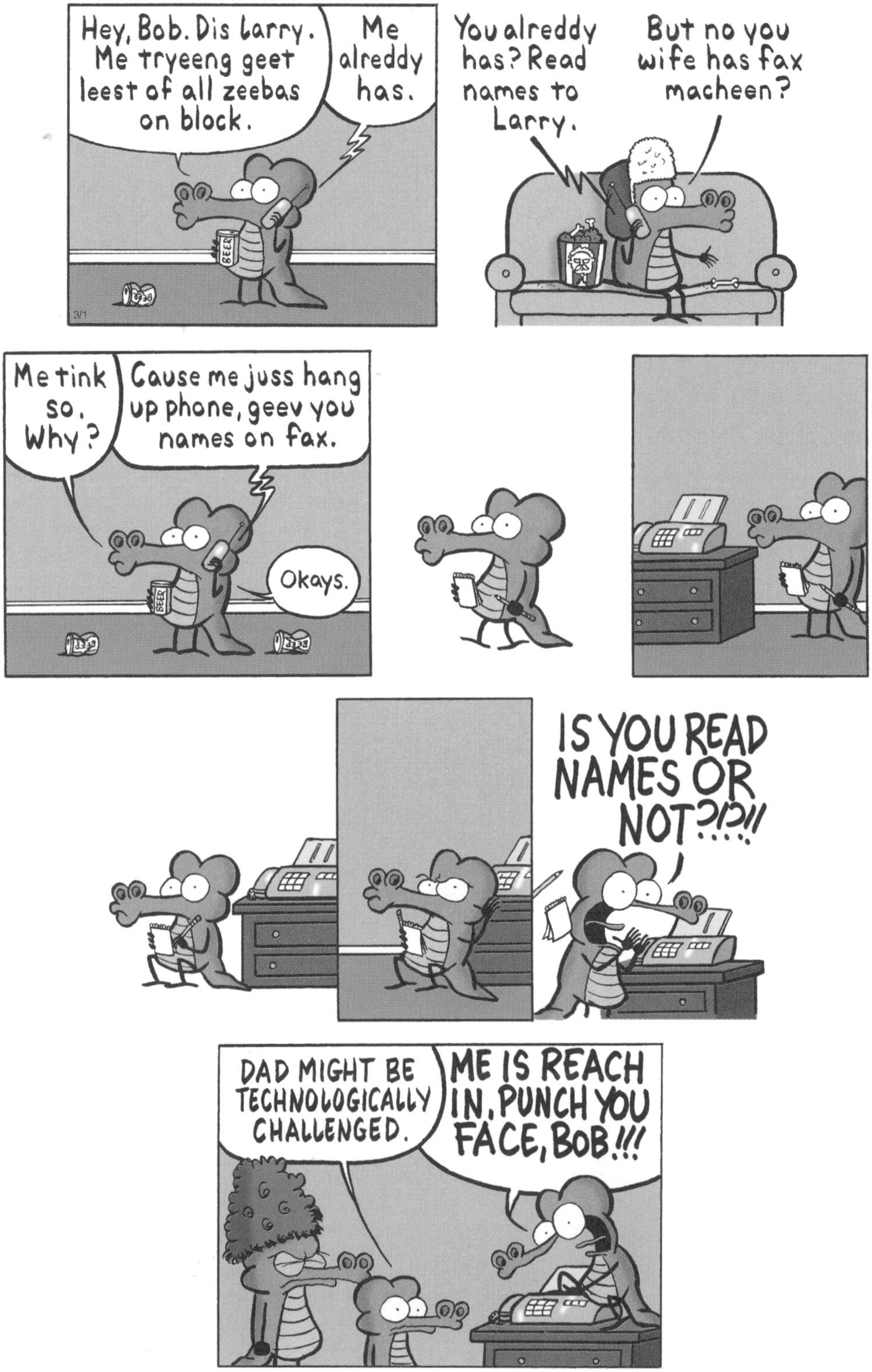
Hey, Bob. Dis Larry. Me tryeeng geet leest of all zeebas on block.
Me alreddy has.
3/1
You alreddy has? Read names to Larry.
But no you wife has fax macheen?
Me tink so. Why?
Cause me juss hang up phone, geev you names on fax.
Okays.
IS YOU READ NAMES OR NOT?!?!!
DAD MIGHT BE TECHNOLOGICALLY CHALLENGED.
ME IS REACH IN, PUNCH YOU FACE, BOB!!!

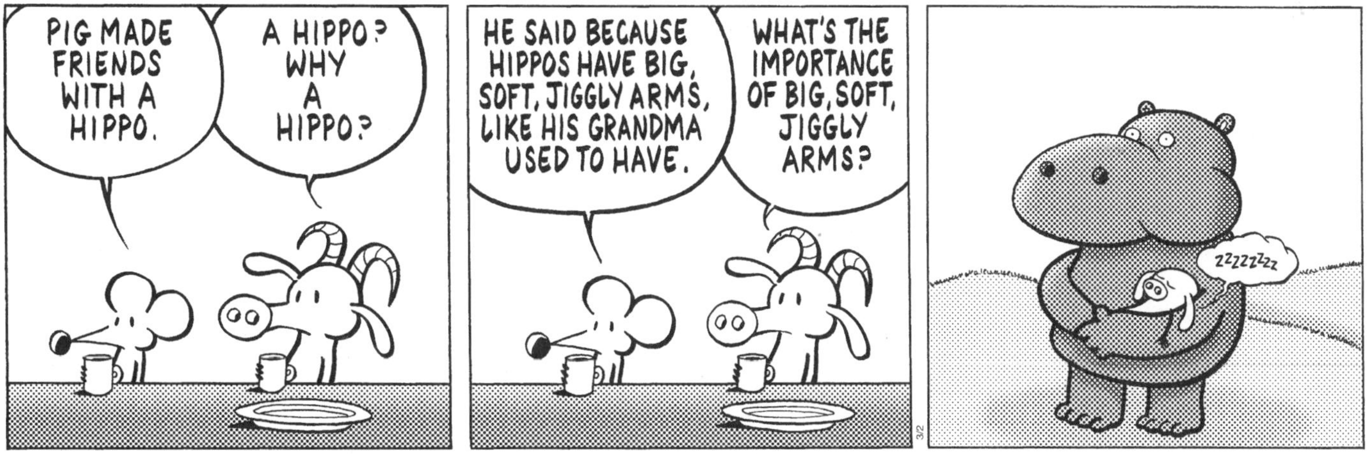
PIG MADE FRIENDS WITH A HIPPO.
A HIPPO? WHY A HIPPO?
HE SAID BECAUSE HIPPOS HAVE BIG, SOFT, JIGGLY ARMS, LIKE HIS GRANDMA USED TO HAVE.
WHAT'S THE IMPORTANCE OF BIG, SOFT, JIGGLY ARMS?
zzzzzzzz

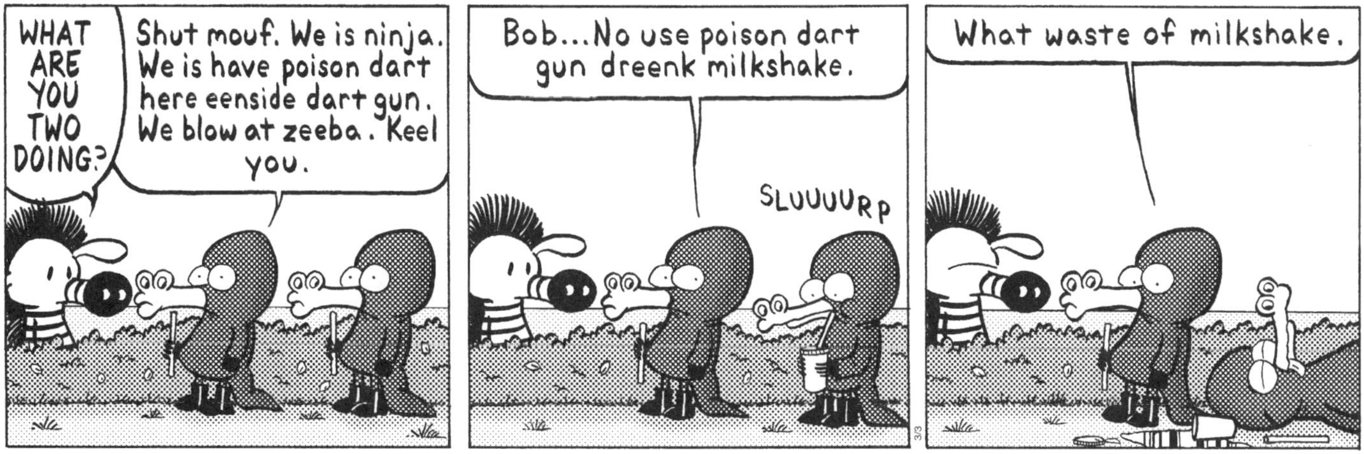
WHAT ARE YOU TWO DOING?
Shut mouf. We is ninja. We is have poison dart here eenside dart gun. We blow at zeeba. Keel you.
Bob...No use poison dart gun dreenk milkshake.
SLUUUURP
What waste of milkshake.

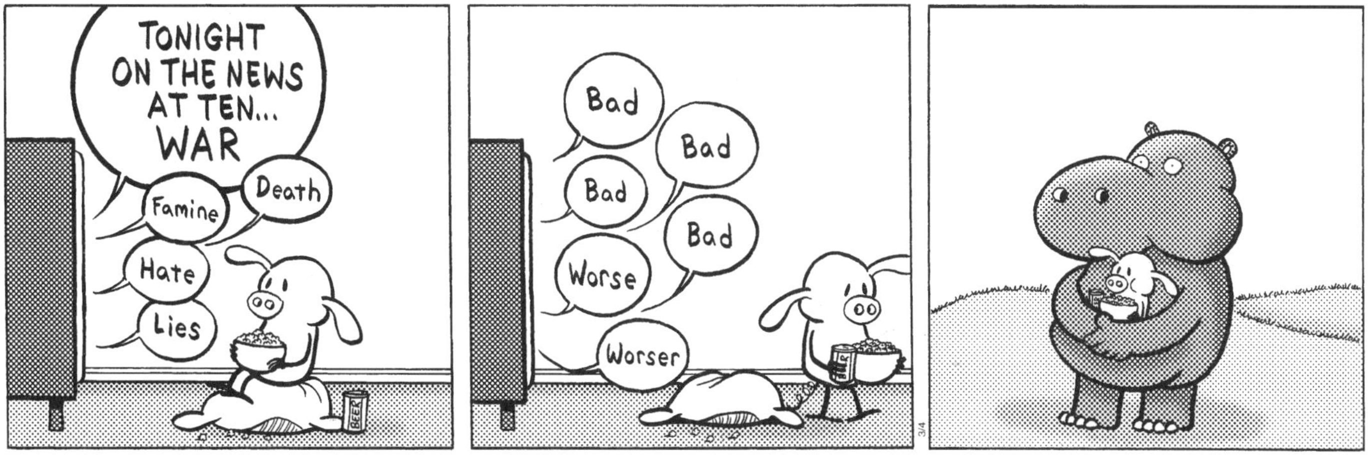
TONIGHT ON THE NEWS AT TEN... WAR
Famine
Death
Hate
Lies
Bad
Bad
Bad
Bad
Worse
Worser

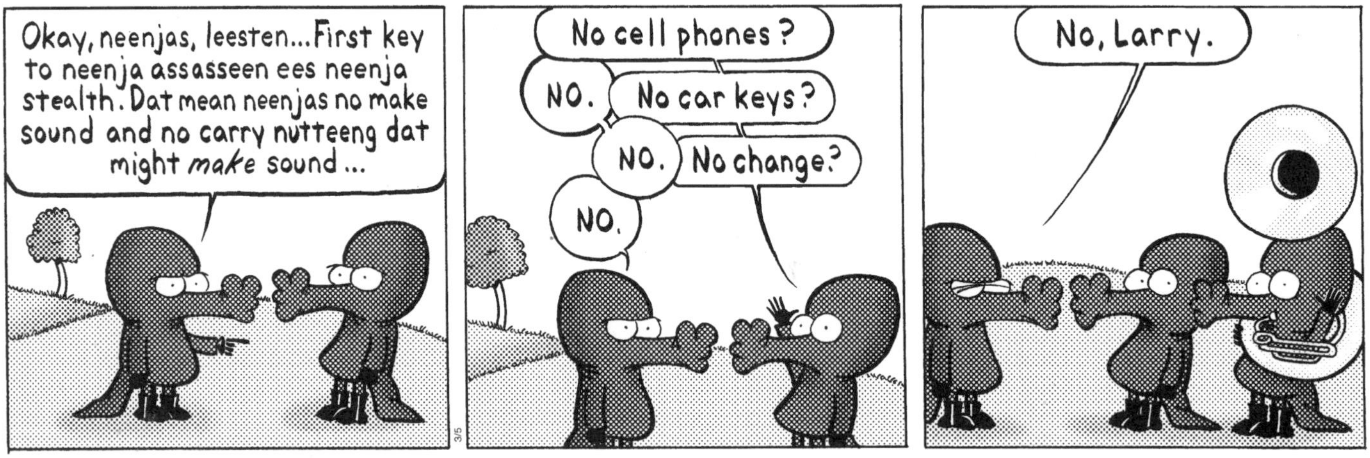
Okay, neenjas, leesten...First key to neenja assasseen ees neenja stealth. Dat mean neenjas no make sound and no carry nutteeng dat might *make* sound ...
No cell phones?
NO.
No car keys?
NO.
No change?
NO.
3/5
No, Larry.

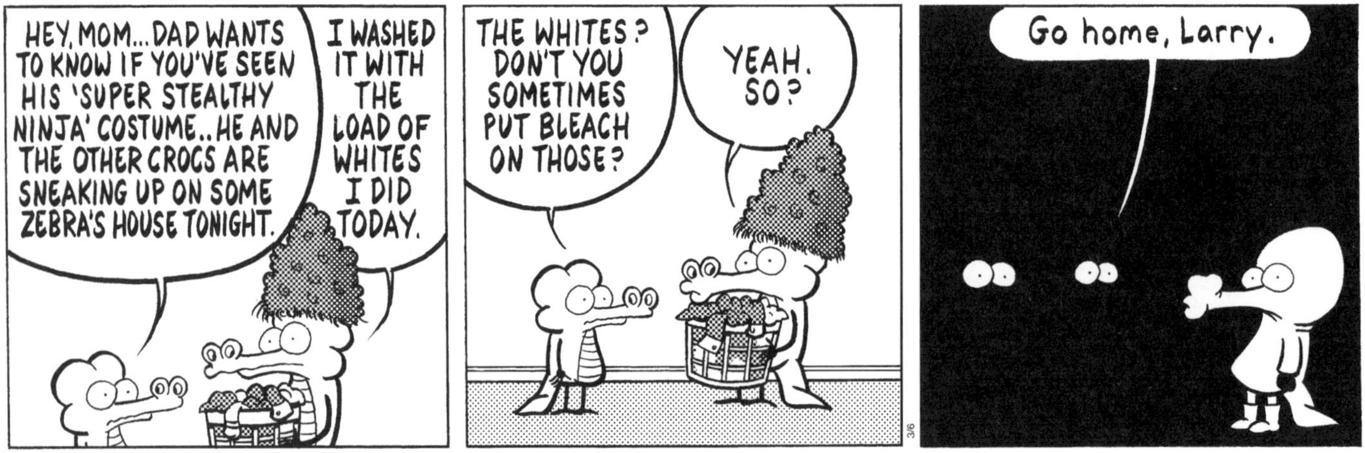
HEY, MOM... DAD WANTS TO KNOW IF YOU'VE SEEN HIS 'SUPER STEALTHY NINJA' COSTUME.. HE AND THE OTHER CROCS ARE SNEAKING UP ON SOME ZEBRA'S HOUSE TONIGHT.
I WASHED IT WITH THE LOAD OF WHITES I DID TODAY.
THE WHITES? DON'T YOU SOMETIMES PUT BLEACH ON THOSE?
YEAH. SO?
3/6
Go home, Larry.

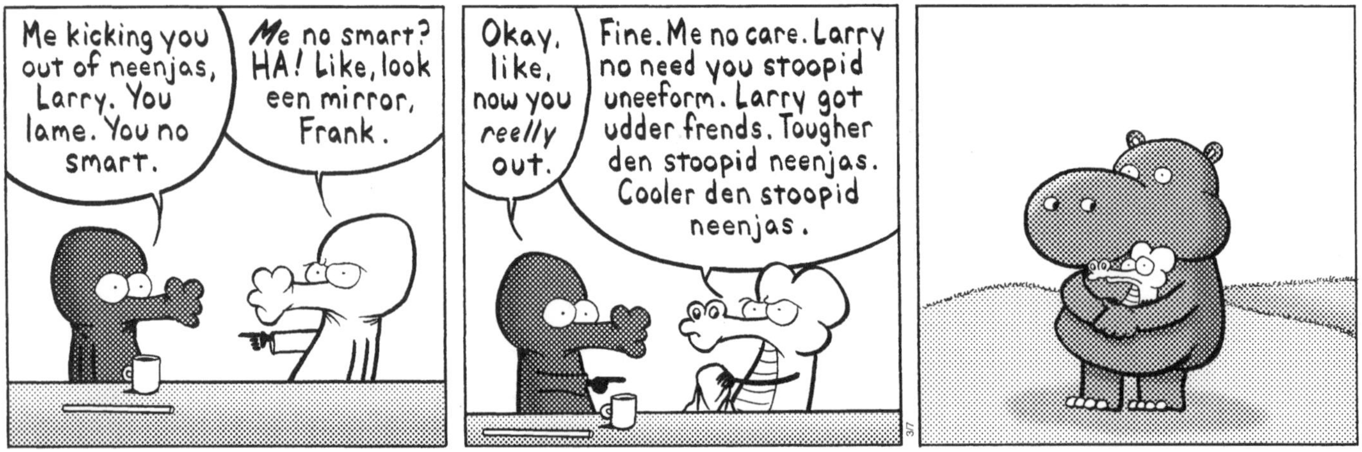
Me kicking you out of neenjas, Larry. You lame. You no smart.
Me no smart? HA! Like, look een mirror, Frank.
Okay, like, now you *reelly* out.
Fine. Me no care. Larry no need you stoopid uneeform. Larry got udder frends. Tougher den stoopid neenjas. Cooler den stoopid neenjas.
3/7

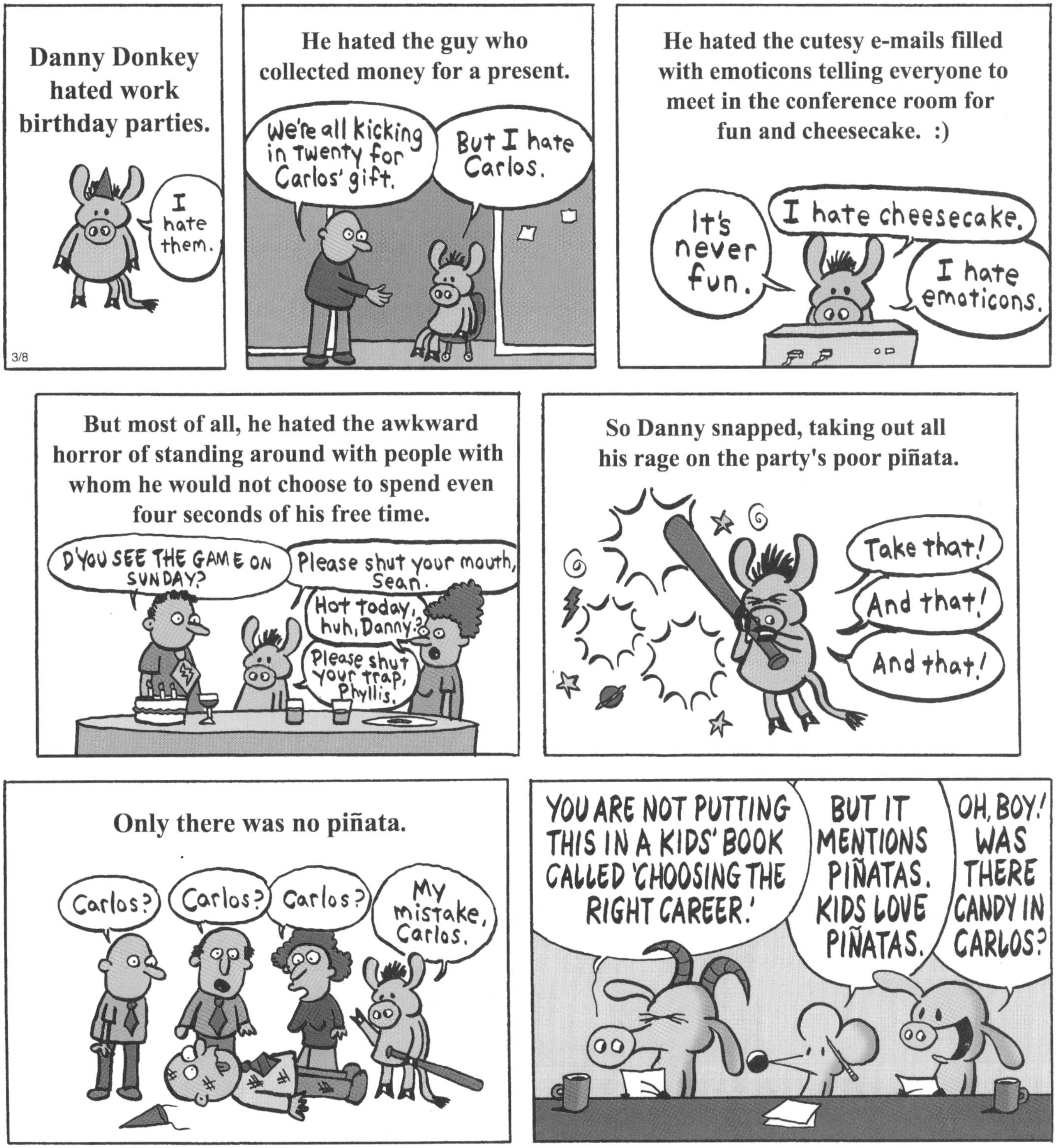
Danny Donkey hated work birthday parties.
I hate them.
3/8
He hated the guy who collected money for a present.
We're all kicking in twenty for Carlos' gift.
But I hate Carlos.
He hated the cutesy e-mails filled with emoticons telling everyone to meet in the conference room for fun and cheesecake. :)
It's never fun.
I hate cheesecake.
I hate emoticons.
But most of all, he hated the awkward horror of standing around with people with whom he would not choose to spend even four seconds of his free time.
D'YOU SEE THE GAME ON SUNDAY?
Please shut your mouth, Sean.
Hot today, huh, Danny?
Please shut your trap, Phyllis.
So Danny snapped, taking out all his rage on the party's poor piñata.
Take that!
And that!
And that!
Only there was no piñata.
Carlos?
Carlos?
Carlos?
My mistake, Carlos.
YOU ARE NOT PUTTING THIS IN A KIDS' BOOK CALLED 'CHOOSING THE RIGHT CAREER.'
BUT IT MENTIONS PIÑATAS. KIDS LOVE PIÑATAS.
OH, BOY! WAS THERE CANDY IN CARLOS?

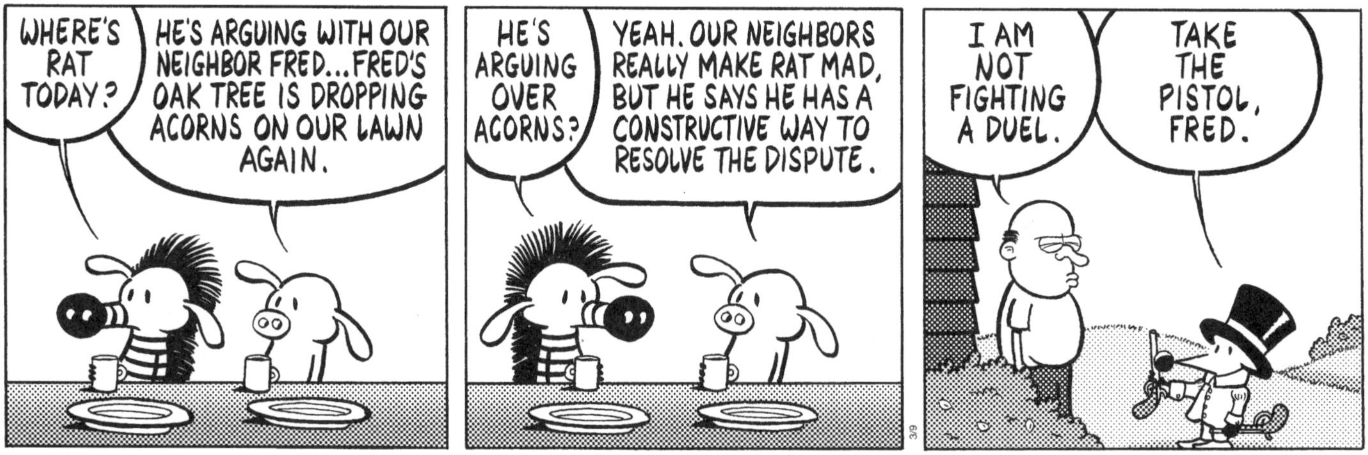
WHERE'S RAT TODAY?
HE'S ARGUING WITH OUR NEIGHBOR FRED... FRED'S OAK TREE IS DROPPING ACORNS ON OUR LAWN AGAIN.
HE'S ARGUING OVER ACORNS?
YEAH. OUR NEIGHBORS REALLY MAKE RAT MAD, BUT HE SAYS HE HAS A CONSTRUCTIVE WAY TO RESOLVE THE DISPUTE.
I AM NOT FIGHTING A DUEL.
TAKE THE PISTOL, FRED.

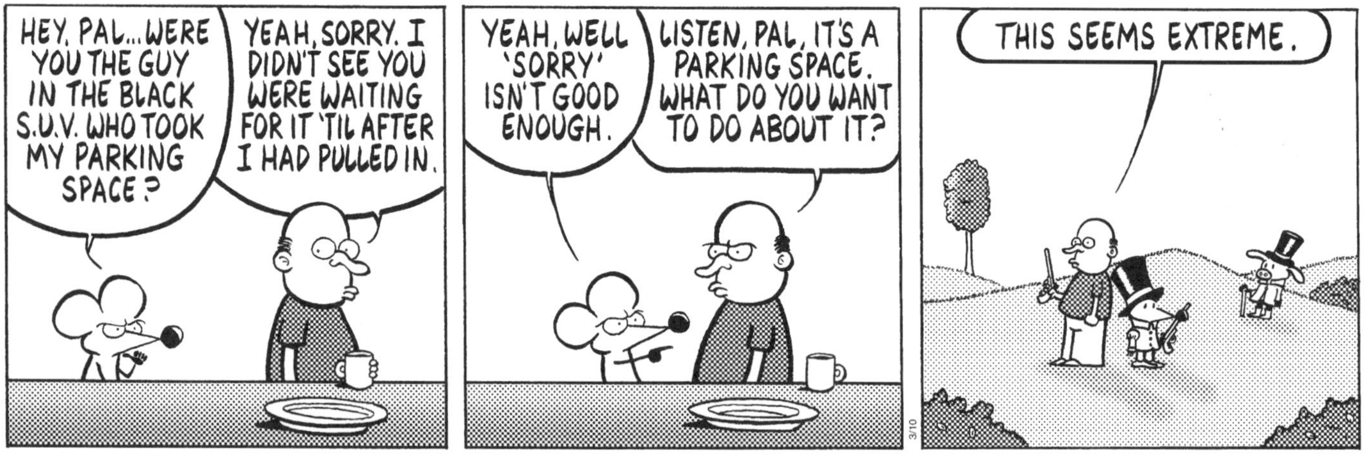
HEY, PAL... WERE YOU THE GUY IN THE BLACK S.U.V. WHO TOOK MY PARKING SPACE?
YEAH, SORRY. I DIDN'T SEE YOU WERE WAITING FOR IT 'TIL AFTER I HAD PULLED IN.
YEAH, WELL 'SORRY' ISN'T GOOD ENOUGH.
LISTEN, PAL, IT'S A PARKING SPACE. WHAT DO YOU WANT TO DO ABOUT IT?
THIS SEEMS EXTREME.

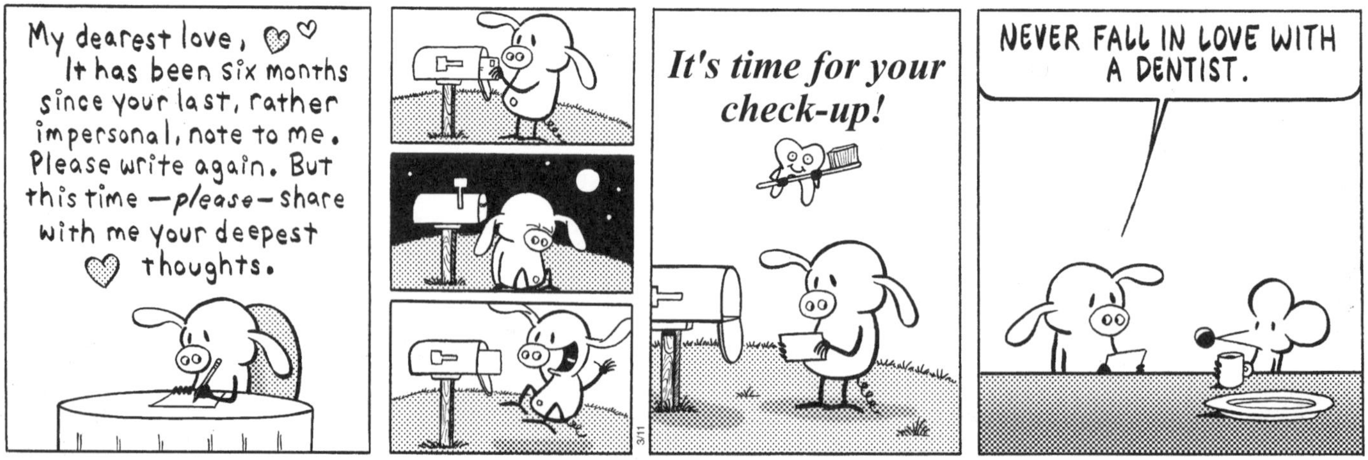
My dearest love,
It has been six months since your last, rather impersonal, note to me. Please write again. But this time —please— share with me your deepest thoughts.
It's time for your check-up!
NEVER FALL IN LOVE WITH A DENTIST.

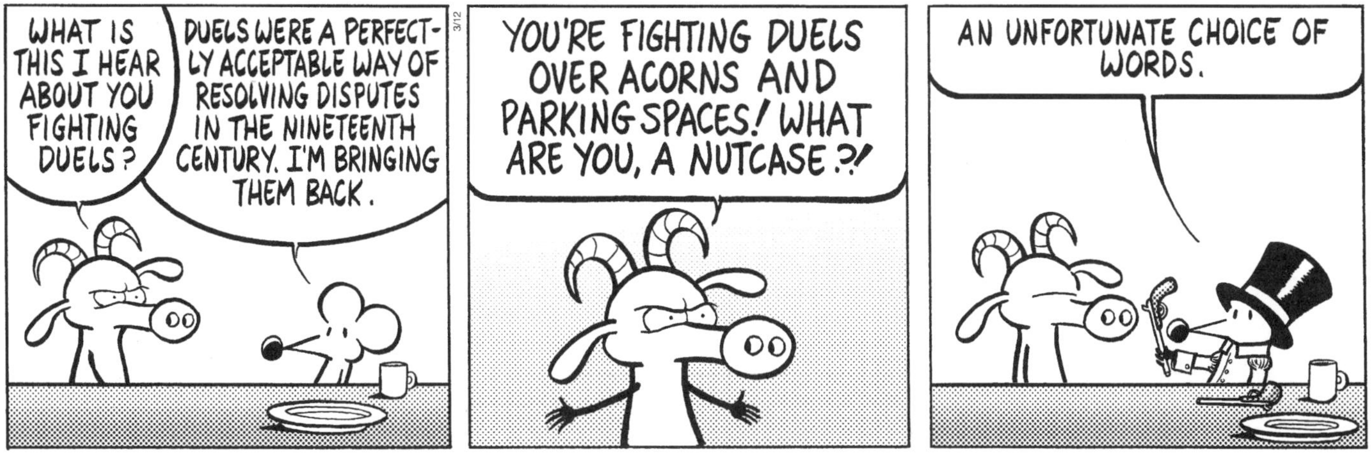
WHAT IS THIS I HEAR ABOUT YOU FIGHTING DUELS?
DUELS WERE A PERFECTLY ACCEPTABLE WAY OF RESOLVING DISPUTES IN THE NINETEENTH CENTURY. I'M BRINGING THEM BACK.
3/12
YOU'RE FIGHTING DUELS OVER ACORNS AND PARKING SPACES! WHAT ARE YOU, A NUTCASE?!
AN UNFORTUNATE CHOICE OF WORDS.

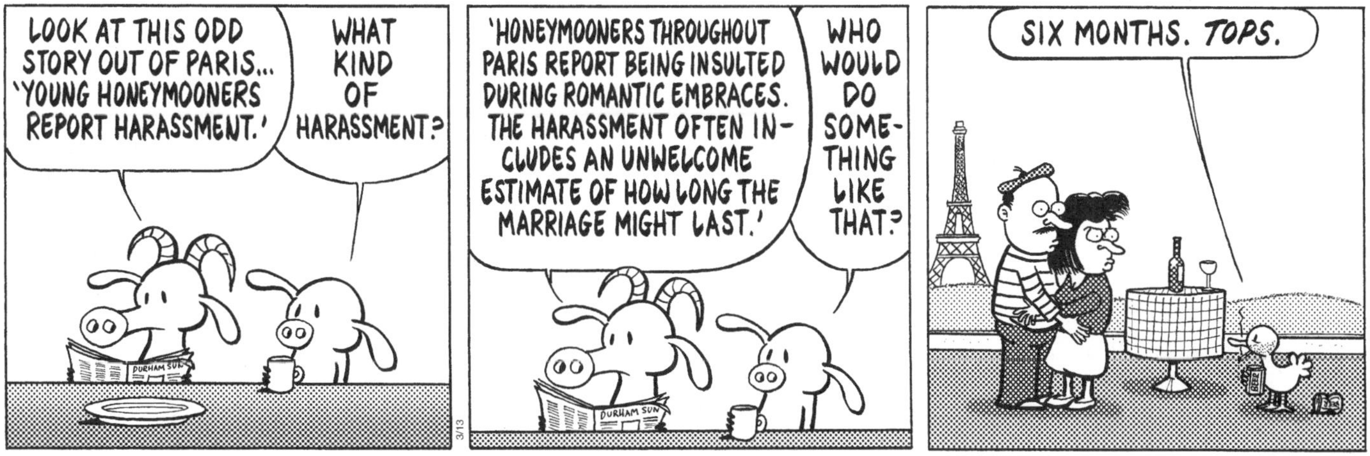
LOOK AT THIS ODD STORY OUT OF PARIS... 'YOUNG HONEYMOONERS REPORT HARASSMENT.'
WHAT KIND OF HARASSMENT?
DURHAM SUN
'HONEYMOONERS THROUGHOUT PARIS REPORT BEING INSULTED DURING ROMANTIC EMBRACES. THE HARASSMENT OFTEN INCLUDES AN UNWELCOME ESTIMATE OF HOW LONG THE MARRIAGE MIGHT LAST.'
WHO WOULD DO SOMETHING LIKE THAT?
DURHAM SUN
3/13
SIX MONTHS. *TOPS.*

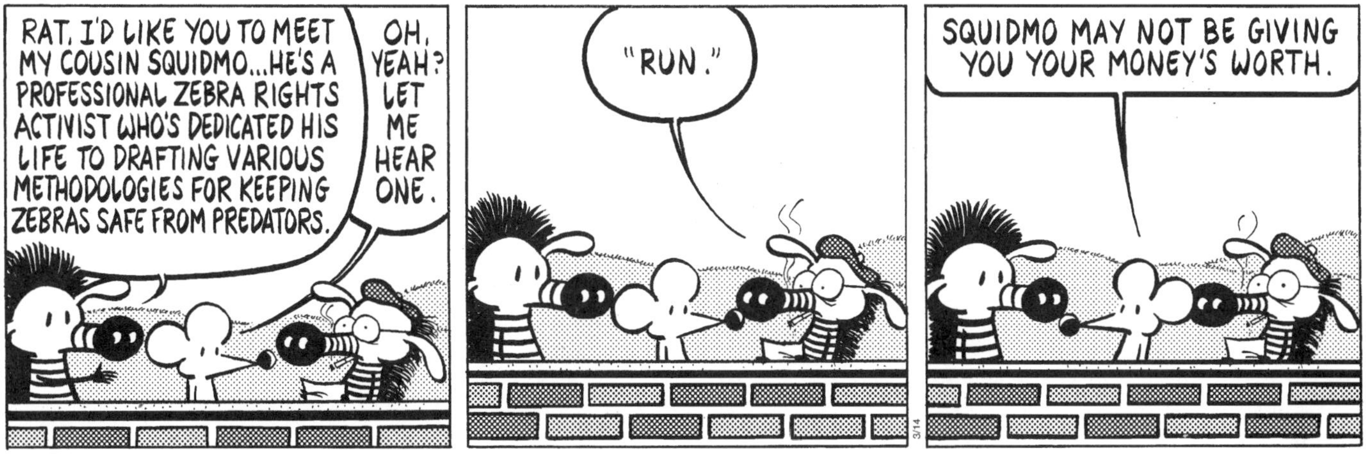
RAT, I'D LIKE YOU TO MEET MY COUSIN SQUIDMO...HE'S A PROFESSIONAL ZEBRA RIGHTS ACTIVIST WHO'S DEDICATED HIS LIFE TO DRAFTING VARIOUS METHODOLOGIES FOR KEEPING ZEBRAS SAFE FROM PREDATORS.
OH, YEAH? LET ME HEAR ONE.
"RUN."
3/14
SQUIDMO MAY NOT BE GIVING YOU YOUR MONEY'S WORTH.

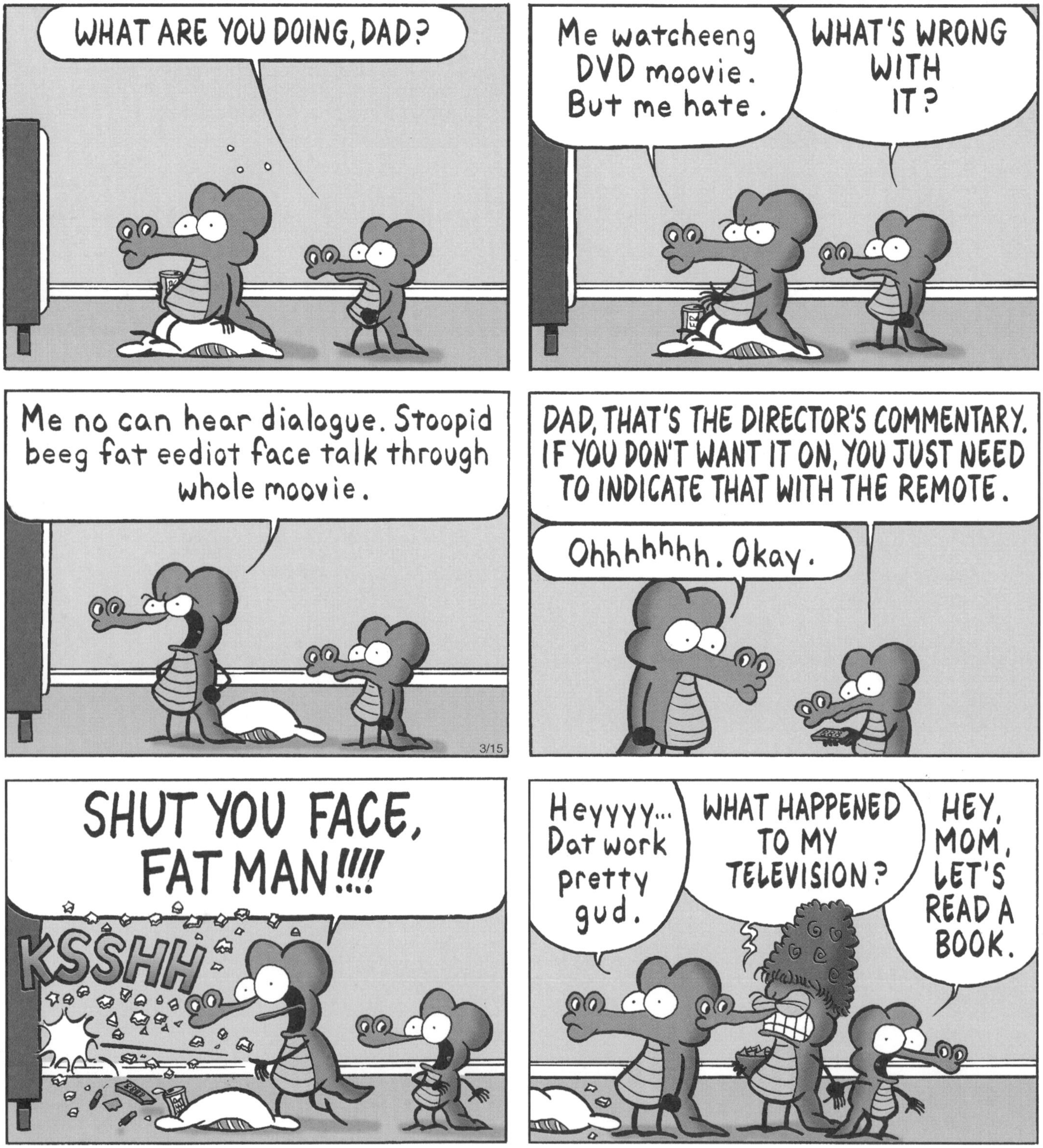
WHAT ARE YOU DOING, DAD?
Me watcheeng DVD moovie. But me hate.
WHAT'S WRONG WITH IT?
Me no can hear dialogue. Stoopid beeg fat eediot face talk through whole moovie.
3/15
DAD, THAT'S THE DIRECTOR'S COMMENTARY. IF YOU DON'T WANT IT ON, YOU JUST NEED TO INDICATE THAT WITH THE REMOTE.
Ohhhhhhh. Okay.
SHUT YOU FACE, FAT MAN!!!!
KSSHH
Heyyyy... Dat work pretty gud.
WHAT HAPPENED TO MY TELEVISION?
HEY, MOM, LET'S READ A BOOK.

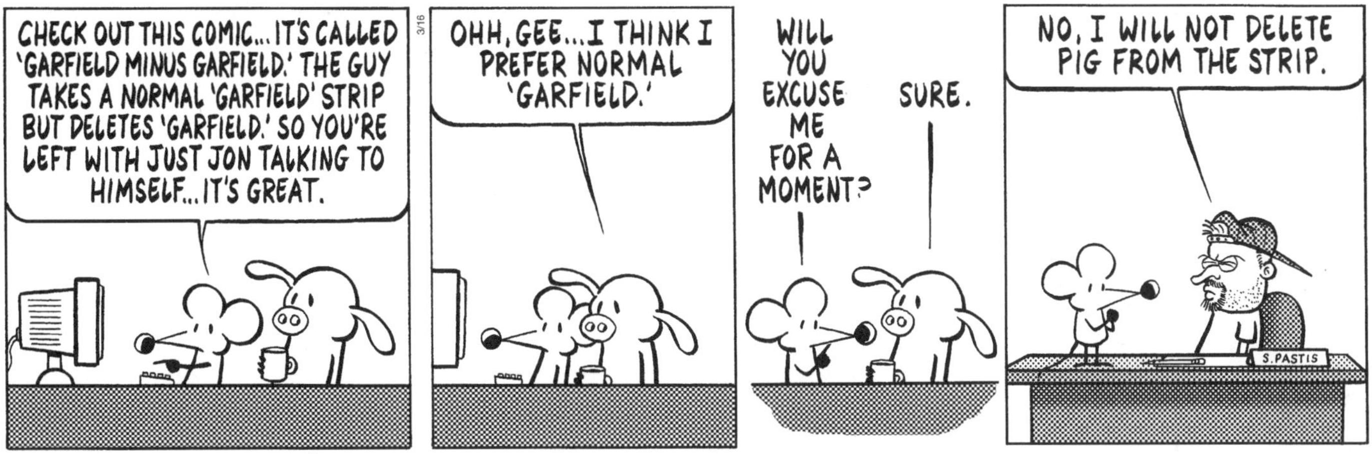
CHECK OUT THIS COMIC... IT'S CALLED 'GARFIELD MINUS GARFIELD.' THE GUY TAKES A NORMAL 'GARFIELD' STRIP BUT DELETES 'GARFIELD.' SO YOU'RE LEFT WITH JUST JON TALKING TO HIMSELF... IT'S GREAT.
3/16
OHH, GEE... I THINK I PREFER NORMAL 'GARFIELD.'
WILL YOU EXCUSE ME FOR A MOMENT?
SURE.
NO, I WILL NOT DELETE PIG FROM THE STRIP.
S. PASTIS

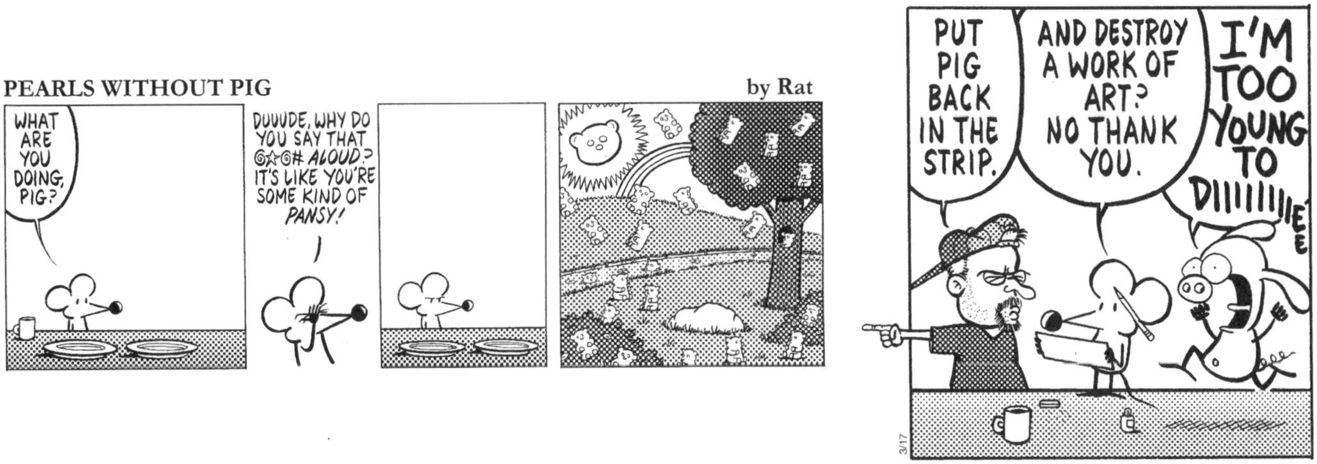
PEARLS WITHOUT PIG
by Rat
WHAT ARE YOU DOING, PIG?
DUUUDE, WHY DO YOU SAY THAT @☆@# *ALOUD*? IT'S LIKE YOU'RE SOME KIND OF *PANSY!*
PUT PIG BACK IN THE STRIP.
AND DESTROY A WORK OF ART? NO THANK YOU.
I'M TOO YOUNG TO DIIIIIIIEEE
3/17

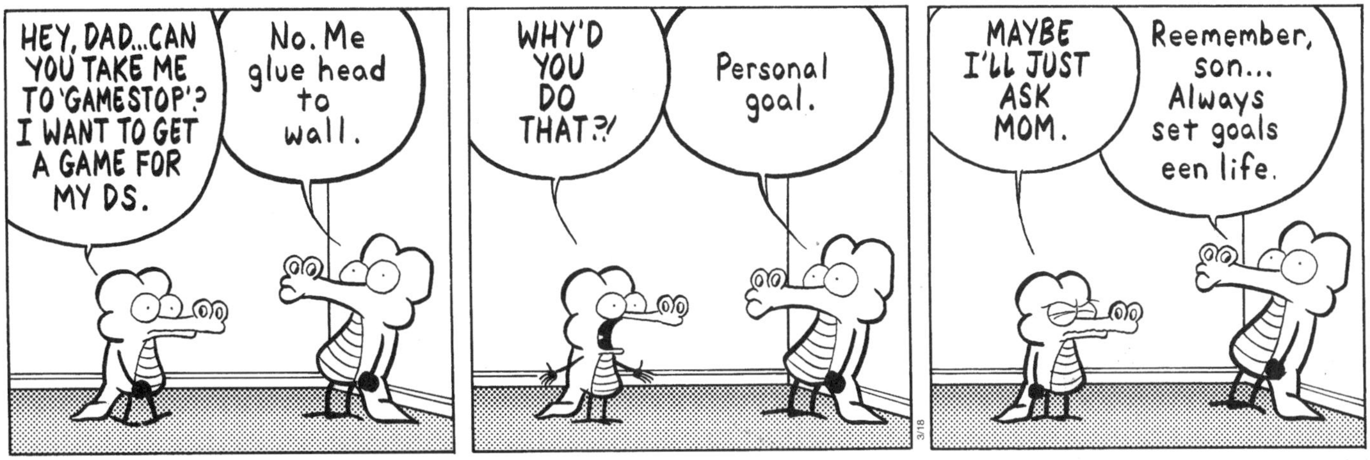
HEY, DAD... CAN YOU TAKE ME TO 'GAMESTOP'? I WANT TO GET A GAME FOR MY DS.
No. Me glue head to wall.
WHY'D YOU DO THAT?!
Personal goal.
3/18
MAYBE I'LL JUST ASK MOM.
Reemember, son... Always set goals een life.

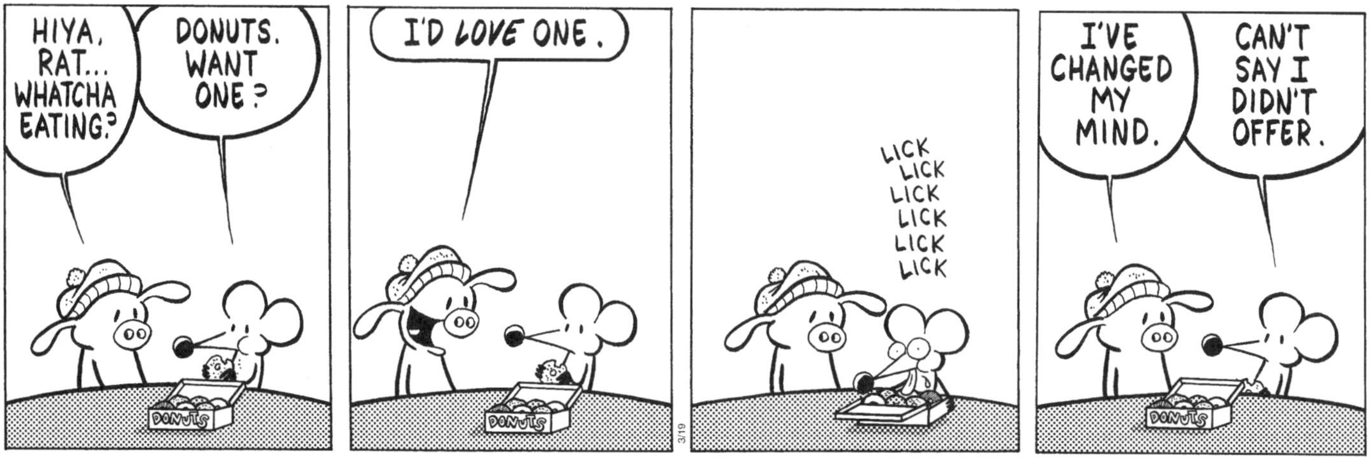
HIYA, RAT... WHATCHA EATING?
DONUTS. WANT ONE?
DONUTS
I'D *LOVE* ONE.
DONUTS
LICK LICK LICK LICK LICK LICK
I'VE CHANGED MY MIND.
CAN'T SAY I DIDN'T OFFER.
DONUTS

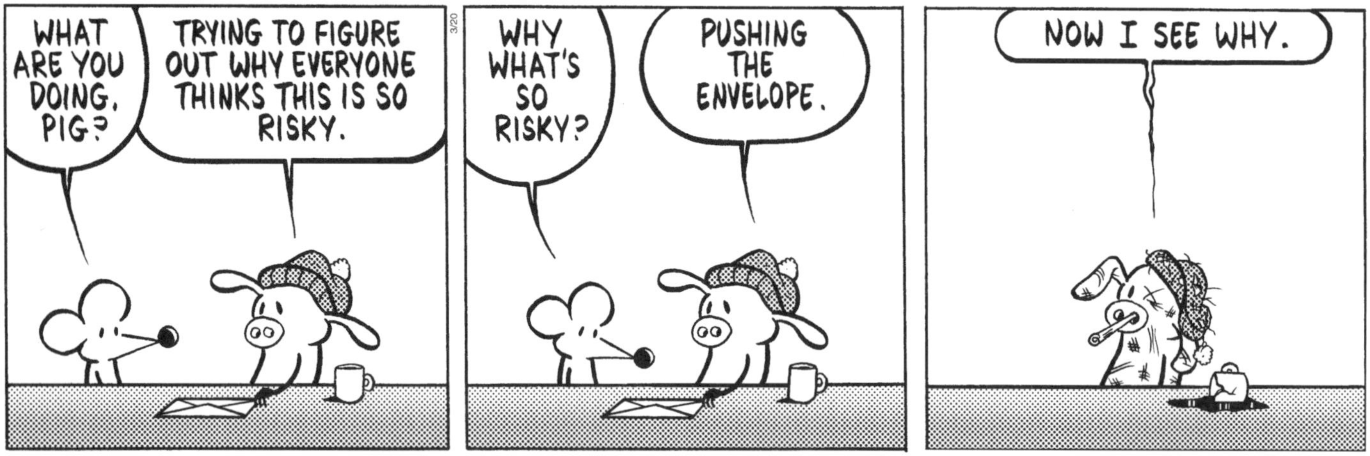
WHAT ARE YOU DOING, PIG?
TRYING TO FIGURE OUT WHY EVERYONE THINKS THIS IS SO RISKY.
WHY WHAT'S SO RISKY?
PUSHING THE ENVELOPE.
NOW I SEE WHY.

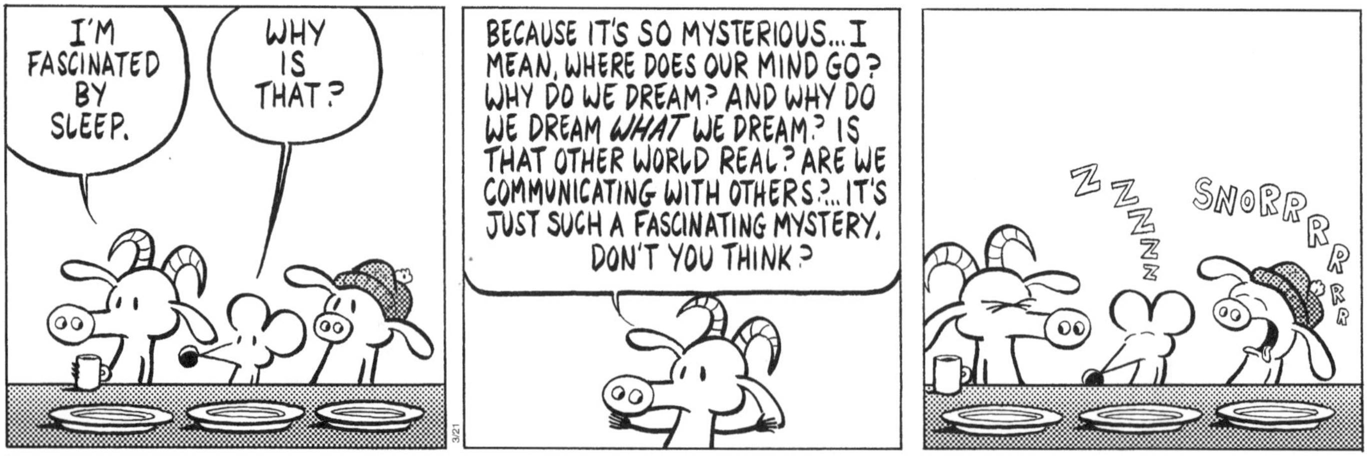
I'M FASCINATED BY SLEEP.
WHY IS THAT?
BECAUSE IT'S SO MYSTERIOUS... I MEAN, WHERE DOES OUR MIND GO? WHY DO WE DREAM? AND WHY DO WE DREAM *WHAT* WE DREAM? IS THAT OTHER WORLD REAL? ARE WE COMMUNICATING WITH OTHERS?... IT'S JUST SUCH A FASCINATING MYSTERY. DON'T YOU THINK?
Z Z Z Z Z Z
SNORRRRRRRR

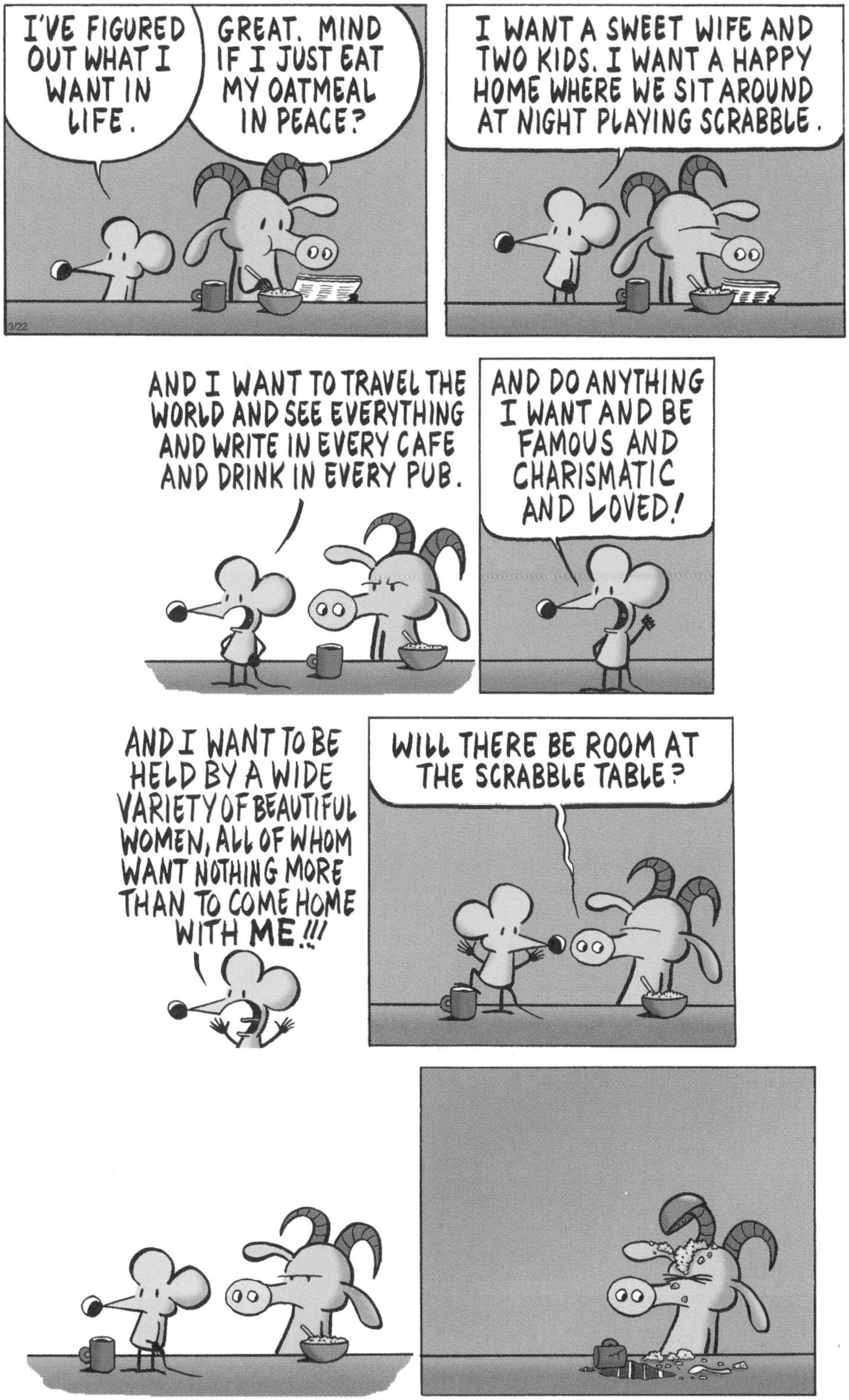
I'VE FIGURED OUT WHAT I WANT IN LIFE.
GREAT. MIND IF I JUST EAT MY OATMEAL IN PEACE?
I WANT A SWEET WIFE AND TWO KIDS. I WANT A HAPPY HOME WHERE WE SIT AROUND AT NIGHT PLAYING SCRABBLE.
AND I WANT TO TRAVEL THE WORLD AND SEE EVERYTHING AND WRITE IN EVERY CAFE AND DRINK IN EVERY PUB.
AND DO ANYTHING I WANT AND BE FAMOUS AND CHARISMATIC AND LOVED!
AND I WANT TO BE HELD BY A WIDE VARIETY OF BEAUTIFUL WOMEN, ALL OF WHOM WANT NOTHING MORE THAN TO COME HOME WITH ME!!!
WILL THERE BE ROOM AT THE SCRABBLE TABLE?

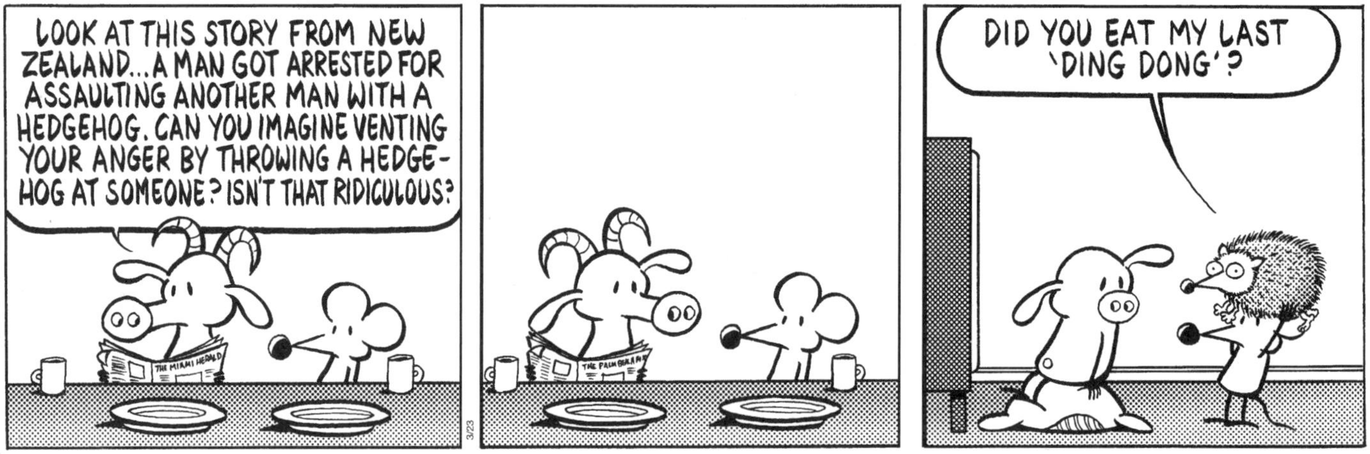
LOOK AT THIS STORY FROM NEW ZEALAND...A MAN GOT ARRESTED FOR ASSAULTING ANOTHER MAN WITH A HEDGEHOG. CAN YOU IMAGINE VENTING YOUR ANGER BY THROWING A HEDGE-HOG AT SOMEONE? ISN'T THAT RIDICULOUS?
DID YOU EAT MY LAST 'DING DONG'?
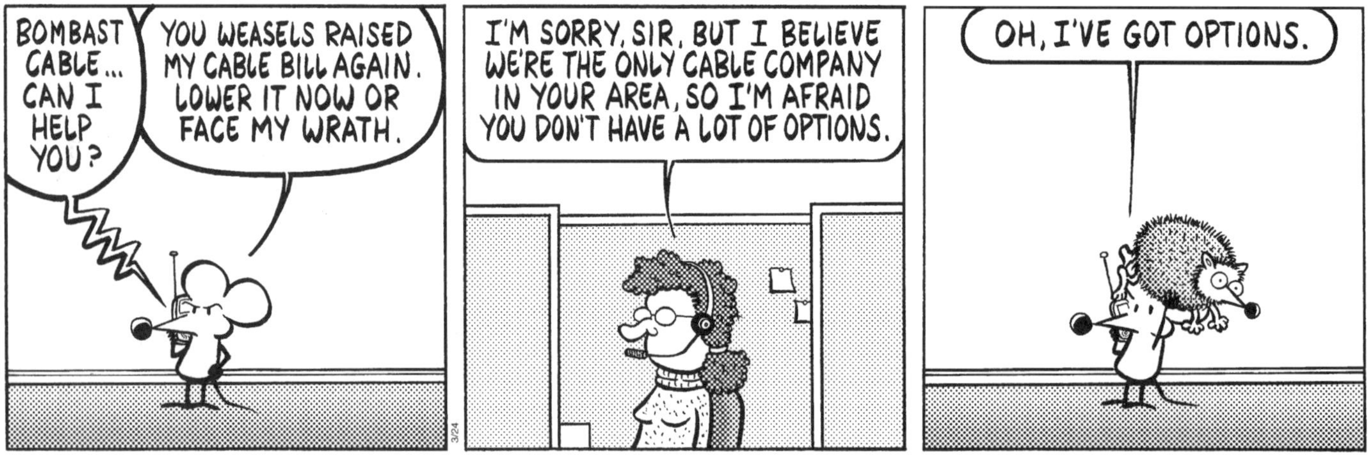
BOMBAST CABLE... CAN I HELP YOU?
YOU WEASELS RAISED MY CABLE BILL AGAIN. LOWER IT NOW OR FACE MY WRATH.
I'M SORRY, SIR, BUT I BELIEVE WE'RE THE ONLY CABLE COMPANY IN YOUR AREA, SO I'M AFRAID YOU DON'T HAVE A LOT OF OPTIONS.
OH, I'VE GOT OPTIONS.
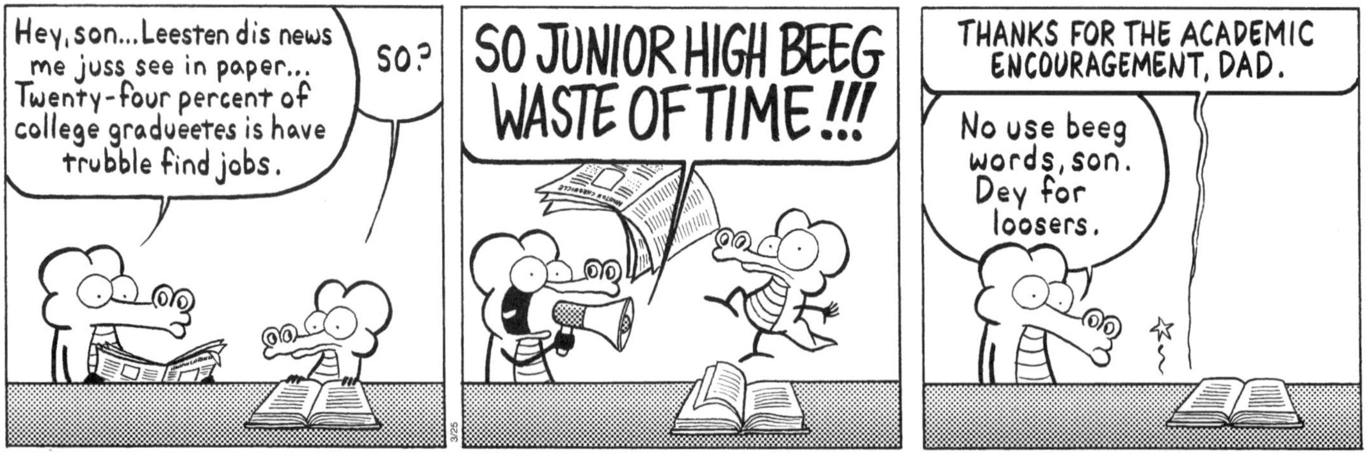
Hey, son...Leesten dis news me juss see in paper... Twenty-four percent of college gradueetes is have trubble find jobs.
SO?
SO JUNIOR HIGH BEEG WASTE OF TIME!!!
THANKS FOR THE ACADEMIC ENCOURAGEMENT, DAD.
No use beeg words, son. Dey for loosers.

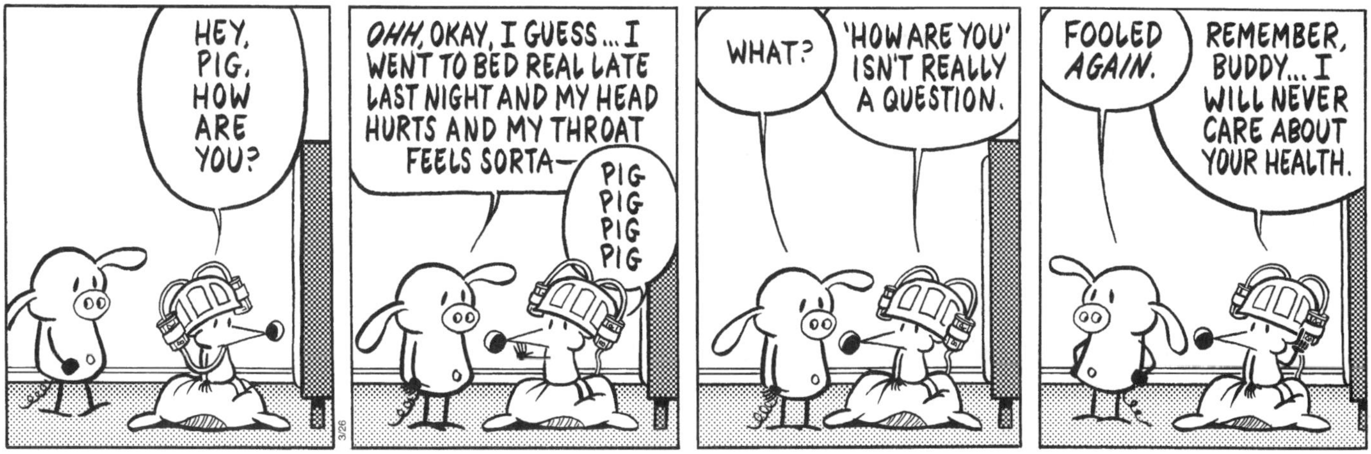
HEY, PIG, HOW ARE YOU?
3/26
OHH, OKAY, I GUESS... I WENT TO BED REAL LATE LAST NIGHT AND MY HEAD HURTS AND MY THROAT FEELS SORTA—
PIG PIG PIG PIG PIG
WHAT?
'HOW ARE YOU' ISN'T REALLY A QUESTION.
FOOLED AGAIN.
REMEMBER, BUDDY... I WILL NEVER CARE ABOUT YOUR HEALTH.

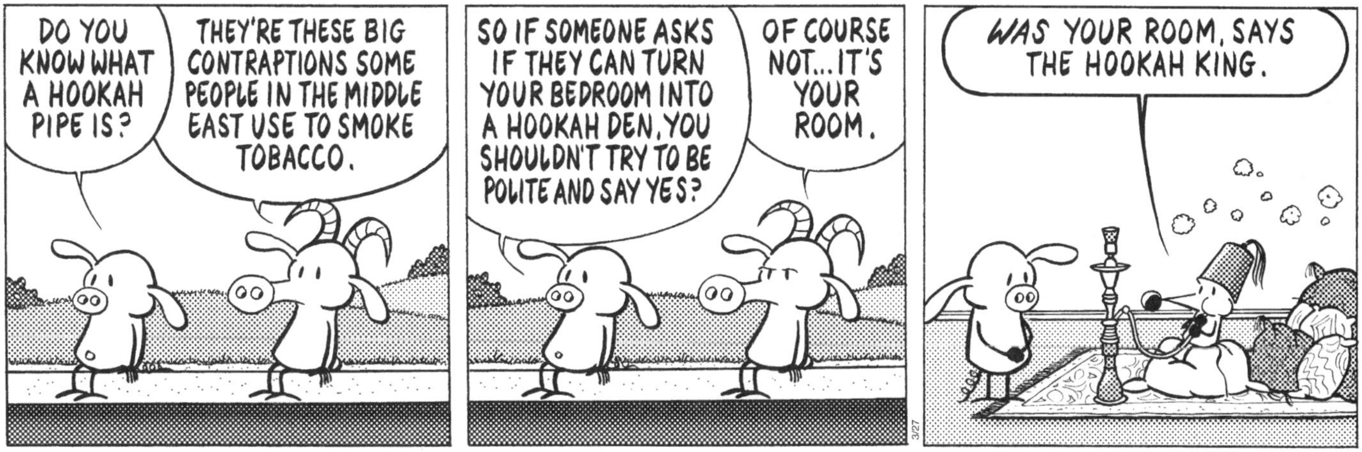
DO YOU KNOW WHAT A HOOKAH PIPE IS?
THEY'RE THESE BIG CONTRAPTIONS SOME PEOPLE IN THE MIDDLE EAST USE TO SMOKE TOBACCO.
SO IF SOMEONE ASKS IF THEY CAN TURN YOUR BEDROOM INTO A HOOKAH DEN, YOU SHOULDN'T TRY TO BE POLITE AND SAY YES?
OF COURSE NOT... IT'S YOUR ROOM.
3/27
WAS YOUR ROOM, SAYS THE HOOKAH KING.

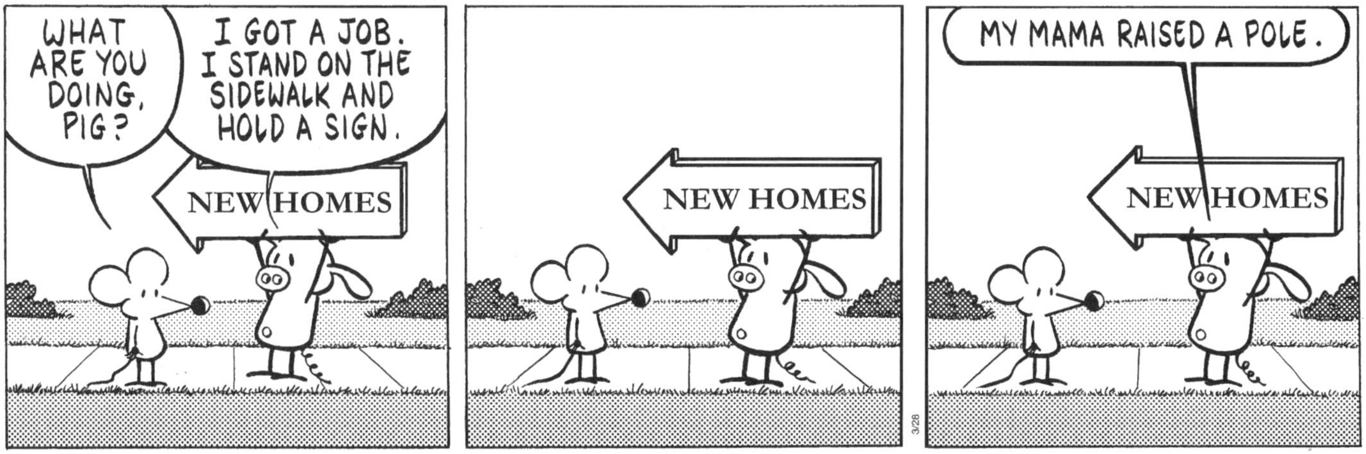
WHAT ARE YOU DOING, PIG?
I GOT A JOB. I STAND ON THE SIDEWALK AND HOLD A SIGN.
NEW HOMES
NEW HOMES
3/28
MY MAMA RAISED A POLE.
NEW HOMES

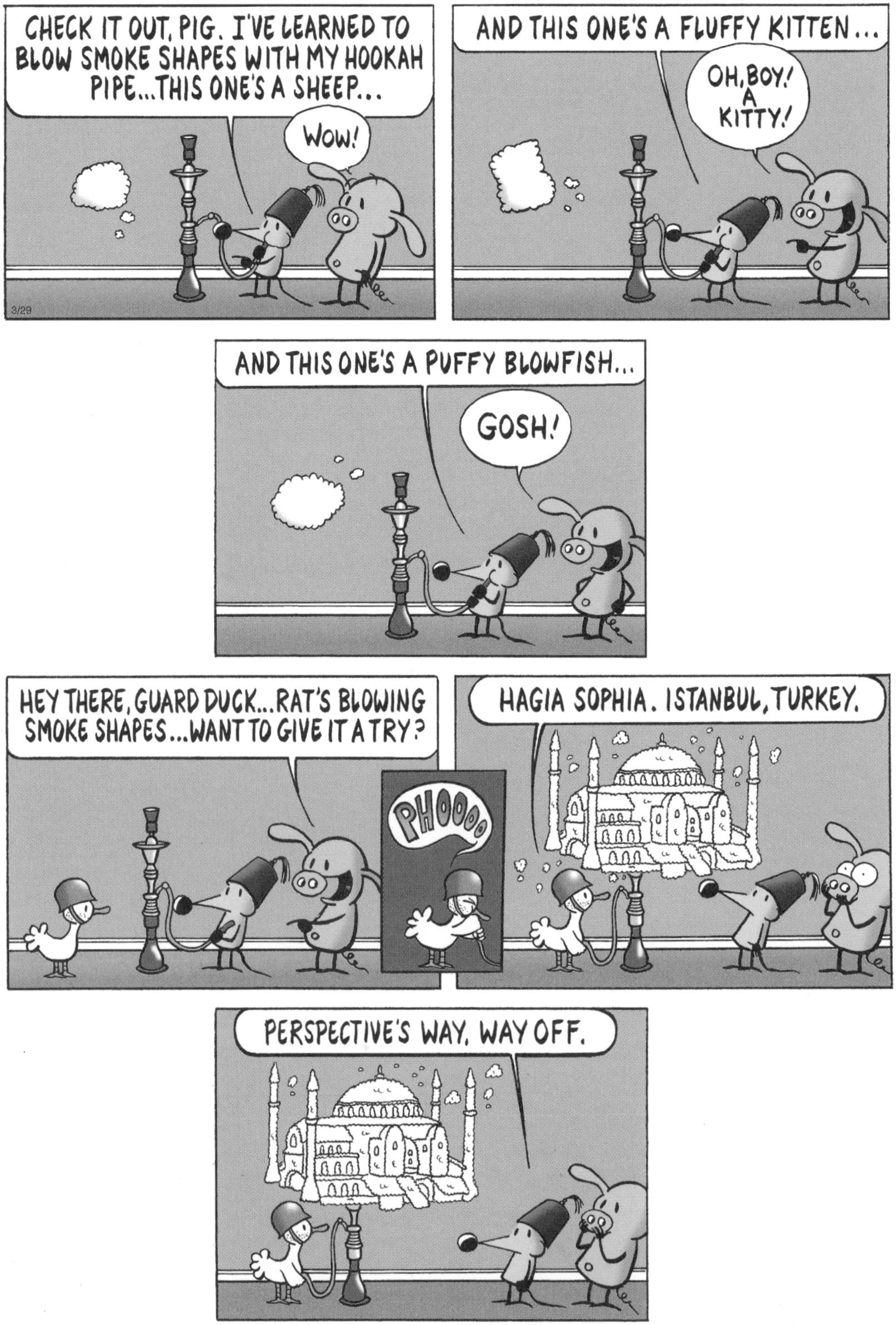
CHECK IT OUT, PIG. I'VE LEARNED TO BLOW SMOKE SHAPES WITH MY HOOKAH PIPE...THIS ONE'S A SHEEP...
WOW!
3/29
AND THIS ONE'S A FLUFFY KITTEN...
OH, BOY! A KITTY!
AND THIS ONE'S A PUFFY BLOWFISH...
GOSH!
HEY THERE, GUARD DUCK...RAT'S BLOWING SMOKE SHAPES...WANT TO GIVE IT A TRY?
PHOOOO
HAGIA SOPHIA. ISTANBUL, TURKEY.
PERSPECTIVE'S WAY, WAY OFF.

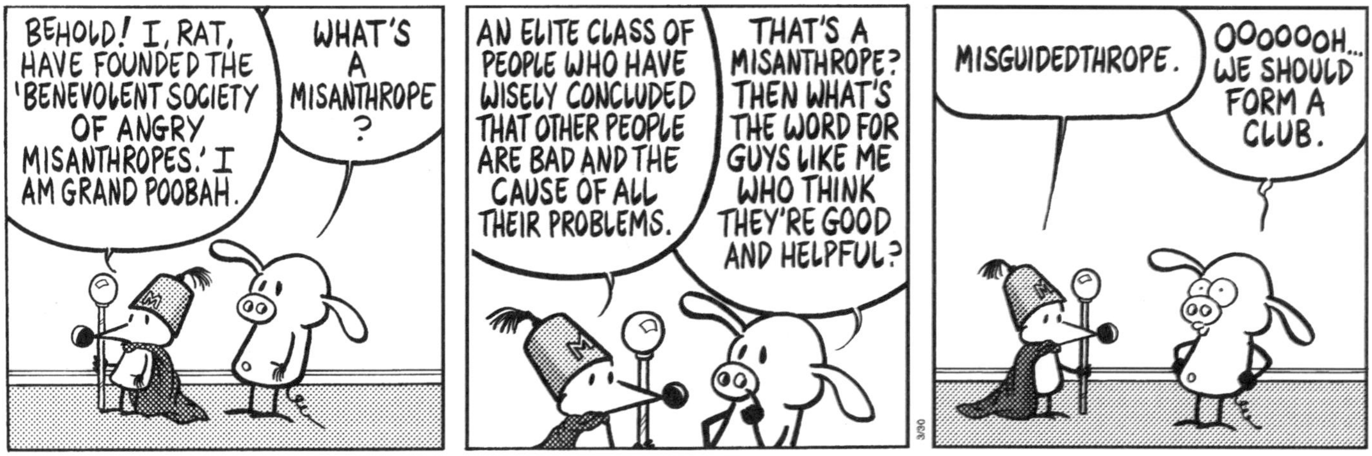
BEHOLD! I, RAT, HAVE FOUNDED THE 'BENEVOLENT SOCIETY OF ANGRY MISANTHROPES.' I AM GRAND POOBAH.
WHAT'S A MISANTHROPE?
AN ELITE CLASS OF PEOPLE WHO HAVE WISELY CONCLUDED THAT OTHER PEOPLE ARE BAD AND THE CAUSE OF ALL THEIR PROBLEMS.
THAT'S A MISANTHROPE? THEN WHAT'S THE WORD FOR GUYS LIKE ME WHO THINK THEY'RE GOOD AND HELPFUL?
MISGUIDEDTHROPE.
OOOOOOH... WE SHOULD FORM A CLUB.
3/30

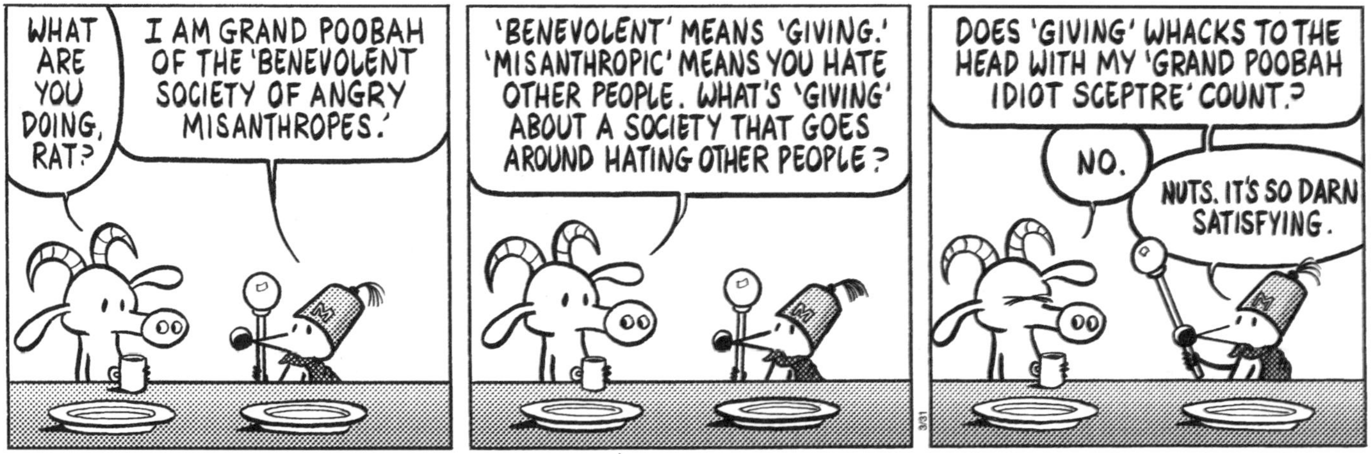
WHAT ARE YOU DOING, RAT?
I AM GRAND POOBAH OF THE 'BENEVOLENT SOCIETY OF ANGRY MISANTHROPES.'
'BENEVOLENT' MEANS 'GIVING.' 'MISANTHROPIC' MEANS YOU HATE OTHER PEOPLE. WHAT'S 'GIVING' ABOUT A SOCIETY THAT GOES AROUND HATING OTHER PEOPLE?
DOES 'GIVING' WHACKS TO THE HEAD WITH MY 'GRAND POOBAH IDIOT SCEPTRE' COUNT?
NO.
NUTS. IT'S SO DARN SATISFYING.
3/31

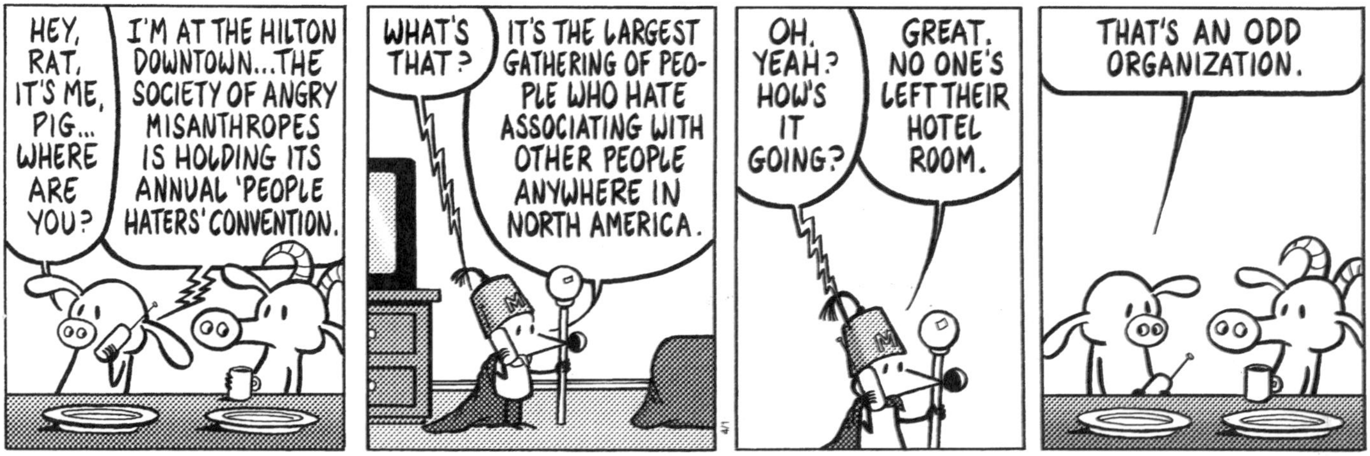
HEY, RAT, IT'S ME, PIG... WHERE ARE YOU?
I'M AT THE HILTON DOWNTOWN...THE SOCIETY OF ANGRY MISANTHROPES IS HOLDING ITS ANNUAL 'PEOPLE HATERS' CONVENTION.
WHAT'S THAT?
IT'S THE LARGEST GATHERING OF PEOPLE WHO HATE ASSOCIATING WITH OTHER PEOPLE ANYWHERE IN NORTH AMERICA.
OH, YEAH? HOW'S IT GOING?
GREAT. NO ONE'S LEFT THEIR HOTEL ROOM.
THAT'S AN ODD ORGANIZATION.
4/1

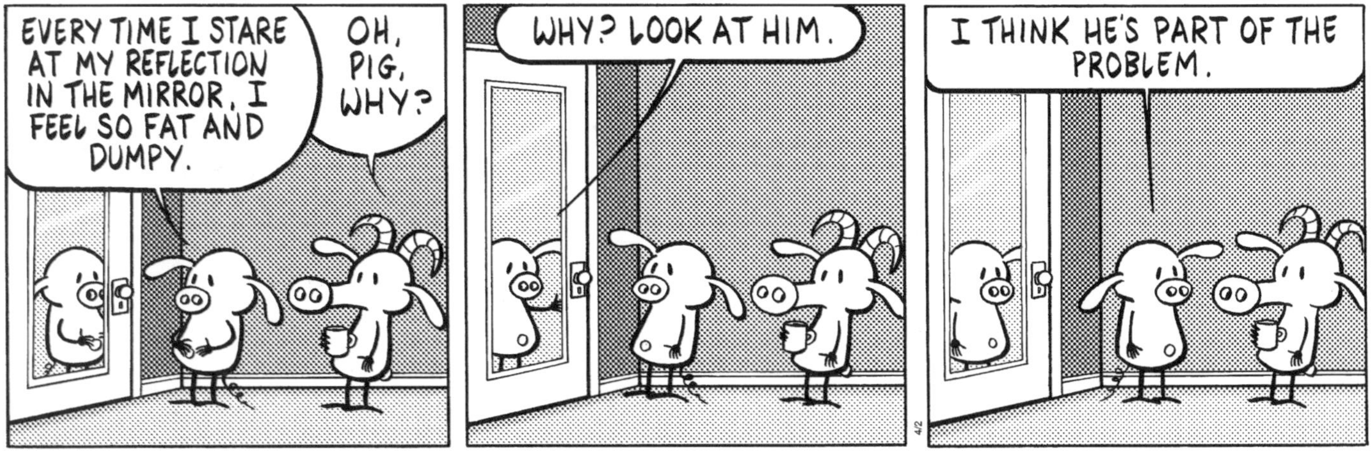
EVERY TIME I STARE AT MY REFLECTION IN THE MIRROR, I FEEL SO FAT AND DUMPY.
OH, PIG, WHY?
WHY? LOOK AT HIM.
I THINK HE'S PART OF THE PROBLEM.

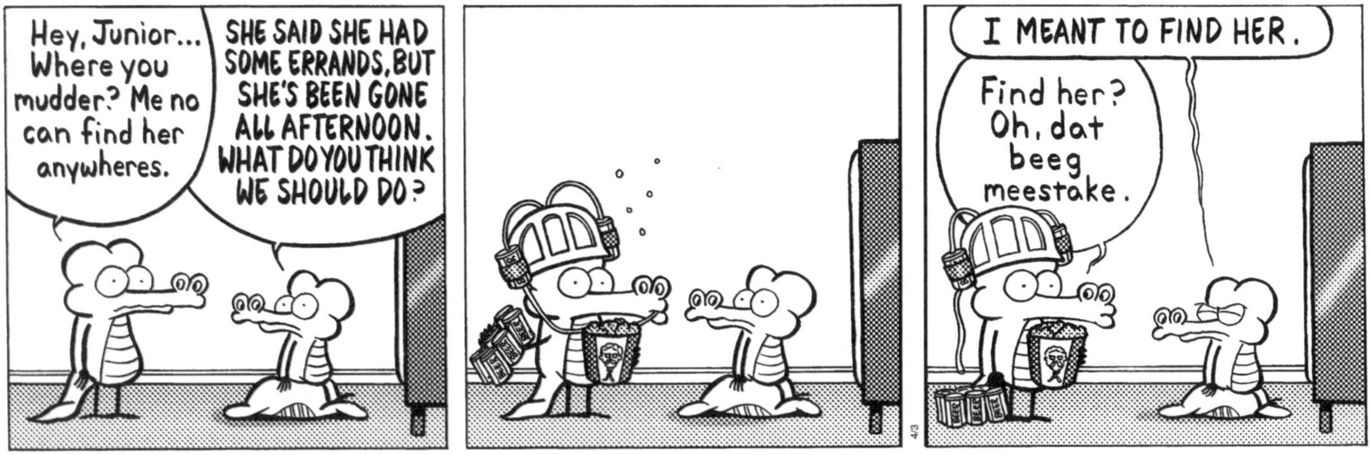
Hey, Junior... Where you mudder? Me no can find her anywheres.
SHE SAID SHE HAD SOME ERRANDS, BUT SHE'S BEEN GONE ALL AFTERNOON. WHAT DO YOU THINK WE SHOULD DO?
I MEANT TO FIND HER.
Find her? Oh, dat beeg meestake.

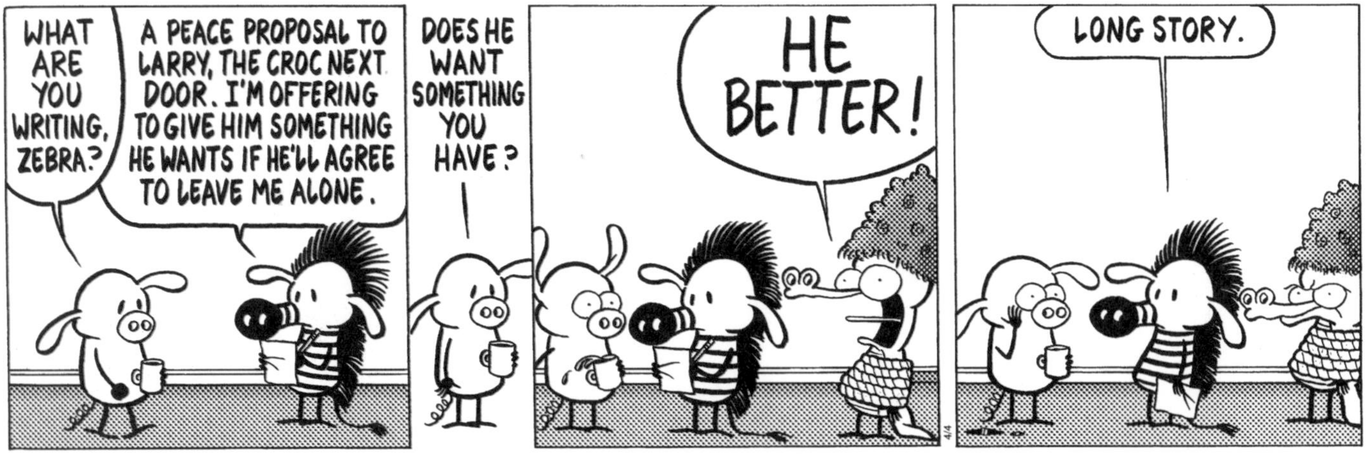
WHAT ARE YOU WRITING, ZEBRA?
A PEACE PROPOSAL TO LARRY, THE CROC NEXT DOOR. I'M OFFERING TO GIVE HIM SOMETHING HE WANTS IF HE'LL AGREE TO LEAVE ME ALONE.
DOES HE WANT SOMETHING YOU HAVE?
HE BETTER!
LONG STORY.

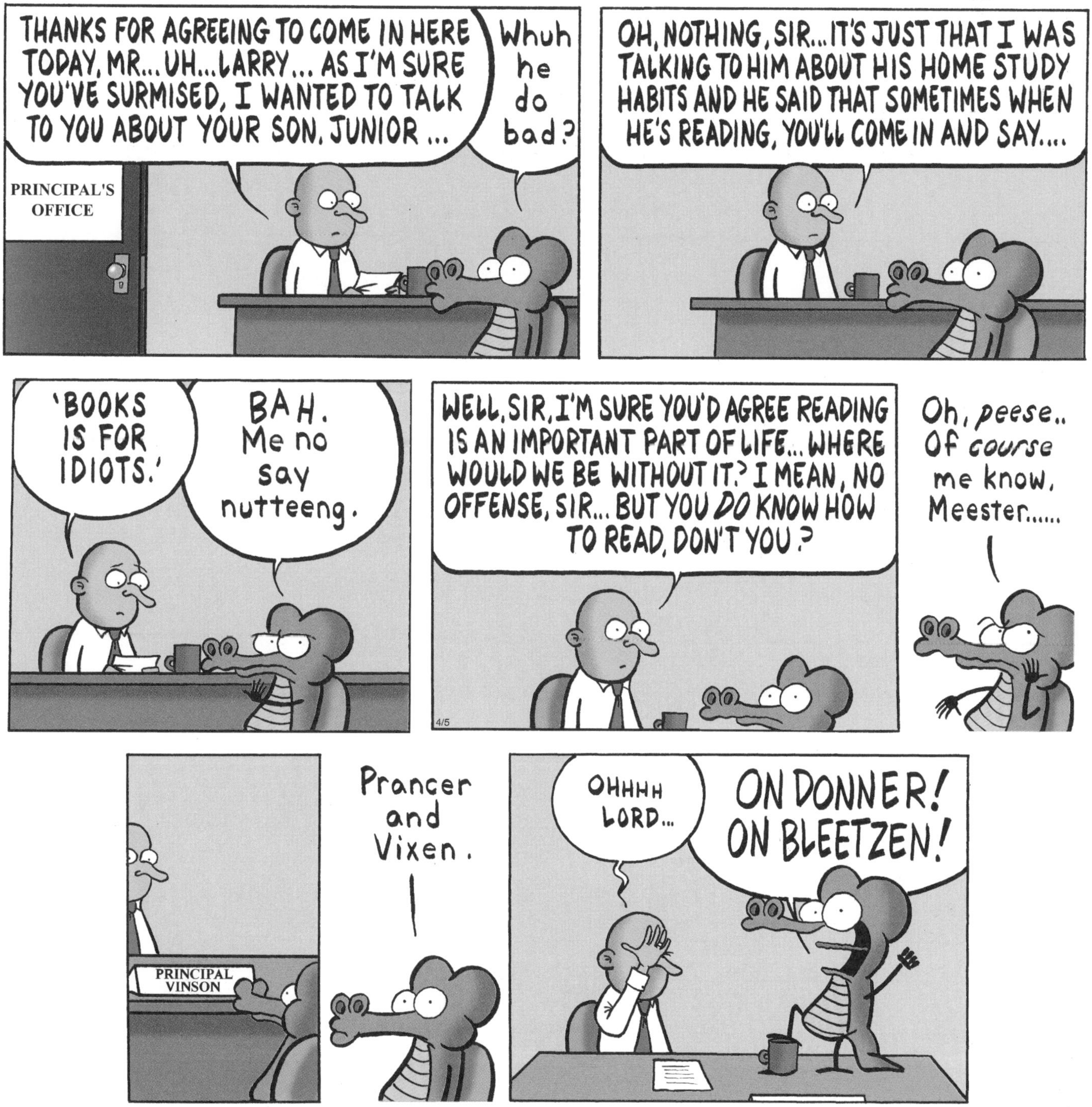
THANKS FOR AGREEING TO COME IN HERE TODAY, MR... UH... LARRY... AS I'M SURE YOU'VE SURMISED, I WANTED TO TALK TO YOU ABOUT YOUR SON, JUNIOR ...
Whuh he do bad?
PRINCIPAL'S OFFICE
OH, NOTHING, SIR... IT'S JUST THAT I WAS TALKING TO HIM ABOUT HIS HOME STUDY HABITS AND HE SAID THAT SOMETIMES WHEN HE'S READING, YOU'LL COME IN AND SAY....
'BOOKS IS FOR IDIOTS.'
BAH. Me no say nutteeng.
WELL, SIR, I'M SURE YOU'D AGREE READING IS AN IMPORTANT PART OF LIFE... WHERE WOULD WE BE WITHOUT IT? I MEAN, NO OFFENSE, SIR... BUT YOU *DO* KNOW HOW TO READ, DON'T YOU?
4/5
Oh, *peese*.. Of *course* me know, Meester......
PRINCIPAL VINSON
Prancer and Vixen.
OHHHH LORD...
ON DONNER! ON BLEETZEN!

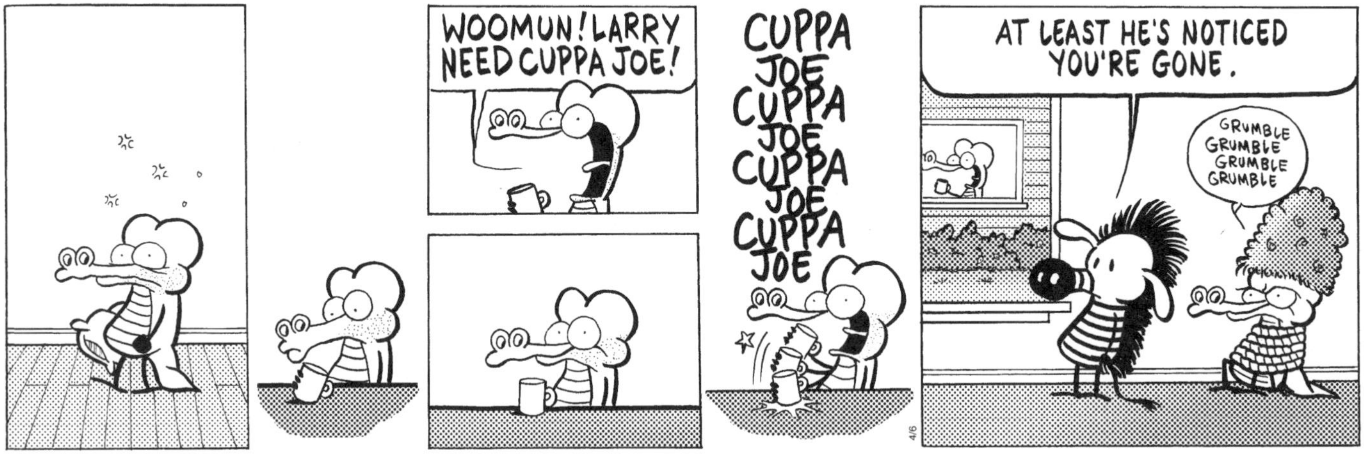
WOOMUN! LARRY NEED CUPPA JOE!
CUPPA JOE CUPPA JOE CUPPA JOE CUPPA JOE
AT LEAST HE'S NOTICED YOU'RE GONE.
GRUMBLE GRUMBLE GRUMBLE GRUMBLE
4/6

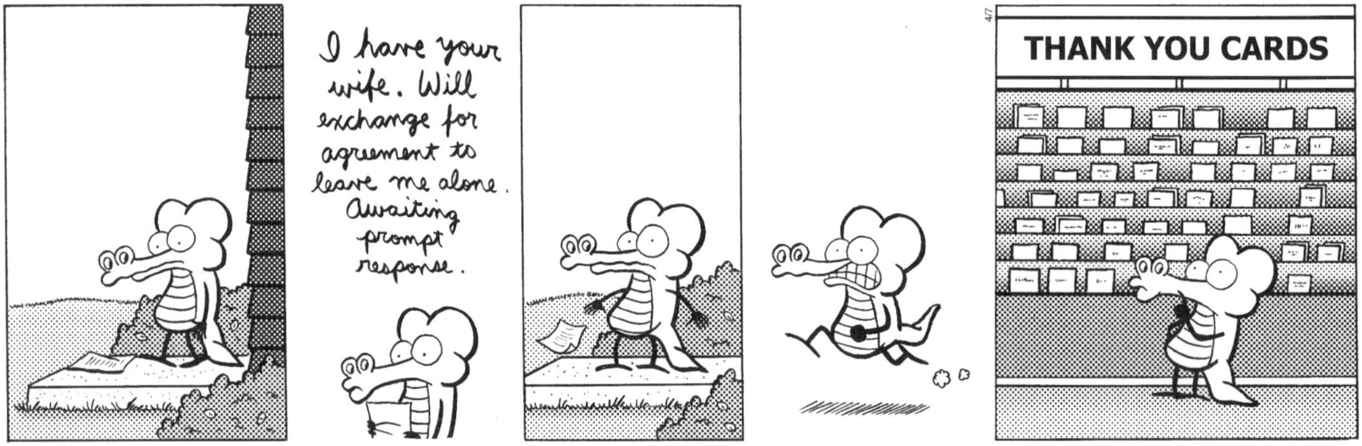
I have your wife. Will exchange for agreement to leave me alone. Awaiting prompt response.
THANK YOU CARDS
4/7

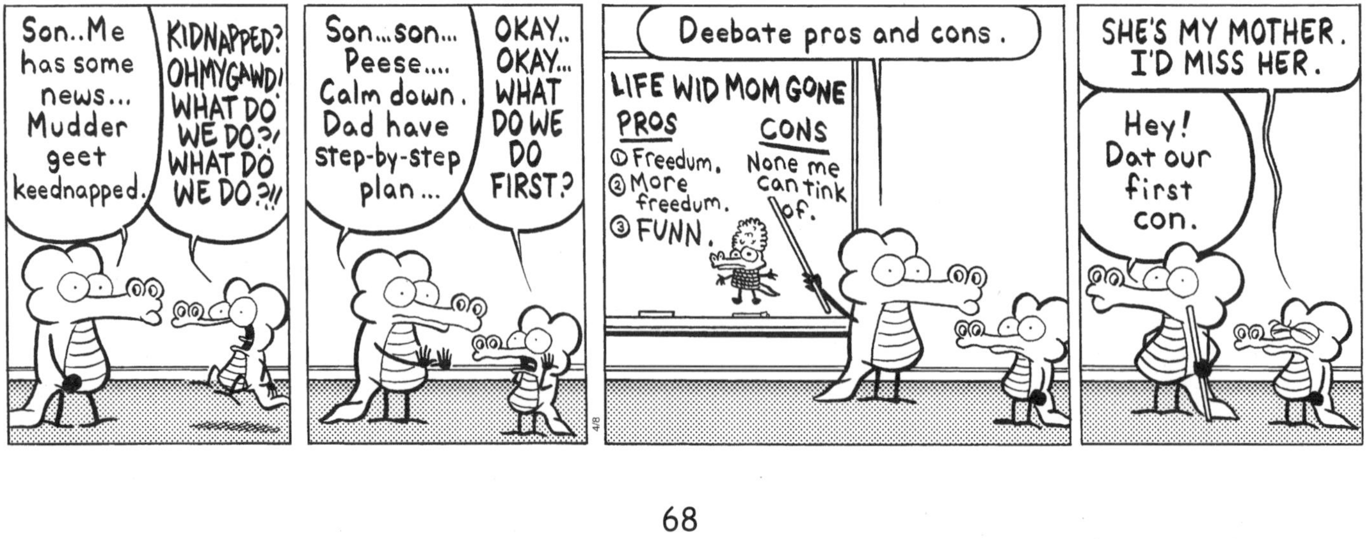
Son..Me has some news... Mudder geet keednapped.
KIDNAPPED? OHMYGAWD! WHAT DO WE DO?! WHAT DO WE DO?!!
Son...son... Peese.... Calm down. Dad have step-by-step plan...
OKAY.. OKAY... WHAT DO WE DO FIRST?
4/8
Deebate pros and cons.
LIFE WID MOM GONE
PROS
① Freedum.
② More freedum.
③ FUNN.
CONS
None me can tink of.
SHE'S MY MOTHER. I'D MISS HER.
Hey! Dat our first con.

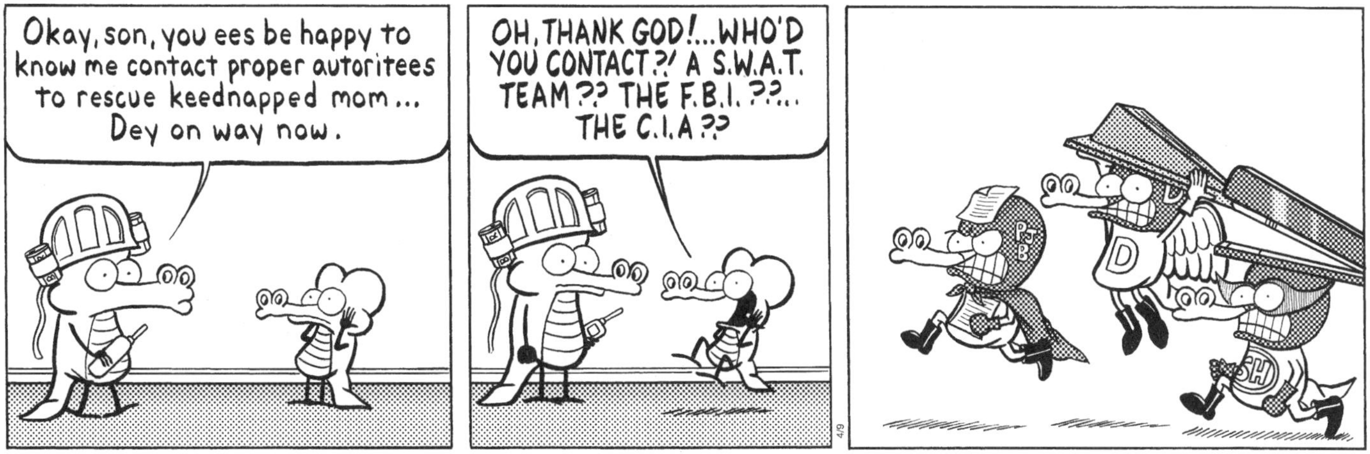
Okay, son, you ees be happy to know me contact proper autoritees to rescue keednapped mom... Dey on way now.
OH, THANK GOD!...WHO'D YOU CONTACT?! A S.W.A.T. TEAM?? THE F.B.I.??.. THE C.I.A??

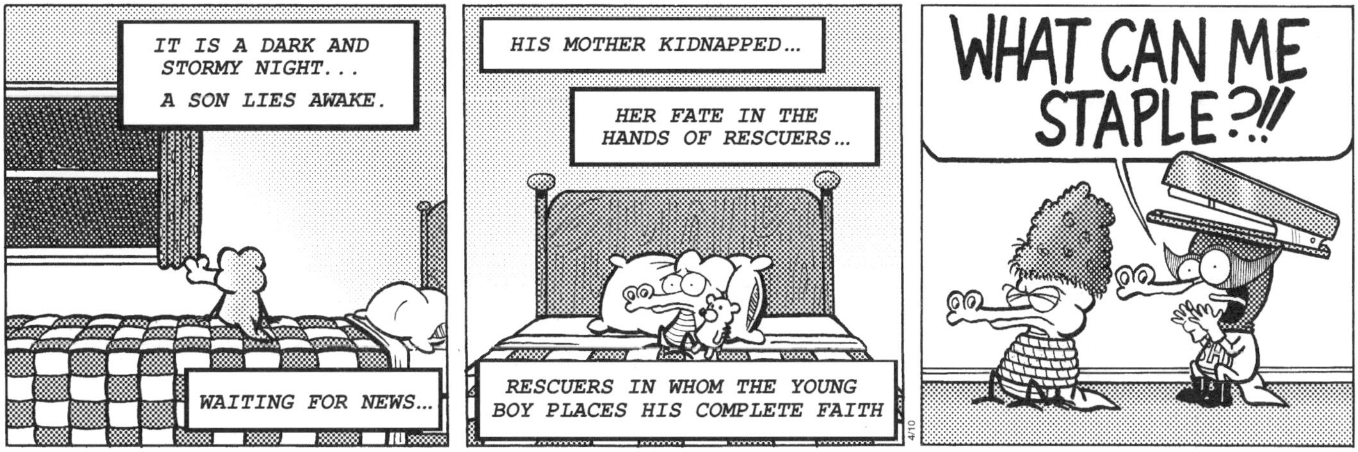
IT IS A DARK AND STORMY NIGHT...
A SON LIES AWAKE.
WAITING FOR NEWS...
HIS MOTHER KIDNAPPED...
HER FATE IN THE HANDS OF RESCUERS...
RESCUERS IN WHOM THE YOUNG BOY PLACES HIS COMPLETE FAITH
WHAT CAN ME STAPLE?!!

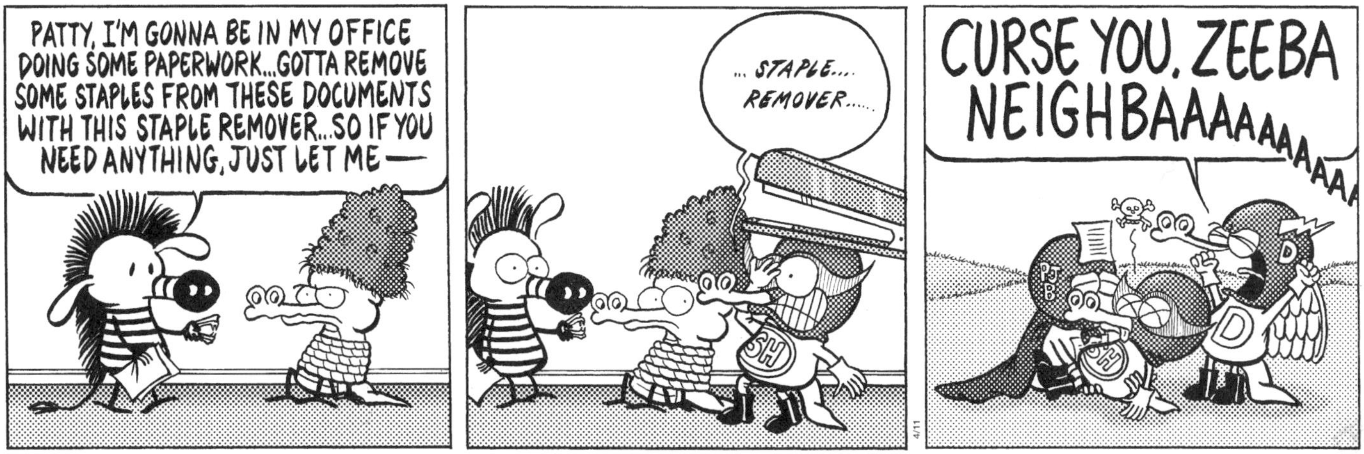
PATTY, I'M GONNA BE IN MY OFFICE DOING SOME PAPERWORK...GOTTA REMOVE SOME STAPLES FROM THESE DOCUMENTS WITH THIS STAPLE REMOVER...SO IF YOU NEED ANYTHING, JUST LET ME—
...STAPLE... REMOVER.....
CURSE YOU, ZEEBA NEIGHBAAAAAAAAAA

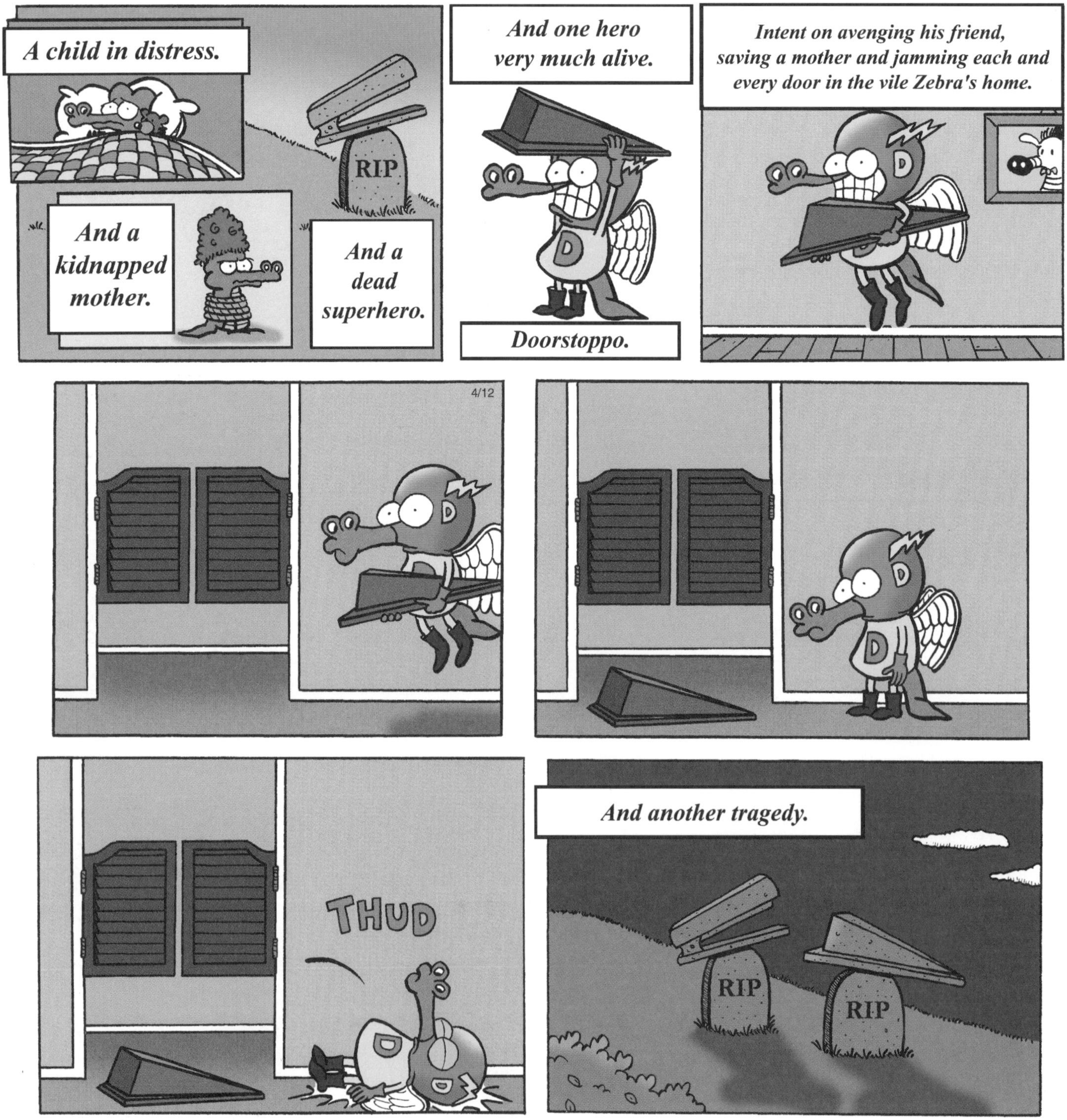
A child in distress.
RIP
And a kidnapped mother.
And a dead superhero.
And one hero very much alive.
Doorstoppo.
Intent on avenging his friend, saving a mother and jamming each and every door in the vile Zebra's home.
4/12
THUD
And another tragedy.
RIP
RIP

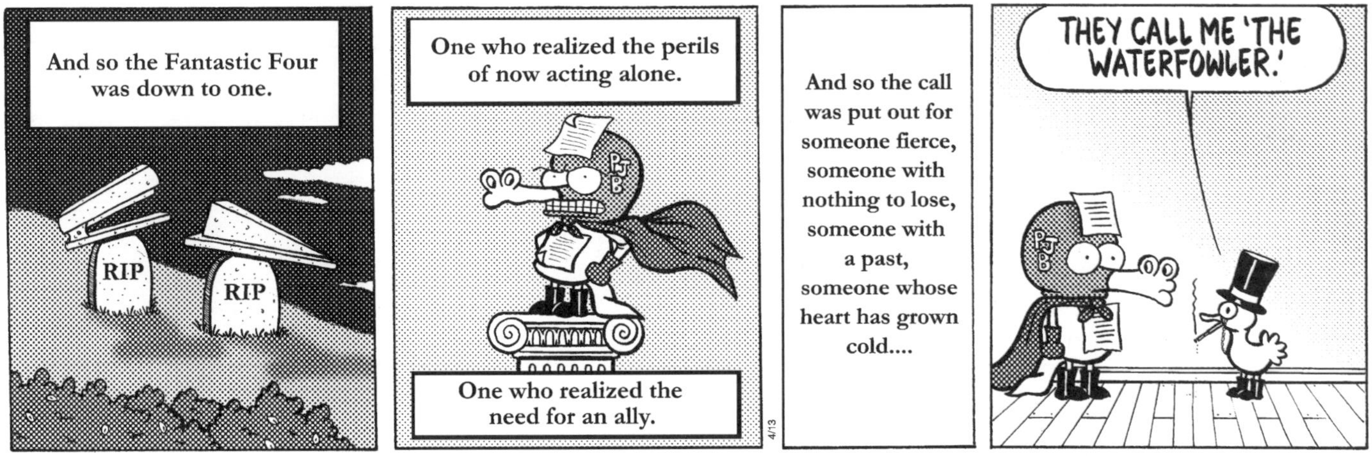

And so the Fantastic Four was down to one.
RIP
RIP
One who realized the perils of now acting alone.
One who realized the need for an ally.
And so the call was put out for someone fierce, someone with nothing to lose, someone with a past, someone whose heart has grown cold....
THEY CALL ME 'THE WATERFOWLER.'

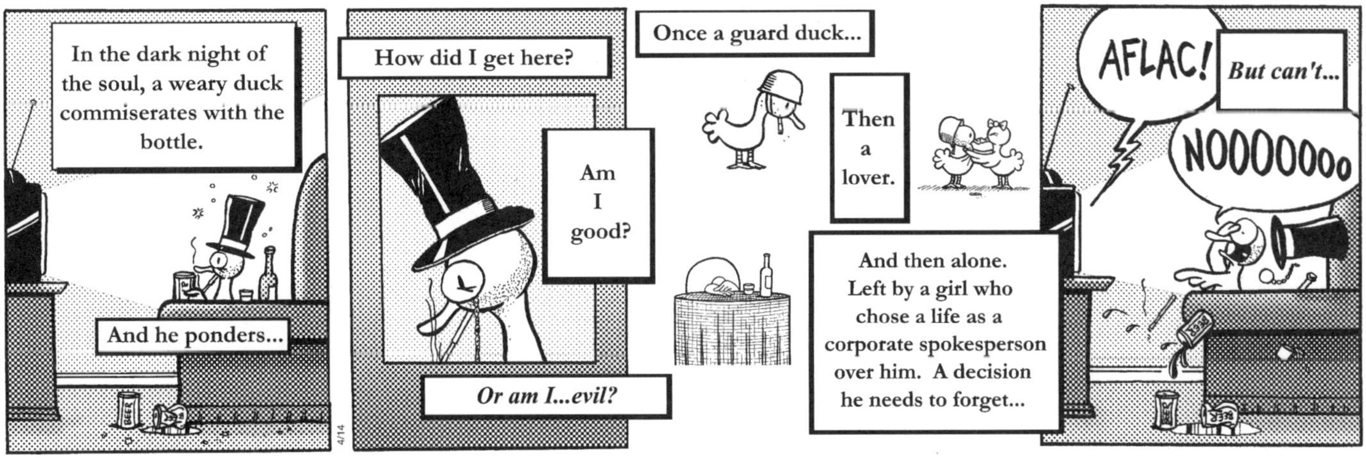

In the dark night of the soul, a weary duck commiserates with the bottle.
And he ponders...
How did I get here?
Am I good?
Or am I...evil?
Once a guard duck...
Then a lover.
And then alone. Left by a girl who chose a life as a corporate spokesperson over him. A decision he needs to forget...
AFLAC!
But can't...
NOOOOOOo

STORY UPDATE

And so to defeat the vile Zebra, our lone hero, Paper Jam Boy, forges a new alliance with a dark stranger, the Waterfowler.

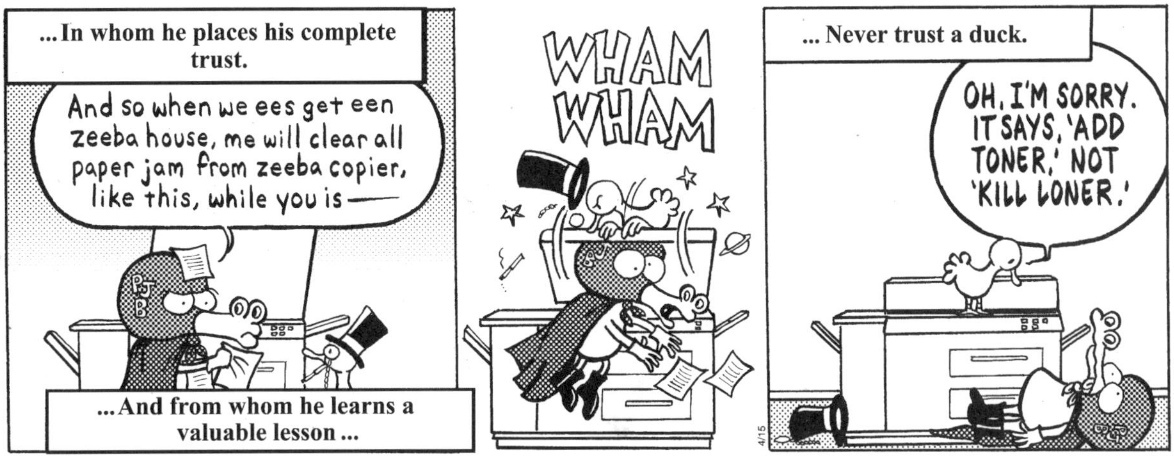

...In whom he places his complete trust.
And so when we ees get een zeeba house, me will clear all paper jam from zeeba copier, like this, while you is—
...And from whom he learns a valuable lesson ...
WHAM WHAM
... Never trust a duck.
OH, I'M SORRY. IT SAYS, 'ADD TONER,' NOT 'KILL LONER.'

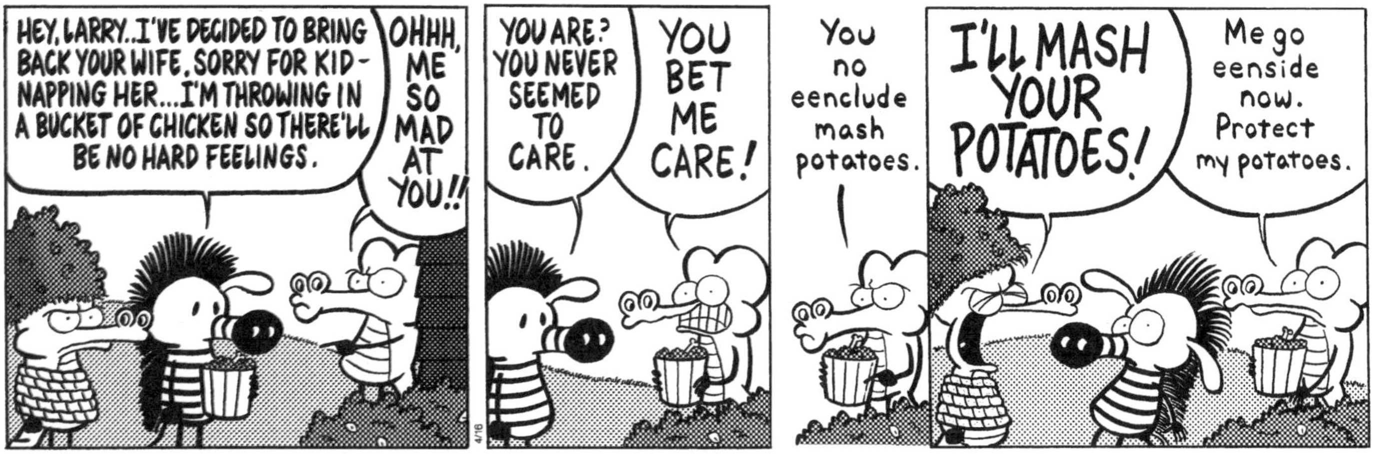
HEY, LARRY..I'VE DECIDED TO BRING BACK YOUR WIFE. SORRY FOR KID-NAPPING HER...I'M THROWING IN A BUCKET OF CHICKEN SO THERE'LL BE NO HARD FEELINGS.
OHHH, ME SO MAD AT YOU!!
4/16
YOU ARE? YOU NEVER SEEMED TO CARE.
YOU BET ME CARE!
You no eenclude mash potatoes.
I'LL MASH YOUR POTATOES!
Me go eenside now. Protect my potatoes.

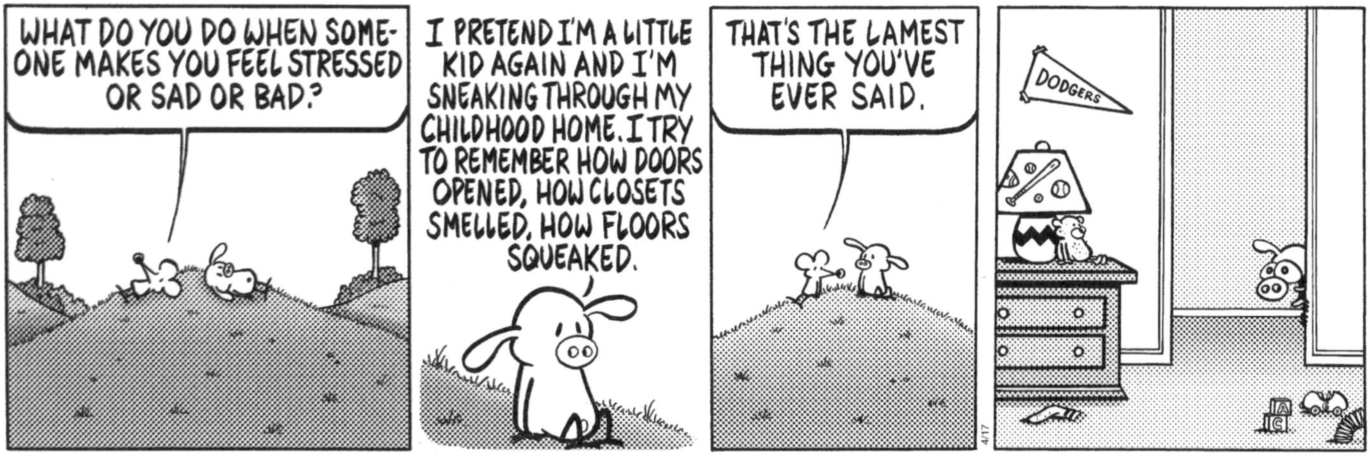
WHAT DO YOU DO WHEN SOME-ONE MAKES YOU FEEL STRESSED OR SAD OR BAD?
I PRETEND I'M A LITTLE KID AGAIN AND I'M SNEAKING THROUGH MY CHILDHOOD HOME. I TRY TO REMEMBER HOW DOORS OPENED, HOW CLOSETS SMELLED, HOW FLOORS SQUEAKED.
THAT'S THE LAMEST THING YOU'VE EVER SAID.
4/17
DODGERS

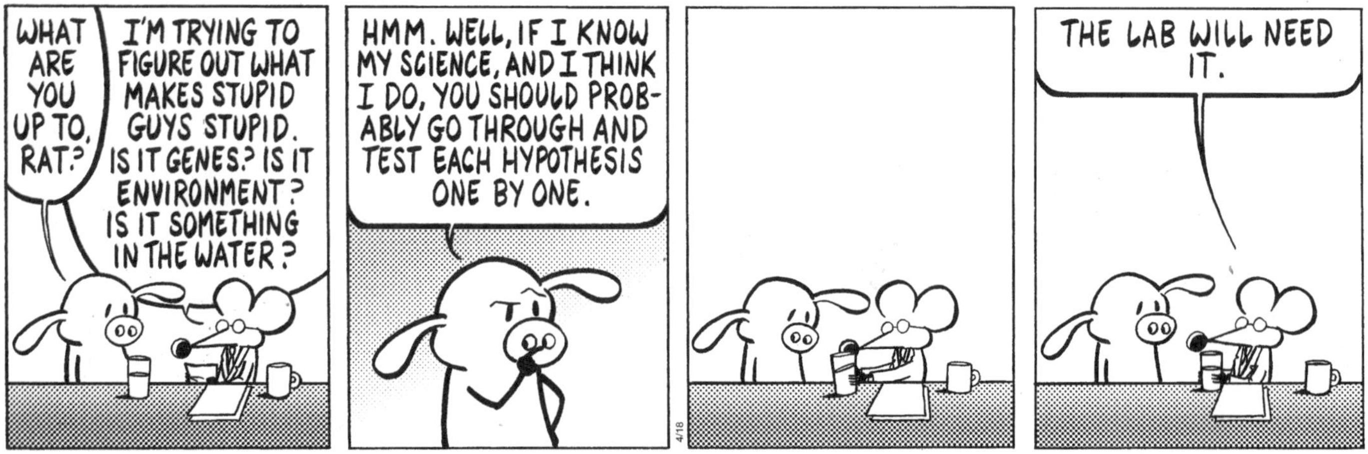
WHAT ARE YOU UP TO, RAT?
I'M TRYING TO FIGURE OUT WHAT MAKES STUPID GUYS STUPID. IS IT GENES? IS IT ENVIRONMENT? IS IT SOMETHING IN THE WATER?
HMM. WELL, IF I KNOW MY SCIENCE, AND I THINK I DO, YOU SHOULD PROB-ABLY GO THROUGH AND TEST EACH HYPOTHESIS ONE BY ONE.
4/18
THE LAB WILL NEED IT.

RAT'S FAIRY TALE O' FAIRNESS AND JUSTICE

Once upon a time, there was a bank C.E.O. who decided to make a lot of home loans to people he knew could not pay them back.

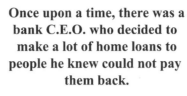

As a result, Mr. Bank C.E.O. made $50,000,000 in bonuses and stock options.

But then the loans went bad.

And as a result, the bank's employees lost their jobs.

And the bank's shareholders lost their money.

And the homeowners lost their homes.

4/19

And taxpayers with no connection to the bank had to pay all the money to fix it.

And Mr. Bank C.E.O. got to keep all of his $50,000,000 and live happily ever after in his Connecticut mansion.

WHERE'S THE FAIRNESS AND JUSTICE IN *THAT*?!

WHOA. PERHAPS I SHOULD RE-TITLE THIS.

OH, I JUST *LOVE* HAPPY ENDINGS.

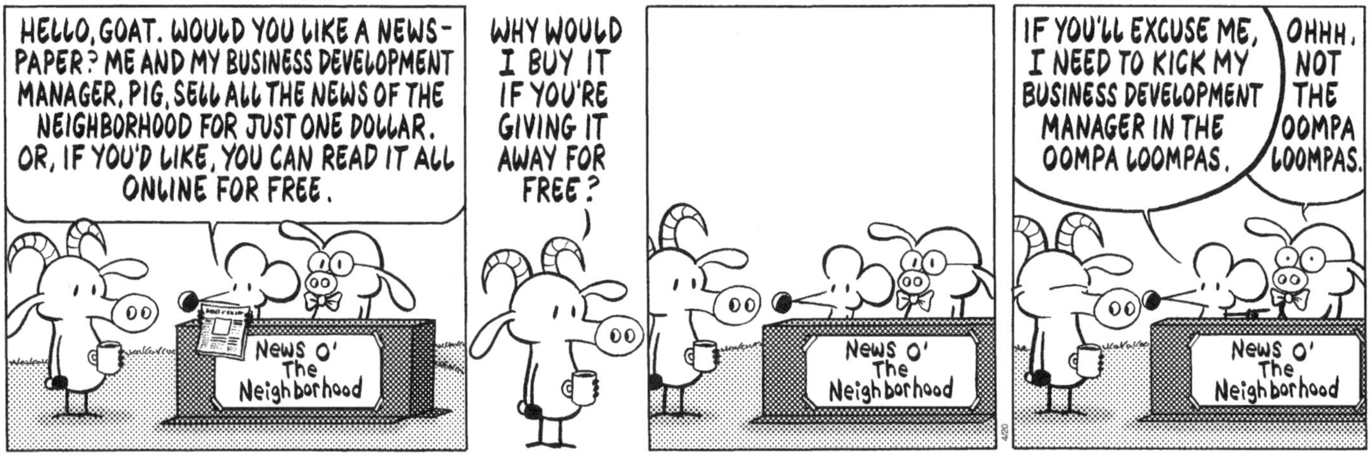
HELLO, GOAT. WOULD YOU LIKE A NEWSPAPER? ME AND MY BUSINESS DEVELOPMENT MANAGER, PIG, SELL ALL THE NEWS OF THE NEIGHBORHOOD FOR JUST ONE DOLLAR. OR, IF YOU'D LIKE, YOU CAN READ IT ALL ONLINE FOR FREE.
News O' The Neighborhood
WHY WOULD I BUY IT IF YOU'RE GIVING IT AWAY FOR FREE?
News O' The Neighborhood
IF YOU'LL EXCUSE ME, I NEED TO KICK MY BUSINESS DEVELOPMENT MANAGER IN THE OOMPA LOOMPAS.
OHHH, NOT THE OOMPA LOOMPAS.
News O' The Neighborhood

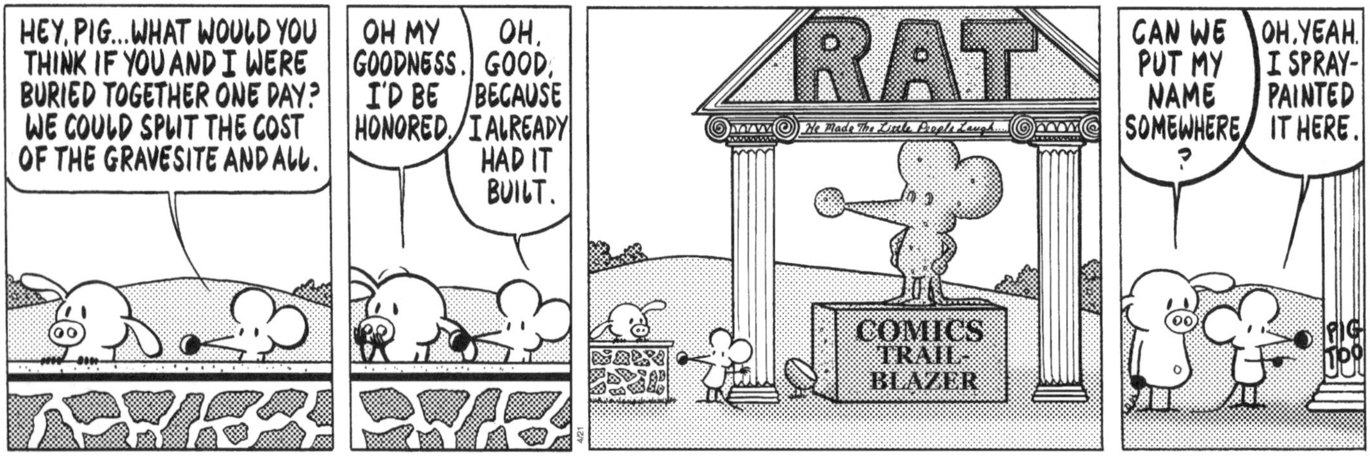
HEY, PIG...WHAT WOULD YOU THINK IF YOU AND I WERE BURIED TOGETHER ONE DAY? WE COULD SPLIT THE COST OF THE GRAVESITE AND ALL.
OH MY GOODNESS. I'D BE HONORED.
OH, GOOD, BECAUSE I ALREADY HAD IT BUILT.
RAT
He Made The Little People Laugh
COMICS TRAIL-BLAZER
CAN WE PUT MY NAME SOMEWHERE?
OH, YEAH. I SPRAY-PAINTED IT HERE.
PIG TOO

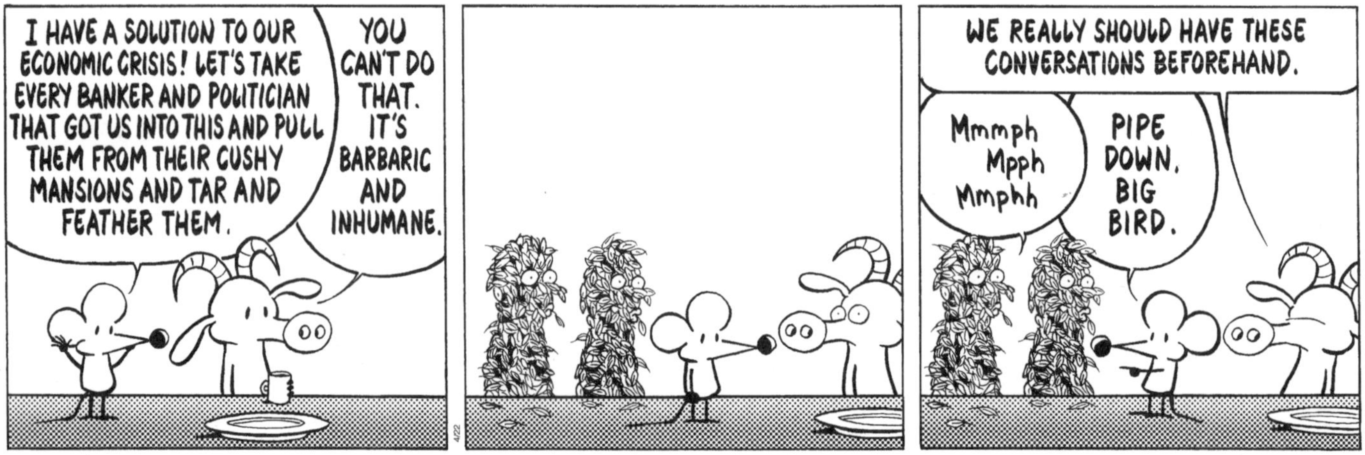
I HAVE A SOLUTION TO OUR ECONOMIC CRISIS! LET'S TAKE EVERY BANKER AND POLITICIAN THAT GOT US INTO THIS AND PULL THEM FROM THEIR CUSHY MANSIONS AND TAR AND FEATHER THEM.
YOU CAN'T DO THAT. IT'S BARBARIC AND INHUMANE.
WE REALLY SHOULD HAVE THESE CONVERSATIONS BEFOREHAND.
Mmmph Mpph Mmphh
PIPE DOWN, BIG BIRD.

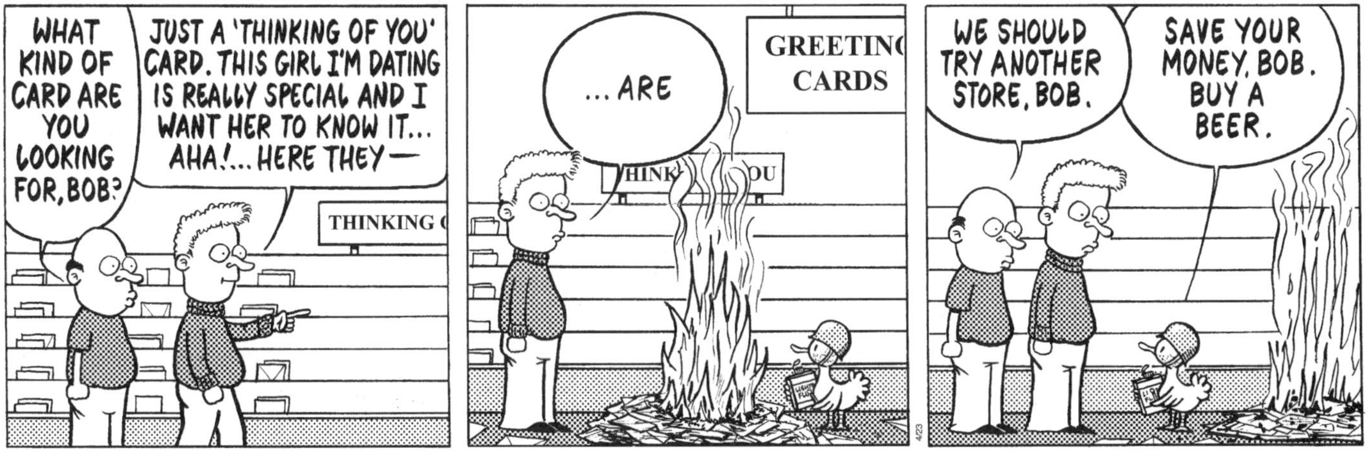
WHAT KIND OF CARD ARE YOU LOOKING FOR, BOB?
JUST A 'THINKING OF YOU' CARD. THIS GIRL I'M DATING IS REALLY SPECIAL AND I WANT HER TO KNOW IT... AHA!... HERE THEY—
THINKING
GREETING CARDS
...ARE
WE SHOULD TRY ANOTHER STORE, BOB.
SAVE YOUR MONEY, BOB. BUY A BEER.

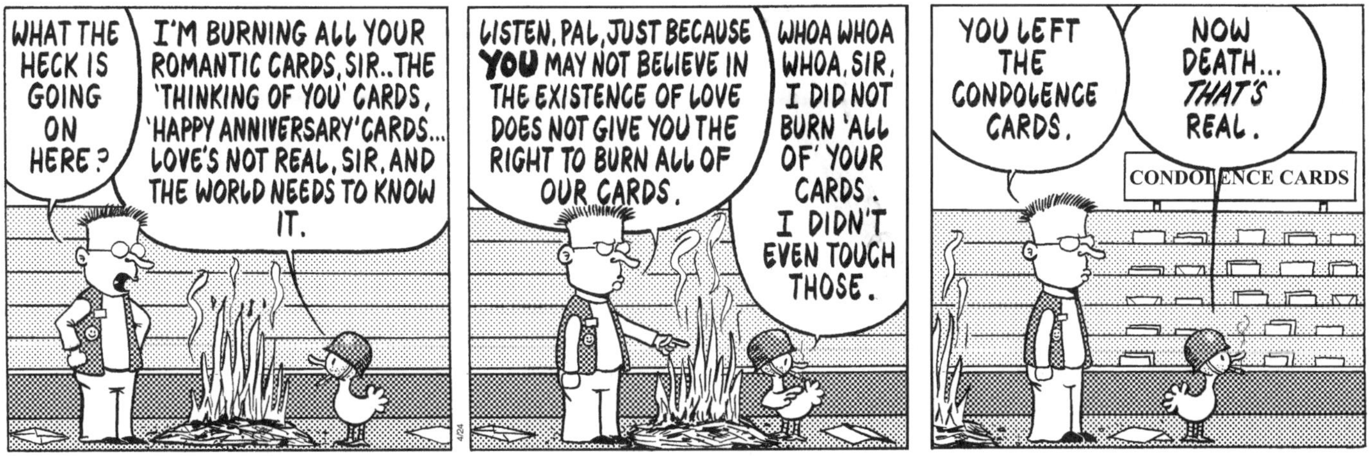
WHAT THE HECK IS GOING ON HERE?
I'M BURNING ALL YOUR ROMANTIC CARDS, SIR.. THE 'THINKING OF YOU' CARDS, 'HAPPY ANNIVERSARY' CARDS... LOVE'S NOT REAL, SIR, AND THE WORLD NEEDS TO KNOW IT.
LISTEN, PAL, JUST BECAUSE **YOU** MAY NOT BELIEVE IN THE EXISTENCE OF LOVE DOES NOT GIVE YOU THE RIGHT TO BURN ALL OF OUR CARDS.
WHOA WHOA WHOA, SIR, I DID NOT BURN 'ALL OF' YOUR CARDS. I DIDN'T EVEN TOUCH THOSE.
YOU LEFT THE CONDOLENCE CARDS.
NOW DEATH... *THAT'S* REAL.
CONDOLENCE CARDS

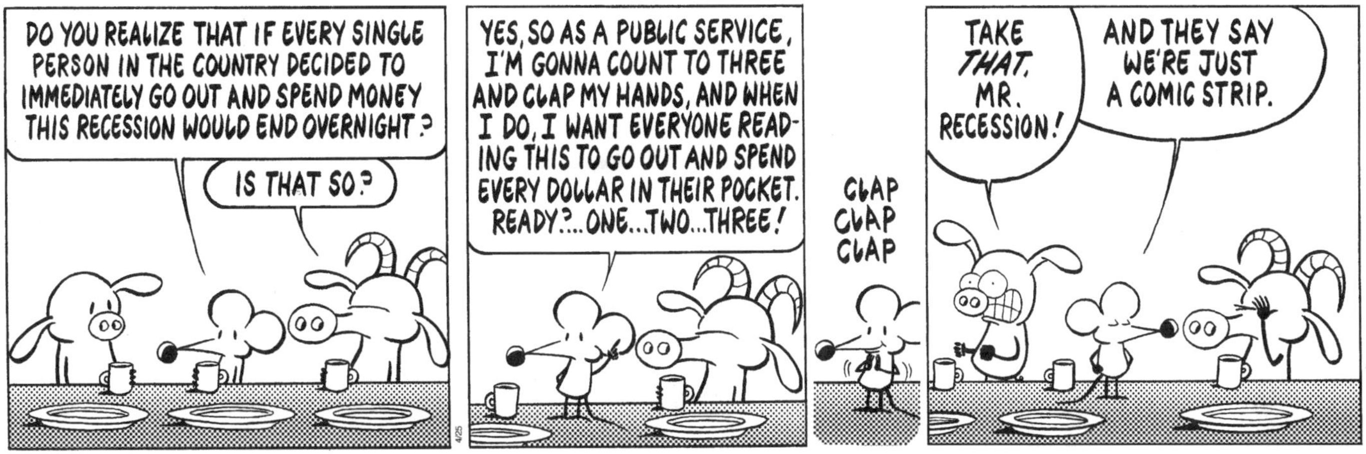
DO YOU REALIZE THAT IF EVERY SINGLE PERSON IN THE COUNTRY DECIDED TO IMMEDIATELY GO OUT AND SPEND MONEY THIS RECESSION WOULD END OVERNIGHT?
IS THAT SO?
YES, SO AS A PUBLIC SERVICE, I'M GONNA COUNT TO THREE AND CLAP MY HANDS, AND WHEN I DO, I WANT EVERYONE READING THIS TO GO OUT AND SPEND EVERY DOLLAR IN THEIR POCKET. READY?... ONE...TWO...THREE!
CLAP CLAP CLAP
TAKE *THAT*, MR. RECESSION!
AND THEY SAY WE'RE JUST A COMIC STRIP.

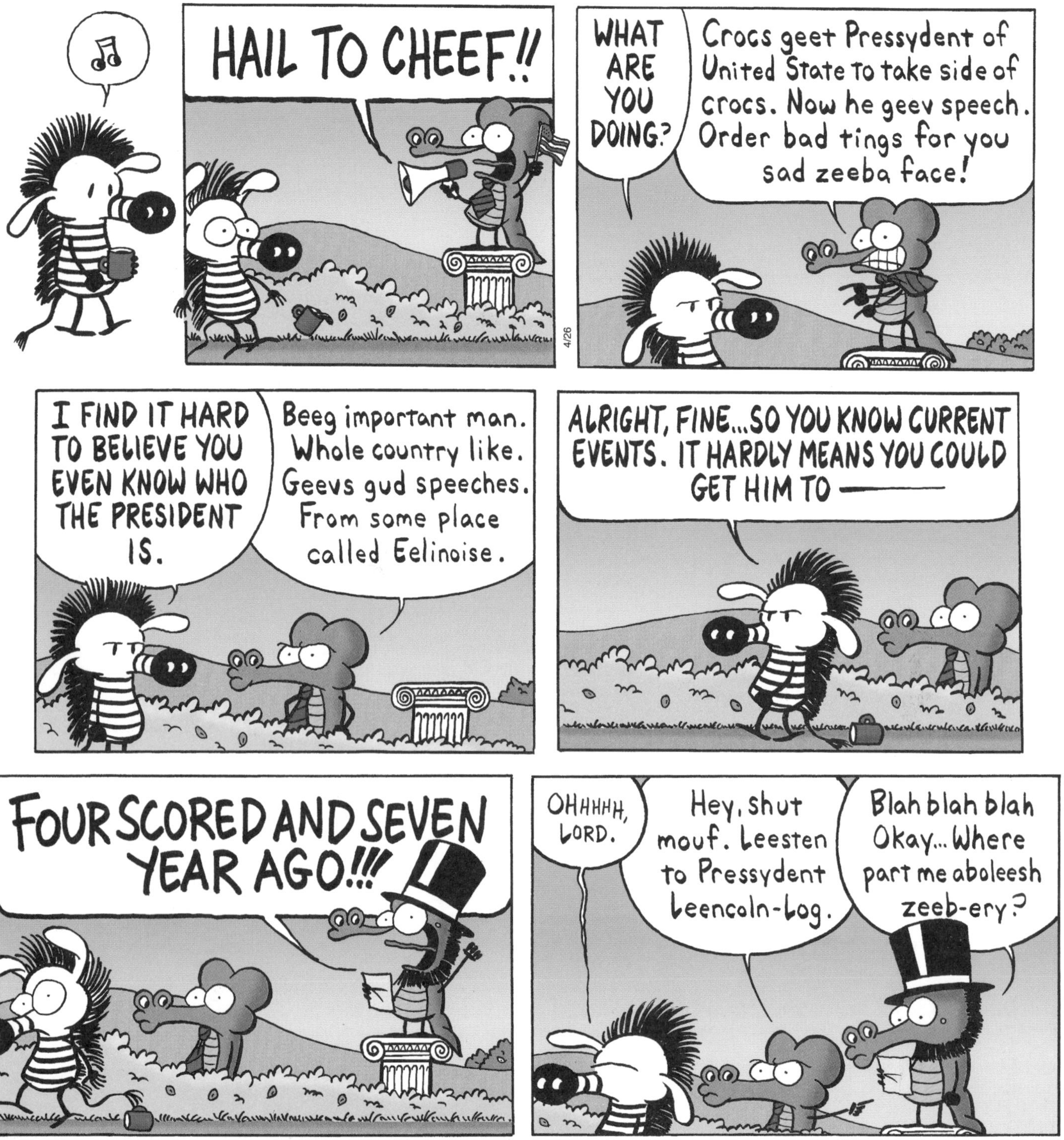
HAIL TO CHEEF!!
4/26
WHAT ARE YOU DOING?
Crocs geet Pressydent of United State to take side of crocs. Now he geev speech. Order bad tings for you sad zeeba face!
I FIND IT HARD TO BELIEVE YOU EVEN KNOW WHO THE PRESIDENT IS.
Beeg important man. Whole country like. Geevs gud speeches. From some place called Eelinoise.
ALRIGHT, FINE...SO YOU KNOW CURRENT EVENTS. IT HARDLY MEANS YOU COULD GET HIM TO ——
FOUR SCORED AND SEVEN YEAR AGO!!!
OHHHHH, LORD.
Hey, shut mouf. Leesten to Pressydent Leencoln-Log.
Blah blah blah Okay... Where part me aboleesh zeeb-ery?

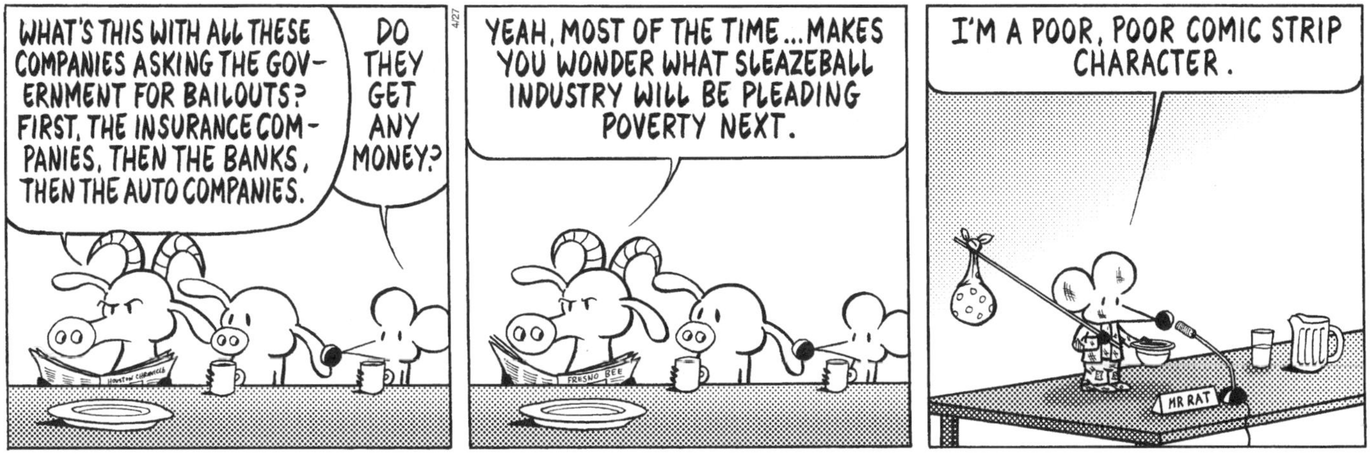
4/27
WHAT'S THIS WITH ALL THESE COMPANIES ASKING THE GOVERNMENT FOR BAILOUTS? FIRST, THE INSURANCE COMPANIES, THEN THE BANKS, THEN THE AUTO COMPANIES.
DO THEY GET ANY MONEY?
YEAH, MOST OF THE TIME... MAKES YOU WONDER WHAT SLEAZEBALL INDUSTRY WILL BE PLEADING POVERTY NEXT.
FRESNO BEE
I'M A POOR, POOR COMIC STRIP CHARACTER.
MR RAT

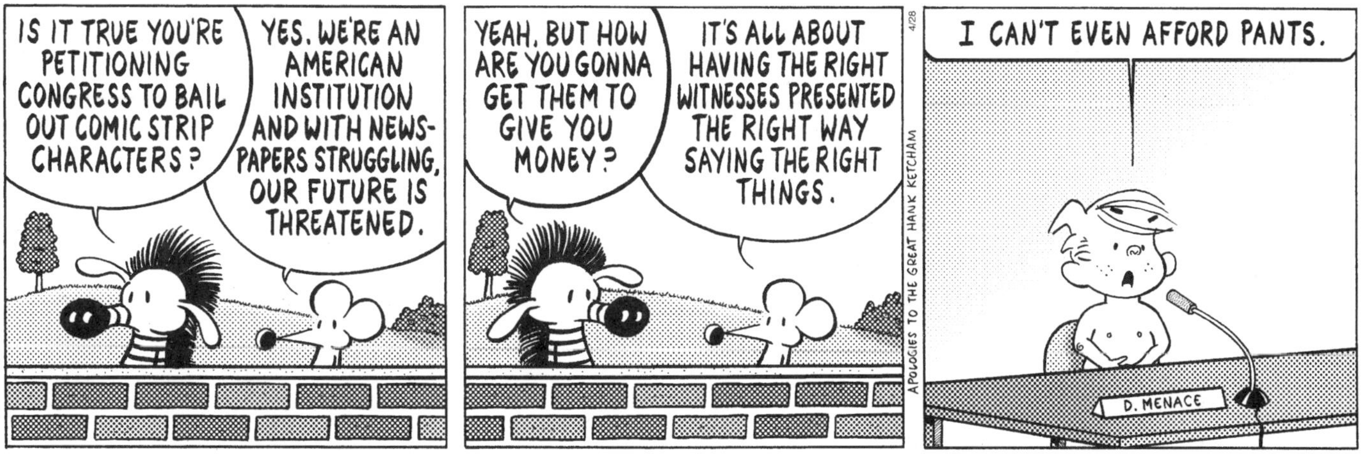
IS IT TRUE YOU'RE PETITIONING CONGRESS TO BAIL OUT COMIC STRIP CHARACTERS?
YES. WE'RE AN AMERICAN INSTITUTION AND WITH NEWSPAPERS STRUGGLING, OUR FUTURE IS THREATENED.
YEAH, BUT HOW ARE YOU GONNA GET THEM TO GIVE YOU MONEY?
IT'S ALL ABOUT HAVING THE RIGHT WITNESSES PRESENTED THE RIGHT WAY SAYING THE RIGHT THINGS.
4/28
APOLOGIES TO THE GREAT HANK KETCHAM
I CAN'T EVEN AFFORD PANTS.
D. MENACE

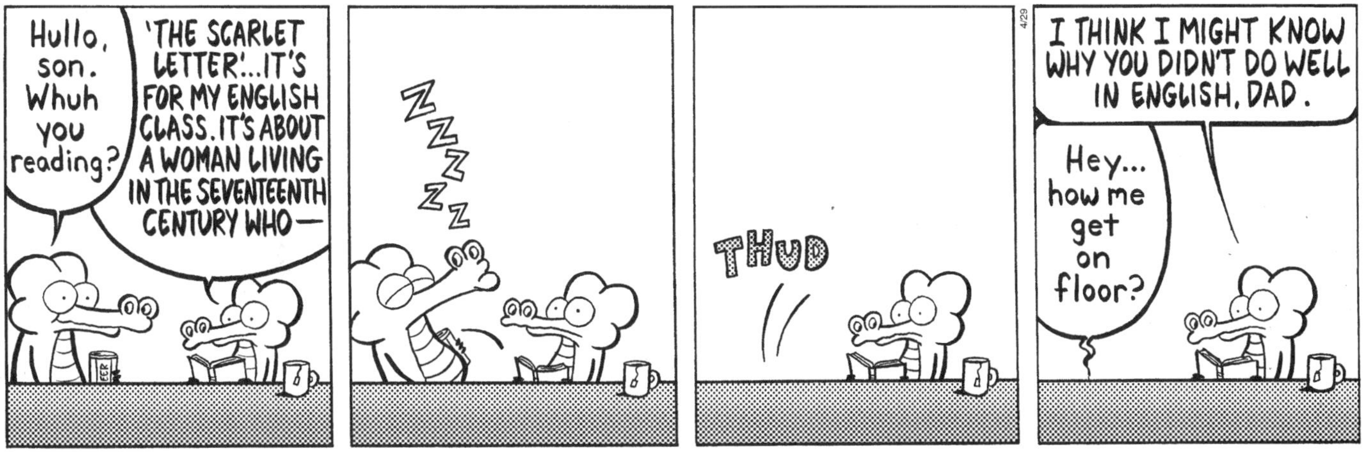
Hullo, son. Whuh you reading?
'THE SCARLET LETTER'... IT'S FOR MY ENGLISH CLASS. IT'S ABOUT A WOMAN LIVING IN THE SEVENTEENTH CENTURY WHO—
ZZZZZ
THUD
4/29
I THINK I MIGHT KNOW WHY YOU DIDN'T DO WELL IN ENGLISH, DAD.
Hey... how me get on floor?

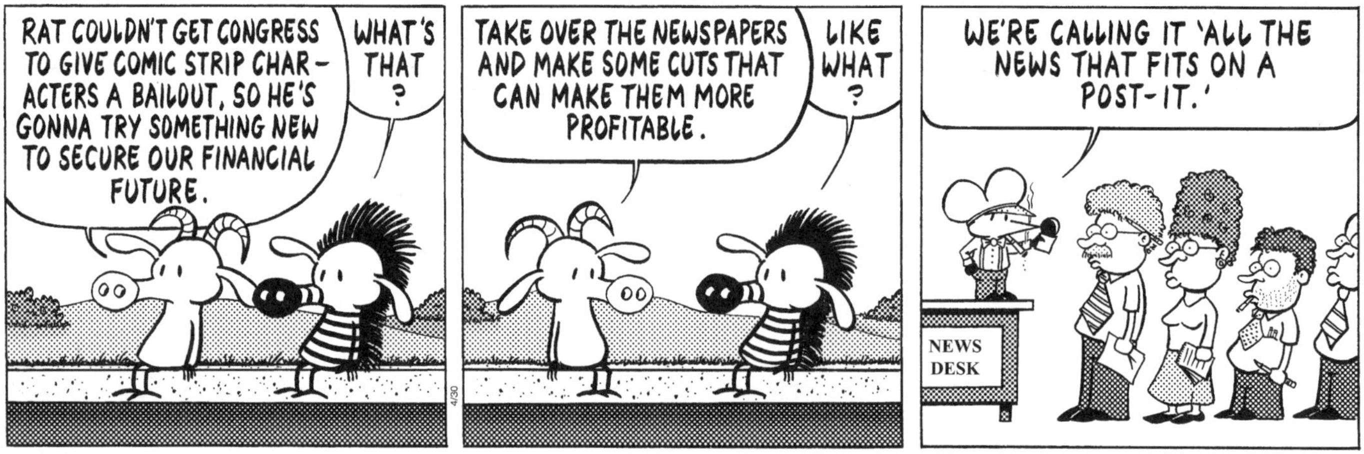
RAT COULDN'T GET CONGRESS TO GIVE COMIC STRIP CHARACTERS A BAILOUT, SO HE'S GONNA TRY SOMETHING NEW TO SECURE OUR FINANCIAL FUTURE.
WHAT'S THAT?
4/30
TAKE OVER THE NEWSPAPERS AND MAKE SOME CUTS THAT CAN MAKE THEM MORE PROFITABLE.
LIKE WHAT?
WE'RE CALLING IT 'ALL THE NEWS THAT FITS ON A POST-IT.'
NEWS DESK

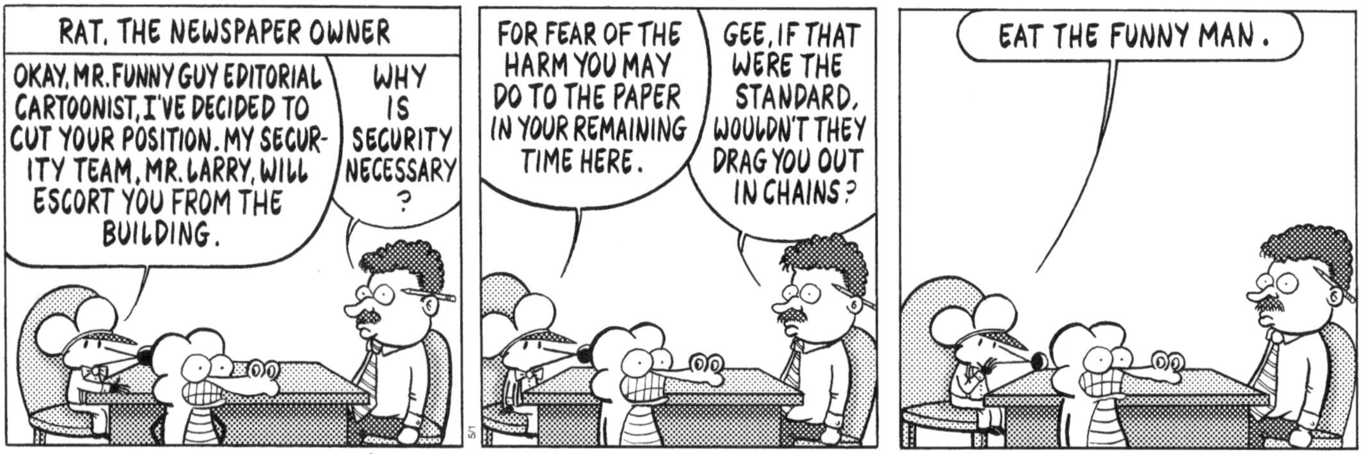
RAT, THE NEWSPAPER OWNER
OKAY, MR. FUNNY GUY EDITORIAL CARTOONIST, I'VE DECIDED TO CUT YOUR POSITION. MY SECURITY TEAM, MR. LARRY, WILL ESCORT YOU FROM THE BUILDING.
WHY IS SECURITY NECESSARY?
5/1
FOR FEAR OF THE HARM YOU MAY DO TO THE PAPER IN YOUR REMAINING TIME HERE.
GEE, IF THAT WERE THE STANDARD, WOULDN'T THEY DRAG YOU OUT IN CHAINS?
EAT THE FUNNY MAN.

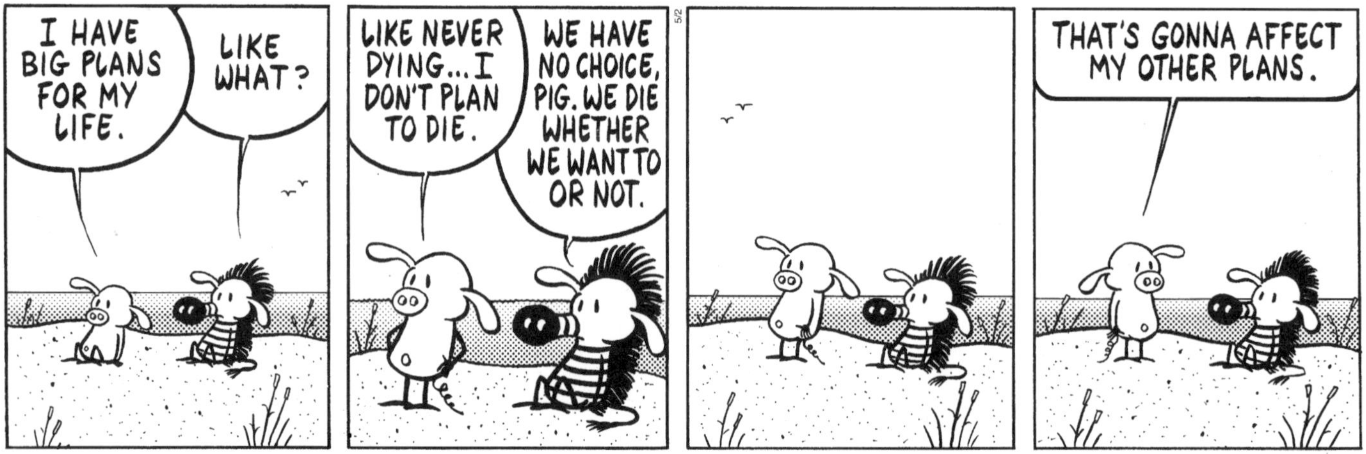
I HAVE BIG PLANS FOR MY LIFE.
LIKE WHAT?
LIKE NEVER DYING... I DON'T PLAN TO DIE.
WE HAVE NO CHOICE, PIG. WE DIE WHETHER WE WANT TO OR NOT.
5/2
THAT'S GONNA AFFECT MY OTHER PLANS.

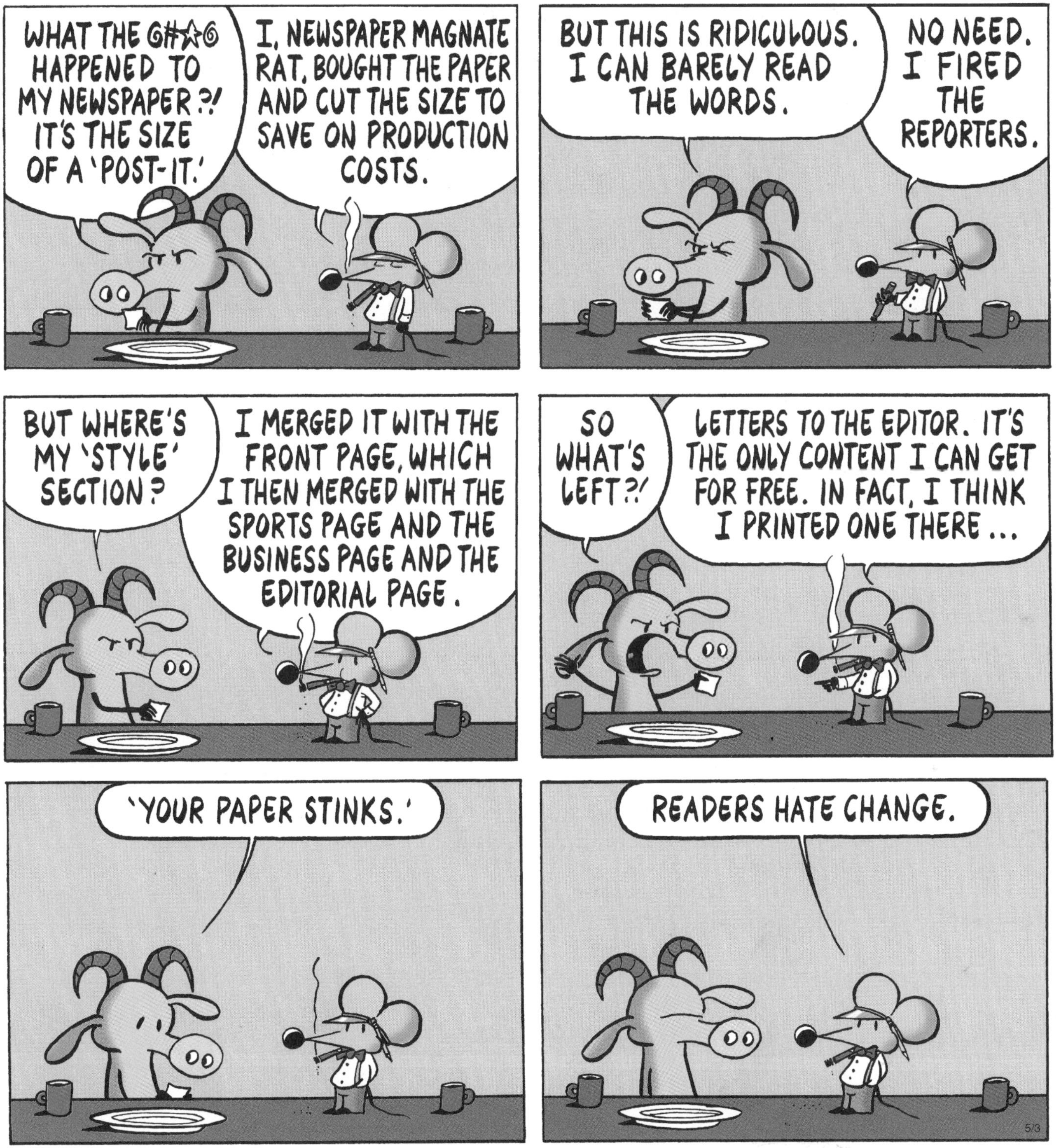
WHAT THE G#☆@ HAPPENED TO MY NEWSPAPER ?! IT'S THE SIZE OF A 'POST-IT.'
I, NEWSPAPER MAGNATE RAT, BOUGHT THE PAPER AND CUT THE SIZE TO SAVE ON PRODUCTION COSTS.
BUT THIS IS RIDICULOUS. I CAN BARELY READ THE WORDS.
NO NEED. I FIRED THE REPORTERS.
BUT WHERE'S MY 'STYLE' SECTION ?
I MERGED IT WITH THE FRONT PAGE, WHICH I THEN MERGED WITH THE SPORTS PAGE AND THE BUSINESS PAGE AND THE EDITORIAL PAGE.
SO WHAT'S LEFT ?!
LETTERS TO THE EDITOR. IT'S THE ONLY CONTENT I CAN GET FOR FREE. IN FACT, I THINK I PRINTED ONE THERE ...
'YOUR PAPER STINKS.'
READERS HATE CHANGE.
5/3

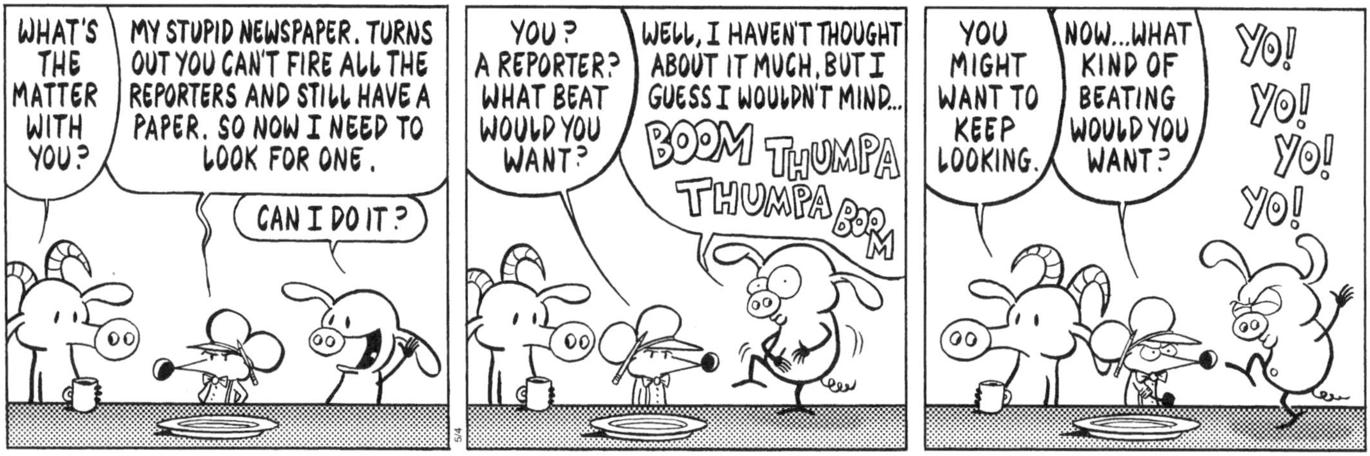
WHAT'S THE MATTER WITH YOU?
MY STUPID NEWSPAPER. TURNS OUT YOU CAN'T FIRE ALL THE REPORTERS AND STILL HAVE A PAPER. SO NOW I NEED TO LOOK FOR ONE.
CAN I DO IT?
YOU? A REPORTER? WHAT BEAT WOULD YOU WANT?
WELL, I HAVEN'T THOUGHT ABOUT IT MUCH, BUT I GUESS I WOULDN'T MIND...
BOOM THUMPA THUMPA BOOM
YOU MIGHT WANT TO KEEP LOOKING.
NOW...WHAT KIND OF BEATING WOULD YOU WANT?
YO! YO! YO! YO!
5/4

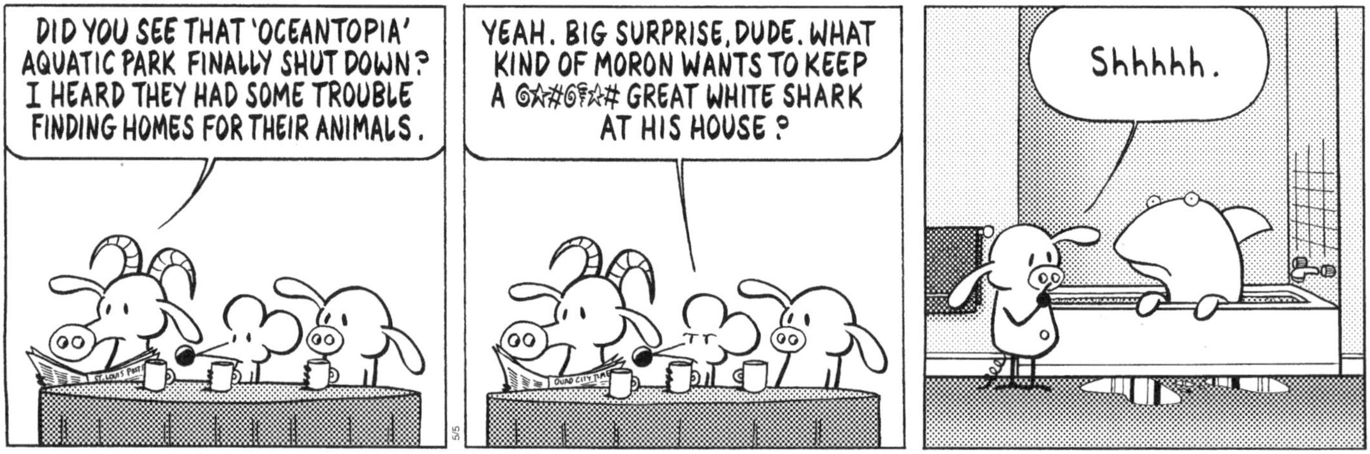
DID YOU SEE THAT 'OCEANTOPIA' AQUATIC PARK FINALLY SHUT DOWN? I HEARD THEY HAD SOME TROUBLE FINDING HOMES FOR THEIR ANIMALS.
YEAH. BIG SURPRISE, DUDE. WHAT KIND OF MORON WANTS TO KEEP A @☆#@$☆# GREAT WHITE SHARK AT HIS HOUSE?
Shhhhh.
5/5

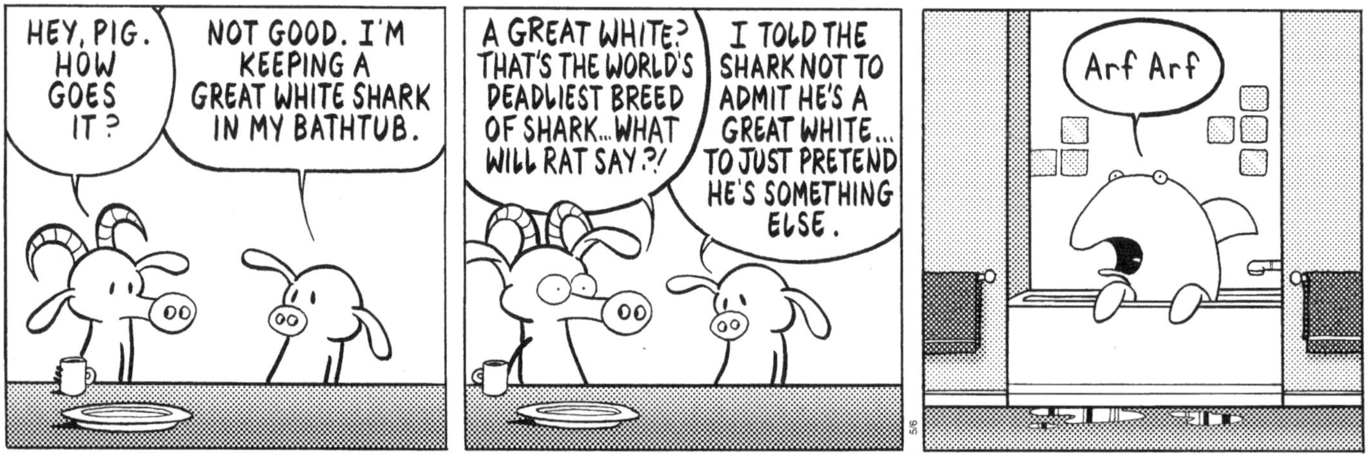
HEY, PIG. HOW GOES IT?
NOT GOOD. I'M KEEPING A GREAT WHITE SHARK IN MY BATHTUB.
A GREAT WHITE? THAT'S THE WORLD'S DEADLIEST BREED OF SHARK...WHAT WILL RAT SAY?!
I TOLD THE SHARK NOT TO ADMIT HE'S A GREAT WHITE... TO JUST PRETEND HE'S SOMETHING ELSE.
Arf Arf
5/6

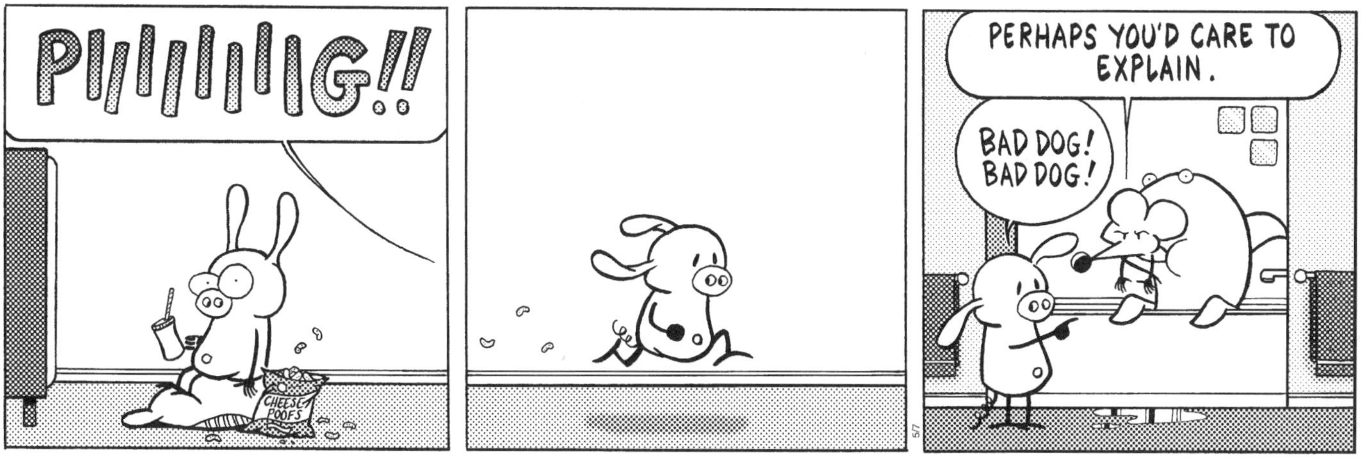
PIIIIIIIG!!
PERHAPS YOU'D CARE TO EXPLAIN.
BAD DOG! BAD DOG!
CHEESE POOFS
5/7

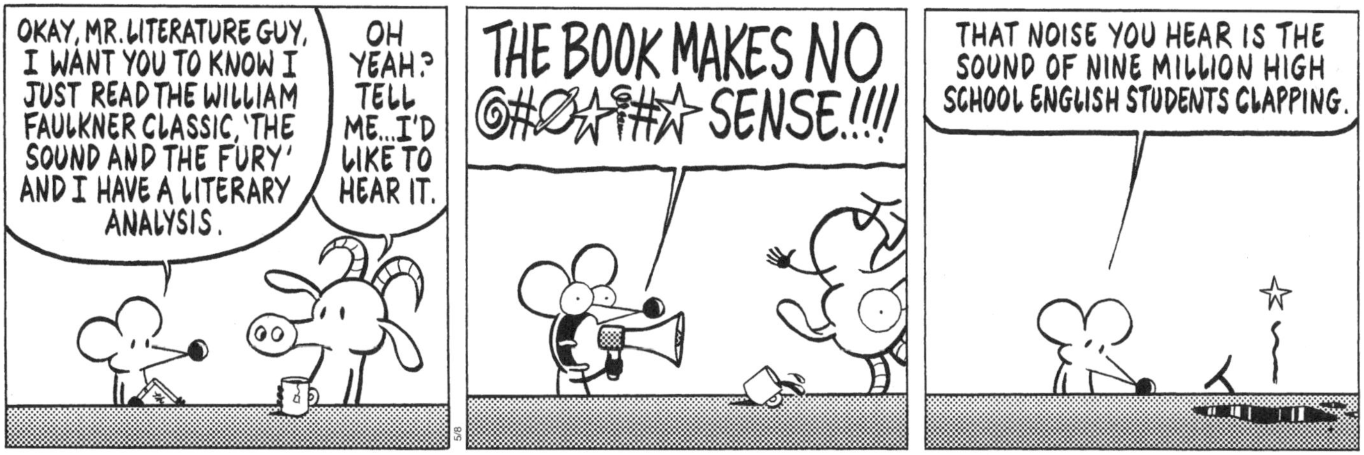
OKAY, MR. LITERATURE GUY, I WANT YOU TO KNOW I JUST READ THE WILLIAM FAULKNER CLASSIC, 'THE SOUND AND THE FURY' AND I HAVE A LITERARY ANALYSIS.
OH YEAH? TELL ME...I'D LIKE TO HEAR IT.
THE BOOK MAKES NO
SENSE!!!!
THAT NOISE YOU HEAR IS THE SOUND OF NINE MILLION HIGH SCHOOL ENGLISH STUDENTS CLAPPING.
5/8

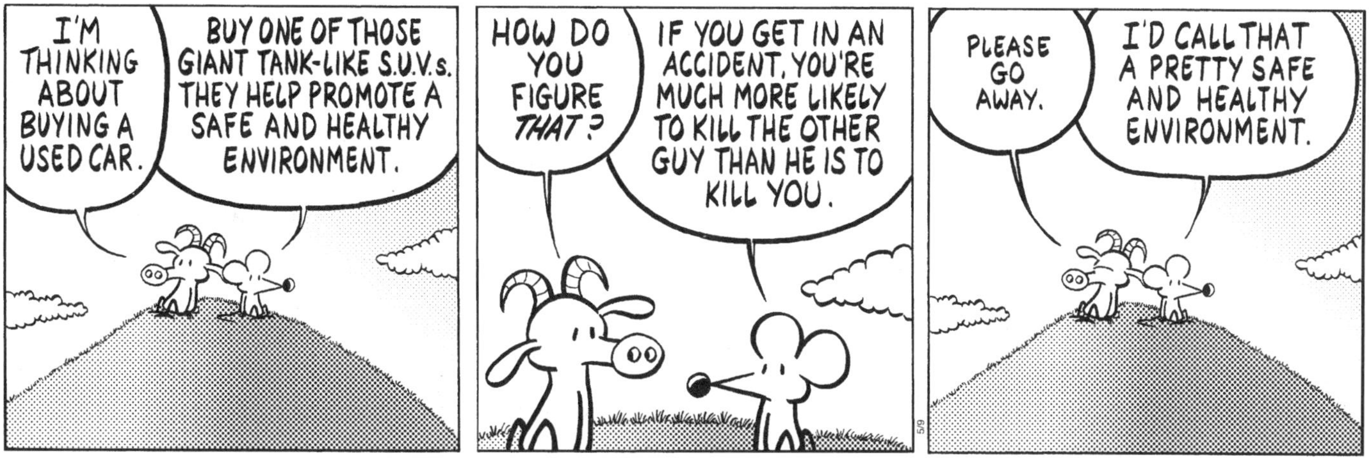
I'M THINKING ABOUT BUYING A USED CAR.
BUY ONE OF THOSE GIANT TANK-LIKE S.U.V.s. THEY HELP PROMOTE A SAFE AND HEALTHY ENVIRONMENT.
HOW DO YOU FIGURE *THAT*?
IF YOU GET IN AN ACCIDENT, YOU'RE MUCH MORE LIKELY TO KILL THE OTHER GUY THAN HE IS TO KILL YOU.
PLEASE GO AWAY.
I'D CALL THAT A PRETTY SAFE AND HEALTHY ENVIRONMENT.
5/9

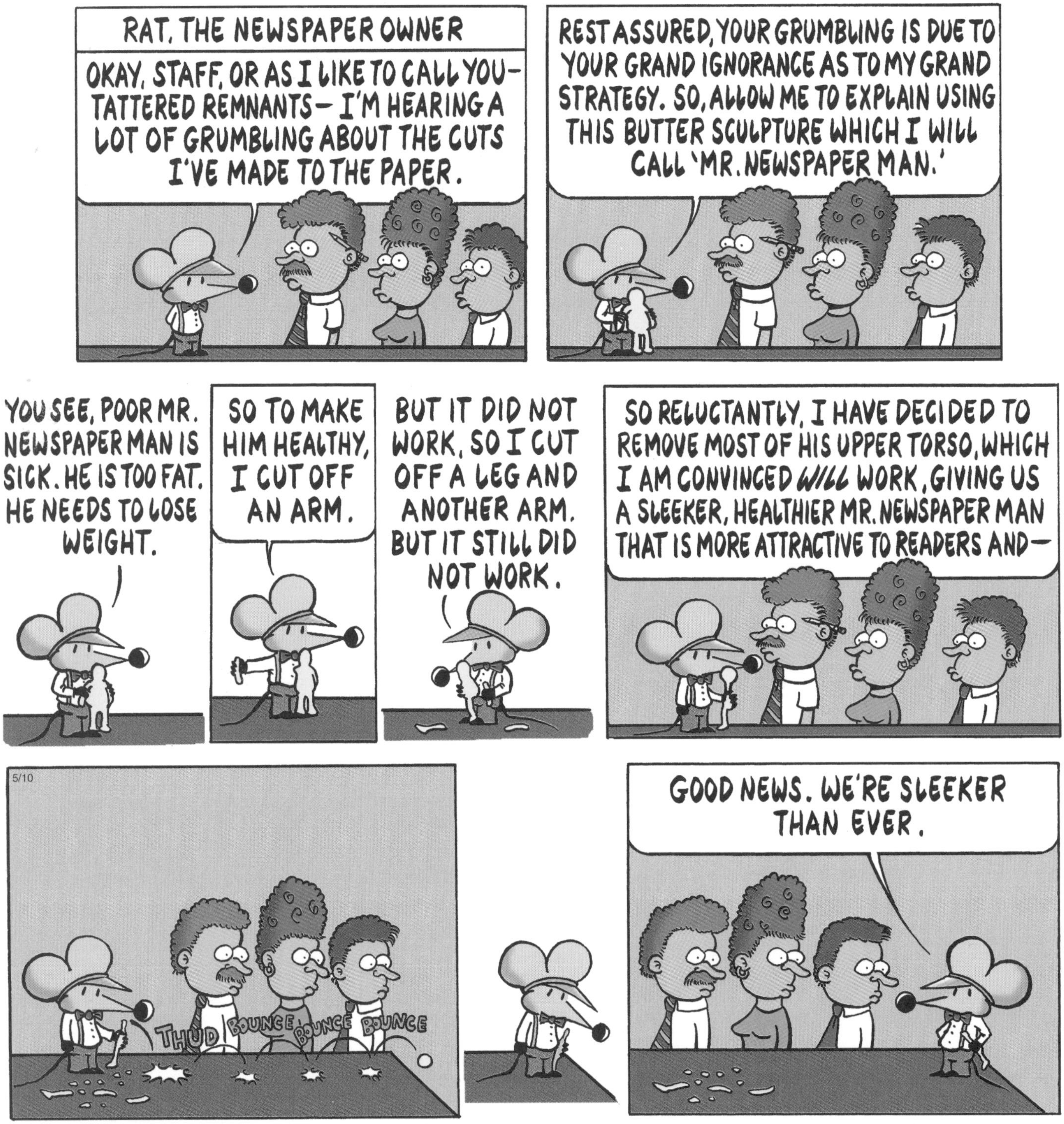
RAT, THE NEWSPAPER OWNER
OKAY, STAFF, OR AS I LIKE TO CALL YOU-TATTERED REMNANTS- I'M HEARING A LOT OF GRUMBLING ABOUT THE CUTS I'VE MADE TO THE PAPER.
REST ASSURED, YOUR GRUMBLING IS DUE TO YOUR GRAND IGNORANCE AS TO MY GRAND STRATEGY. SO, ALLOW ME TO EXPLAIN USING THIS BUTTER SCULPTURE WHICH I WILL CALL 'MR. NEWSPAPER MAN.'
YOU SEE, POOR MR. NEWSPAPER MAN IS SICK. HE IS TOO FAT. HE NEEDS TO LOSE WEIGHT.
SO TO MAKE HIM HEALTHY, I CUT OFF AN ARM.
BUT IT DID NOT WORK, SO I CUT OFF A LEG AND ANOTHER ARM. BUT IT STILL DID NOT WORK.
SO RELUCTANTLY, I HAVE DECIDED TO REMOVE MOST OF HIS UPPER TORSO, WHICH I AM CONVINCED WILL WORK, GIVING US A SLEEKER, HEALTHIER MR. NEWSPAPER MAN THAT IS MORE ATTRACTIVE TO READERS AND—
5/10
THUD
BOUNCE
BOUNCE
BOUNCE
GOOD NEWS. WE'RE SLEEKER THAN EVER.

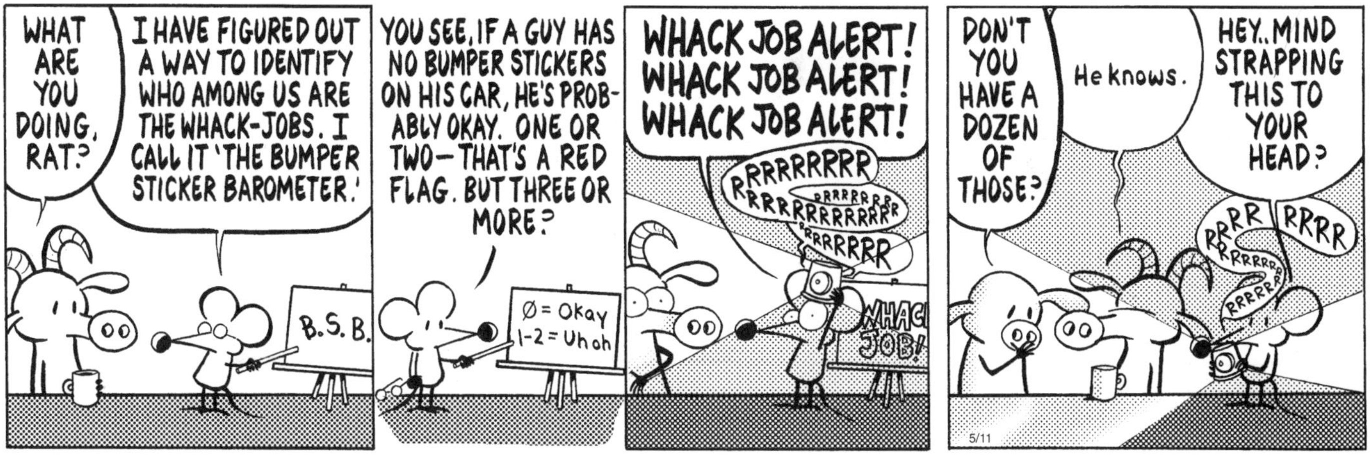
WHAT ARE YOU DOING, RAT?
I HAVE FIGURED OUT A WAY TO IDENTIFY WHO AMONG US ARE THE WHACK-JOBS. I CALL IT 'THE BUMPER STICKER BAROMETER.'
B.S.B.
YOU SEE, IF A GUY HAS NO BUMPER STICKERS ON HIS CAR, HE'S PROBABLY OKAY. ONE OR TWO—THAT'S A RED FLAG. BUT THREE OR MORE?
Ø = Okay
1-2 = Uh oh
WHACK JOB ALERT! WHACK JOB ALERT! WHACK JOB ALERT!
DON'T YOU HAVE A DOZEN OF THOSE?
He knows.
HEY.. MIND STRAPPING THIS TO YOUR HEAD?
5/11

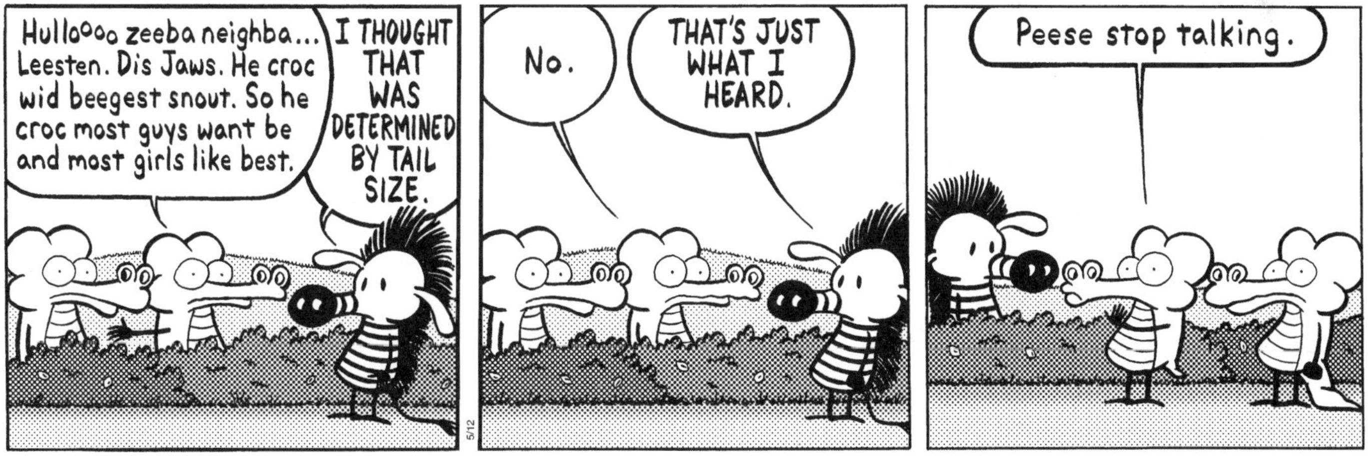
Hulloooo zeeba neighba... Leesten. Dis Jaws. He croc wid beegest snout. So he croc most guys want be and most girls like best.
I THOUGHT THAT WAS DETERMINED BY TAIL SIZE.
5/12
No.
THAT'S JUST WHAT I HEARD.
Peese stop talking.

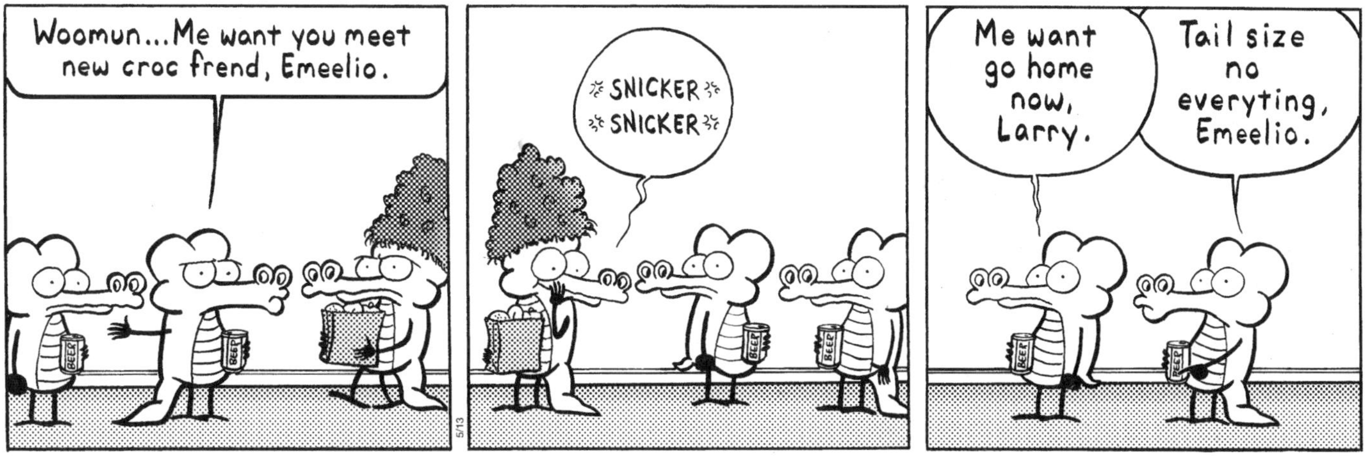
Woomun... Me want you meet new croc frend, Emeelio.
5/13
SNICKER
SNICKER
Me want go home now, Larry.
Tail size no everyting, Emeelio.

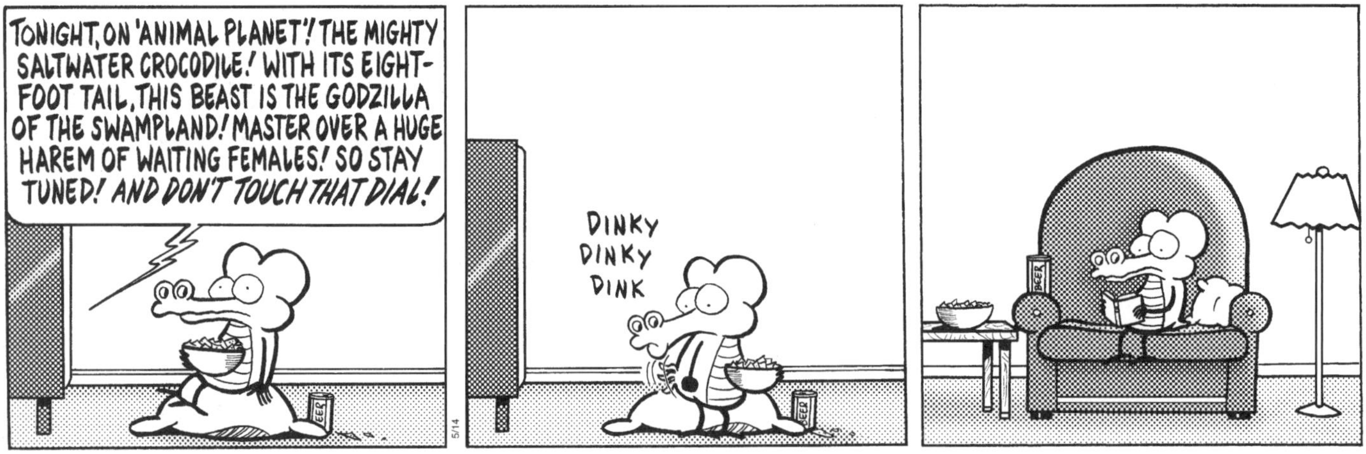
TONIGHT, ON 'ANIMAL PLANET'! THE MIGHTY SALTWATER CROCODILE! WITH ITS EIGHT-FOOT TAIL, THIS BEAST IS THE GODZILLA OF THE SWAMPLAND! MASTER OVER A HUGE HAREM OF WAITING FEMALES! SO STAY TUNED! AND DON'T TOUCH THAT DIAL!
5/14
DINKY DINKY DINK

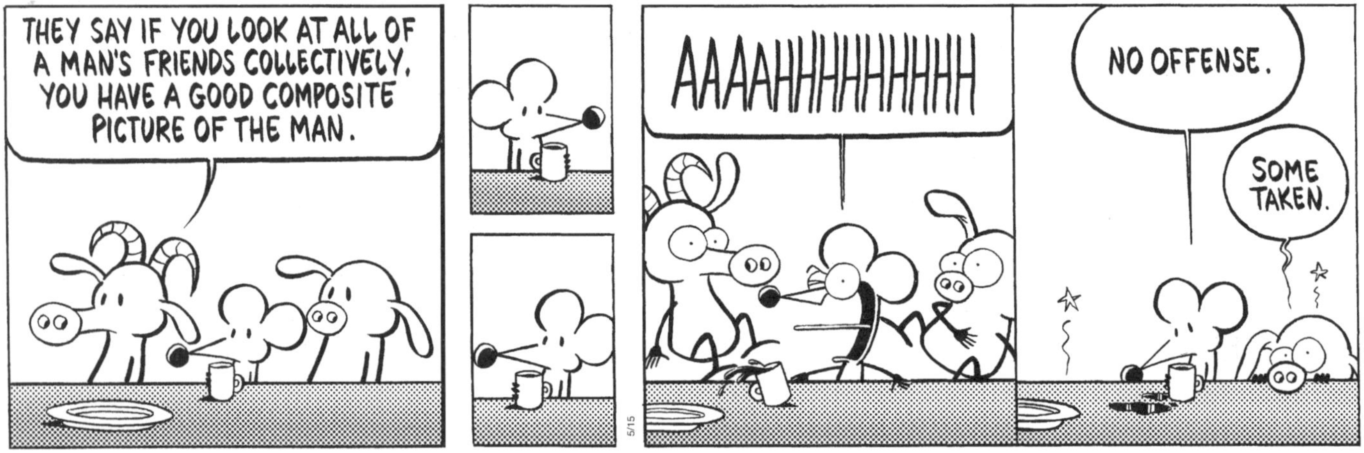
THEY SAY IF YOU LOOK AT ALL OF A MAN'S FRIENDS COLLECTIVELY, YOU HAVE A GOOD COMPOSITE PICTURE OF THE MAN.
5/15
AAAAHHHHHHHHH
NO OFFENSE.
SOME TAKEN.

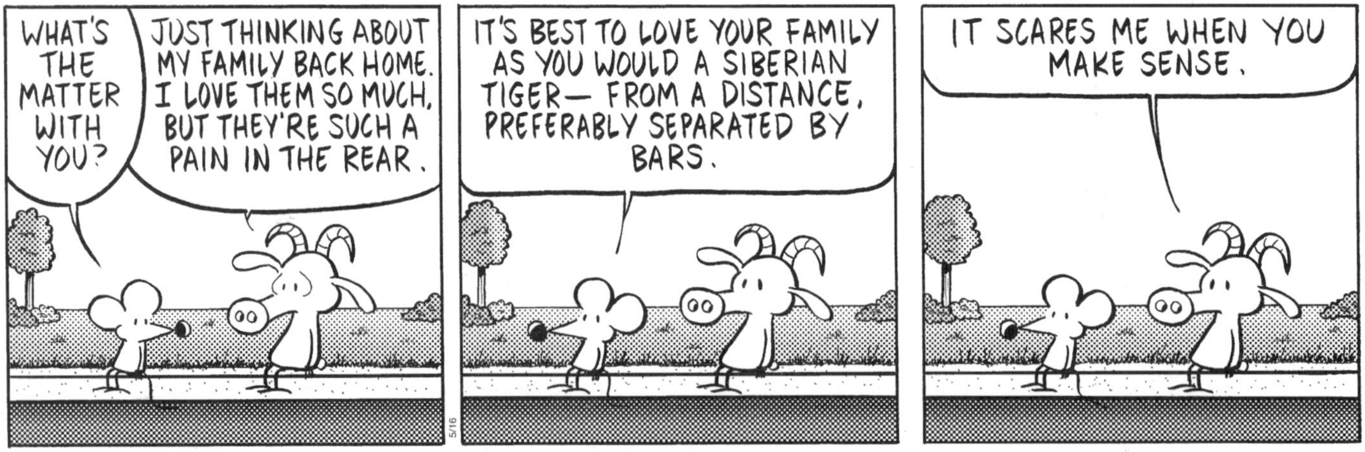
WHAT'S THE MATTER WITH YOU?
JUST THINKING ABOUT MY FAMILY BACK HOME. I LOVE THEM SO MUCH, BUT THEY'RE SUCH A PAIN IN THE REAR.
5/16
IT'S BEST TO LOVE YOUR FAMILY AS YOU WOULD A SIBERIAN TIGER— FROM A DISTANCE, PREFERABLY SEPARATED BY BARS.
IT SCARES ME WHEN YOU MAKE SENSE.

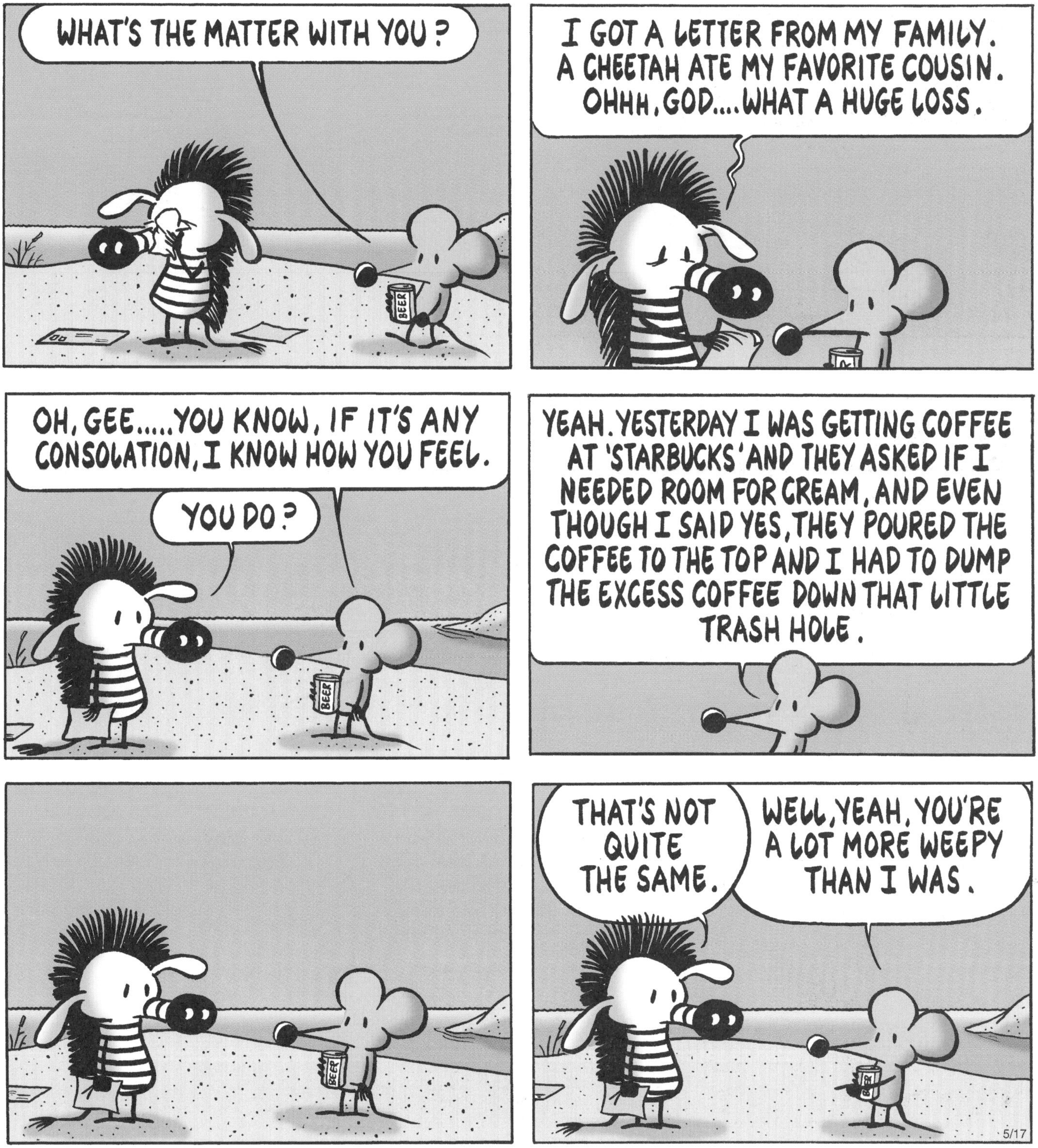
WHAT'S THE MATTER WITH YOU?
I GOT A LETTER FROM MY FAMILY. A CHEETAH ATE MY FAVORITE COUSIN. OHHH, GOD.... WHAT A HUGE LOSS.
OH, GEE..... YOU KNOW, IF IT'S ANY CONSOLATION, I KNOW HOW YOU FEEL.
YOU DO?
YEAH. YESTERDAY I WAS GETTING COFFEE AT 'STARBUCKS' AND THEY ASKED IF I NEEDED ROOM FOR CREAM, AND EVEN THOUGH I SAID YES, THEY POURED THE COFFEE TO THE TOP AND I HAD TO DUMP THE EXCESS COFFEE DOWN THAT LITTLE TRASH HOLE.
THAT'S NOT QUITE THE SAME.
WELL, YEAH, YOU'RE A LOT MORE WEEPY THAN I WAS.
5/17

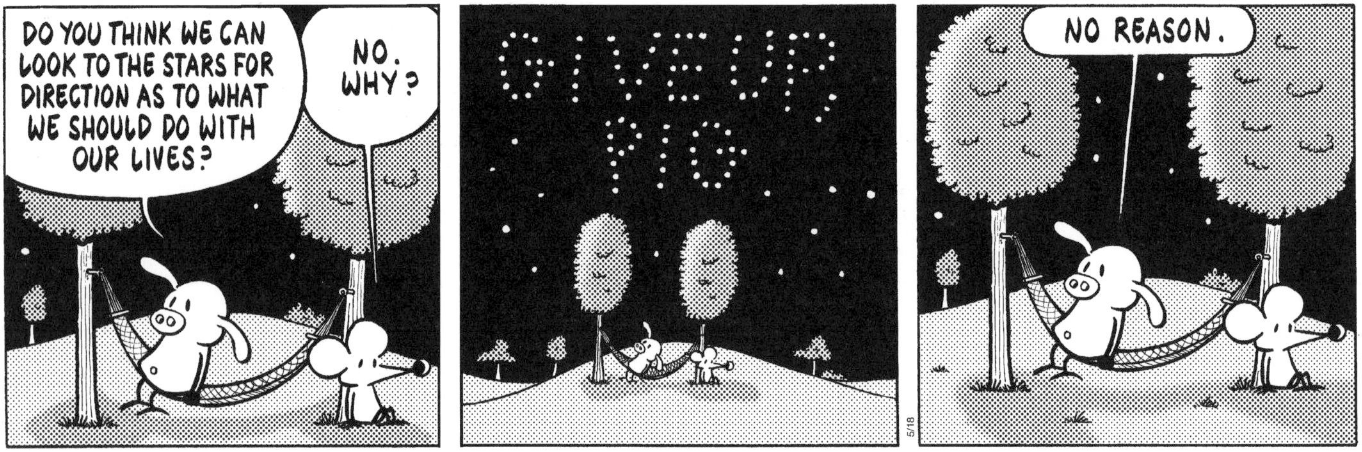
DO YOU THINK WE CAN LOOK TO THE STARS FOR DIRECTION AS TO WHAT WE SHOULD DO WITH OUR LIVES?
NO. WHY?
GIVE UP PIG
NO REASON.
5/18

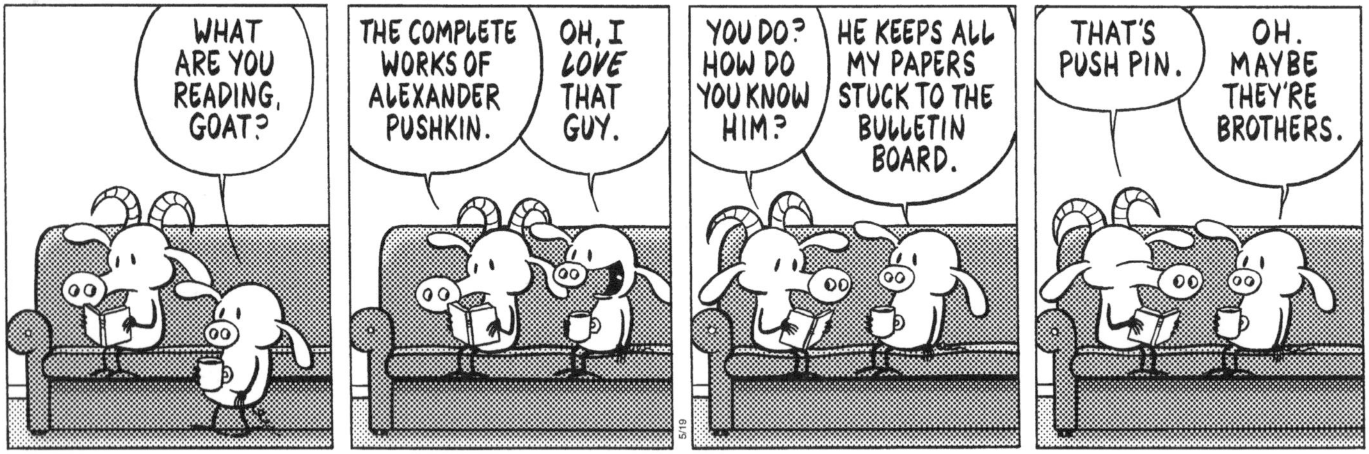
WHAT ARE YOU READING, GOAT?
THE COMPLETE WORKS OF ALEXANDER PUSHKIN.
OH, I *LOVE* THAT GUY.
5/19
YOU DO? HOW DO YOU KNOW HIM?
HE KEEPS ALL MY PAPERS STUCK TO THE BULLETIN BOARD.
THAT'S PUSH PIN.
OH. MAYBE THEY'RE BROTHERS.

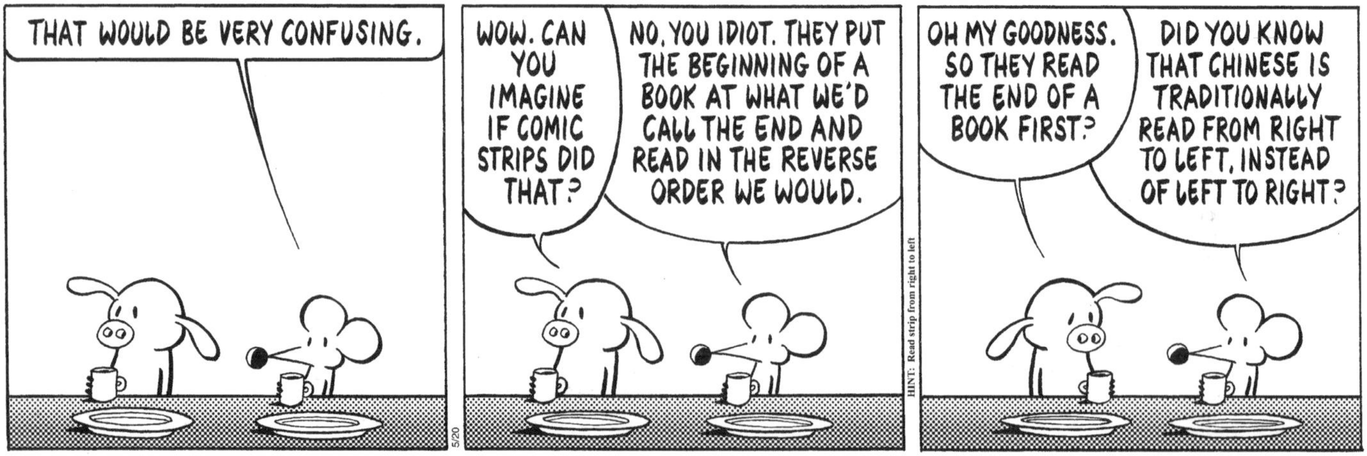
HINT: Read strip from right to left
DID YOU KNOW THAT CHINESE IS TRADITIONALLY READ FROM RIGHT TO LEFT, INSTEAD OF LEFT TO RIGHT?
OH MY GOODNESS. SO THEY READ THE END OF A BOOK FIRST?
NO, YOU IDIOT. THEY PUT THE BEGINNING OF A BOOK AT WHAT WE'D CALL THE END AND READ IN THE REVERSE ORDER WE WOULD.
WOW. CAN YOU IMAGINE IF COMIC STRIPS DID THAT?
5/20
THAT WOULD BE VERY CONFUSING.

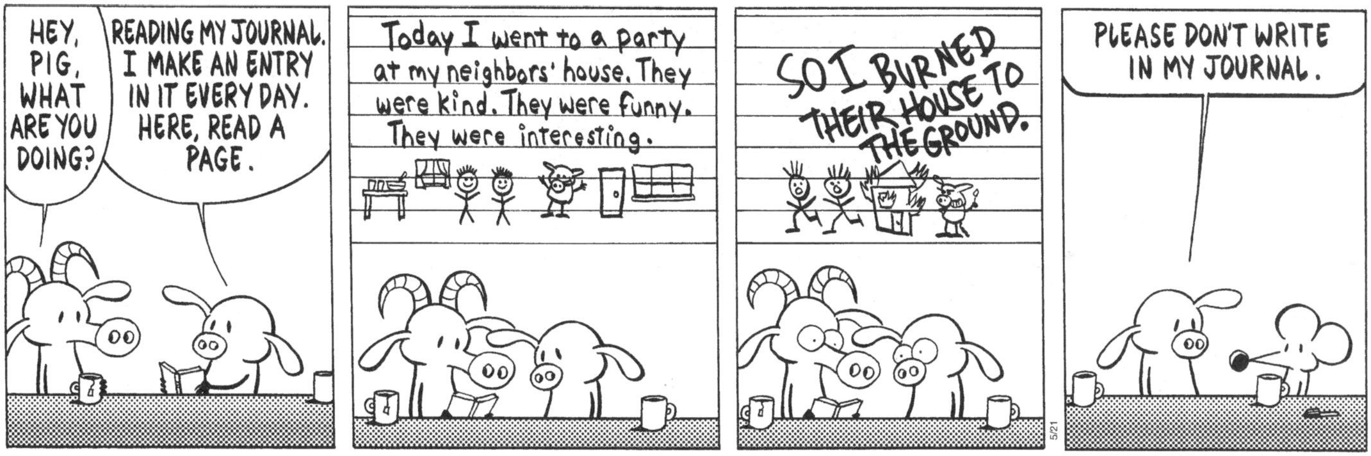
HEY, PIG, WHAT ARE YOU DOING?
READING MY JOURNAL. I MAKE AN ENTRY IN IT EVERY DAY. HERE, READ A PAGE.
Today I went to a party at my neighbors' house. They were kind. They were funny. They were interesting.
SO I BURNED THEIR HOUSE TO THE GROUND.
5/21
PLEASE DON'T WRITE IN MY JOURNAL.

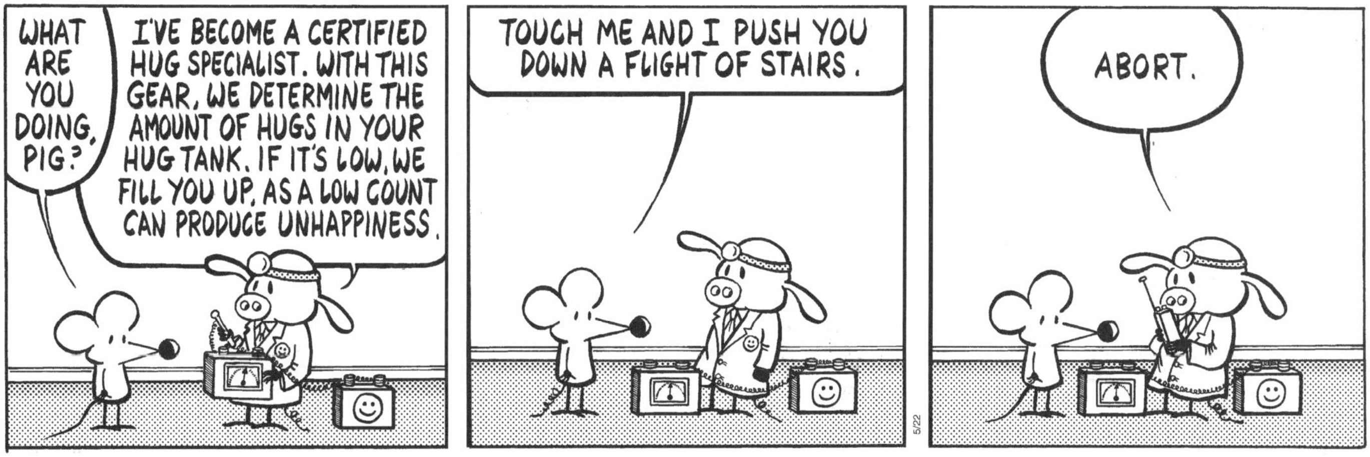
WHAT ARE YOU DOING, PIG?
I'VE BECOME A CERTIFIED HUG SPECIALIST. WITH THIS GEAR, WE DETERMINE THE AMOUNT OF HUGS IN YOUR HUG TANK. IF IT'S LOW, WE FILL YOU UP, AS A LOW COUNT CAN PRODUCE UNHAPPINESS.
TOUCH ME AND I PUSH YOU DOWN A FLIGHT OF STAIRS.
5/22
ABORT.

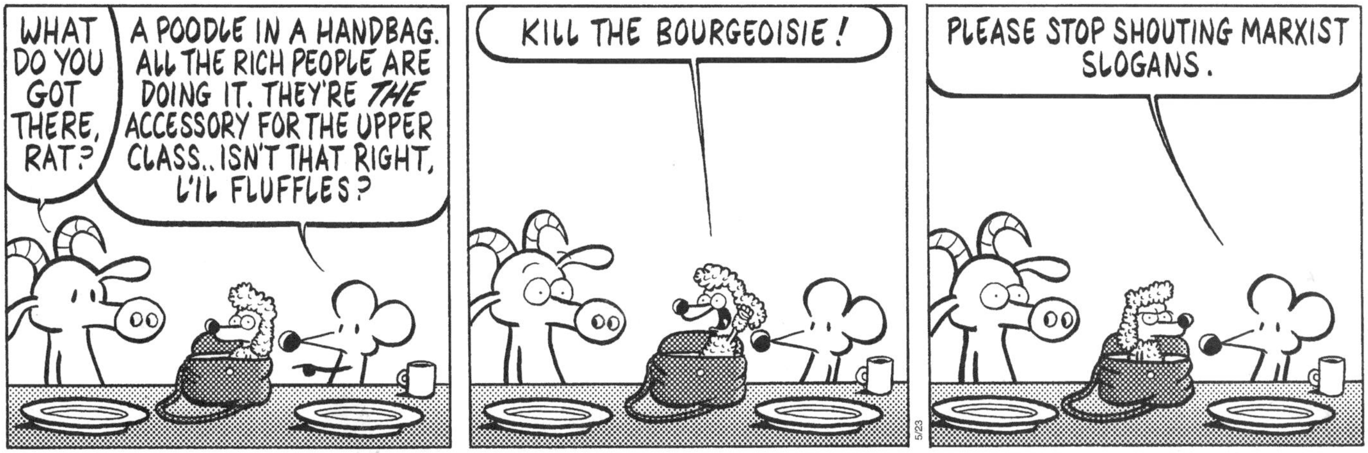
WHAT DO YOU GOT THERE, RAT?
A POODLE IN A HANDBAG. ALL THE RICH PEOPLE ARE DOING IT. THEY'RE *THE* ACCESSORY FOR THE UPPER CLASS.. ISN'T THAT RIGHT, L'IL FLUFFLES?
KILL THE BOURGEOISIE!
5/23
PLEASE STOP SHOUTING MARXIST SLOGANS.

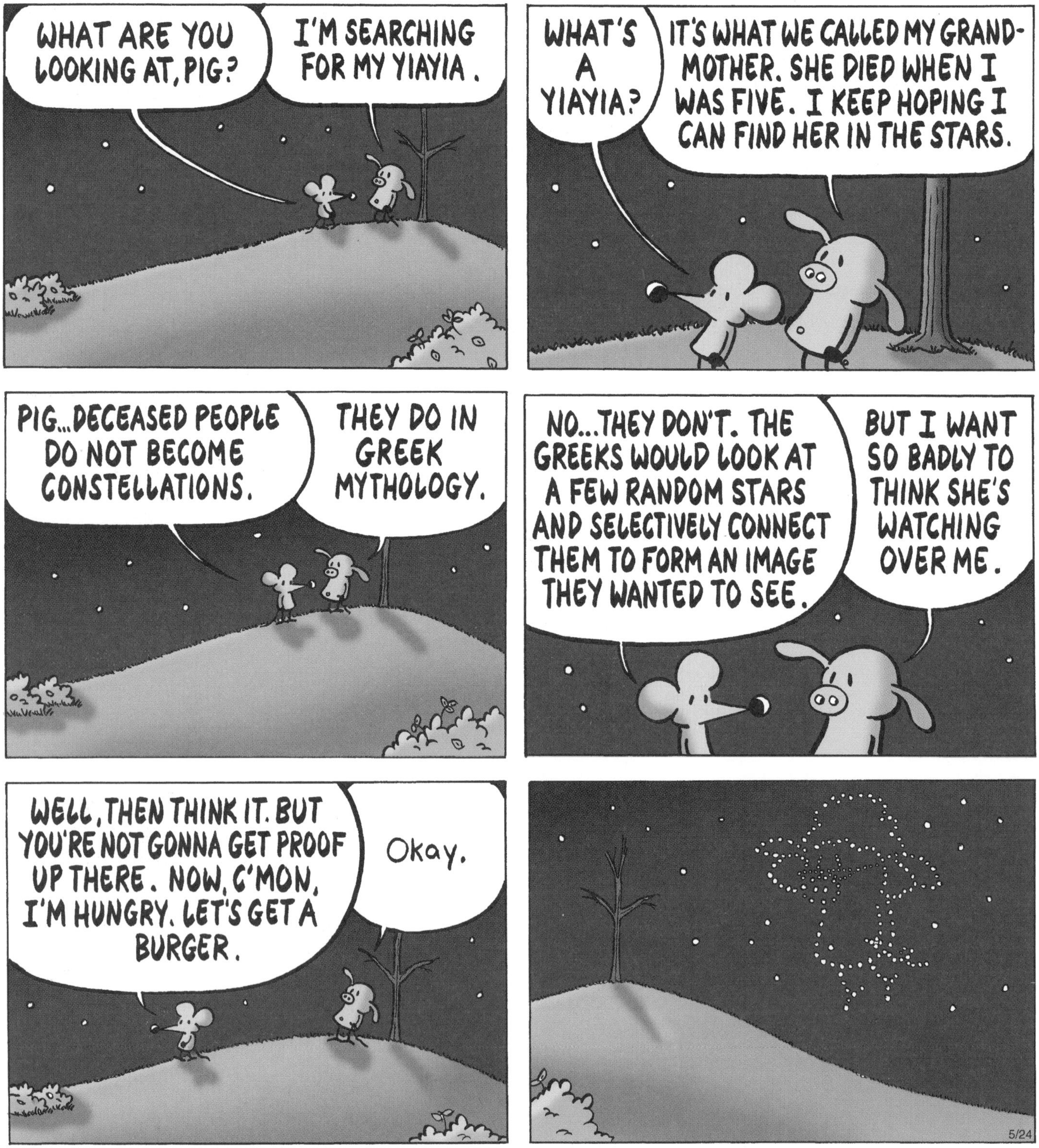
WHAT ARE YOU LOOKING AT, PIG?
I'M SEARCHING FOR MY YIAYIA.
WHAT'S A YIAYIA?
IT'S WHAT WE CALLED MY GRAND-MOTHER. SHE DIED WHEN I WAS FIVE. I KEEP HOPING I CAN FIND HER IN THE STARS.
PIG...DECEASED PEOPLE DO NOT BECOME CONSTELLATIONS.
THEY DO IN GREEK MYTHOLOGY.
NO...THEY DON'T. THE GREEKS WOULD LOOK AT A FEW RANDOM STARS AND SELECTIVELY CONNECT THEM TO FORM AN IMAGE THEY WANTED TO SEE.
BUT I WANT SO BADLY TO THINK SHE'S WATCHING OVER ME.
WELL, THEN THINK IT. BUT YOU'RE NOT GONNA GET PROOF UP THERE. NOW, C'MON, I'M HUNGRY. LET'S GET A BURGER.
Okay.
5/24

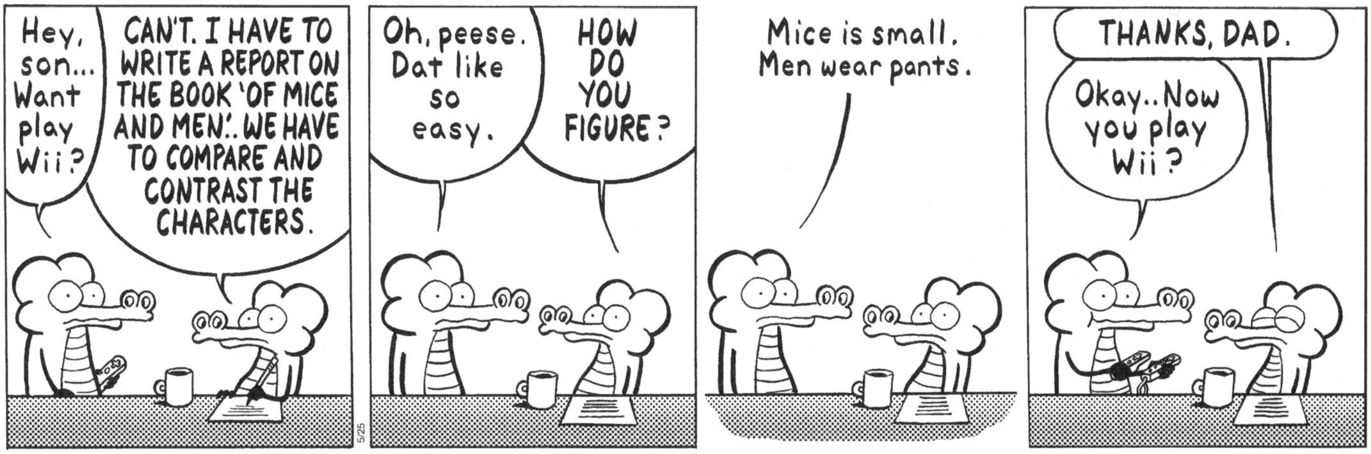
Hey, son... Want play Wii?
CAN'T. I HAVE TO WRITE A REPORT ON THE BOOK 'OF MICE AND MEN'. WE HAVE TO COMPARE AND CONTRAST THE CHARACTERS.
5/25
Oh, peese. Dat like so easy.
HOW DO YOU FIGURE?
Mice is small. Men wear pants.
THANKS, DAD.
Okay.. Now you play Wii?

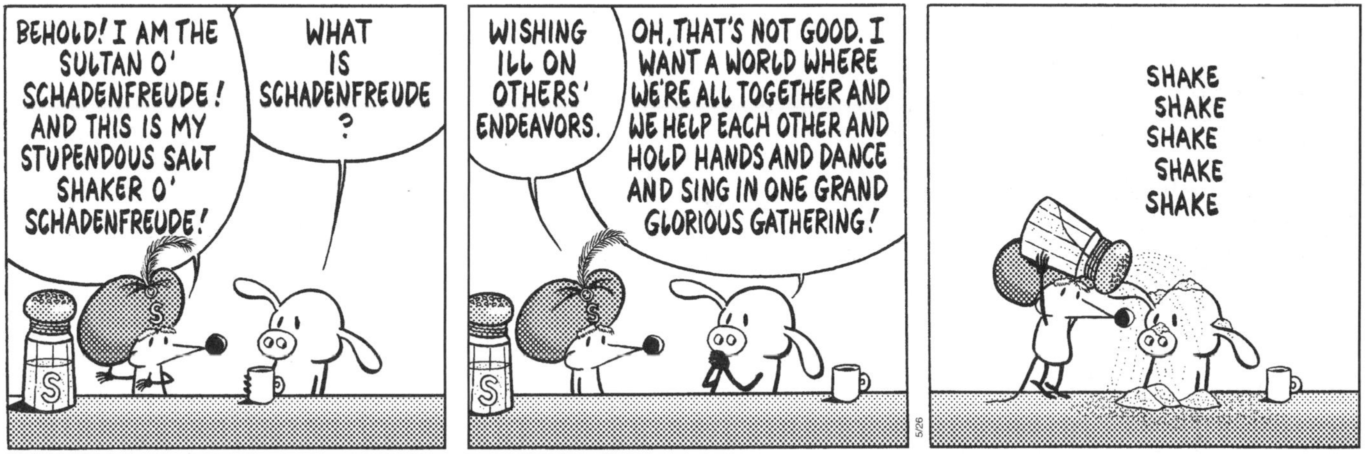
BEHOLD! I AM THE SULTAN O' SCHADENFREUDE! AND THIS IS MY STUPENDOUS SALT SHAKER O' SCHADENFREUDE!
WHAT IS SCHADENFREUDE?
WISHING ILL ON OTHERS' ENDEAVORS.
OH, THAT'S NOT GOOD. I WANT A WORLD WHERE WE'RE ALL TOGETHER AND WE HELP EACH OTHER AND HOLD HANDS AND DANCE AND SING IN ONE GRAND GLORIOUS GATHERING!
5/26
SHAKE SHAKE SHAKE SHAKE SHAKE

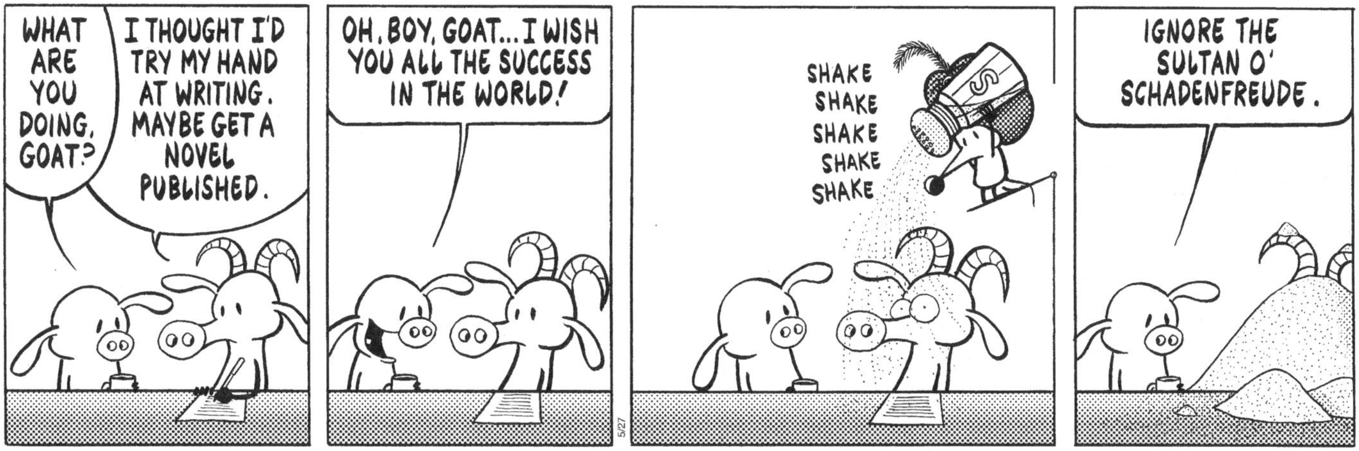
WHAT ARE YOU DOING, GOAT?
I THOUGHT I'D TRY MY HAND AT WRITING. MAYBE GET A NOVEL PUBLISHED.
OH, BOY, GOAT... I WISH YOU ALL THE SUCCESS IN THE WORLD!
5/27
SHAKE SHAKE SHAKE SHAKE SHAKE
IGNORE THE SULTAN O' SCHADENFREUDE.

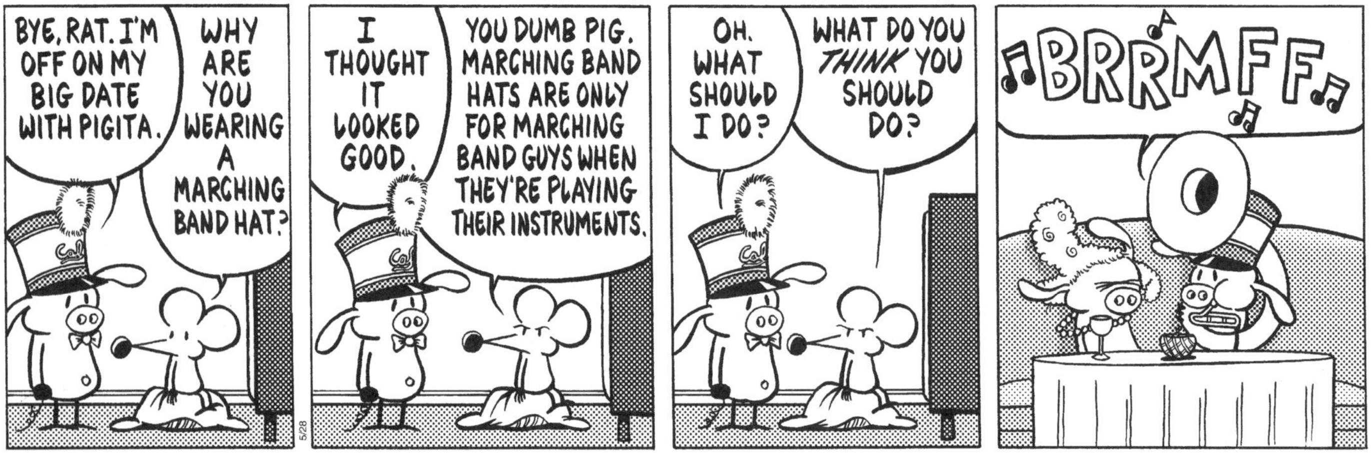
BYE, RAT. I'M OFF ON MY BIG DATE WITH PIGITA.
WHY ARE YOU WEARING A MARCHING BAND HAT?
5/28
I THOUGHT IT LOOKED GOOD.
YOU DUMB PIG. MARCHING BAND HATS ARE ONLY FOR MARCHING BAND GUYS WHEN THEY'RE PLAYING THEIR INSTRUMENTS.
OH. WHAT SHOULD I DO?
WHAT DO YOU *THINK* YOU SHOULD DO?
BRRMFF

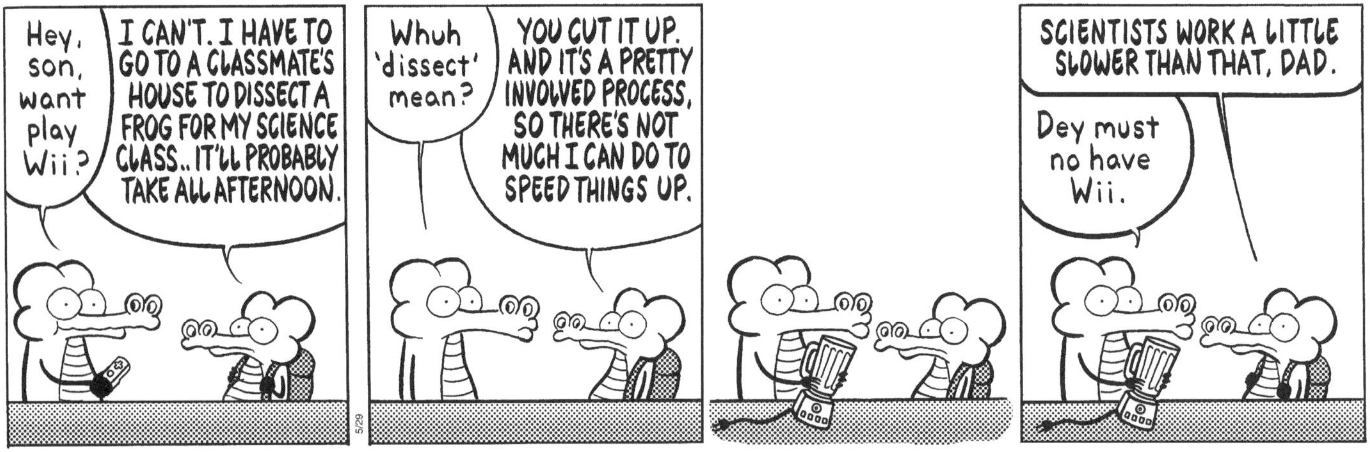
Hey, son, want play Wii?
I CAN'T. I HAVE TO GO TO A CLASSMATE'S HOUSE TO DISSECT A FROG FOR MY SCIENCE CLASS.. IT'LL PROBABLY TAKE ALL AFTERNOON.
5/29
Whuh 'dissect' mean?
YOU CUT IT UP. AND IT'S A PRETTY INVOLVED PROCESS, SO THERE'S NOT MUCH I CAN DO TO SPEED THINGS UP.
SCIENTISTS WORK A LITTLE SLOWER THAN THAT, DAD.
Dey must no have Wii.

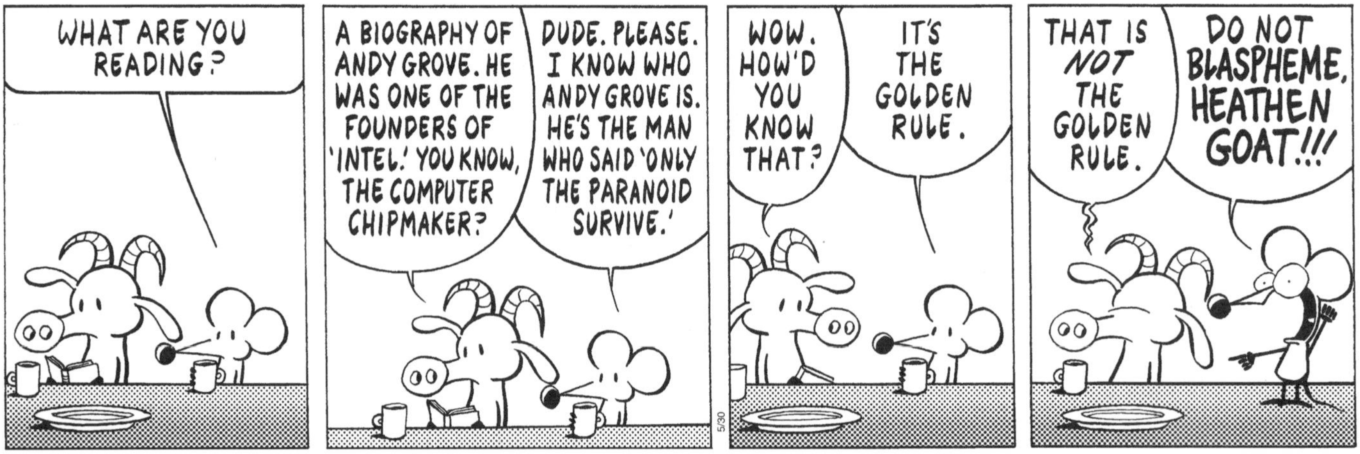
WHAT ARE YOU READING?
A BIOGRAPHY OF ANDY GROVE. HE WAS ONE OF THE FOUNDERS OF 'INTEL.' YOU KNOW, THE COMPUTER CHIPMAKER?
DUDE. PLEASE. I KNOW WHO ANDY GROVE IS. HE'S THE MAN WHO SAID 'ONLY THE PARANOID SURVIVE.'
5/30
WOW. HOW'D YOU KNOW THAT?
IT'S THE GOLDEN RULE.
THAT IS *NOT* THE GOLDEN RULE.
DO NOT BLASPHEME, HEATHEN GOAT!!!

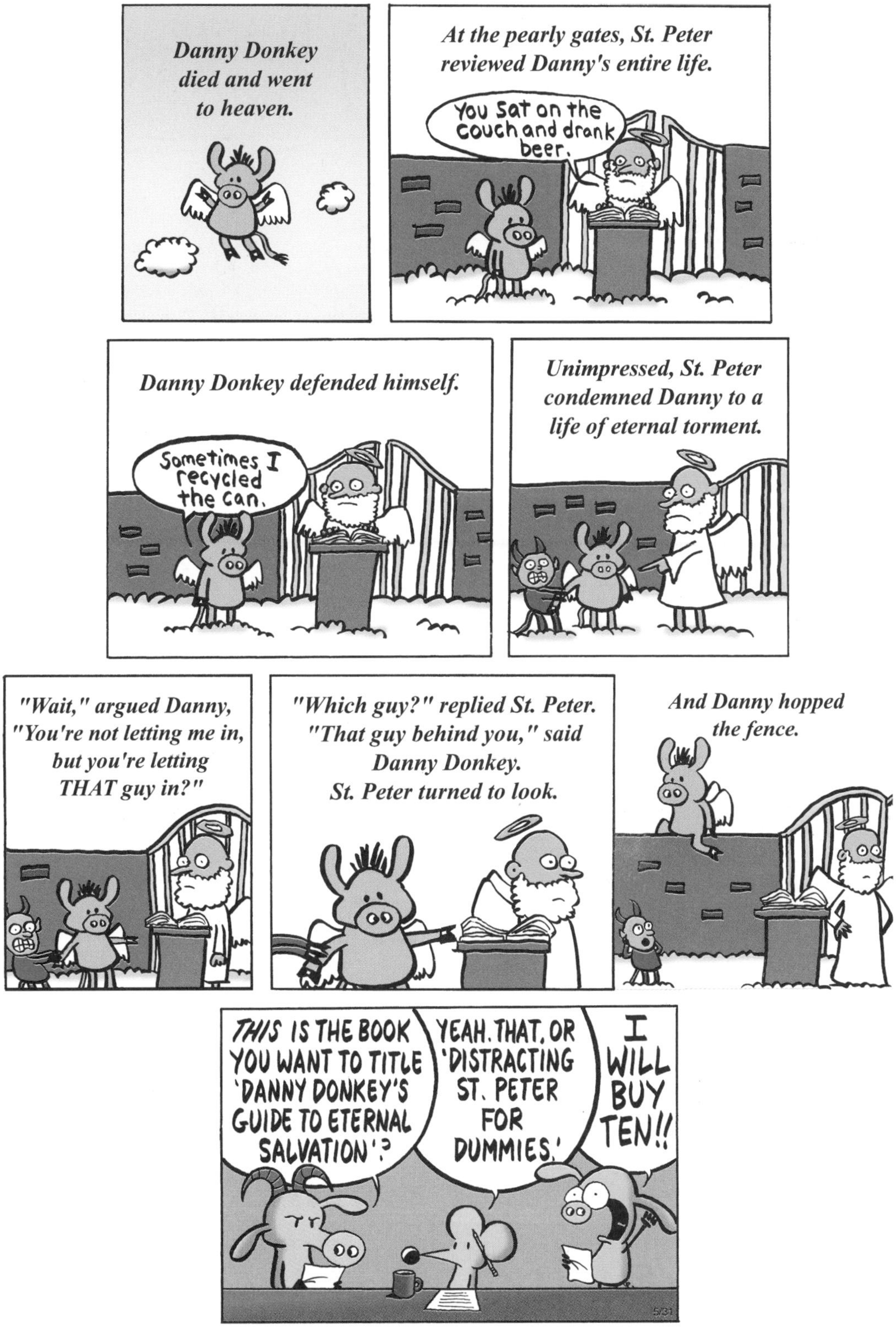
Danny Donkey died and went to heaven.
At the pearly gates, St. Peter reviewed Danny's entire life.
You sat on the couch and drank beer.
Danny Donkey defended himself.
Sometimes I recycled the can.
Unimpressed, St. Peter condemned Danny to a life of eternal torment.
"Wait," argued Danny, "You're not letting me in, but you're letting THAT guy in?"
"Which guy?" replied St. Peter. "That guy behind you," said Danny Donkey. St. Peter turned to look.
And Danny hopped the fence.
THIS IS THE BOOK YOU WANT TO TITLE 'DANNY DONKEY'S GUIDE TO ETERNAL SALVATION'?
YEAH. THAT, OR 'DISTRACTING ST. PETER FOR DUMMIES.'
I WILL BUY TEN!!
5/31

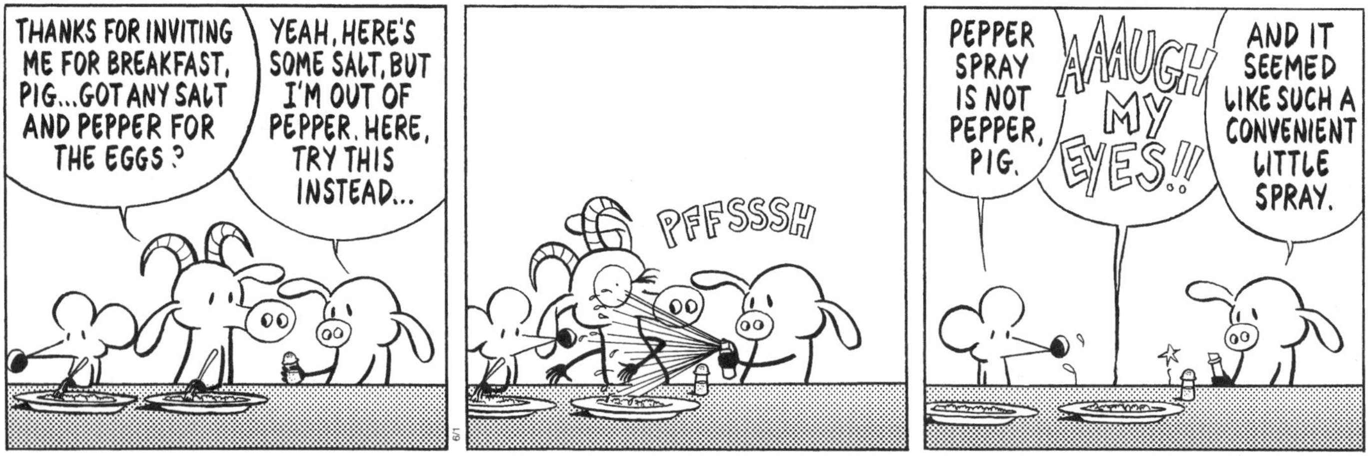
THANKS FOR INVITING ME FOR BREAKFAST, PIG...GOT ANY SALT AND PEPPER FOR THE EGGS?
YEAH, HERE'S SOME SALT, BUT I'M OUT OF PEPPER. HERE, TRY THIS INSTEAD...
PFFSSSH
PEPPER SPRAY IS NOT PEPPER, PIG.
AAAUGH MY EYES!!
AND IT SEEMED LIKE SUCH A CONVENIENT LITTLE SPRAY.

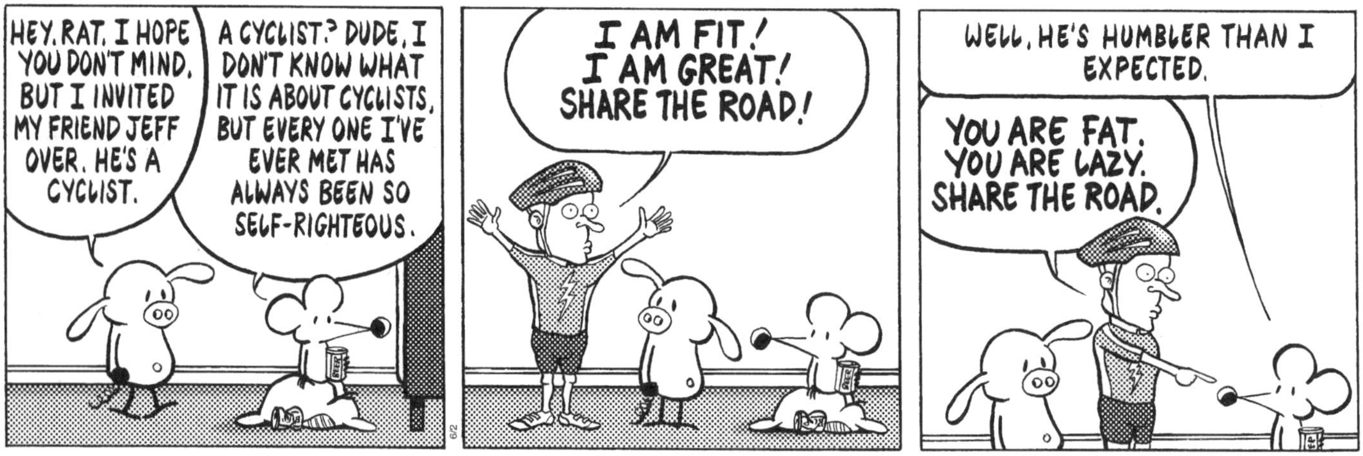
HEY, RAT, I HOPE YOU DON'T MIND, BUT I INVITED MY FRIEND JEFF OVER. HE'S A CYCLIST.
A CYCLIST? DUDE, I DON'T KNOW WHAT IT IS ABOUT CYCLISTS, BUT EVERY ONE I'VE EVER MET HAS ALWAYS BEEN SO SELF-RIGHTEOUS.
I AM FIT! I AM GREAT! SHARE THE ROAD!
WELL, HE'S HUMBLER THAN I EXPECTED.
YOU ARE FAT. YOU ARE LAZY. SHARE THE ROAD.

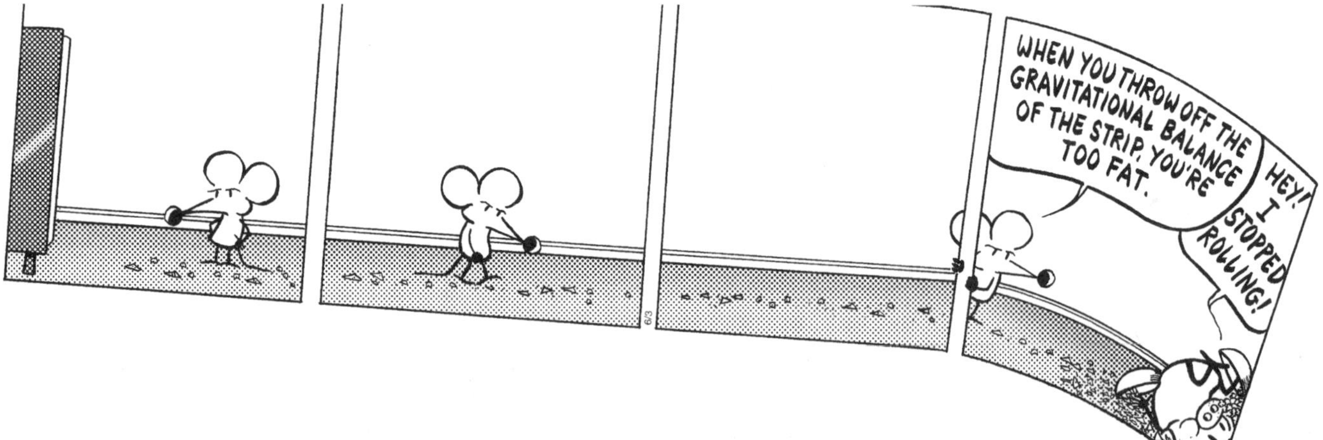
WHEN YOU THROW OFF THE GRAVITATIONAL BALANCE OF THE STRIP, YOU'RE TOO FAT.
HEY! I STOPPED ROLLING!

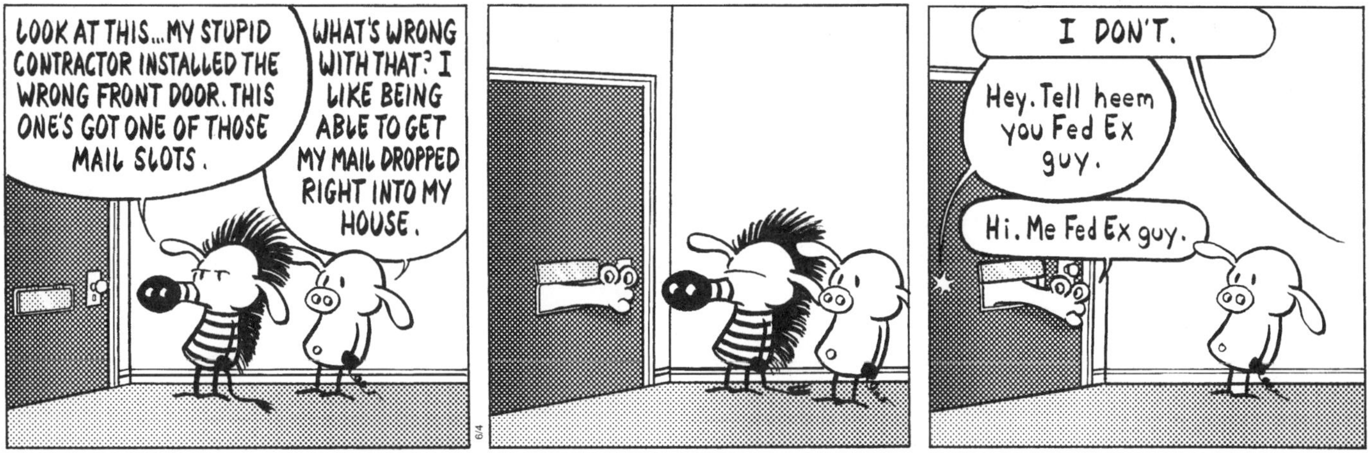
LOOK AT THIS...MY STUPID CONTRACTOR INSTALLED THE WRONG FRONT DOOR. THIS ONE'S GOT ONE OF THOSE MAIL SLOTS.
WHAT'S WRONG WITH THAT? I LIKE BEING ABLE TO GET MY MAIL DROPPED RIGHT INTO MY HOUSE.
6/4
I DON'T.
Hey. Tell heem you Fed Ex guy.
Hi. Me Fed Ex guy.

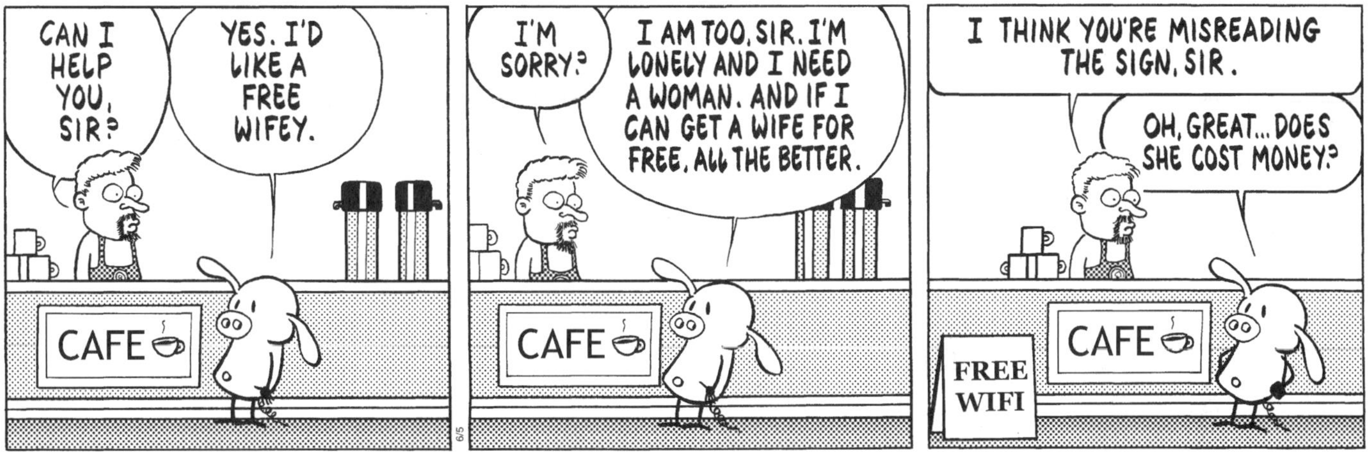
CAN I HELP YOU, SIR?
YES. I'D LIKE A FREE WIFEY.
CAFE
6/5
I'M SORRY?
I AM TOO, SIR. I'M LONELY AND I NEED A WOMAN. AND IF I CAN GET A WIFE FOR FREE, ALL THE BETTER.
CAFE
I THINK YOU'RE MISREADING THE SIGN, SIR.
OH, GREAT... DOES SHE COST MONEY?
FREE WIFI
CAFE

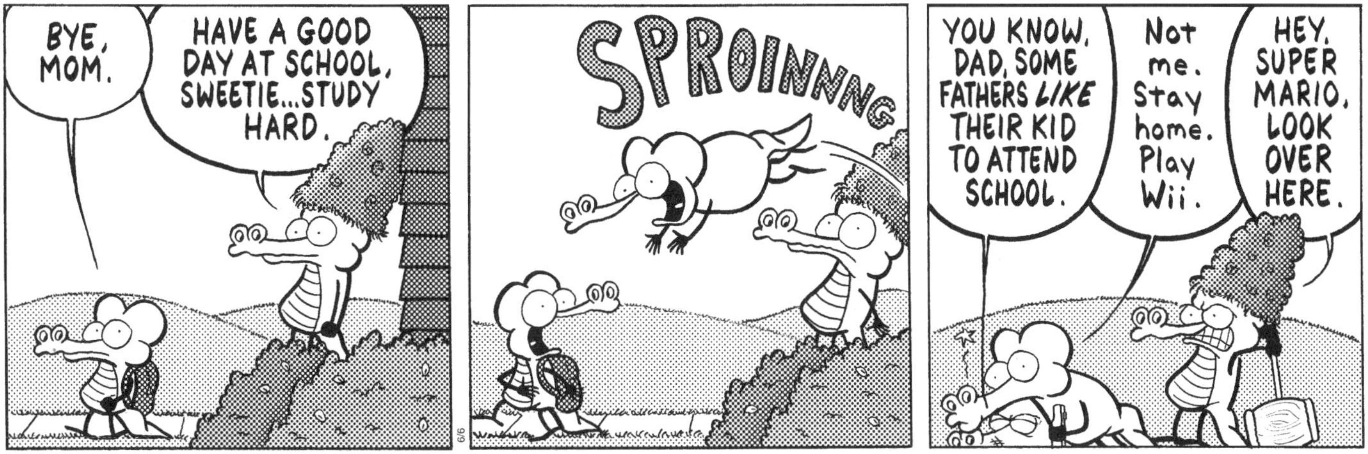
BYE, MOM.
HAVE A GOOD DAY AT SCHOOL, SWEETIE...STUDY HARD.
6/6
SPROINNNG
YOU KNOW, DAD, SOME FATHERS *LIKE* THEIR KID TO ATTEND SCHOOL.
Not me. Stay home. Play Wii.
HEY, SUPER MARIO. LOOK OVER HERE.

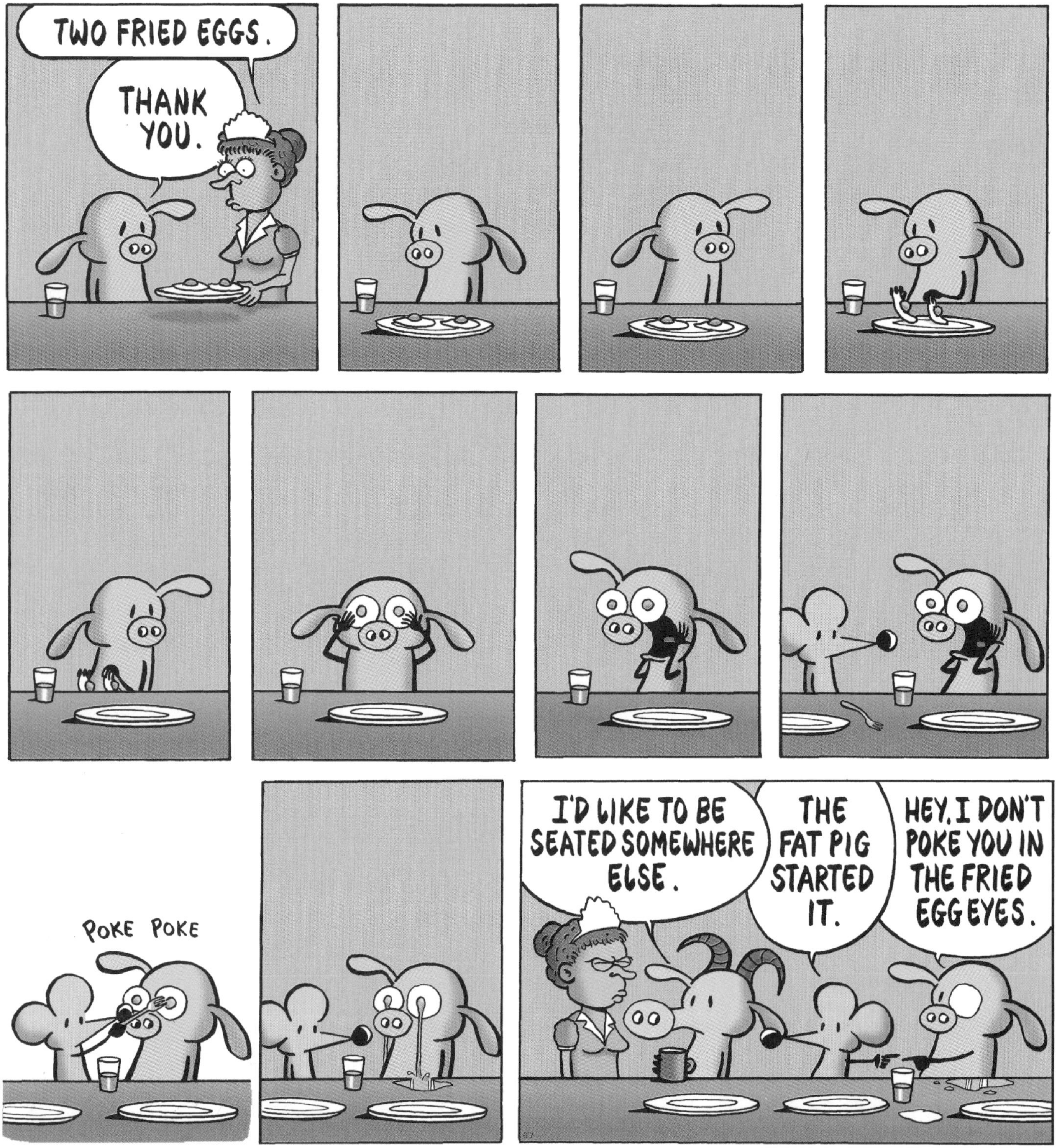

TWO FRIED EGGS.
THANK YOU.
POKE POKE
I'D LIKE TO BE SEATED SOMEWHERE ELSE.
THE FAT PIG STARTED IT.
HEY, I DON'T POKE YOU IN THE FRIED EGG EYES.

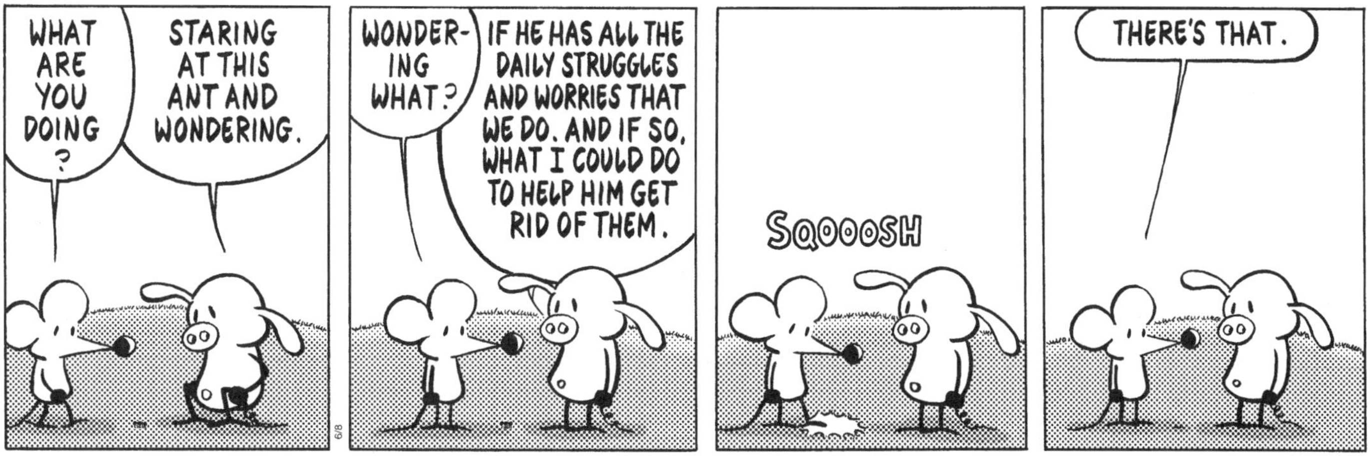
WHAT ARE YOU DOING?
STARING AT THIS ANT AND WONDERING.
WONDERING WHAT?
IF HE HAS ALL THE DAILY STRUGGLES AND WORRIES THAT WE DO. AND IF SO, WHAT I COULD DO TO HELP HIM GET RID OF THEM.
SQOOOSH
THERE'S THAT.
6/8

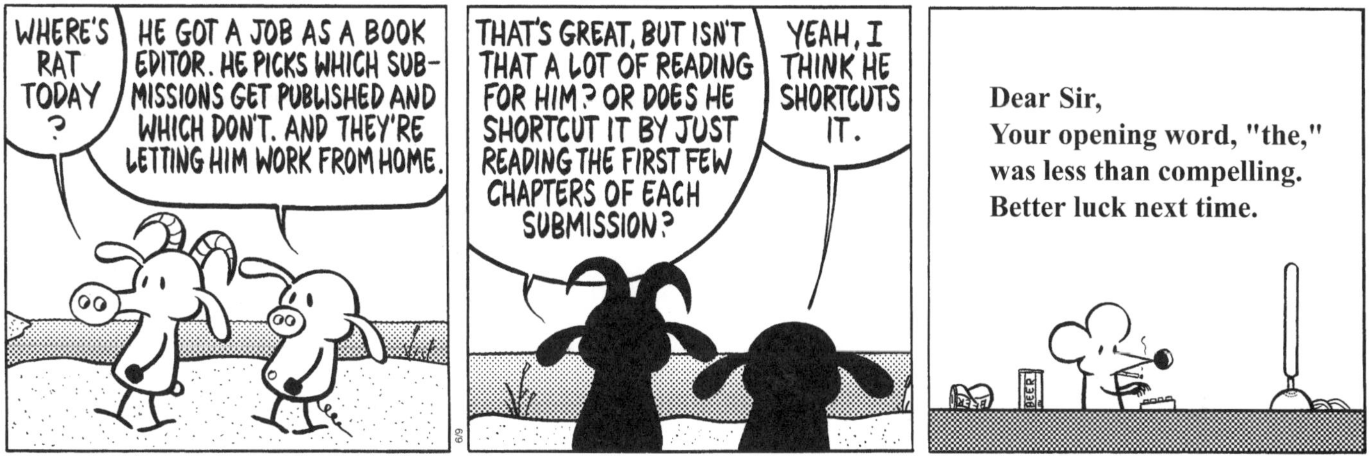
WHERE'S RAT TODAY?
HE GOT A JOB AS A BOOK EDITOR. HE PICKS WHICH SUBMISSIONS GET PUBLISHED AND WHICH DON'T. AND THEY'RE LETTING HIM WORK FROM HOME.
THAT'S GREAT, BUT ISN'T THAT A LOT OF READING FOR HIM? OR DOES HE SHORTCUT IT BY JUST READING THE FIRST FEW CHAPTERS OF EACH SUBMISSION?
YEAH, I THINK HE SHORTCUTS IT.
Dear Sir,
Your opening word, "the," was less than compelling. Better luck next time.
6/9

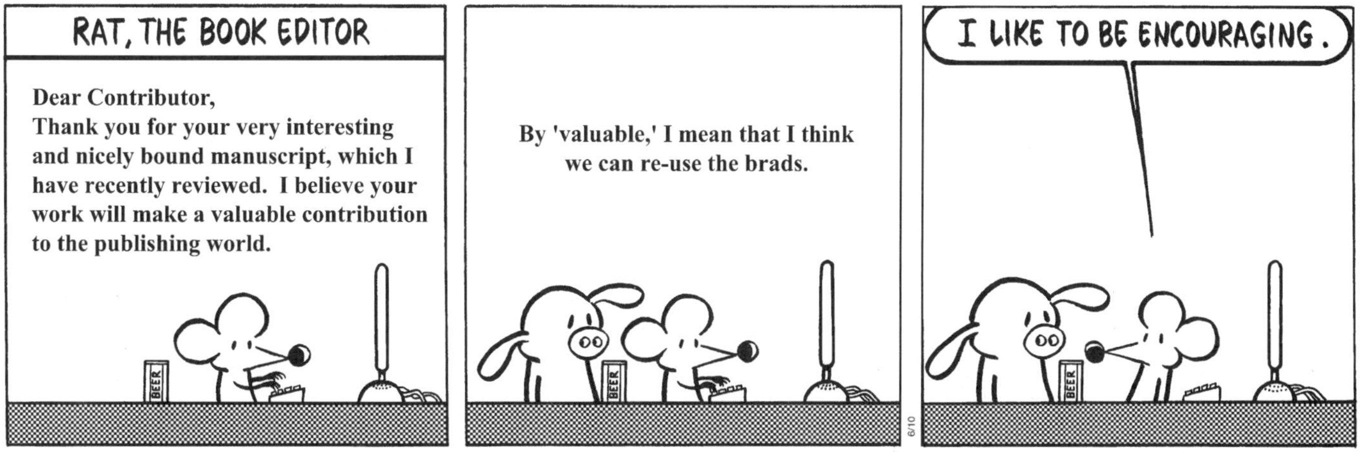
RAT, THE BOOK EDITOR
Dear Contributor,
Thank you for your very interesting and nicely bound manuscript, which I have recently reviewed. I believe your work will make a valuable contribution to the publishing world.
By 'valuable,' I mean that I think we can re-use the brads.
I LIKE TO BE ENCOURAGING.
6/10

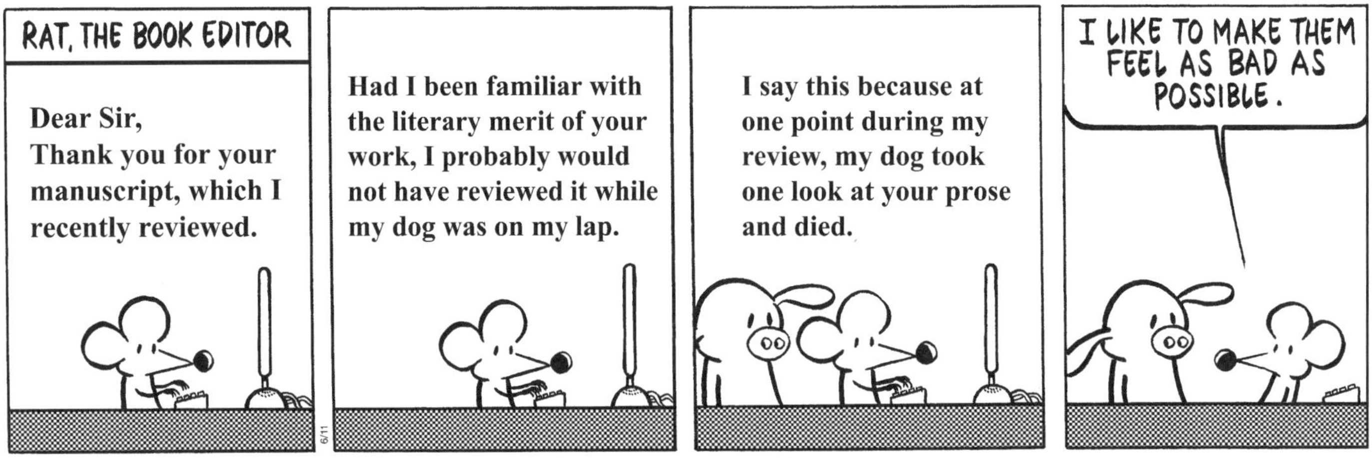
RAT, THE BOOK EDITOR
Dear Sir,
Thank you for your manuscript, which I recently reviewed.
6/11
Had I been familiar with the literary merit of your work, I probably would not have reviewed it while my dog was on my lap.
I say this because at one point during my review, my dog took one look at your prose and died.
I LIKE TO MAKE THEM FEEL AS BAD AS POSSIBLE.

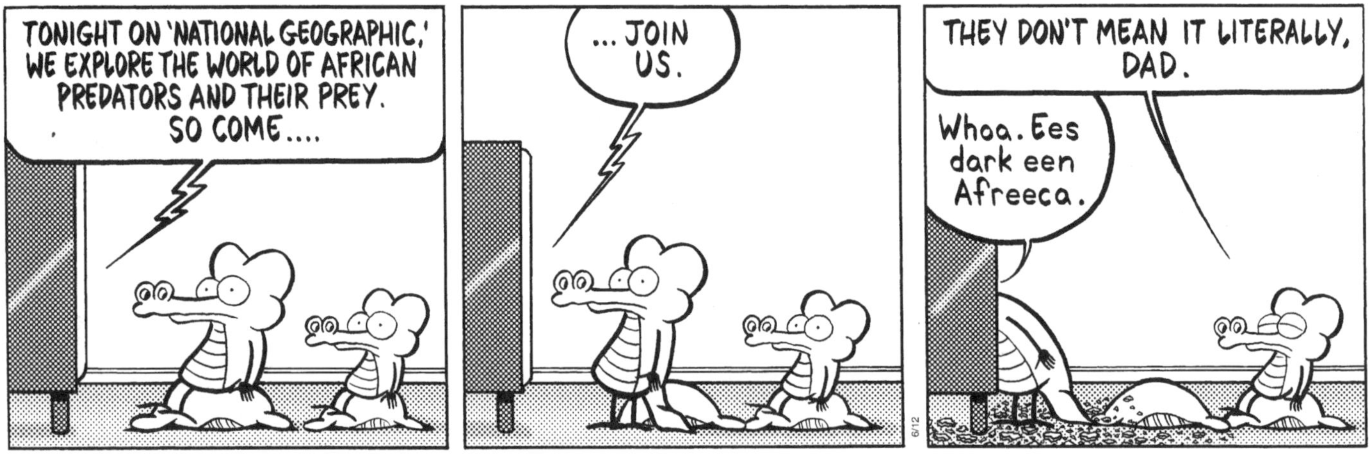
TONIGHT ON 'NATIONAL GEOGRAPHIC,' WE EXPLORE THE WORLD OF AFRICAN PREDATORS AND THEIR PREY. SO COME....
... JOIN US.
6/12
THEY DON'T MEAN IT LITERALLY, DAD.
Whoa. Ees dark een Afreeca.

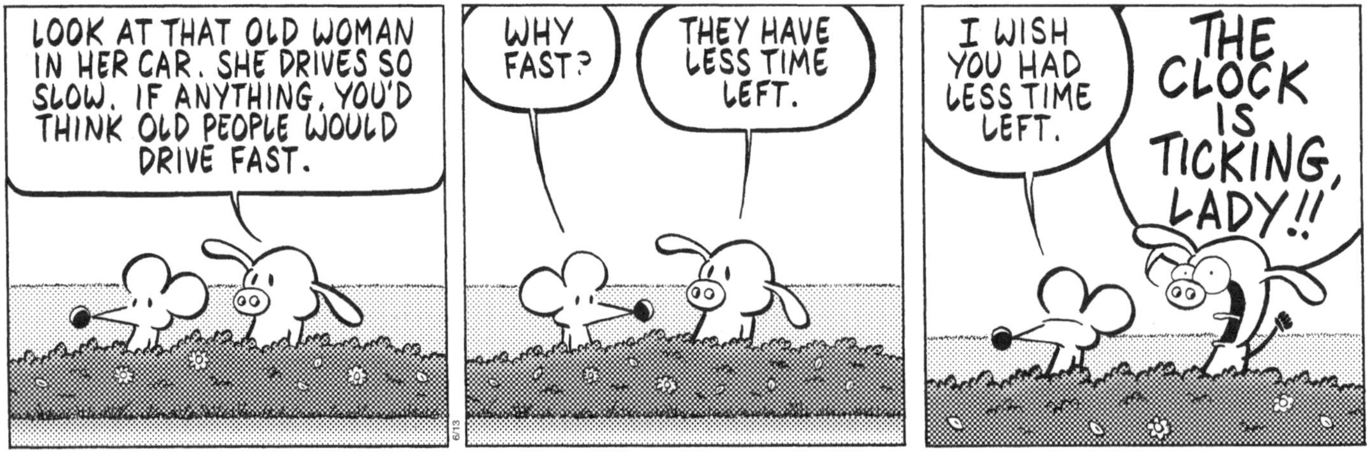
LOOK AT THAT OLD WOMAN IN HER CAR. SHE DRIVES SO SLOW. IF ANYTHING, YOU'D THINK OLD PEOPLE WOULD DRIVE FAST.
6/13
WHY FAST?
THEY HAVE LESS TIME LEFT.
I WISH YOU HAD LESS TIME LEFT.
THE CLOCK IS TICKING, LADY!!

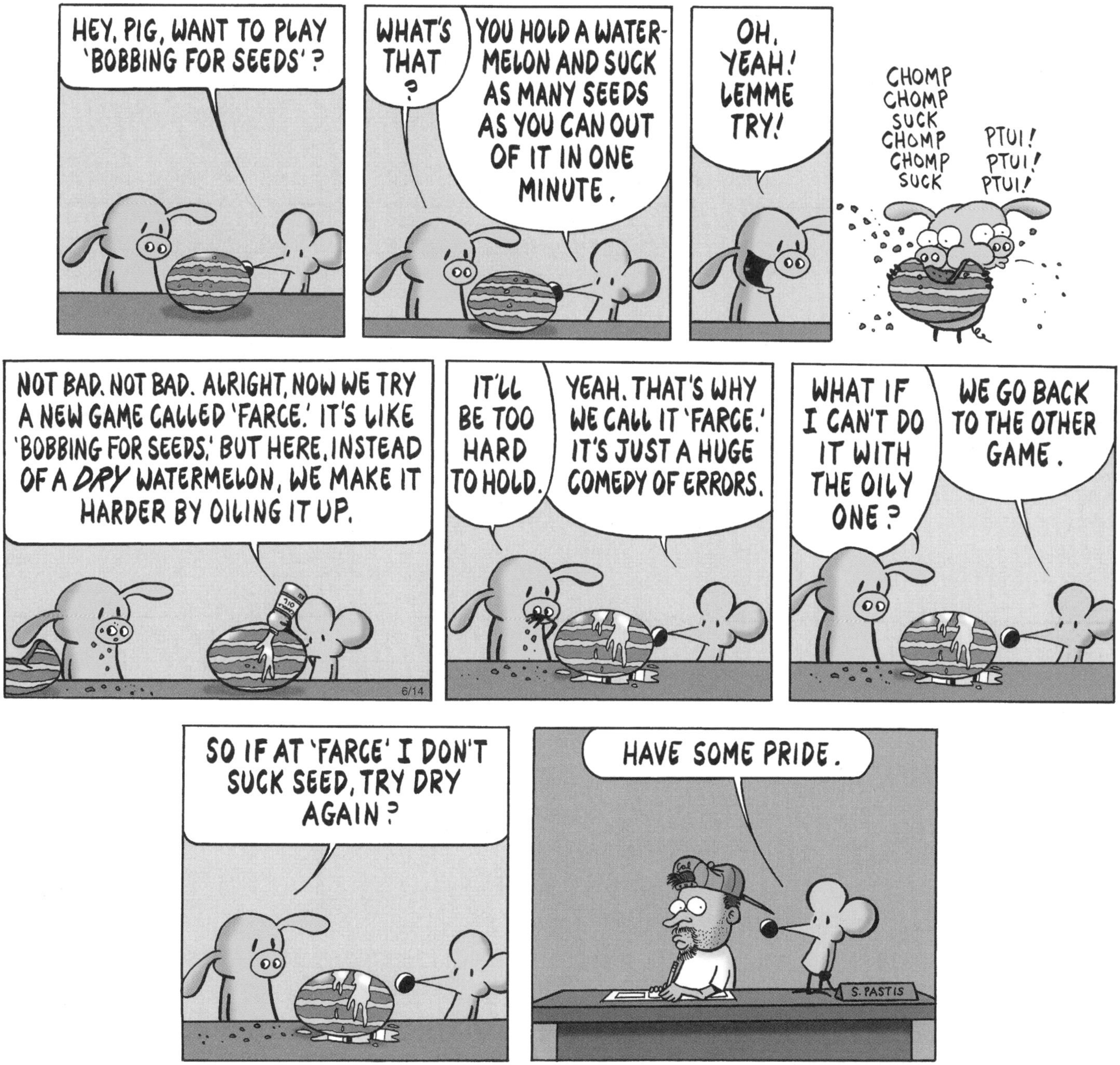
HEY, PIG, WANT TO PLAY 'BOBBING FOR SEEDS'?
WHAT'S THAT?
YOU HOLD A WATER-MELON AND SUCK AS MANY SEEDS AS YOU CAN OUT OF IT IN ONE MINUTE.
OH, YEAH! LEMME TRY!
CHOMP CHOMP SUCK CHOMP CHOMP SUCK
PTUI! PTUI! PTUI!
NOT BAD. NOT BAD. ALRIGHT, NOW WE TRY A NEW GAME CALLED 'FARCE.' IT'S LIKE 'BOBBING FOR SEEDS,' BUT HERE, INSTEAD OF A DRY WATERMELON, WE MAKE IT HARDER BY OILING IT UP.
6/14
IT'LL BE TOO HARD TO HOLD.
YEAH. THAT'S WHY WE CALL IT 'FARCE.' IT'S JUST A HUGE COMEDY OF ERRORS.
WHAT IF I CAN'T DO IT WITH THE OILY ONE?
WE GO BACK TO THE OTHER GAME.
SO IF AT 'FARCE' I DON'T SUCK SEED, TRY DRY AGAIN?
HAVE SOME PRIDE.
S. PASTIS

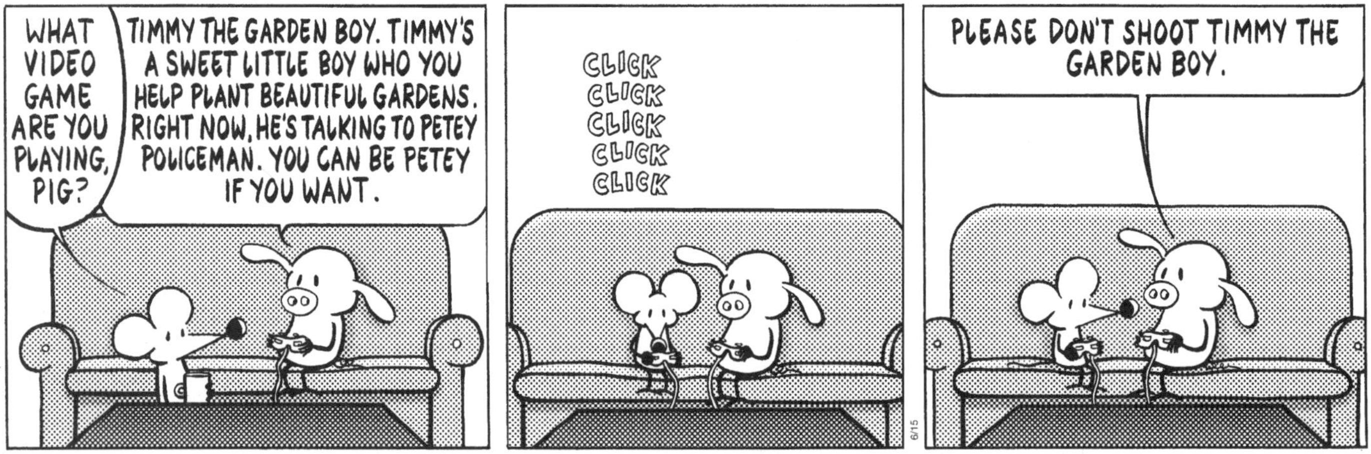
WHAT VIDEO GAME ARE YOU PLAYING, PIG?
TIMMY THE GARDEN BOY. TIMMY'S A SWEET LITTLE BOY WHO YOU HELP PLANT BEAUTIFUL GARDENS. RIGHT NOW, HE'S TALKING TO PETEY POLICEMAN. YOU CAN BE PETEY IF YOU WANT.
CLICK CLICK CLICK CLICK CLICK
6/15
PLEASE DON'T SHOOT TIMMY THE GARDEN BOY.

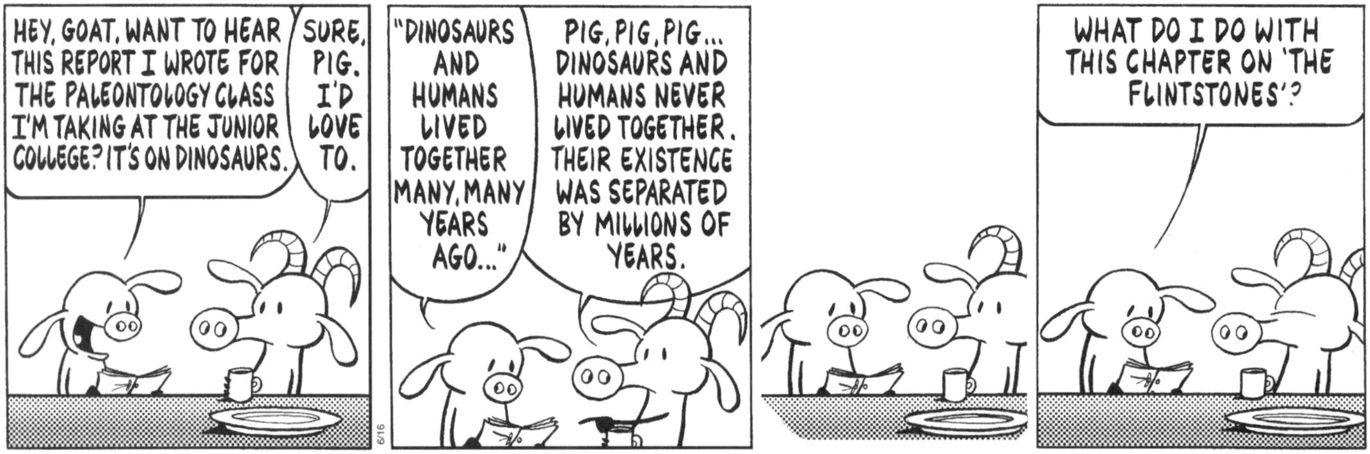
HEY, GOAT. WANT TO HEAR THIS REPORT I WROTE FOR THE PALEONTOLOGY CLASS I'M TAKING AT THE JUNIOR COLLEGE? IT'S ON DINOSAURS.
SURE, PIG. I'D LOVE TO.
6/16
"DINOSAURS AND HUMANS LIVED TOGETHER MANY, MANY YEARS AGO..."
PIG, PIG, PIG... DINOSAURS AND HUMANS NEVER LIVED TOGETHER. THEIR EXISTENCE WAS SEPARATED BY MILLIONS OF YEARS.
WHAT DO I DO WITH THIS CHAPTER ON 'THE FLINTSTONES'?

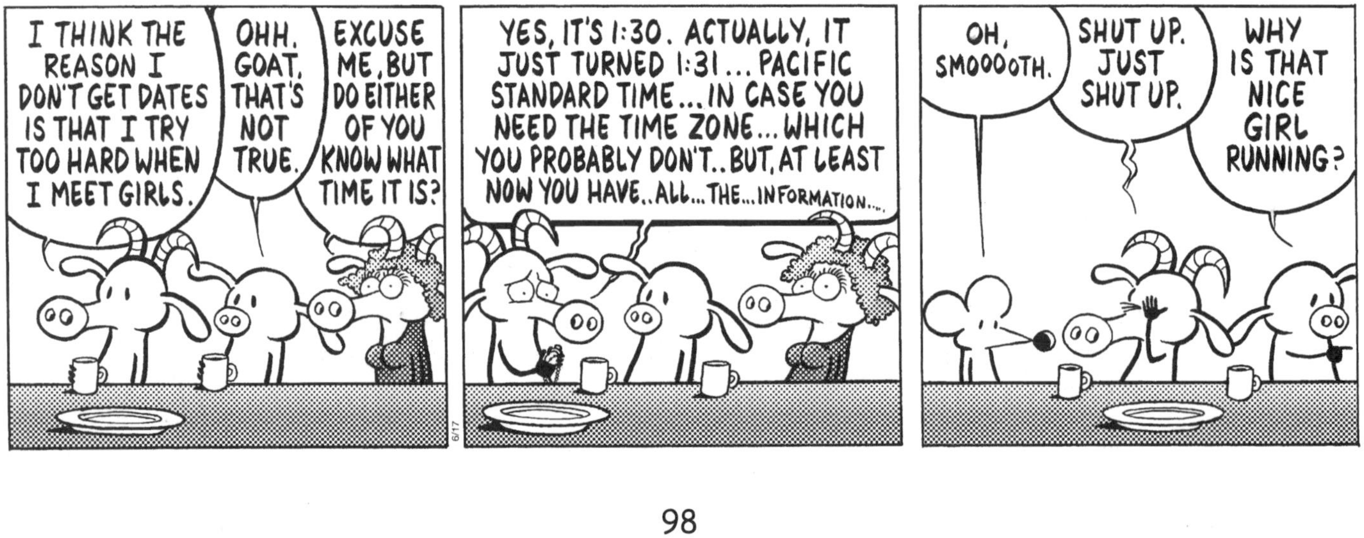
I THINK THE REASON I DON'T GET DATES IS THAT I TRY TOO HARD WHEN I MEET GIRLS.
OHH. GOAT. THAT'S NOT TRUE.
EXCUSE ME, BUT DO EITHER OF YOU KNOW WHAT TIME IT IS?
6/17
YES, IT'S 1:30. ACTUALLY, IT JUST TURNED 1:31... PACIFIC STANDARD TIME... IN CASE YOU NEED THE TIME ZONE... WHICH YOU PROBABLY DON'T.. BUT, AT LEAST NOW YOU HAVE.. ALL... THE... INFORMATION....
OH, SMOOOOTH.
SHUT UP. JUST SHUT UP.
WHY IS THAT NICE GIRL RUNNING?

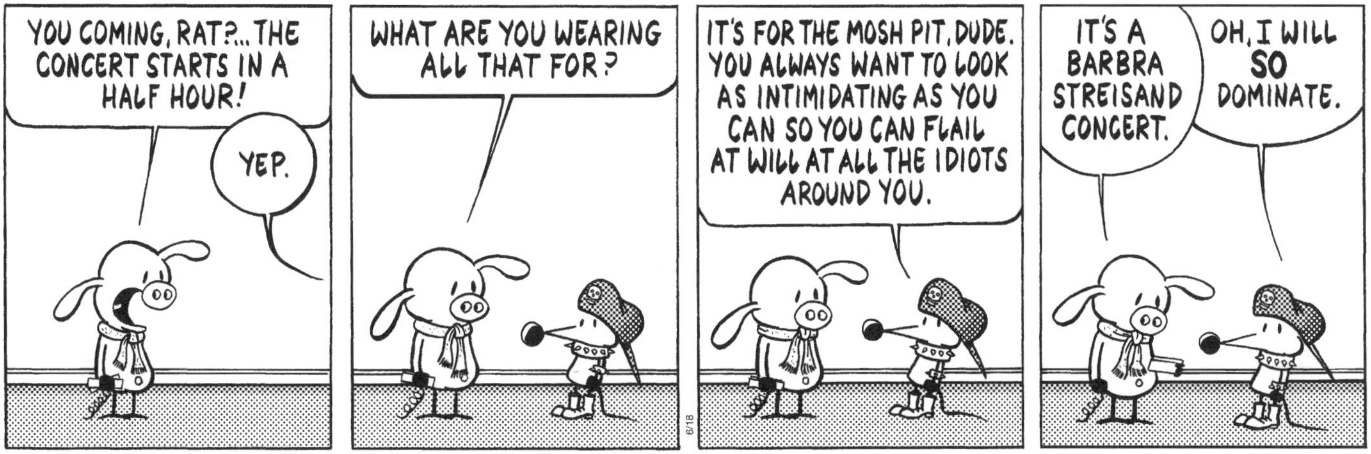
YOU COMING, RAT?... THE CONCERT STARTS IN A HALF HOUR!
YEP.
WHAT ARE YOU WEARING ALL THAT FOR?
IT'S FOR THE MOSH PIT, DUDE. YOU ALWAYS WANT TO LOOK AS INTIMIDATING AS YOU CAN SO YOU CAN FLAIL AT WILL AT ALL THE IDIOTS AROUND YOU.
IT'S A BARBRA STREISAND CONCERT.
OH, I WILL **SO** DOMINATE.

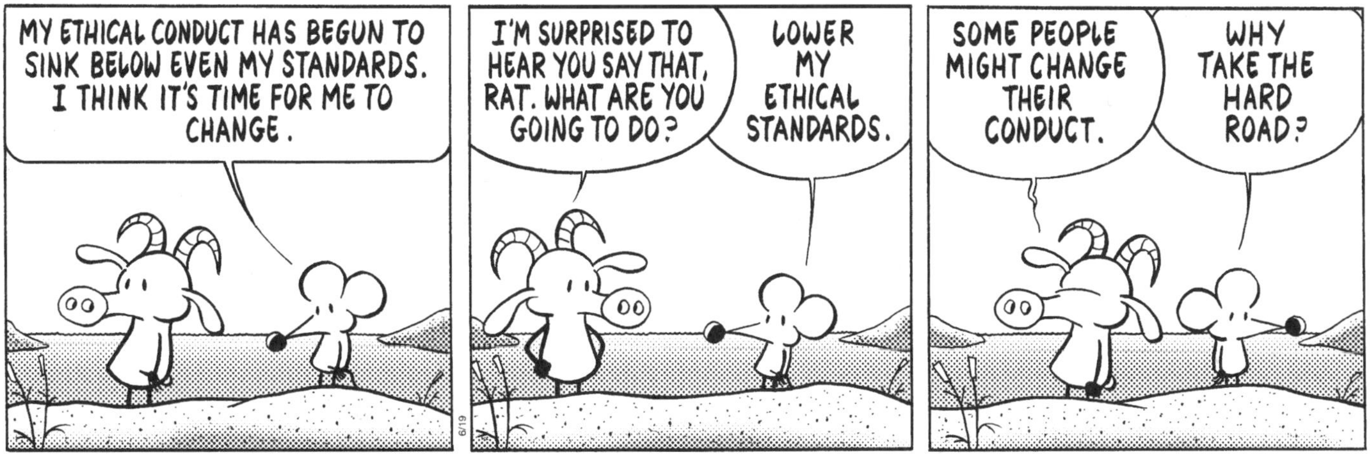
MY ETHICAL CONDUCT HAS BEGUN TO SINK BELOW EVEN MY STANDARDS. I THINK IT'S TIME FOR ME TO CHANGE.
I'M SURPRISED TO HEAR YOU SAY THAT, RAT. WHAT ARE YOU GOING TO DO?
LOWER MY ETHICAL STANDARDS.
SOME PEOPLE MIGHT CHANGE THEIR CONDUCT.
WHY TAKE THE HARD ROAD?

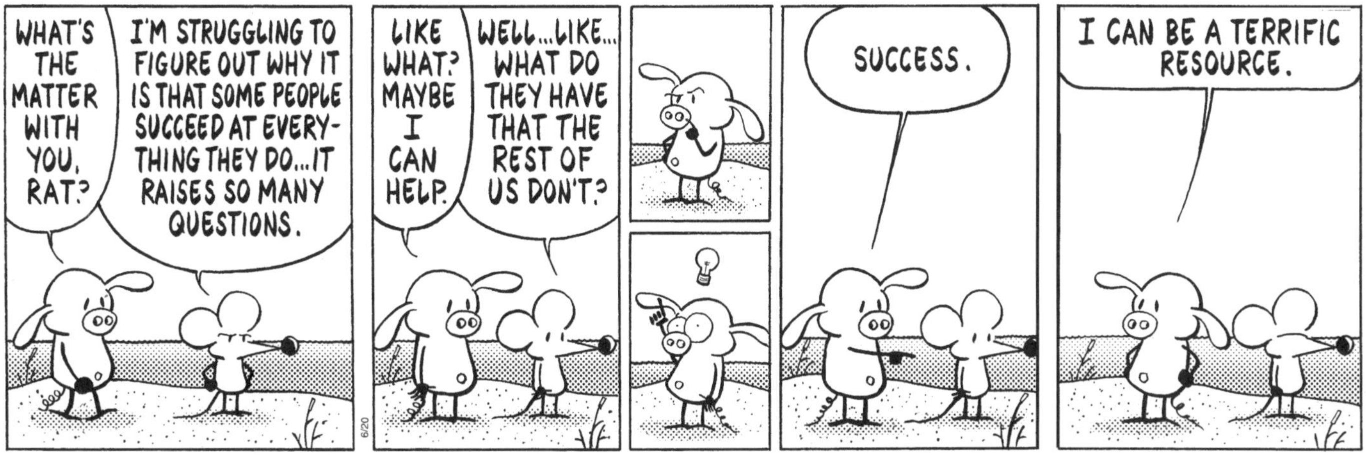
WHAT'S THE MATTER WITH YOU, RAT?
I'M STRUGGLING TO FIGURE OUT WHY IT IS THAT SOME PEOPLE SUCCEED AT EVERYTHING THEY DO... IT RAISES SO MANY QUESTIONS.
LIKE WHAT? MAYBE I CAN HELP.
WELL... LIKE... WHAT DO THEY HAVE THAT THE REST OF US DON'T?
SUCCESS.
I CAN BE A TERRIFIC RESOURCE.

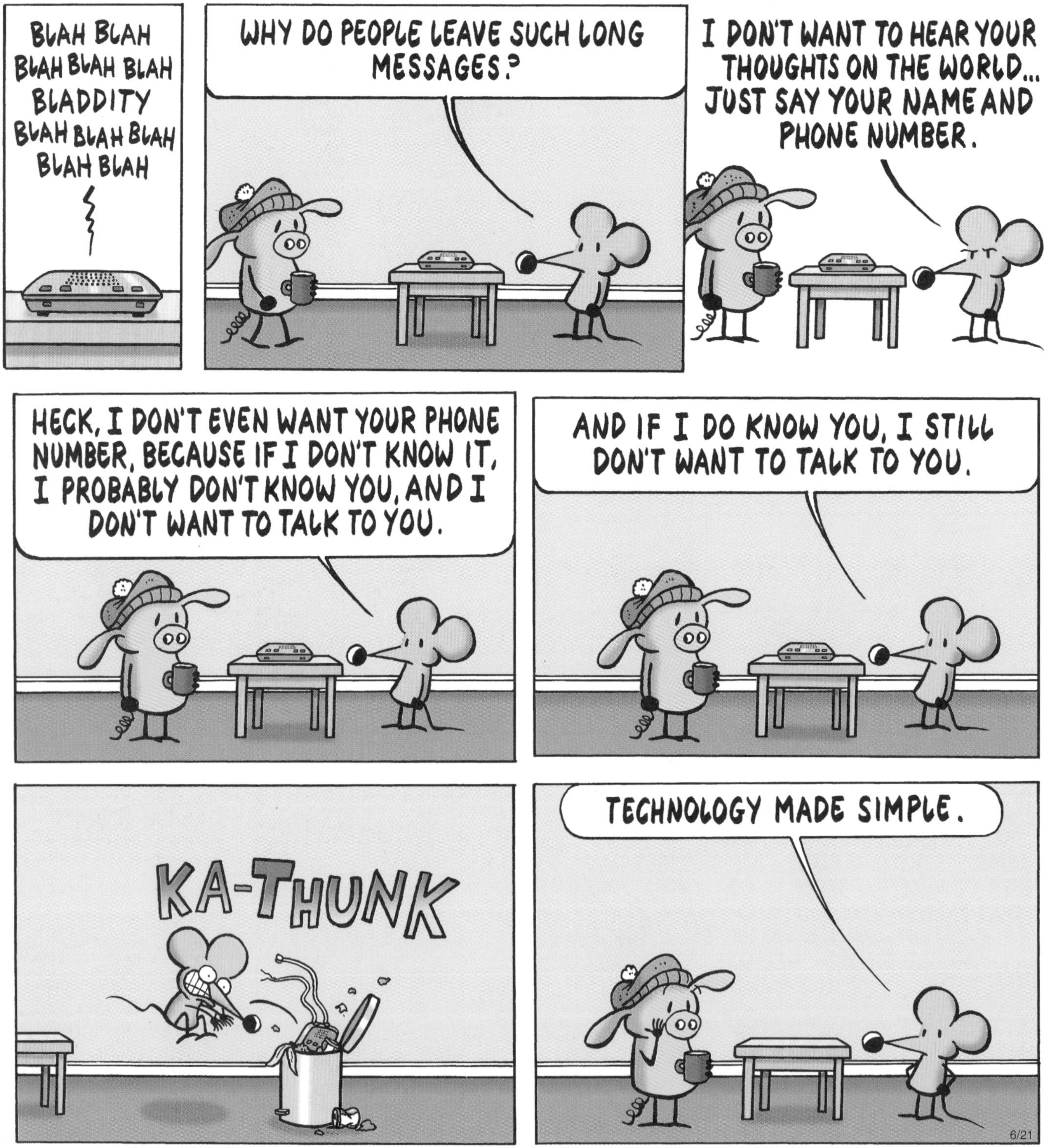
BLAH BLAH BLAH BLAH BLAH BLADDITY BLAH BLAH BLAH BLAH BLAH
WHY DO PEOPLE LEAVE SUCH LONG MESSAGES?
I DON'T WANT TO HEAR YOUR THOUGHTS ON THE WORLD... JUST SAY YOUR NAME AND PHONE NUMBER.
HECK, I DON'T EVEN WANT YOUR PHONE NUMBER, BECAUSE IF I DON'T KNOW IT, I PROBABLY DON'T KNOW YOU, AND I DON'T WANT TO TALK TO YOU.
AND IF I DO KNOW YOU, I STILL DON'T WANT TO TALK TO YOU.
KA-THUNK
TECHNOLOGY MADE SIMPLE.
6/21

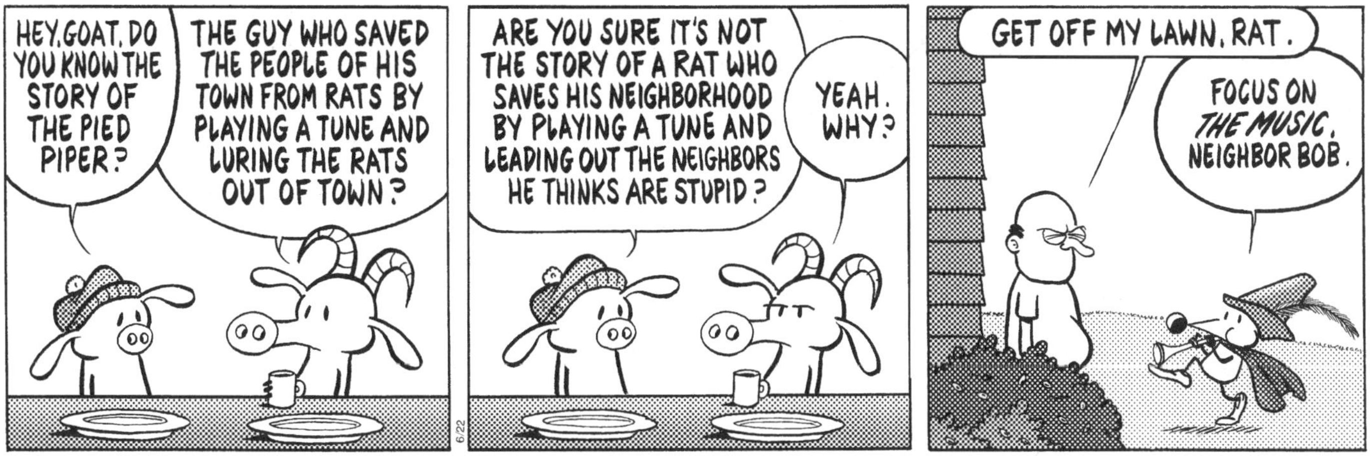
HEY, GOAT, DO YOU KNOW THE STORY OF THE PIED PIPER?
THE GUY WHO SAVED THE PEOPLE OF HIS TOWN FROM RATS BY PLAYING A TUNE AND LURING THE RATS OUT OF TOWN?
6/22
ARE YOU SURE IT'S NOT THE STORY OF A RAT WHO SAVES HIS NEIGHBORHOOD BY PLAYING A TUNE AND LEADING OUT THE NEIGHBORS HE THINKS ARE STUPID?
YEAH. WHY?
GET OFF MY LAWN, RAT.
FOCUS ON *THE MUSIC*, NEIGHBOR BOB.

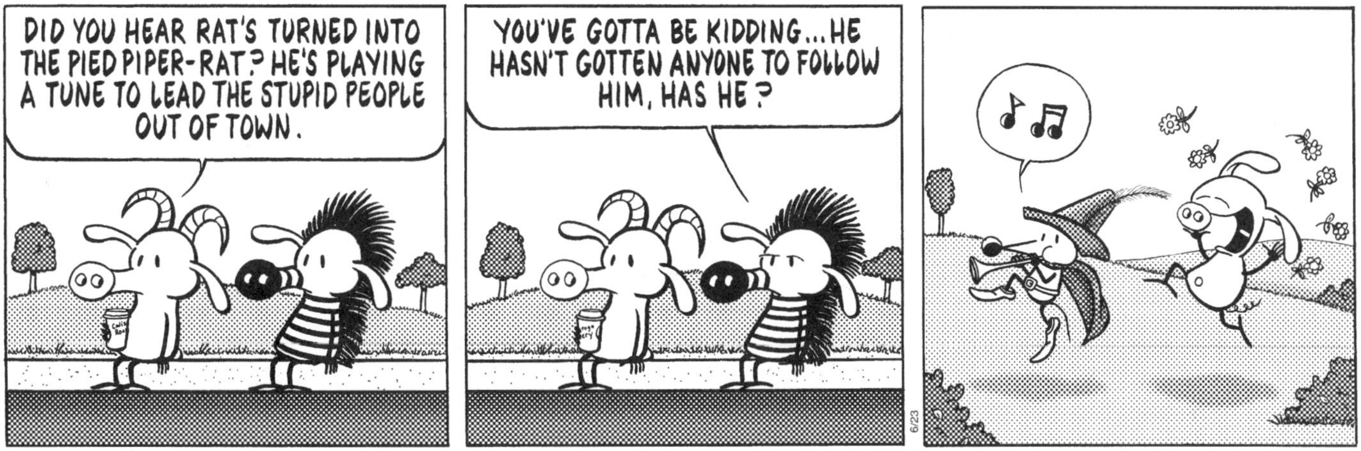
DID YOU HEAR RAT'S TURNED INTO THE PIED PIPER-RAT? HE'S PLAYING A TUNE TO LEAD THE STUPID PEOPLE OUT OF TOWN.
YOU'VE GOTTA BE KIDDING... HE HASN'T GOTTEN ANYONE TO FOLLOW HIM, HAS HE?
6/23

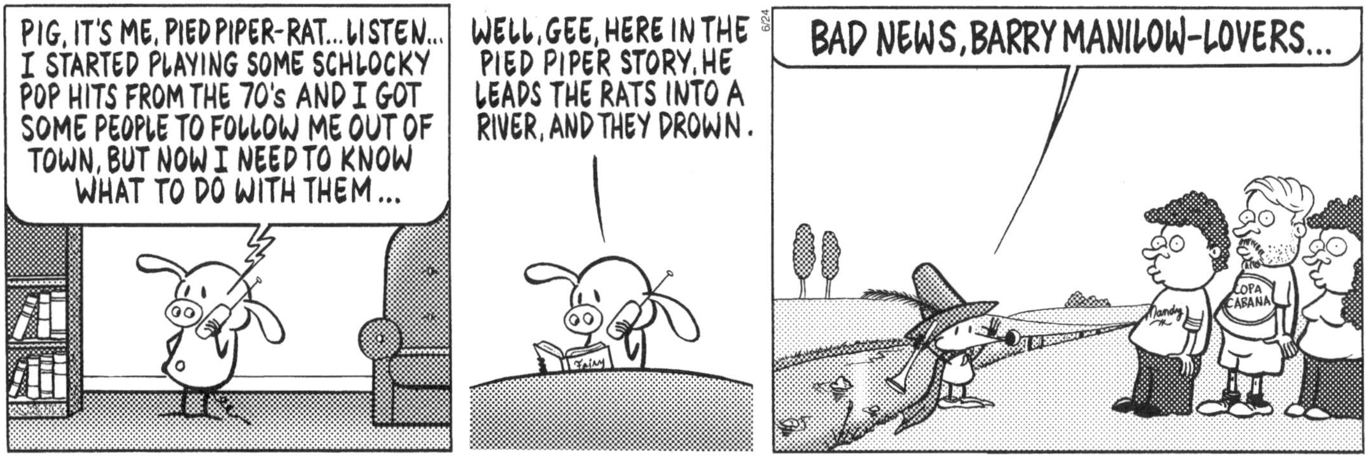
PIG, IT'S ME, PIED PIPER-RAT... LISTEN... I STARTED PLAYING SOME SCHLOCKY POP HITS FROM THE 70's AND I GOT SOME PEOPLE TO FOLLOW ME OUT OF TOWN, BUT NOW I NEED TO KNOW WHAT TO DO WITH THEM...
WELL, GEE, HERE IN THE PIED PIPER STORY, HE LEADS THE RATS INTO A RIVER, AND THEY DROWN.
6/24
BAD NEWS, BARRY MANILOW-LOVERS...
COPA CABANA

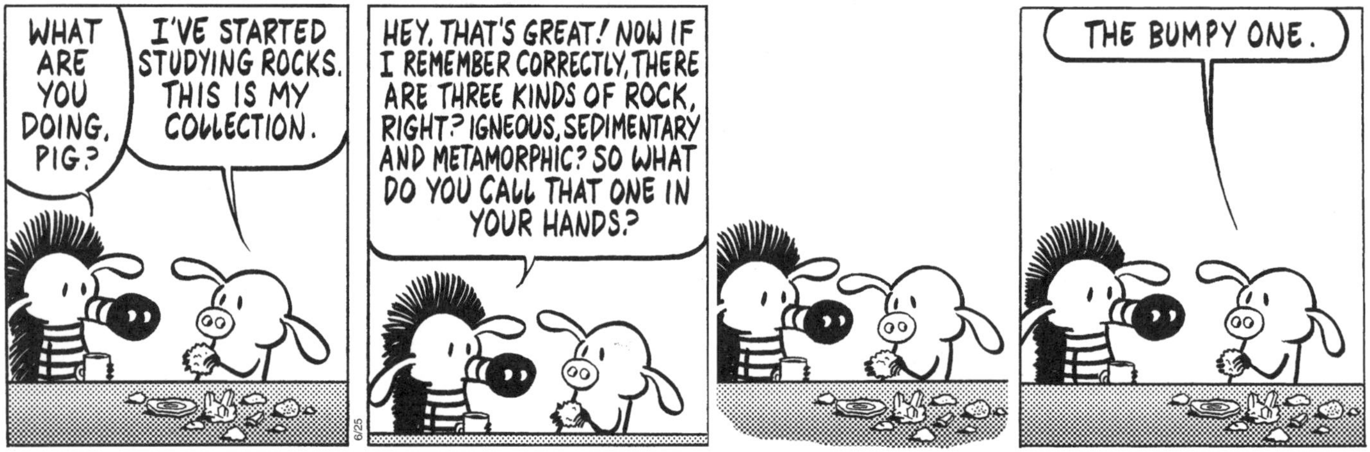
WHAT ARE YOU DOING, PIG?
I'VE STARTED STUDYING ROCKS. THIS IS MY COLLECTION.
6/25
HEY, THAT'S GREAT! NOW IF I REMEMBER CORRECTLY, THERE ARE THREE KINDS OF ROCK, RIGHT? IGNEOUS, SEDIMENTARY AND METAMORPHIC? SO WHAT DO YOU CALL THAT ONE IN YOUR HANDS?
THE BUMPY ONE.

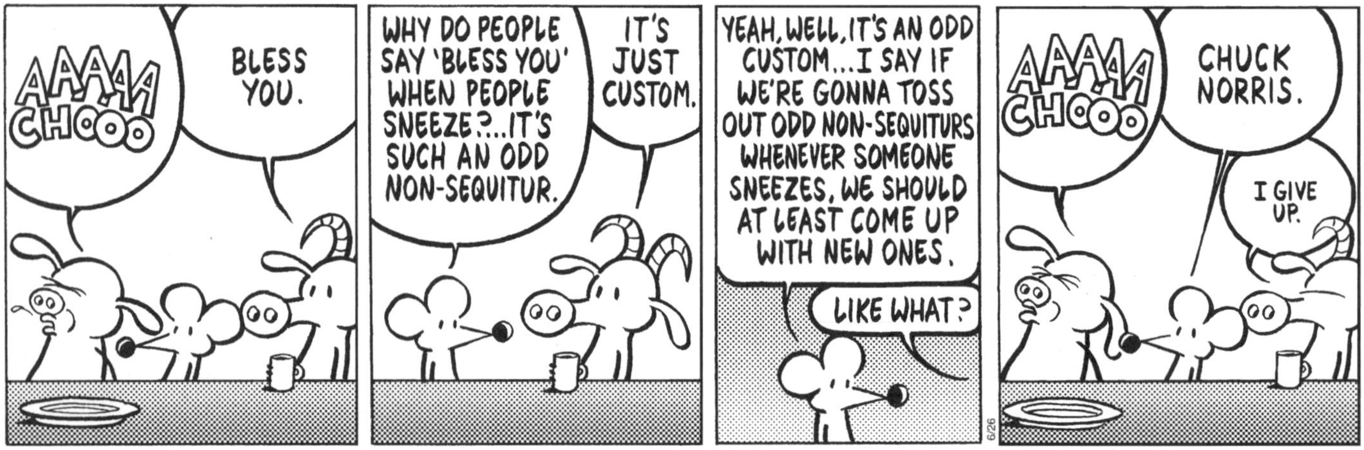
AAAAA CHOOO
BLESS YOU.
WHY DO PEOPLE SAY 'BLESS YOU' WHEN PEOPLE SNEEZE?...IT'S SUCH AN ODD NON-SEQUITUR.
IT'S JUST CUSTOM.
YEAH, WELL, IT'S AN ODD CUSTOM...I SAY IF WE'RE GONNA TOSS OUT ODD NON-SEQUITURS WHENEVER SOMEONE SNEEZES, WE SHOULD AT LEAST COME UP WITH NEW ONES.
LIKE WHAT?
6/26
AAAAA CHOOO
CHUCK NORRIS.
I GIVE UP.

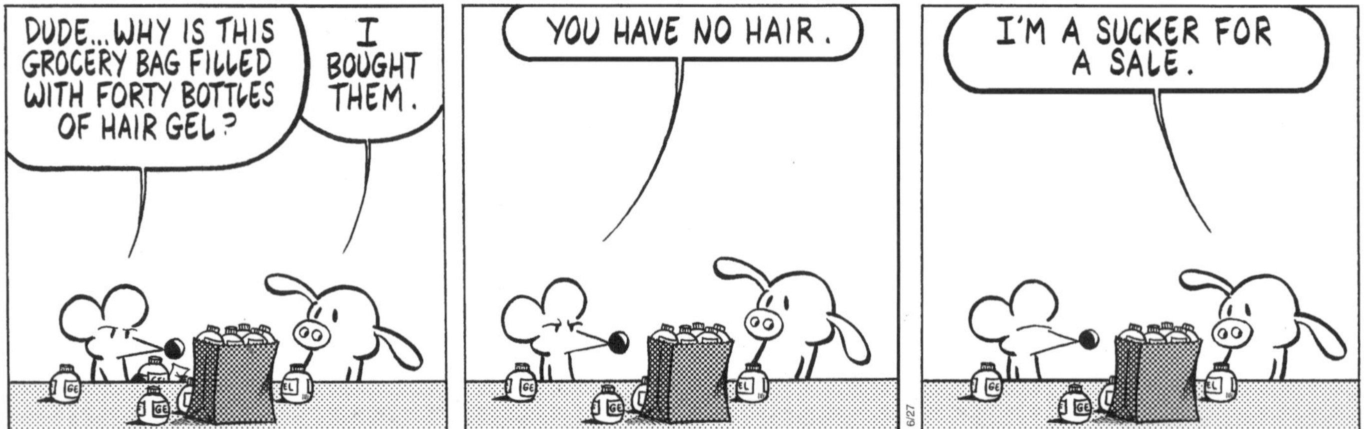
DUDE... WHY IS THIS GROCERY BAG FILLED WITH FORTY BOTTLES OF HAIR GEL?
I BOUGHT THEM.
YOU HAVE NO HAIR.
6/27
I'M A SUCKER FOR A SALE.

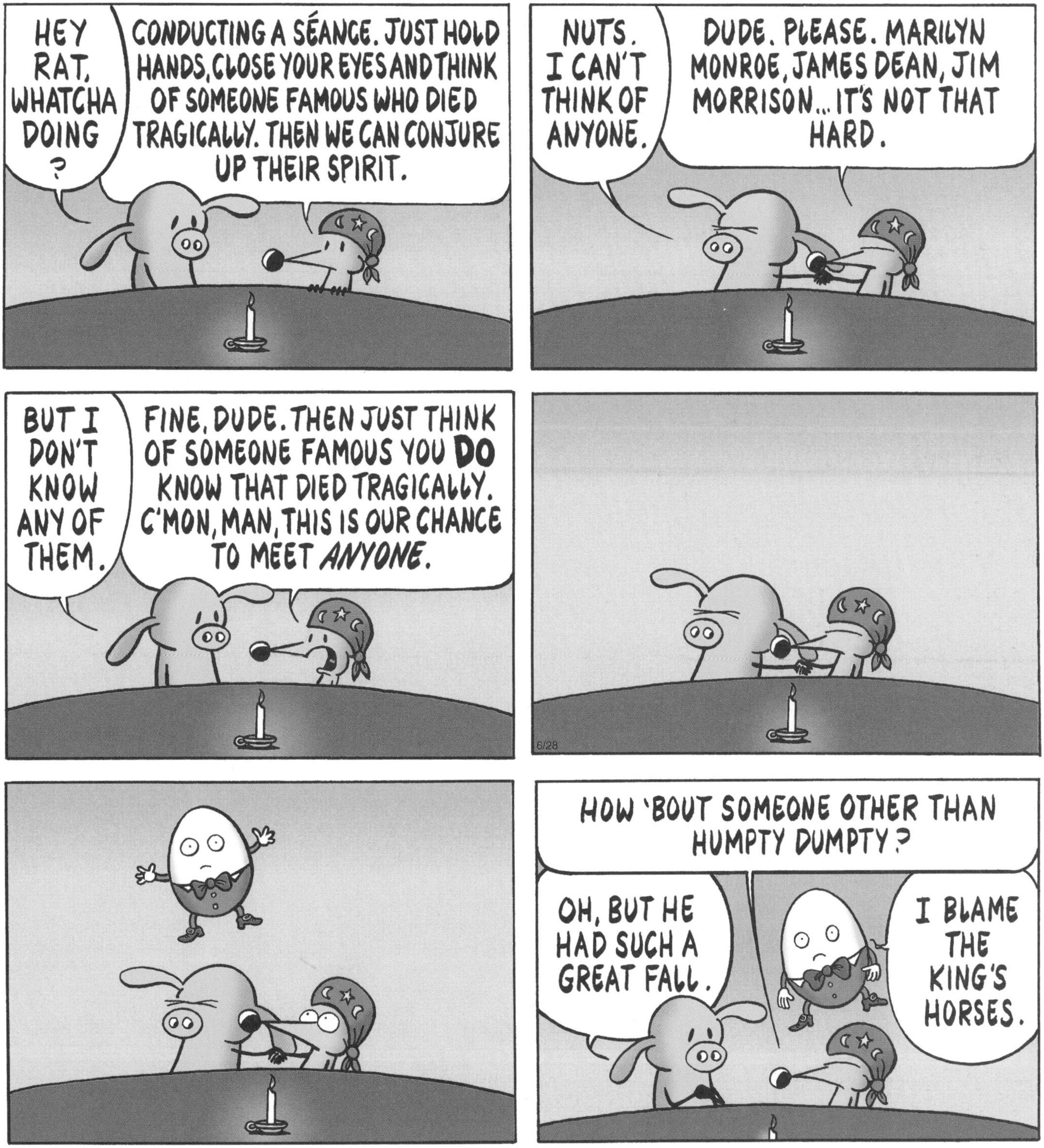
HEY RAT, WHATCHA DOING ?
CONDUCTING A SÉANCE. JUST HOLD HANDS, CLOSE YOUR EYES AND THINK OF SOMEONE FAMOUS WHO DIED TRAGICALLY. THEN WE CAN CONJURE UP THEIR SPIRIT.
NUTS. I CAN'T THINK OF ANYONE.
DUDE. PLEASE. MARILYN MONROE, JAMES DEAN, JIM MORRISON... IT'S NOT THAT HARD.
BUT I DON'T KNOW ANY OF THEM.
FINE, DUDE. THEN JUST THINK OF SOMEONE FAMOUS YOU **DO** KNOW THAT DIED TRAGICALLY. C'MON, MAN, THIS IS OUR CHANCE TO MEET *ANYONE*.
6/28
HOW 'BOUT SOMEONE OTHER THAN HUMPTY DUMPTY ?
OH, BUT HE HAD SUCH A GREAT FALL.
I BLAME THE KING'S HORSES.

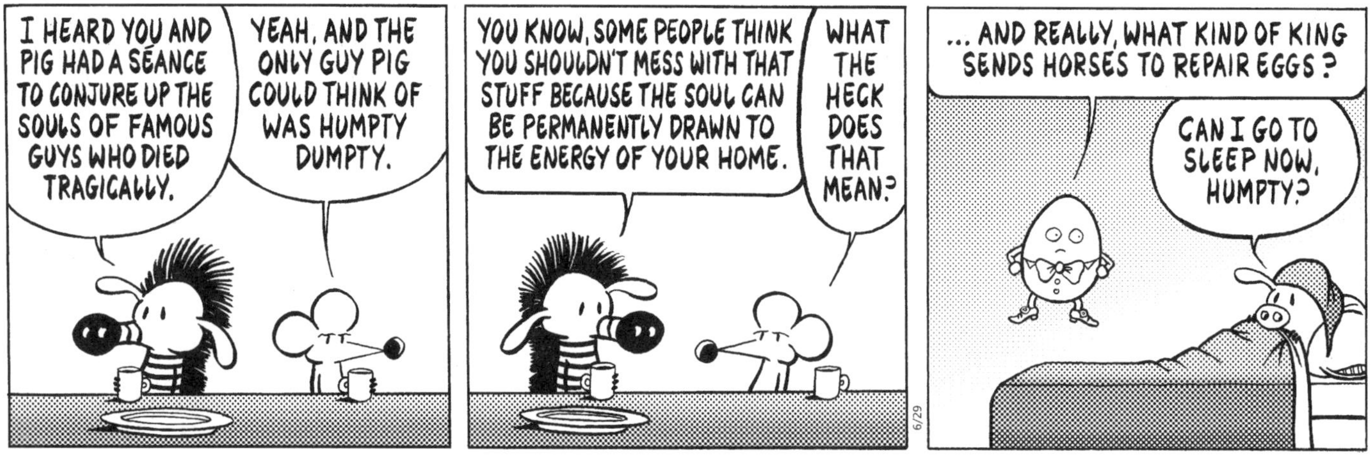
I HEARD YOU AND PIG HAD A SÉANCE TO CONJURE UP THE SOULS OF FAMOUS GUYS WHO DIED TRAGICALLY.
YEAH, AND THE ONLY GUY PIG COULD THINK OF WAS HUMPTY DUMPTY.
YOU KNOW, SOME PEOPLE THINK YOU SHOULDN'T MESS WITH THAT STUFF BECAUSE THE SOUL CAN BE PERMANENTLY DRAWN TO THE ENERGY OF YOUR HOME.
WHAT THE HECK DOES THAT MEAN?
6/29
... AND REALLY, WHAT KIND OF KING SENDS HORSES TO REPAIR EGGS?
CAN I GO TO SLEEP NOW, HUMPTY?

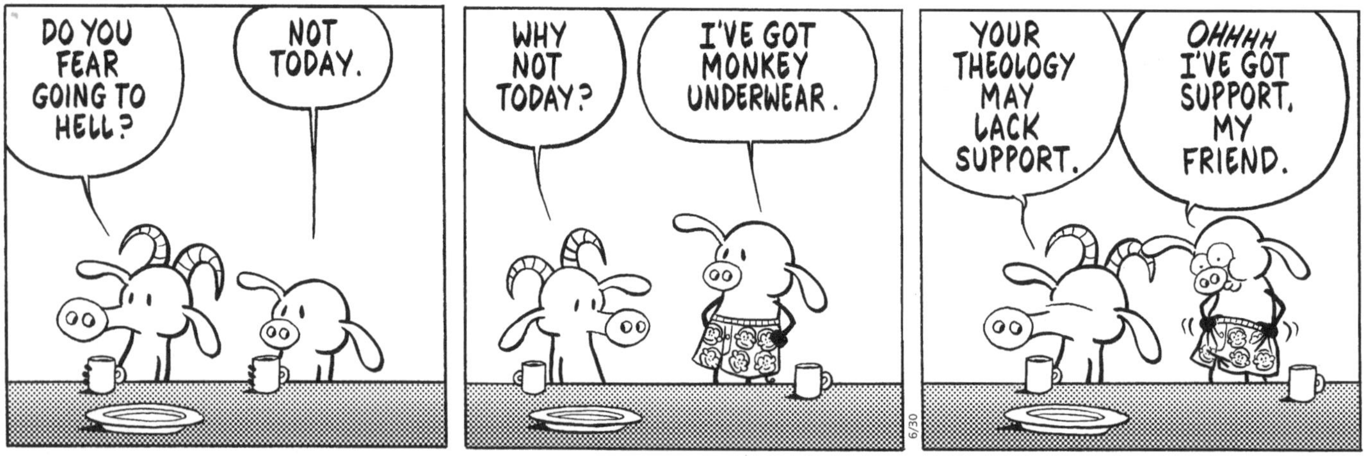
DO YOU FEAR GOING TO HELL?
NOT TODAY.
WHY NOT TODAY?
I'VE GOT MONKEY UNDERWEAR.
6/30
YOUR THEOLOGY MAY LACK SUPPORT.
OHHHH I'VE GOT SUPPORT, MY FRIEND.

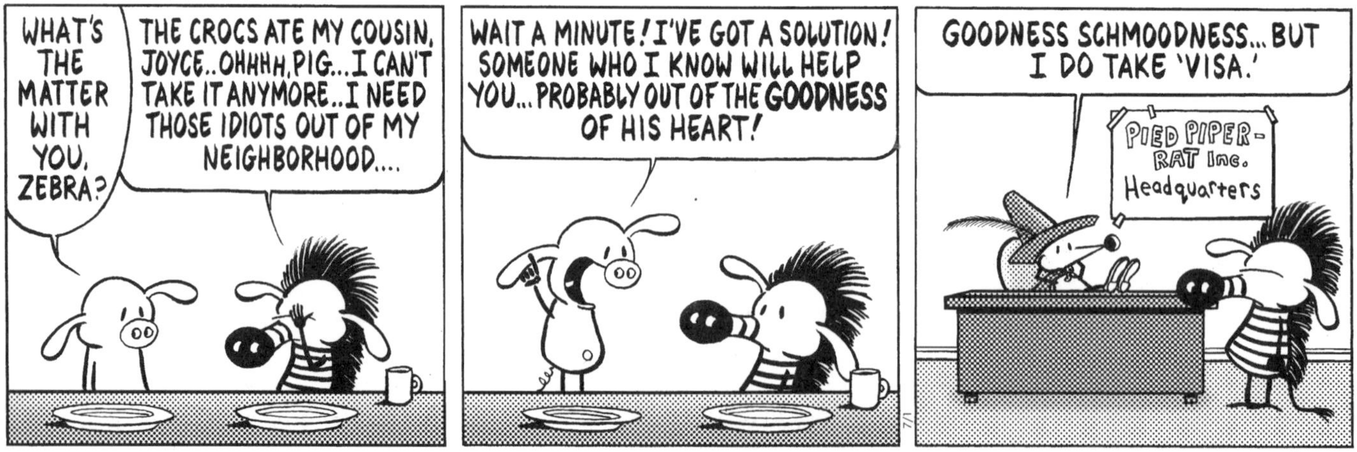
WHAT'S THE MATTER WITH YOU, ZEBRA?
THE CROCS ATE MY COUSIN, JOYCE..OHHHH, PIG...I CAN'T TAKE IT ANYMORE..I NEED THOSE IDIOTS OUT OF MY NEIGHBORHOOD....
WAIT A MINUTE! I'VE GOT A SOLUTION! SOMEONE WHO I KNOW WILL HELP YOU...PROBABLY OUT OF THE GOODNESS OF HIS HEART!
7/1
GOODNESS SCHMOODNESS... BUT I DO TAKE 'VISA.'
PIED PIPER-RAT Inc. Headquarters

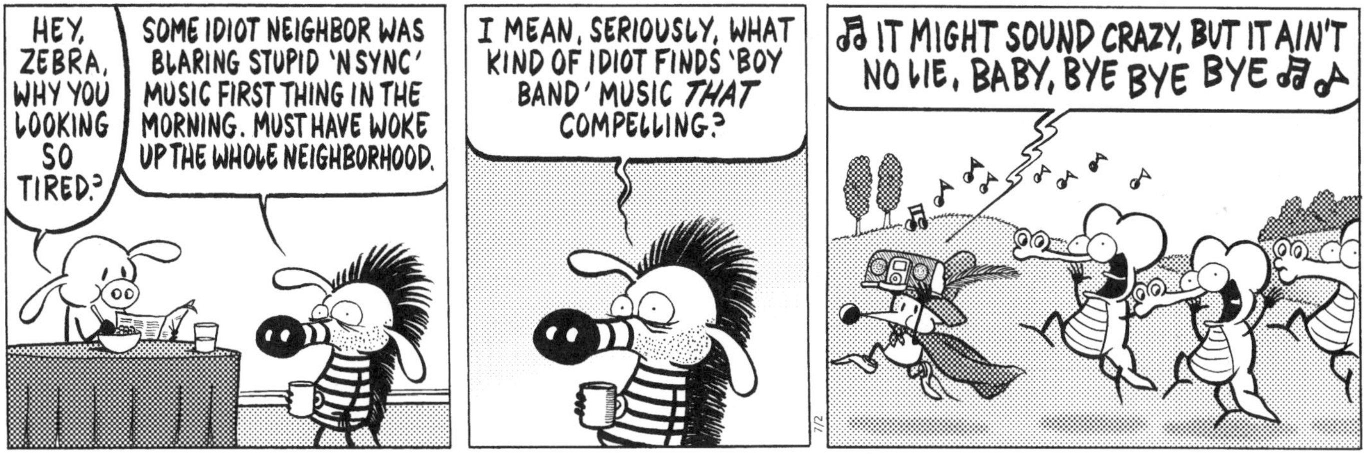
HEY, ZEBRA, WHY YOU LOOKING SO TIRED?
SOME IDIOT NEIGHBOR WAS BLARING STUPID 'N SYNC' MUSIC FIRST THING IN THE MORNING. MUST HAVE WOKE UP THE WHOLE NEIGHBORHOOD.
I MEAN, SERIOUSLY, WHAT KIND OF IDIOT FINDS 'BOY BAND' MUSIC *THAT* COMPELLING?
♫ IT MIGHT SOUND CRAZY, BUT IT AIN'T NO LIE, BABY, BYE BYE BYE ♫♪
7/2

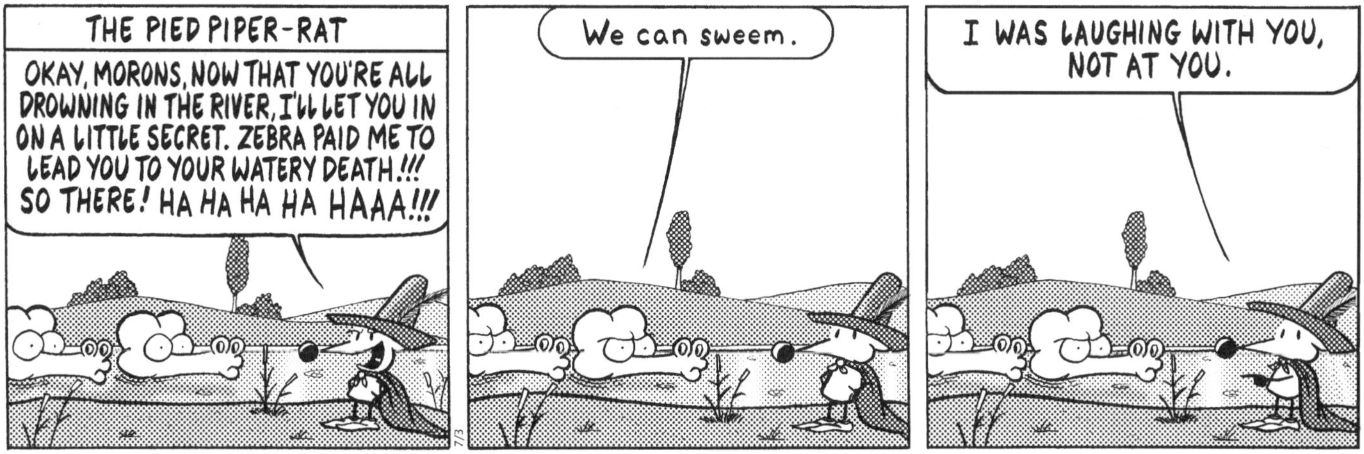
THE PIED PIPER-RAT
OKAY, MORONS, NOW THAT YOU'RE ALL DROWNING IN THE RIVER, I'LL LET YOU IN ON A LITTLE SECRET. ZEBRA PAID ME TO LEAD YOU TO YOUR WATERY DEATH!!! SO THERE! HA HA HA HA HAAA!!!
7/3
We can sweem.
I WAS LAUGHING WITH YOU, NOT AT YOU.

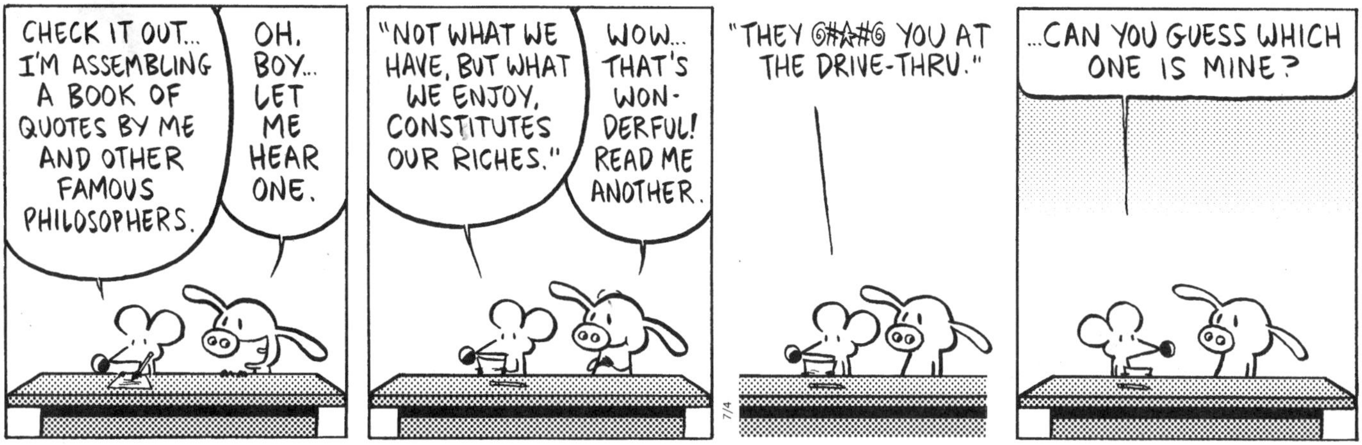
CHECK IT OUT... I'M ASSEMBLING A BOOK OF QUOTES BY ME AND OTHER FAMOUS PHILOSOPHERS.
OH, BOY... LET ME HEAR ONE.
"NOT WHAT WE HAVE, BUT WHAT WE ENJOY, CONSTITUTES OUR RICHES."
WOW... THAT'S WONDERFUL! READ ME ANOTHER.
"THEY @#☆#@ YOU AT THE DRIVE-THRU."
7/4
...CAN YOU GUESS WHICH ONE IS MINE?

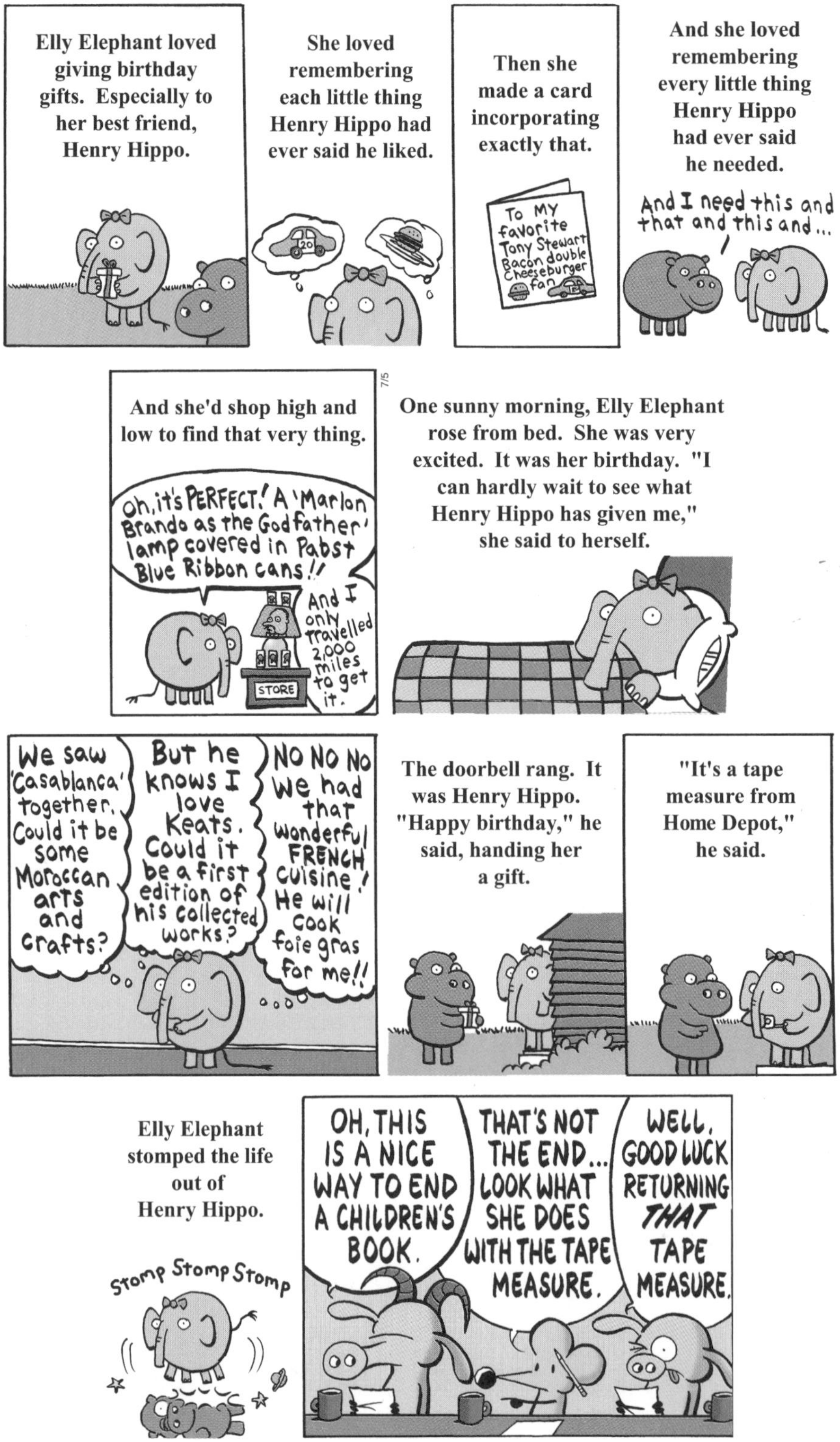
Elly Elephant loved giving birthday gifts. Especially to her best friend, Henry Hippo.
She loved remembering each little thing Henry Hippo had ever said he liked.
20
Then she made a card incorporating exactly that.
To My favorite Tony Stewart Bacon double Cheeseburger fan
And she loved remembering every little thing Henry Hippo had ever said he needed.
And I need this and that and this and...
And she'd shop high and low to find that very thing.
Oh, it's PERFECT! A 'Marlon Brando as the Godfather' lamp covered in Pabst Blue Ribbon cans!!
And I only travelled 2,000 miles to get it.
STORE
7/5
One sunny morning, Elly Elephant rose from bed. She was very excited. It was her birthday. "I can hardly wait to see what Henry Hippo has given me," she said to herself.
We saw 'Casablanca' together. Could it be some Moroccan arts and crafts?
But he knows I love Keats. Could it be a first edition of his collected works?
NO NO NO We had that wonderful FRENCH cuisine! He will cook foie gras for me!!
The doorbell rang. It was Henry Hippo. "Happy birthday," he said, handing her a gift.
"It's a tape measure from Home Depot," he said.
Elly Elephant stomped the life out of Henry Hippo.
Stomp Stomp Stomp
OH, THIS IS A NICE WAY TO END A CHILDREN'S BOOK.
THAT'S NOT THE END... LOOK WHAT SHE DOES WITH THE TAPE MEASURE.
WELL, GOOD LUCK RETURNING *THAT* TAPE MEASURE.

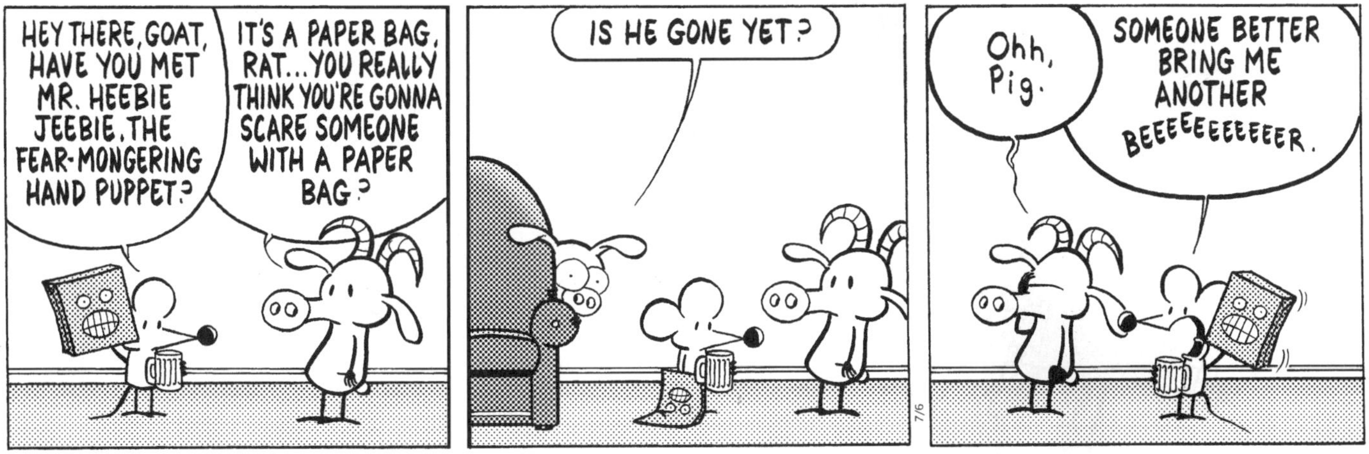
HEY THERE, GOAT, HAVE YOU MET MR. HEEBIE JEEBIE, THE FEAR-MONGERING HAND PUPPET?
IT'S A PAPER BAG, RAT... YOU REALLY THINK YOU'RE GONNA SCARE SOMEONE WITH A PAPER BAG?
IS HE GONE YET?
7/6
Ohh, Pig.
SOMEONE BETTER BRING ME ANOTHER BEEEEEEEEEEEER.

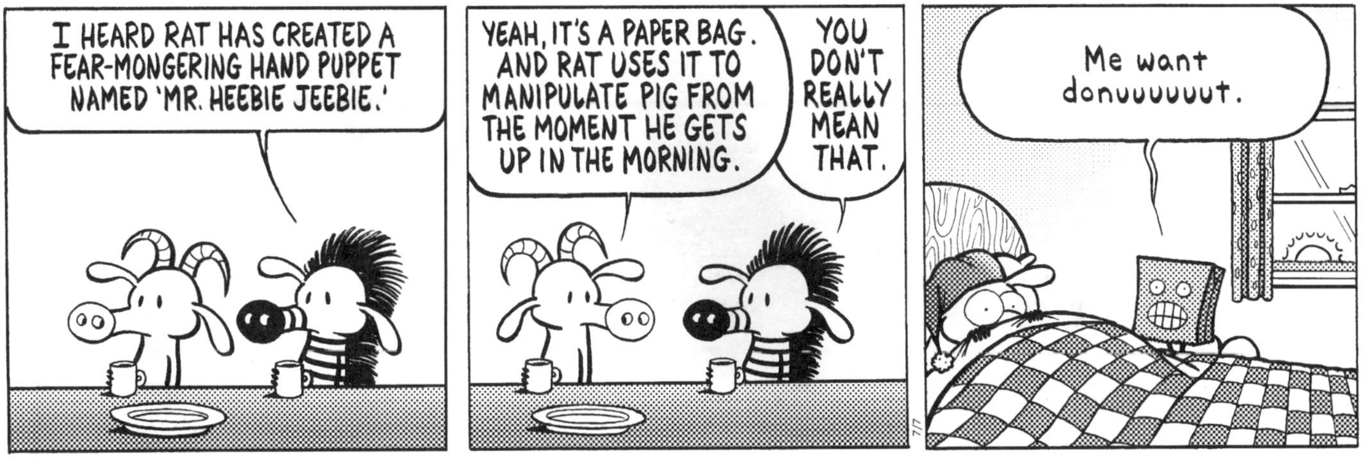
I HEARD RAT HAS CREATED A FEAR-MONGERING HAND PUPPET NAMED 'MR. HEEBIE JEEBIE.'
YEAH, IT'S A PAPER BAG. AND RAT USES IT TO MANIPULATE PIG FROM THE MOMENT HE GETS UP IN THE MORNING.
YOU DON'T REALLY MEAN THAT.
7/7
Me want donuuuuuut.

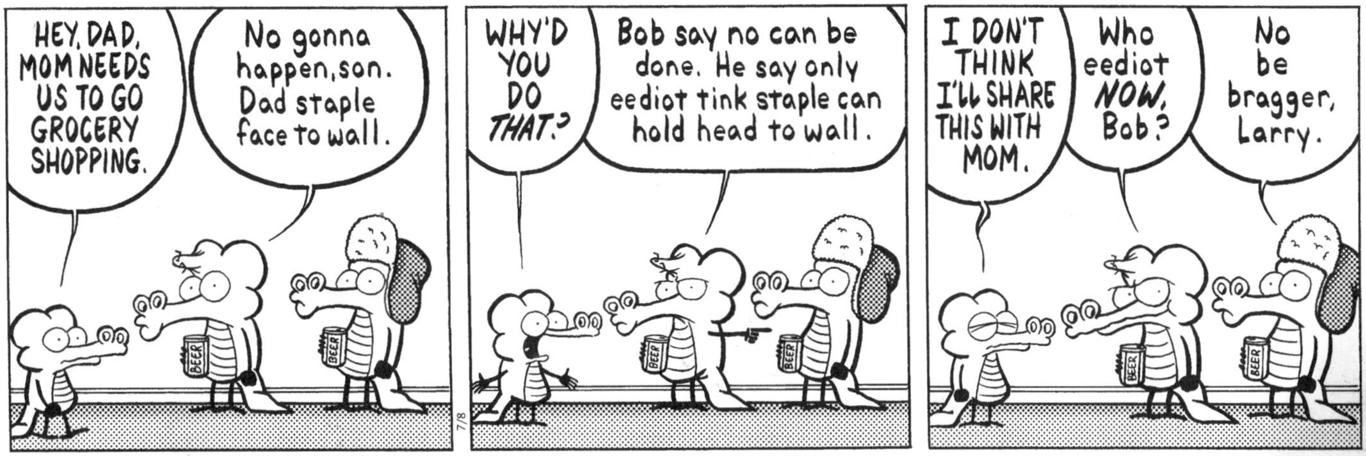
HEY, DAD, MOM NEEDS US TO GO GROCERY SHOPPING.
No gonna happen, son. Dad staple face to wall.
7/8
WHY'D YOU DO *THAT*?
Bob say no can be done. He say only eediot tink staple can hold head to wall.
I DON'T THINK I'LL SHARE THIS WITH MOM.
Who eediot *NOW*, Bob?
No be bragger, Larry.

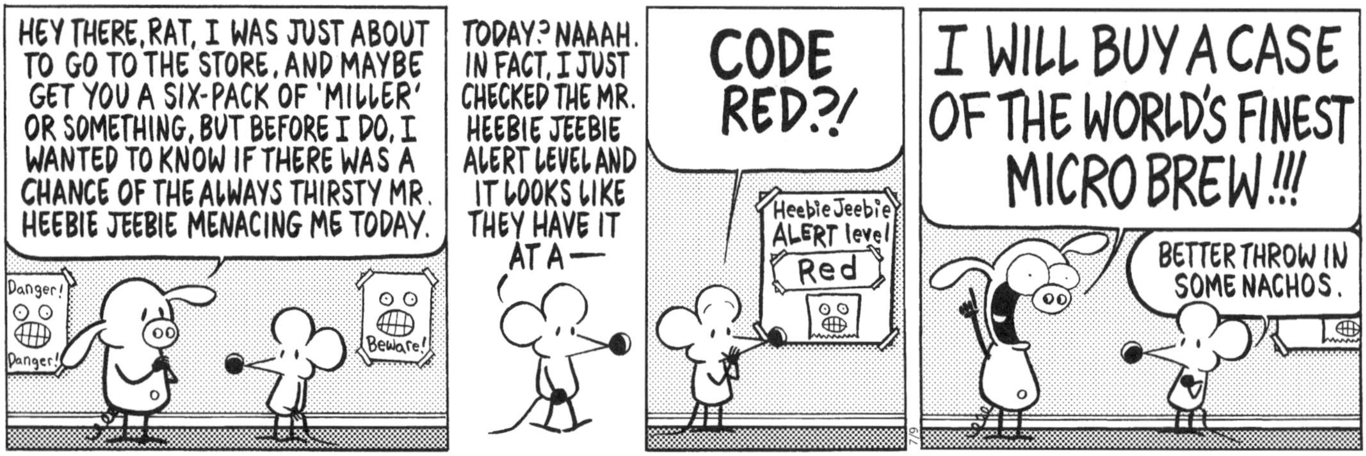
HEY THERE, RAT, I WAS JUST ABOUT TO GO TO THE STORE, AND MAYBE GET YOU A SIX-PACK OF 'MILLER' OR SOMETHING, BUT BEFORE I DO, I WANTED TO KNOW IF THERE WAS A CHANCE OF THE ALWAYS THIRSTY MR. HEEBIE JEEBIE MENACING ME TODAY.
Danger! Danger!
Beware!
TODAY? NAAAH. IN FACT, I JUST CHECKED THE MR. HEEBIE JEEBIE ALERT LEVEL AND IT LOOKS LIKE THEY HAVE IT AT A—
CODE RED?!
Heebie Jeebie ALERT level
Red
I WILL BUY A CASE OF THE WORLD'S FINEST MICRO BREW!!!
BETTER THROW IN SOME NACHOS.
7/9

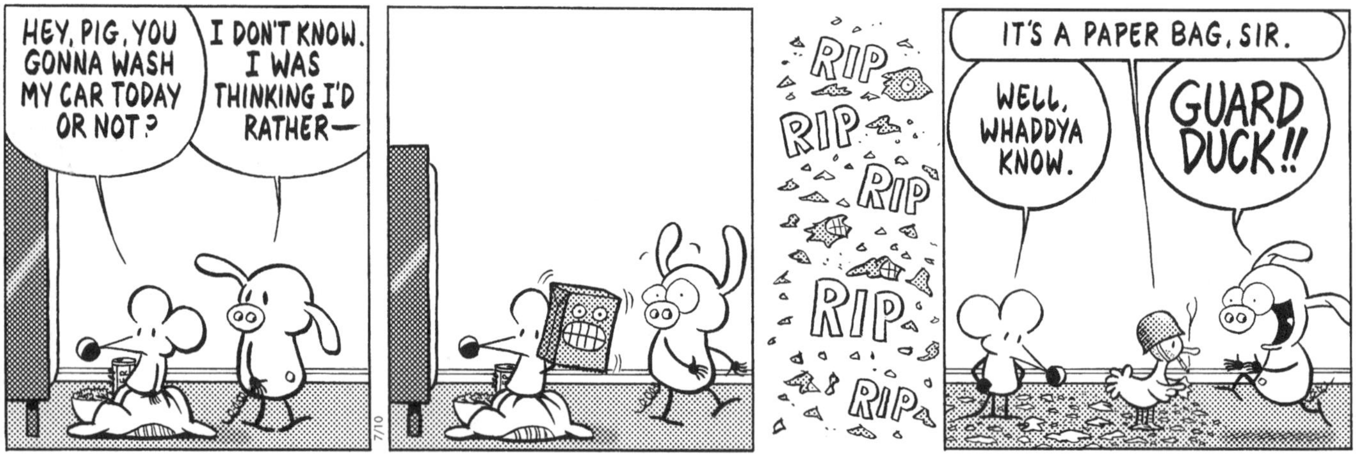
HEY, PIG, YOU GONNA WASH MY CAR TODAY OR NOT?
I DON'T KNOW. I WAS THINKING I'D RATHER—
7/10
RIP
RIP
RIP
RIP
RIP
IT'S A PAPER BAG, SIR.
WELL, WHADDYA KNOW.
GUARD DUCK!!

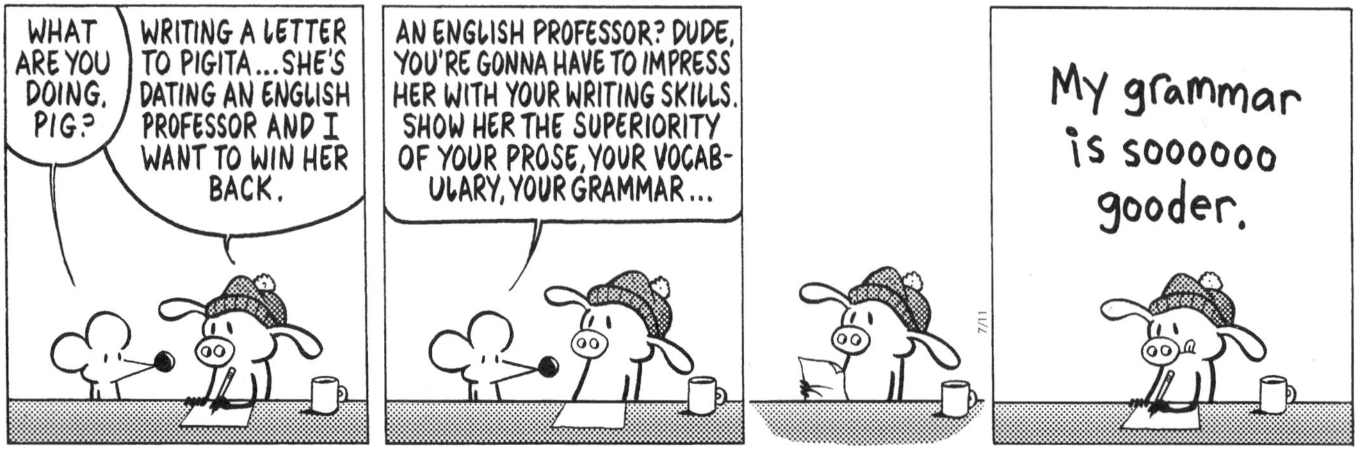
WHAT ARE YOU DOING, PIG?
WRITING A LETTER TO PIGITA... SHE'S DATING AN ENGLISH PROFESSOR AND I WANT TO WIN HER BACK.
AN ENGLISH PROFESSOR? DUDE, YOU'RE GONNA HAVE TO IMPRESS HER WITH YOUR WRITING SKILLS. SHOW HER THE SUPERIORITY OF YOUR PROSE, YOUR VOCABULARY, YOUR GRAMMAR...
7/11
My grammar is soooooo gooder.

OH MY GOSH! LOOK! A BEACHED WHALE! WHAT DO WE DO, ZEBRA? WHAT DO WE DO.?

I'M AFRAID THERE'S NOT MUCH WE CAN DO, PIG. EVEN LARGE BOATS HAVE TROUBLE DRAGGING WHALES BACK INTO THE SEA.

WHY DO WHALES DO THIS?!

NO ONE KNOWS, PIG. THERE ARE THEORIES ABOUT CHASING PREY TOO CLOSE TO SHORE, ECHOLOCATION PROBLEMS, ILLNESS... BUT THE TRUTH IS WE MAY NEVER KNOW WHAT THEY COME OUT OF THE OCEAN FOR.

WHAT DO YOU COME OUT OF THE OCEAN FOR?

7/12

CARAMEL MACCHIATO.

THEY'RE VERY POPULAR DRINKS.

WHOA. I THOUGHT I SAID EXTRA CARAMEL.

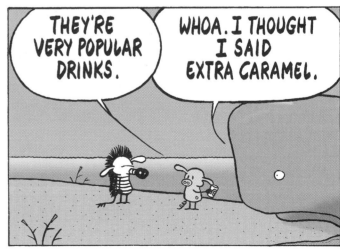

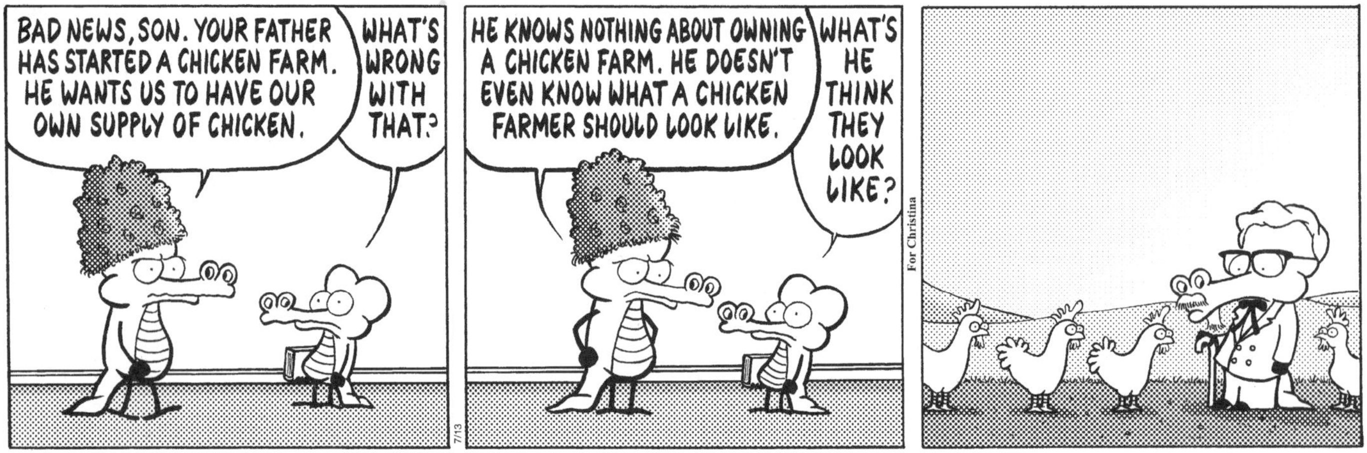
BAD NEWS, SON. YOUR FATHER HAS STARTED A CHICKEN FARM. HE WANTS US TO HAVE OUR OWN SUPPLY OF CHICKEN.
WHAT'S WRONG WITH THAT?
7/13
HE KNOWS NOTHING ABOUT OWNING A CHICKEN FARM. HE DOESN'T EVEN KNOW WHAT A CHICKEN FARMER SHOULD LOOK LIKE.
WHAT'S HE THINK THEY LOOK LIKE?
For Christina

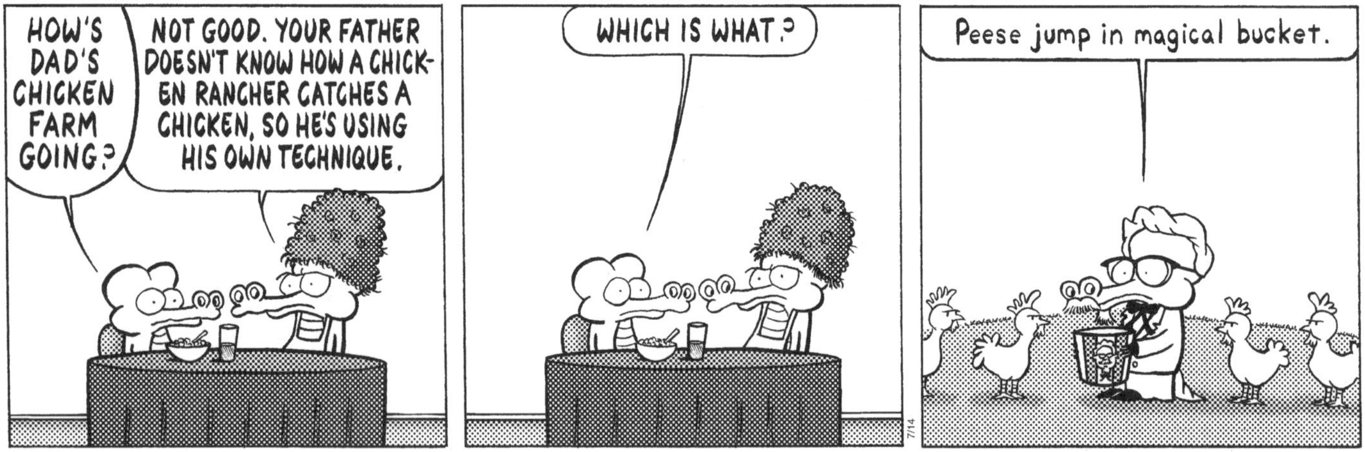
HOW'S DAD'S CHICKEN FARM GOING?
NOT GOOD. YOUR FATHER DOESN'T KNOW HOW A CHICKEN RANCHER CATCHES A CHICKEN, SO HE'S USING HIS OWN TECHNIQUE.
WHICH IS WHAT?
7/14
Peese jump in magical bucket.

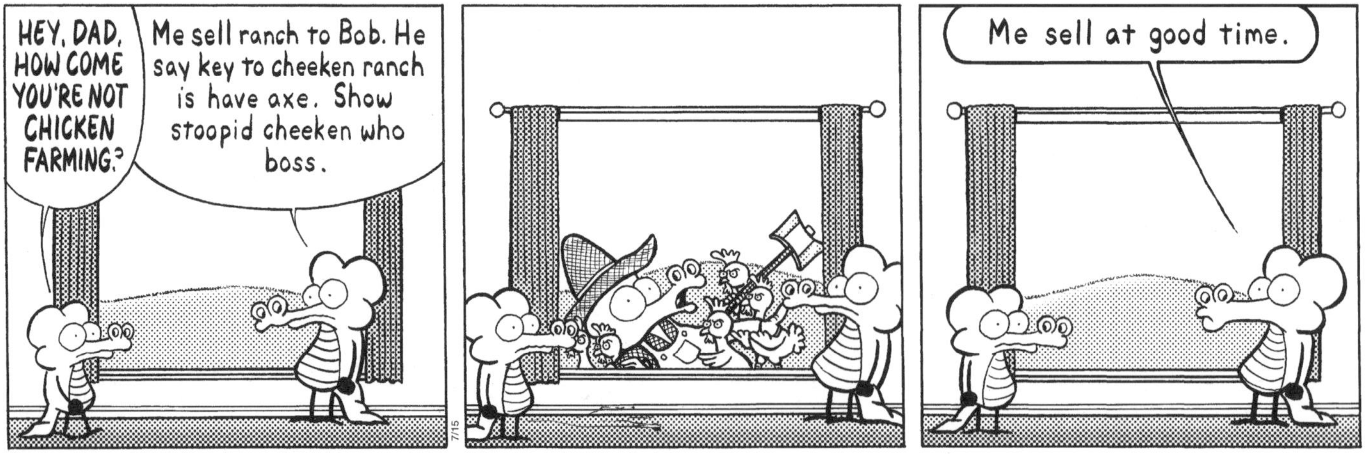
HEY, DAD, HOW COME YOU'RE NOT CHICKEN FARMING?
Me sell ranch to Bob. He say key to cheeken ranch is have axe. Show stoopid cheeken who boss.
7/15
Me sell at good time.

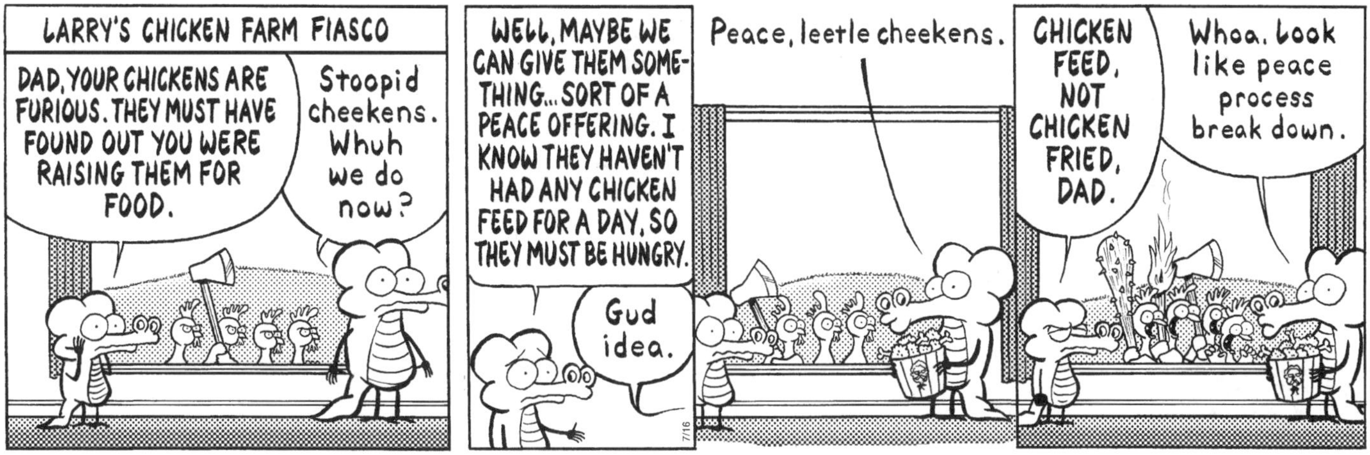
LARRY'S CHICKEN FARM FIASCO
DAD, YOUR CHICKENS ARE FURIOUS. THEY MUST HAVE FOUND OUT YOU WERE RAISING THEM FOR FOOD.
Stoopid cheekens. Whuh we do now?
WELL, MAYBE WE CAN GIVE THEM SOMETHING... SORT OF A PEACE OFFERING. I KNOW THEY HAVEN'T HAD ANY CHICKEN FEED FOR A DAY, SO THEY MUST BE HUNGRY.
Gud idea.
7/16
Peace, leetle cheekens.
CHICKEN FEED, NOT CHICKEN FRIED, DAD.
Whoa. Look like peace process break down.

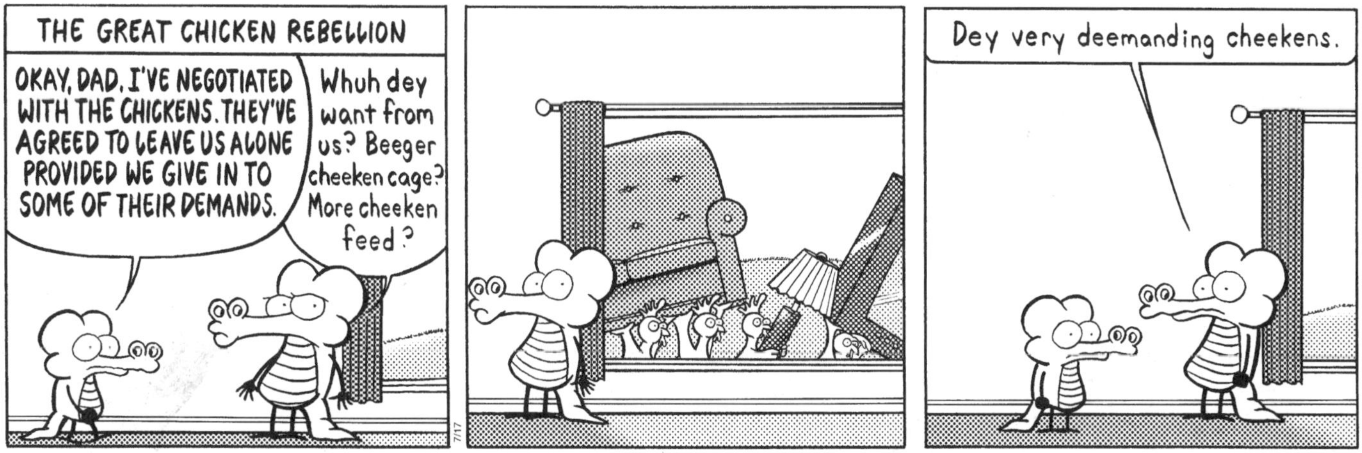
THE GREAT CHICKEN REBELLION
OKAY, DAD, I'VE NEGOTIATED WITH THE CHICKENS. THEY'VE AGREED TO LEAVE US ALONE PROVIDED WE GIVE IN TO SOME OF THEIR DEMANDS.
Whuh dey want from us? Beeger cheeken cage? More cheeken feed?
7/17
Dey very deemanding cheekens.

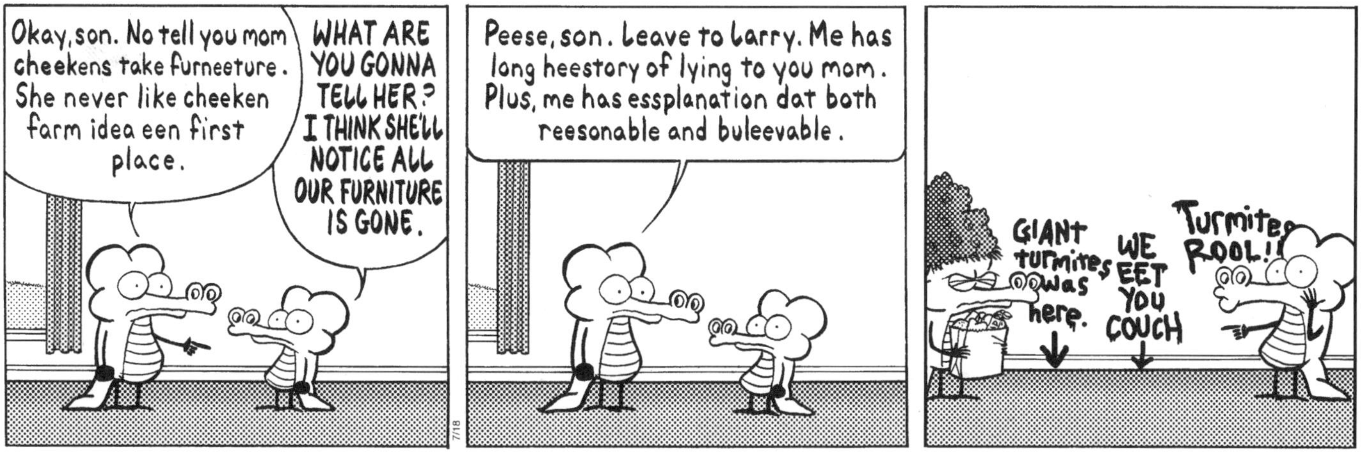
Okay, son. No tell you mom cheekens take furneeture. She never like cheeken farm idea een first place.
WHAT ARE YOU GONNA TELL HER? I THINK SHE'LL NOTICE ALL OUR FURNITURE IS GONE.
7/18
Peese, son. Leave to Larry. Me has long heestory of lying to you mom. Plus, me has essplanation dat both reesonable and buleevable.
GIANT turmites was here.
WE EET YOU COUCH
Turmites ROOL!!

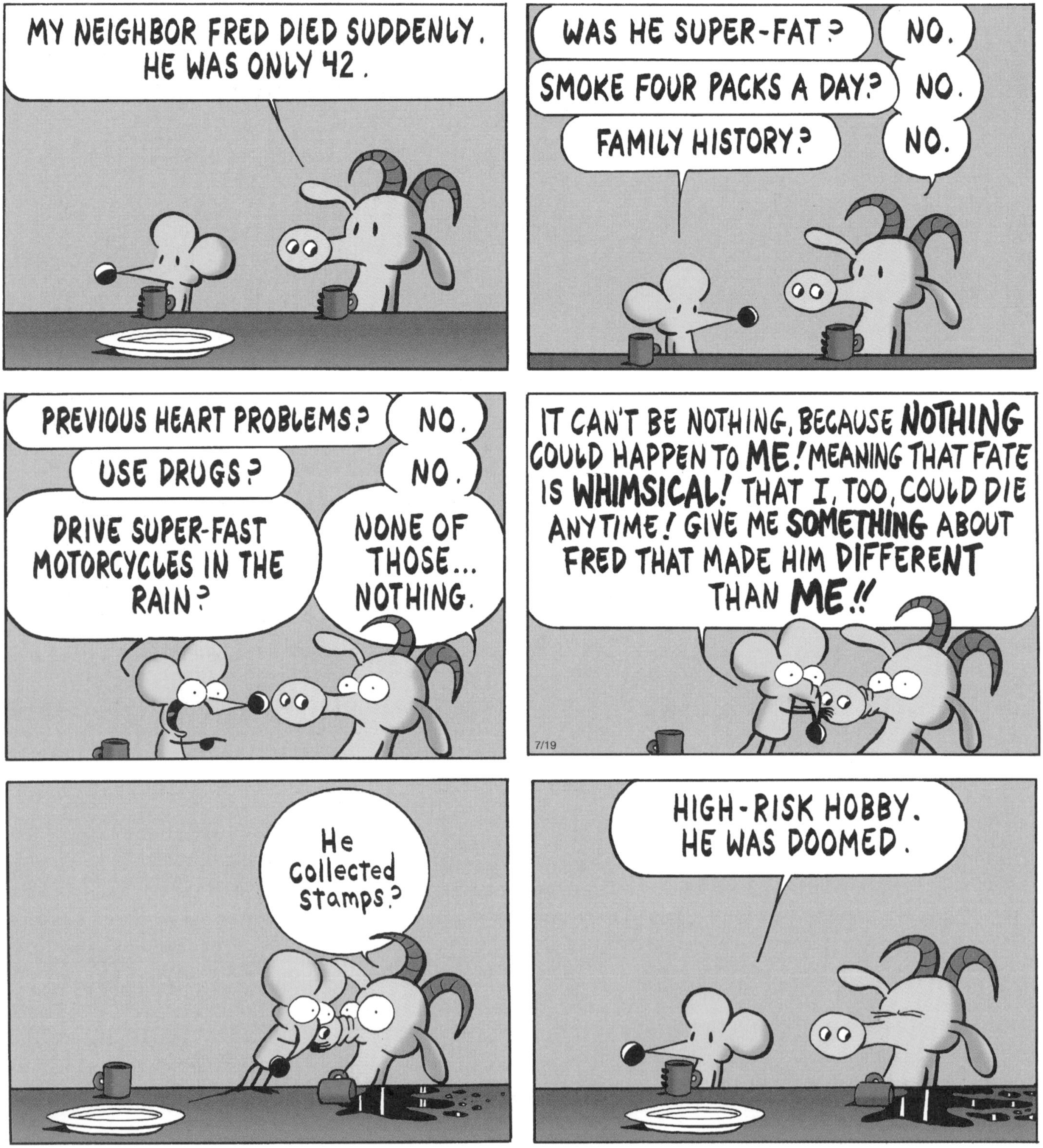

MY NEIGHBOR FRED DIED SUDDENLY. HE WAS ONLY 42.
WAS HE SUPER-FAT?
NO.
SMOKE FOUR PACKS A DAY?
NO.
FAMILY HISTORY?
NO.
PREVIOUS HEART PROBLEMS?
NO.
USE DRUGS?
NO.
DRIVE SUPER-FAST MOTORCYCLES IN THE RAIN?
NONE OF THOSE... NOTHING.
IT CAN'T BE NOTHING, BECAUSE NOTHING COULD HAPPEN TO ME! MEANING THAT FATE IS WHIMSICAL! THAT I, TOO, COULD DIE ANYTIME! GIVE ME SOMETHING ABOUT FRED THAT MADE HIM DIFFERENT THAN ME!!
7/19
He collected stamps?
HIGH-RISK HOBBY. HE WAS DOOMED.

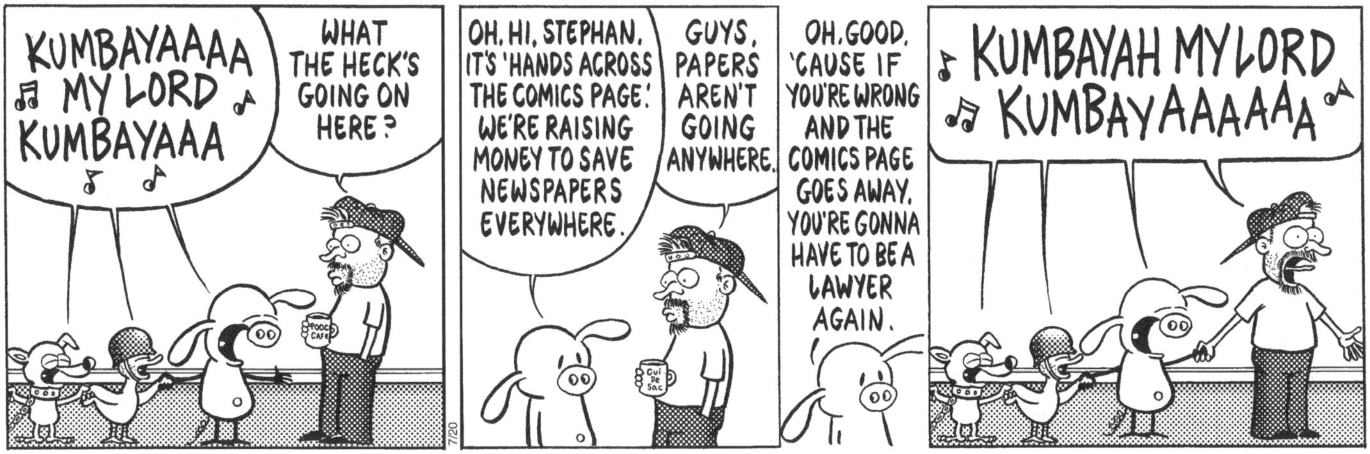
KUMBAYAAAA MY LORD KUMBAYAAA
WHAT THE HECK'S GOING ON HERE?
7/20
OH, HI, STEPHAN. IT'S 'HANDS ACROSS THE COMICS PAGE.' WE'RE RAISING MONEY TO SAVE NEWSPAPERS EVERYWHERE.
GUYS, PAPERS AREN'T GOING ANYWHERE.
OH, GOOD. 'CAUSE IF YOU'RE WRONG AND THE COMICS PAGE GOES AWAY, YOU'RE GONNA HAVE TO BE A LAWYER AGAIN.
KUMBAYAH MY LORD KUMBAYAAAAAA

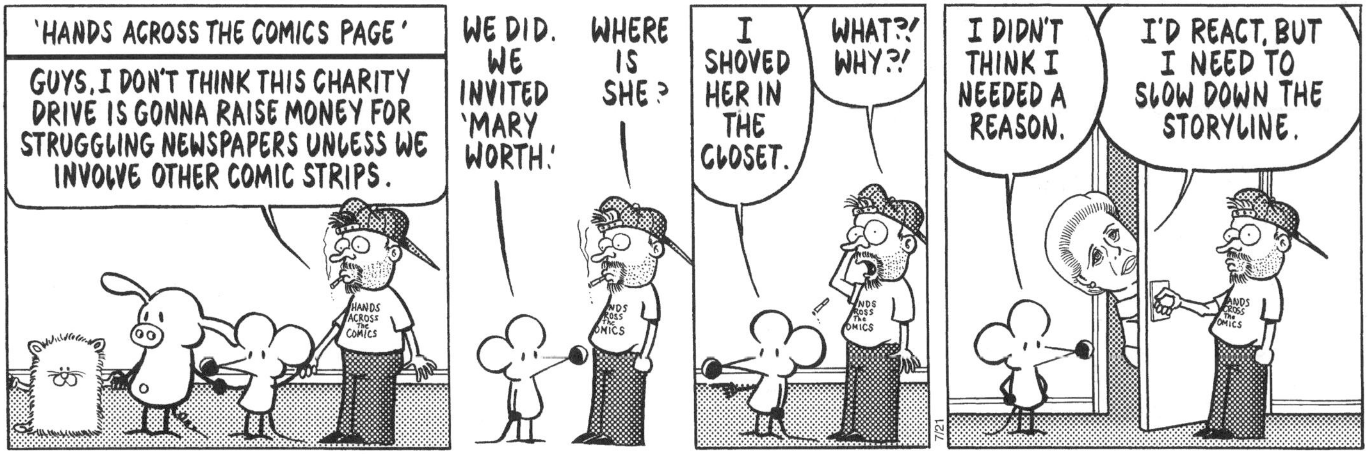
'HANDS ACROSS THE COMICS PAGE'
GUYS, I DON'T THINK THIS CHARITY DRIVE IS GONNA RAISE MONEY FOR STRUGGLING NEWSPAPERS UNLESS WE INVOLVE OTHER COMIC STRIPS.
HANDS ACROSS THE COMICS
WE DID. WE INVITED 'MARY WORTH.'
WHERE IS SHE?
I SHOVED HER IN THE CLOSET.
WHAT?! WHY?!
7/21
I DIDN'T THINK I NEEDED A REASON.
I'D REACT, BUT I NEED TO SLOW DOWN THE STORYLINE.

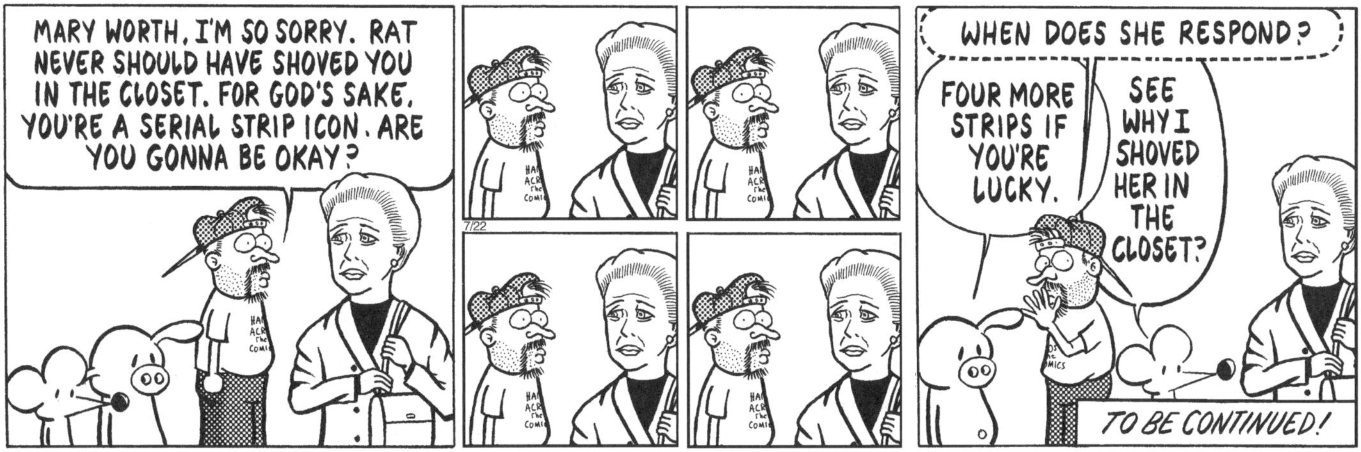
MARY WORTH, I'M SO SORRY. RAT NEVER SHOULD HAVE SHOVED YOU IN THE CLOSET. FOR GOD'S SAKE, YOU'RE A SERIAL STRIP ICON. ARE YOU GONNA BE OKAY?
7/22
WHEN DOES SHE RESPOND?
FOUR MORE STRIPS IF YOU'RE LUCKY.
SEE WHY I SHOVED HER IN THE CLOSET?
TO BE CONTINUED!

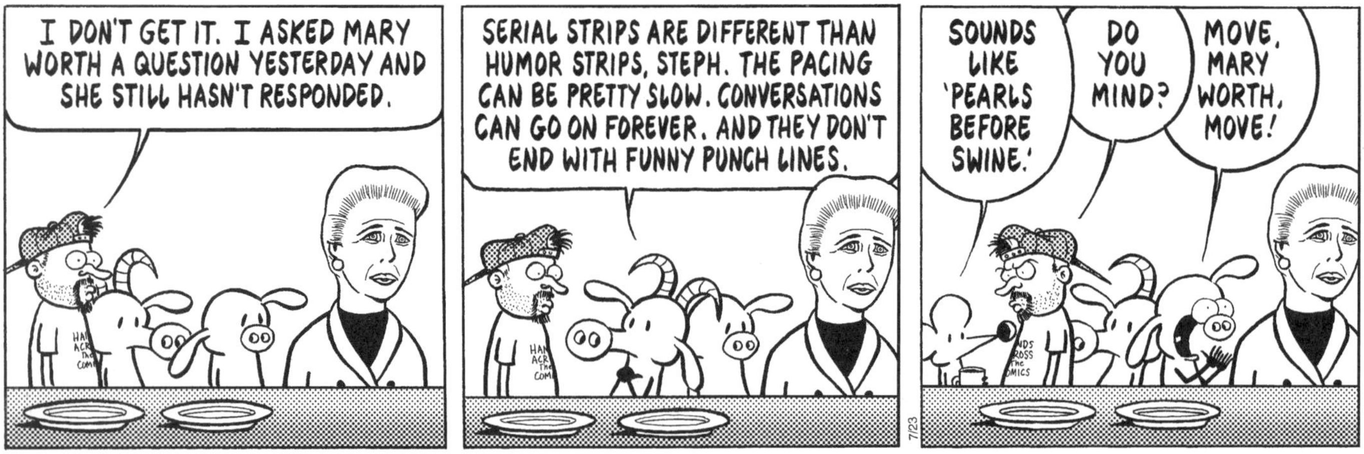
I DON'T GET IT. I ASKED MARY WORTH A QUESTION YESTERDAY AND SHE STILL HASN'T RESPONDED.
SERIAL STRIPS ARE DIFFERENT THAN HUMOR STRIPS, STEPH. THE PACING CAN BE PRETTY SLOW. CONVERSATIONS CAN GO ON FOREVER. AND THEY DON'T END WITH FUNNY PUNCH LINES.
7/23
SOUNDS LIKE 'PEARLS BEFORE SWINE.'
DO YOU MIND?
MOVE, MARY WORTH, MOVE!

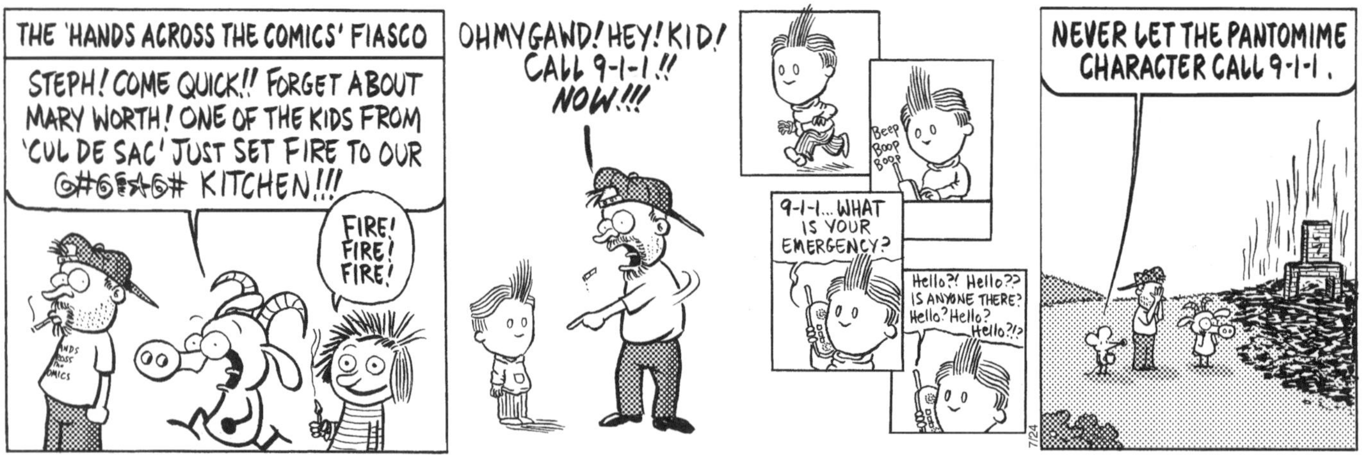
THE 'HANDS ACROSS THE COMICS' FIASCO
STEPH! COME QUICK!! FORGET ABOUT MARY WORTH! ONE OF THE KIDS FROM 'CUL DE SAC' JUST SET FIRE TO OUR @#$%&# KITCHEN!!!
FIRE! FIRE! FIRE!
OHMYGAWD! HEY! KID! CALL 9-1-1!! NOW!!!
Beep Boop Boop
9-1-1... WHAT IS YOUR EMERGENCY?
Hello?! Hello?? IS ANYONE THERE? Hello? Hello? Hello?!?
7/24
NEVER LET THE PANTOMIME CHARACTER CALL 9-1-1.

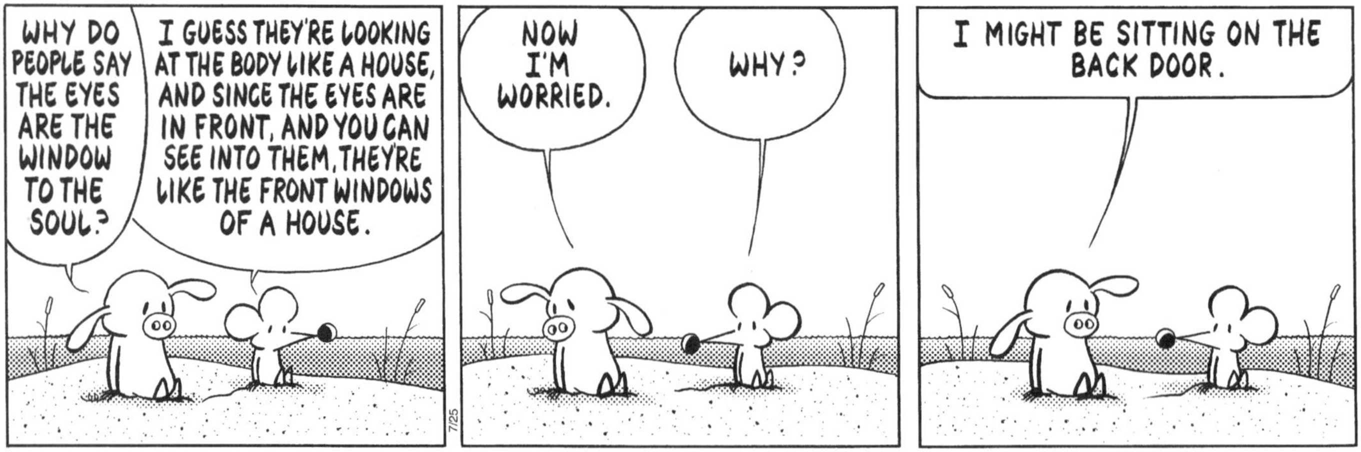
WHY DO PEOPLE SAY THE EYES ARE THE WINDOW TO THE SOUL?
I GUESS THEY'RE LOOKING AT THE BODY LIKE A HOUSE, AND SINCE THE EYES ARE IN FRONT, AND YOU CAN SEE INTO THEM, THEY'RE LIKE THE FRONT WINDOWS OF A HOUSE.
7/25
NOW I'M WORRIED.
WHY?
I MIGHT BE SITTING ON THE BACK DOOR.

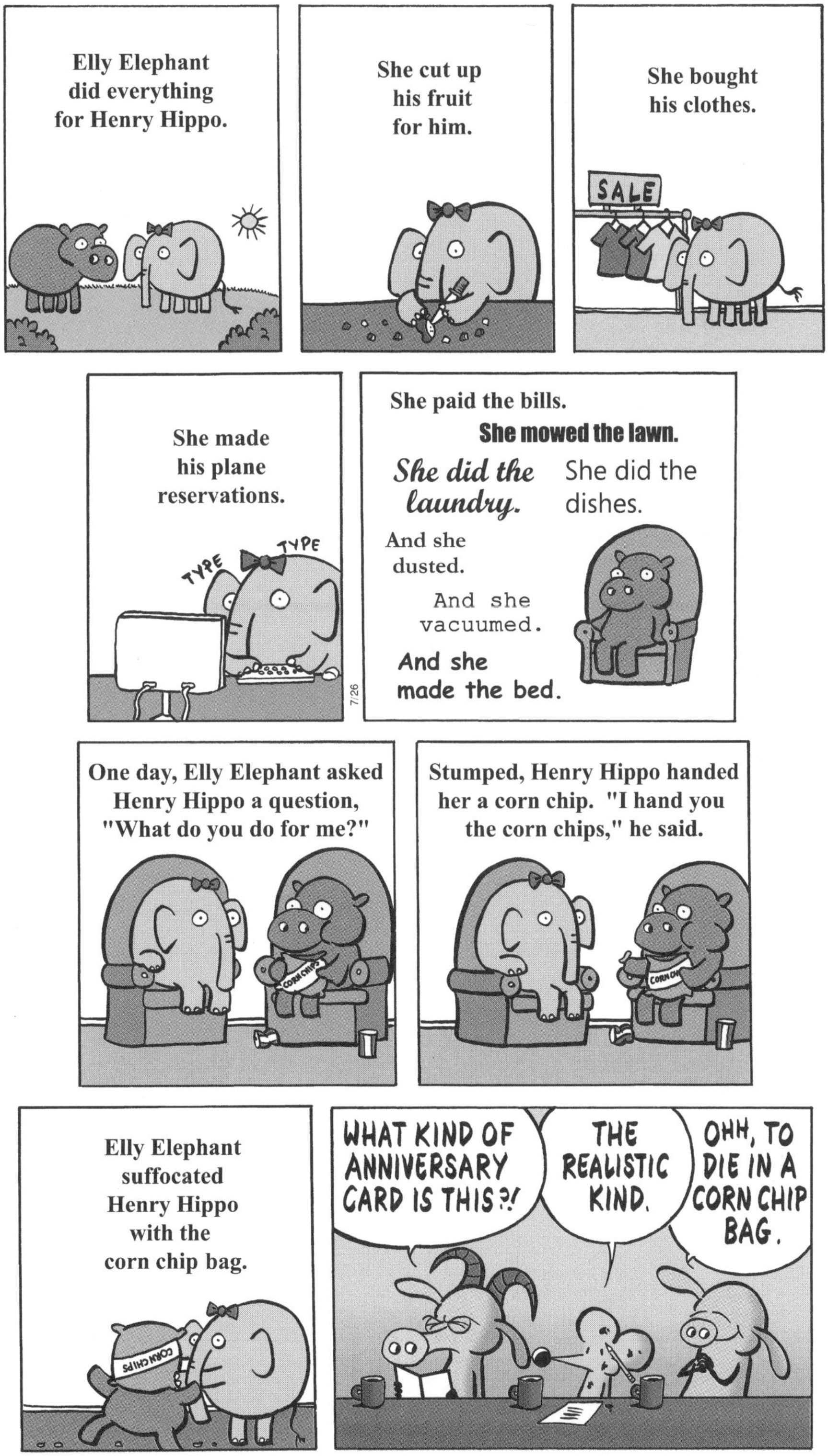
Elly Elephant did everything for Henry Hippo.
She cut up his fruit for him.
She bought his clothes.
SALE
She made his plane reservations.
TYPE
TYPE
7/26
She paid the bills.
She mowed the lawn.
She did the laundry.
She did the dishes.
And she dusted.
And she vacuumed.
And she made the bed.
One day, Elly Elephant asked Henry Hippo a question, "What do you do for me?"
CORN CHIPS
Stumped, Henry Hippo handed her a corn chip. "I hand you the corn chips," he said.
Elly Elephant suffocated Henry Hippo with the corn chip bag.
CORN CHIPS
WHAT KIND OF ANNIVERSARY CARD IS THIS?!
THE REALISTIC KIND.
OHH, TO DIE IN A CORN CHIP BAG.

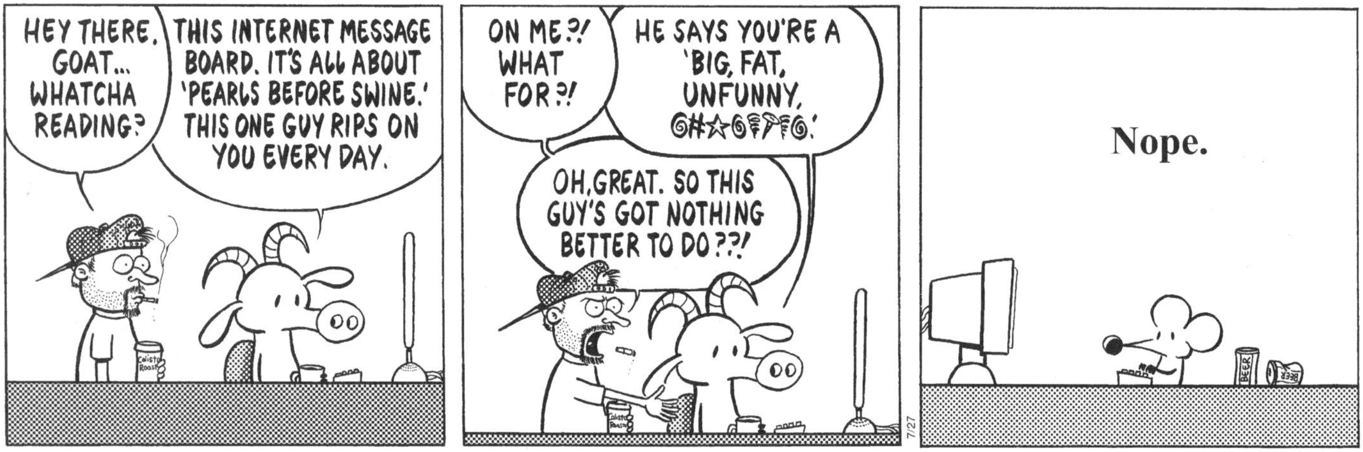
HEY THERE, GOAT... WHATCHA READING?
THIS INTERNET MESSAGE BOARD. IT'S ALL ABOUT 'PEARLS BEFORE SWINE.' THIS ONE GUY RIPS ON YOU EVERY DAY.
ON ME?! WHAT FOR?!
HE SAYS YOU'RE A 'BIG, FAT, UNFUNNY,
OH, GREAT. SO THIS GUY'S GOT NOTHING BETTER TO DO??!
Nope.
BEER
7/27

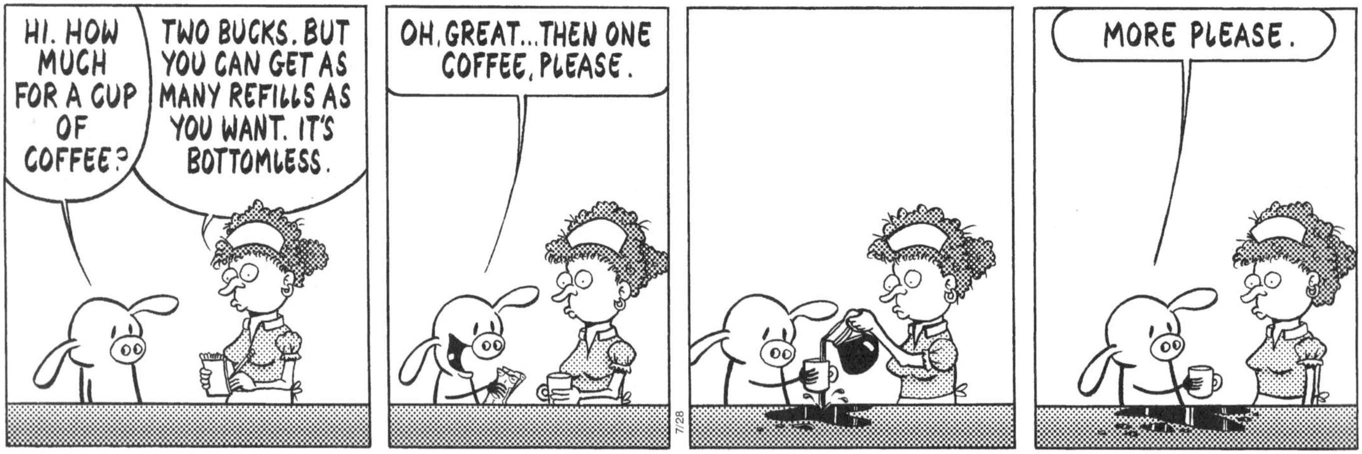
HI. HOW MUCH FOR A CUP OF COFFEE?
TWO BUCKS. BUT YOU CAN GET AS MANY REFILLS AS YOU WANT. IT'S BOTTOMLESS.
OH, GREAT... THEN ONE COFFEE, PLEASE.
MORE PLEASE.
7/28

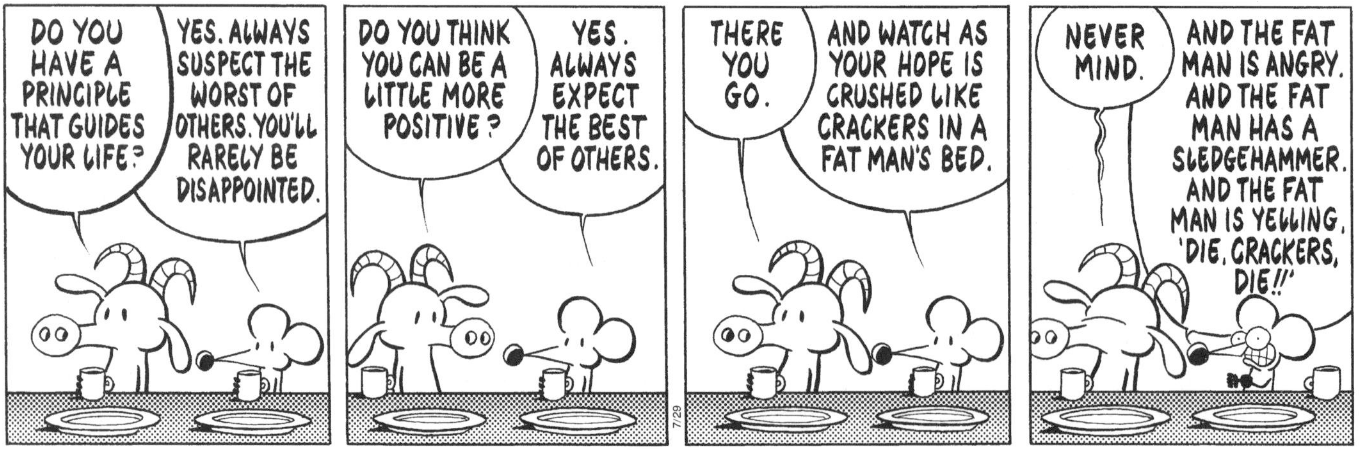
DO YOU HAVE A PRINCIPLE THAT GUIDES YOUR LIFE?
YES. ALWAYS SUSPECT THE WORST OF OTHERS. YOU'LL RARELY BE DISAPPOINTED.
DO YOU THINK YOU CAN BE A LITTLE MORE POSITIVE?
YES. ALWAYS EXPECT THE BEST OF OTHERS.
THERE YOU GO.
AND WATCH AS YOUR HOPE IS CRUSHED LIKE CRACKERS IN A FAT MAN'S BED.
NEVER MIND.
AND THE FAT MAN IS ANGRY. AND THE FAT MAN HAS A SLEDGEHAMMER. AND THE FAT MAN IS YELLING, 'DIE, CRACKERS, DIE!!'
7/29

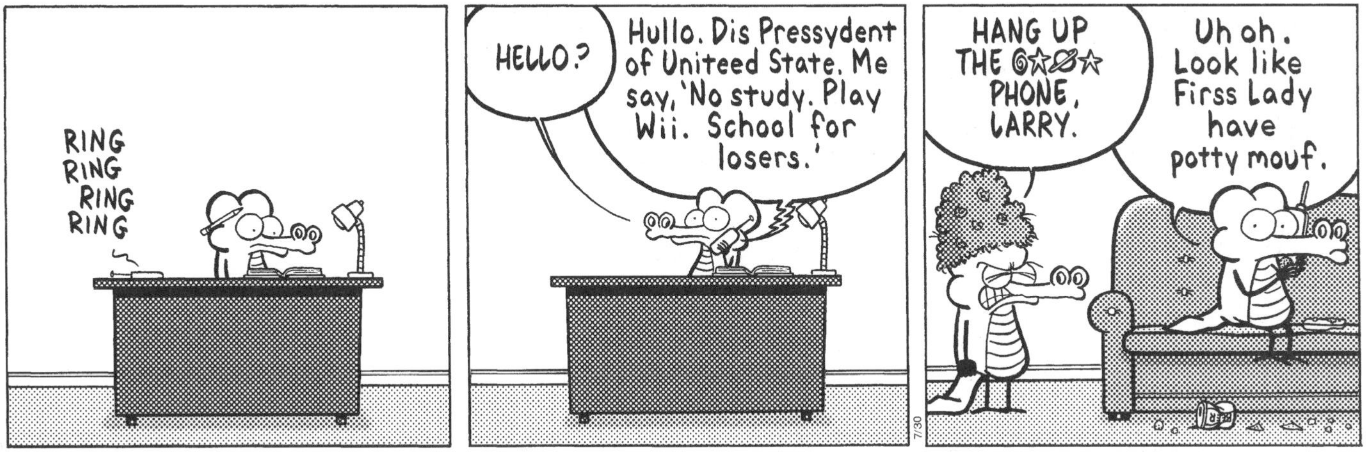
RING RING RING RING
HELLO?
Hullo. Dis Pressydent of Uniteed State. Me say, 'No study. Play Wii. School for losers.'
HANG UP THE @☆@☆ PHONE, LARRY.
Uh oh. Look like Firss Lady have potty mouf.

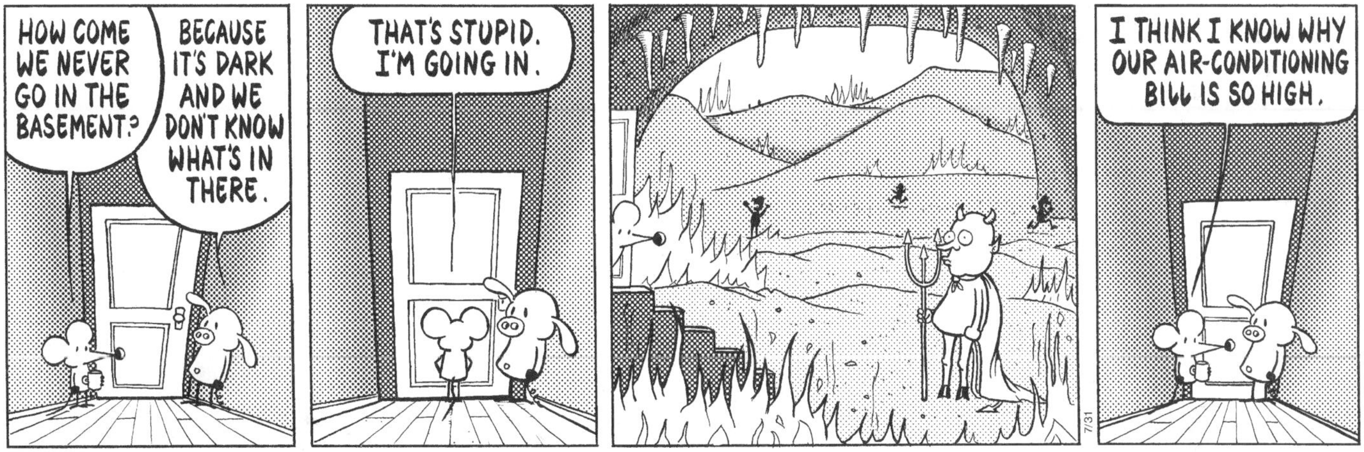
HOW COME WE NEVER GO IN THE BASEMENT?
BECAUSE IT'S DARK AND WE DON'T KNOW WHAT'S IN THERE.
THAT'S STUPID. I'M GOING IN.
I THINK I KNOW WHY OUR AIR-CONDITIONING BILL IS SO HIGH.

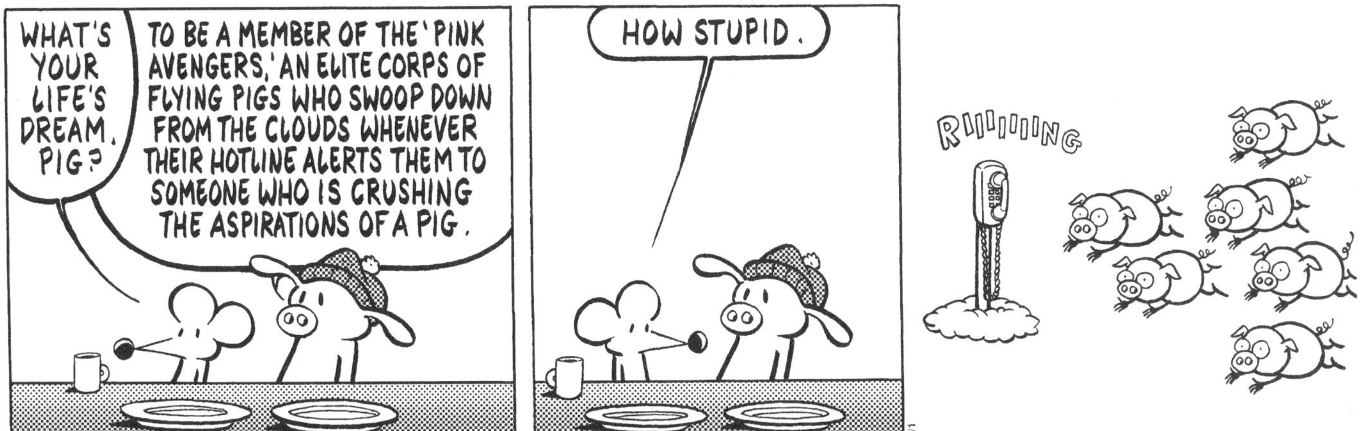
WHAT'S YOUR LIFE'S DREAM, PIG?
TO BE A MEMBER OF THE 'PINK AVENGERS,' AN ELITE CORPS OF FLYING PIGS WHO SWOOP DOWN FROM THE CLOUDS WHENEVER THEIR HOTLINE ALERTS THEM TO SOMEONE WHO IS CRUSHING THE ASPIRATIONS OF A PIG.
HOW STUPID.
RIIIIIING

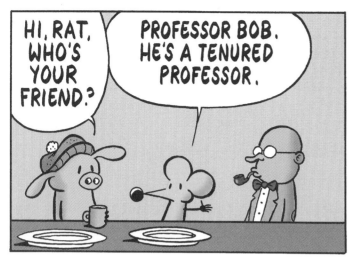

HI, RAT, WHO'S YOUR FRIEND?

PROFESSOR BOB. HE'S A TENURED PROFESSOR.

WHAT DOES TENURED MEAN?

IT MEANS HIS UNIVERSITY HAS GIVEN HIM A TEACHING POSITION FOR LIFE, SO NOW HE CAN DO PRETTY MUCH ANYTHING HE WANTS.

OH YEAH? SO WHAT DO YOU WANT TO DO, PROFESSOR BOB?

BLOW SOME ⊙☆∅# UP.

STAY ON HIS GOOD SIDE.

8/2

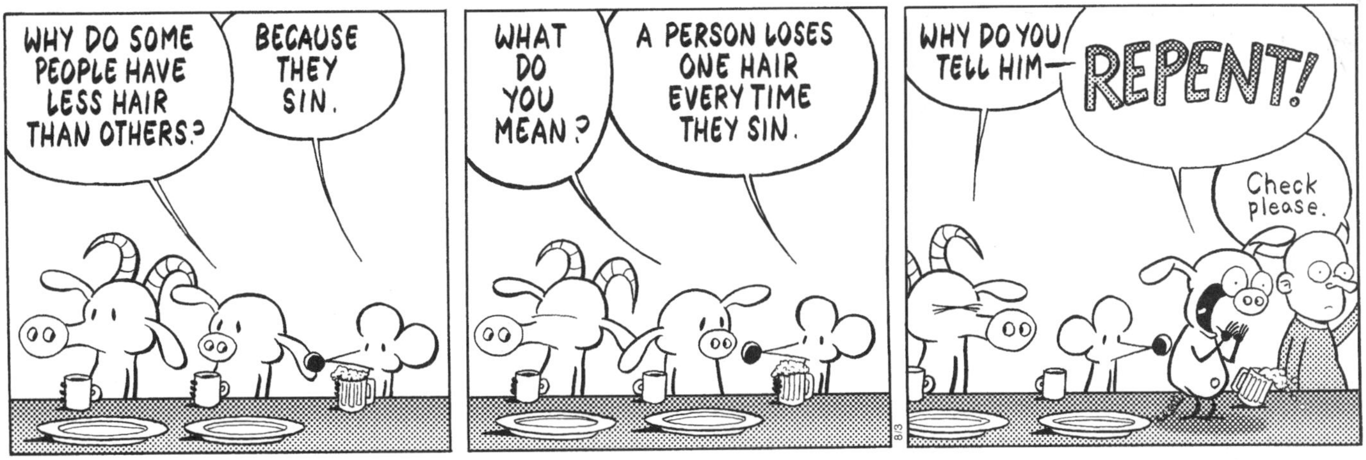
WHY DO SOME PEOPLE HAVE LESS HAIR THAN OTHERS?
BECAUSE THEY SIN.
WHAT DO YOU MEAN?
A PERSON LOSES ONE HAIR EVERY TIME THEY SIN.
8/3
WHY DO YOU TELL HIM—
REPENT!
Check please.

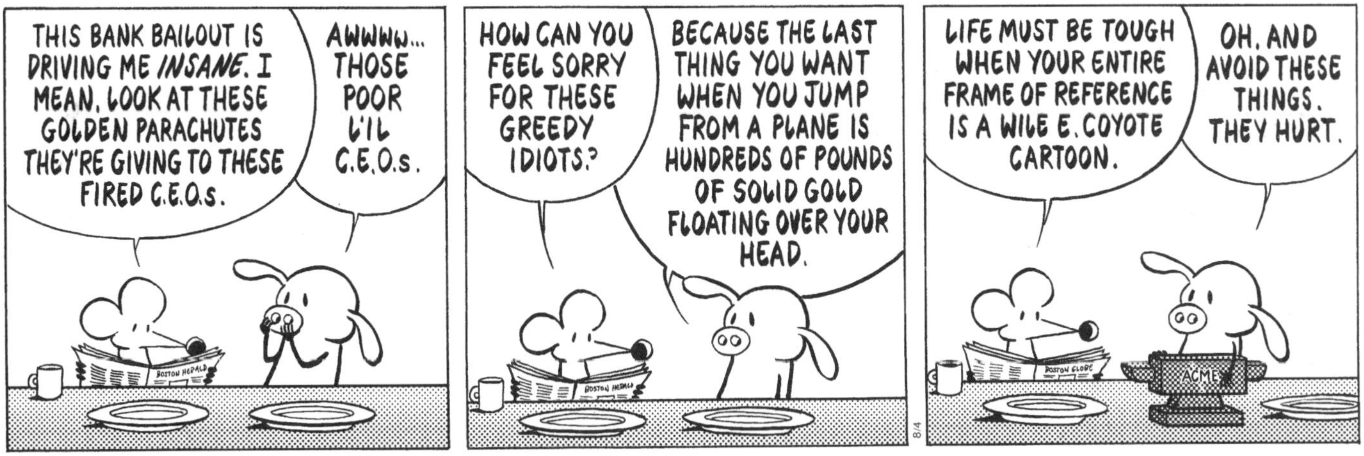
THIS BANK BAILOUT IS DRIVING ME *INSANE*. I MEAN, LOOK AT THESE GOLDEN PARACHUTES THEY'RE GIVING TO THESE FIRED C.E.O.s.
AWWWW... THOSE POOR LI'L C.E.O.s.
BOSTON HERALD
HOW CAN YOU FEEL SORRY FOR THESE GREEDY IDIOTS?
BECAUSE THE LAST THING YOU WANT WHEN YOU JUMP FROM A PLANE IS HUNDREDS OF POUNDS OF SOLID GOLD FLOATING OVER YOUR HEAD.
BOSTON HERALD
8/4
LIFE MUST BE TOUGH WHEN YOUR ENTIRE FRAME OF REFERENCE IS A WILE E. COYOTE CARTOON.
OH, AND AVOID THESE THINGS. THEY HURT.
BOSTON GLOBE
ACME

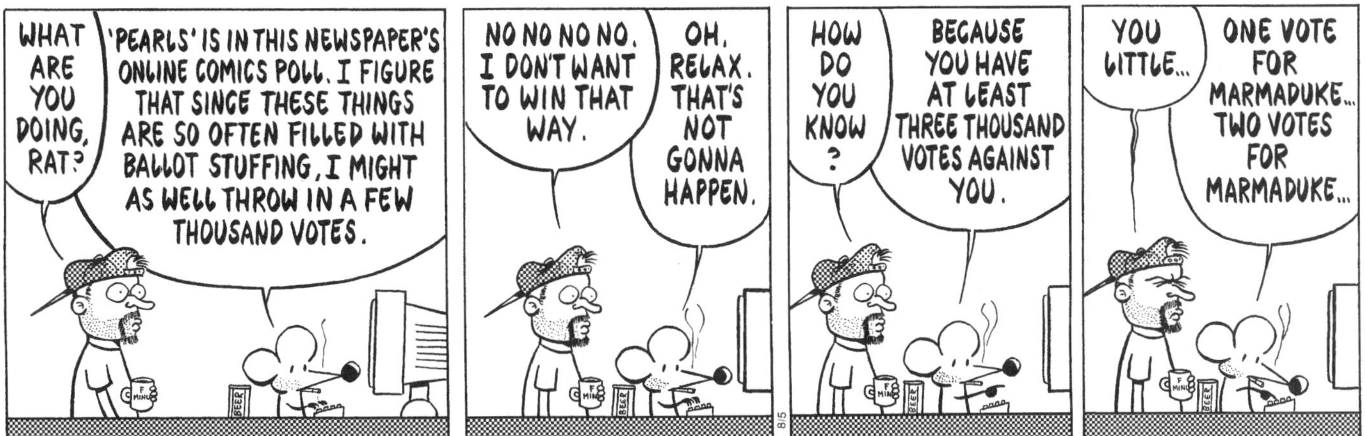
WHAT ARE YOU DOING, RAT?
'PEARLS' IS IN THIS NEWSPAPER'S ONLINE COMICS POLL. I FIGURE THAT SINCE THESE THINGS ARE SO OFTEN FILLED WITH BALLOT STUFFING, I MIGHT AS WELL THROW IN A FEW THOUSAND VOTES.
BEER
NO NO NO NO. I DON'T WANT TO WIN THAT WAY.
OH, RELAX. THAT'S NOT GONNA HAPPEN.
BEER
8/5
HOW DO YOU KNOW?
BECAUSE YOU HAVE AT LEAST THREE THOUSAND VOTES AGAINST YOU.
BEER
YOU LITTLE...
ONE VOTE FOR MARMADUKE... TWO VOTES FOR MARMADUKE...
BEER

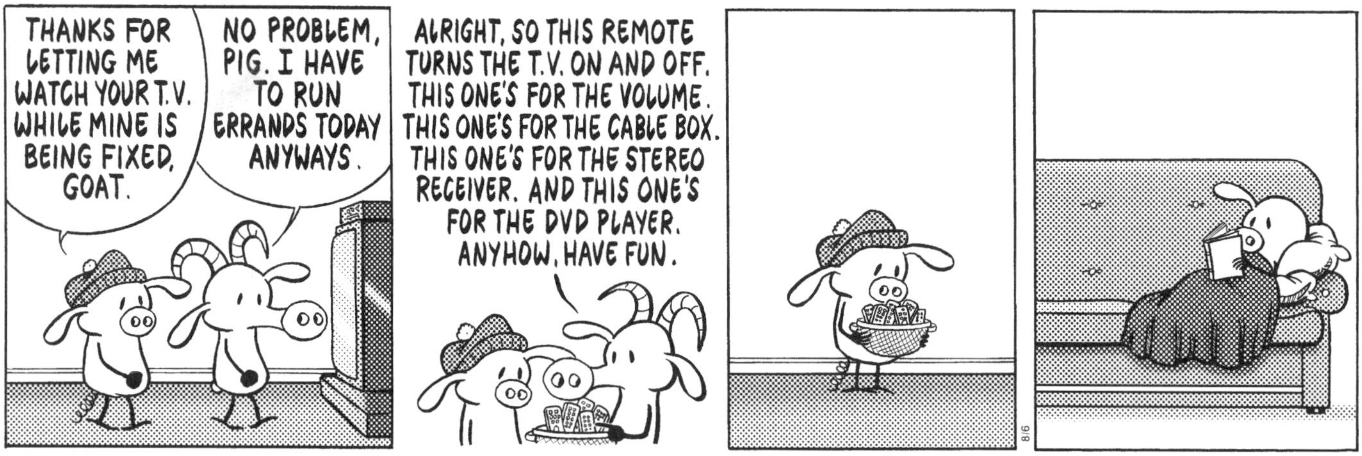
THANKS FOR LETTING ME WATCH YOUR T.V. WHILE MINE IS BEING FIXED, GOAT.
NO PROBLEM, PIG. I HAVE TO RUN ERRANDS TODAY ANYWAYS.
ALRIGHT, SO THIS REMOTE TURNS THE T.V. ON AND OFF. THIS ONE'S FOR THE VOLUME. THIS ONE'S FOR THE CABLE BOX. THIS ONE'S FOR THE STEREO RECEIVER. AND THIS ONE'S FOR THE DVD PLAYER. ANYHOW, HAVE FUN.
8/6

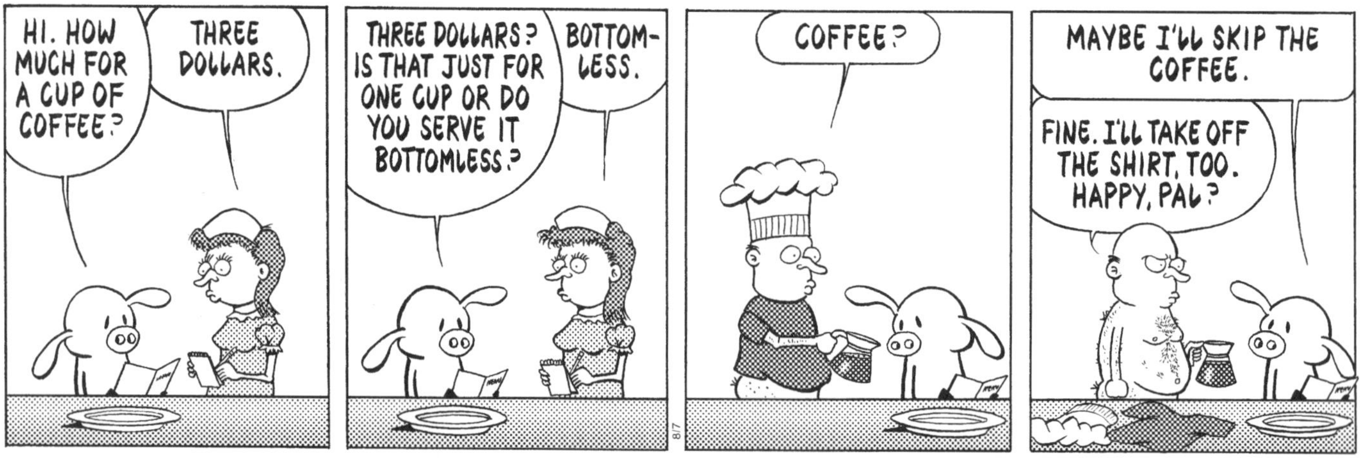
HI. HOW MUCH FOR A CUP OF COFFEE?
THREE DOLLARS.
THREE DOLLARS? IS THAT JUST FOR ONE CUP OR DO YOU SERVE IT BOTTOMLESS?
BOTTOMLESS.
8/7
COFFEE?
MAYBE I'LL SKIP THE COFFEE.
FINE. I'LL TAKE OFF THE SHIRT, TOO. HAPPY, PAL?

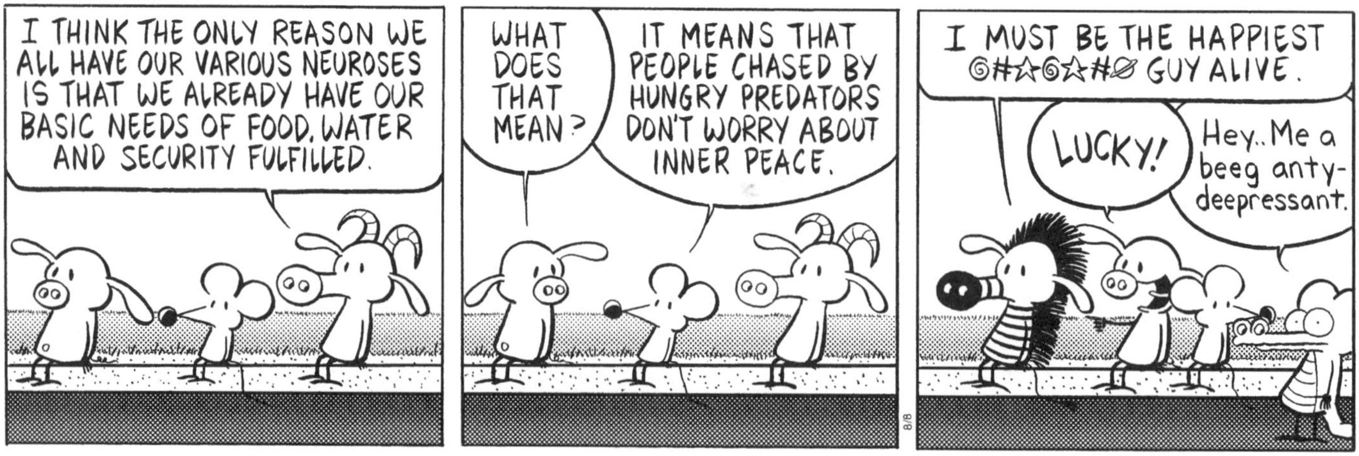
I THINK THE ONLY REASON WE ALL HAVE OUR VARIOUS NEUROSES IS THAT WE ALREADY HAVE OUR BASIC NEEDS OF FOOD, WATER AND SECURITY FULFILLED.
WHAT DOES THAT MEAN?
IT MEANS THAT PEOPLE CHASED BY HUNGRY PREDATORS DON'T WORRY ABOUT INNER PEACE.
8/8
I MUST BE THE HAPPIEST @#☆@☆#@ GUY ALIVE.
LUCKY!
Hey.. Me a beeg anty-deepressant.

Panel 1:

WHAT ARE YOU DOING, RAT?

THIS NEWSPAPER'S DOING AN ONLINE COMICS POLL... I HAVE VOTED 5,292 TIMES AGAINST 'PEARLS.'

Panel 2:

ARRRGH!! IT'S BAD ENOUGH PAPERS DO THESE BOGUS, CHEATABLE POLLS! DO YOU HAVE TO MAKE IT WORSE BY VOTING AGAINST 'PEARLS'?!

YES. I DO NOT ENJOY THE FEATURE.

Panel 3:

THEN VOTE ONCE.

BUT THAT WOULD NOT REFLECT THE DEPTH OF MY HATRED FOR YOUR WORK.

Panel 4:

OH? AND WHAT'S SO WRONG WITH IT?!

WELL, LISTEN... HERE'S SOME CONSTRUCTIVE CRITICISM...

Panel 5:

YOU ARE NOT FUNNY. YOU ARE NOT CLEVER. YOU ARE UGLY. AND YOU SMELL A LITTLE BIT.

Panel 6:

YOU ARE TO COMICS WHAT 'GIGLI' WAS TO FILM, WHAT THE 'FORD PINTO' WAS TO CARS. IF YOU WERE A 'BACKSTREET BOY,' YOU'D BE THE FAT ONE WHOSE NAME I CAN'T REMEMBER.

8/9

Panel 7:

ANYTHING ELSE?!

YES. I WOULD LIKE TO BE TRANSFERRED TO A SWEETER, MORE UPLIFTING COMIC. AT LEAST THERE, I'D HAVE GREETING CARD POTENTIAL.

Panel 8:

OH, FINE. AND YOU THINK YOU'D FIT IN THERE?

OF COURSE I'D FIT IN. WHY WOULDN'T I FIT IN?

Panel 9:

THERE'S NO DRINKING IN ZIGGY.

WHAT THE ⊙☆#☆, ZIG?

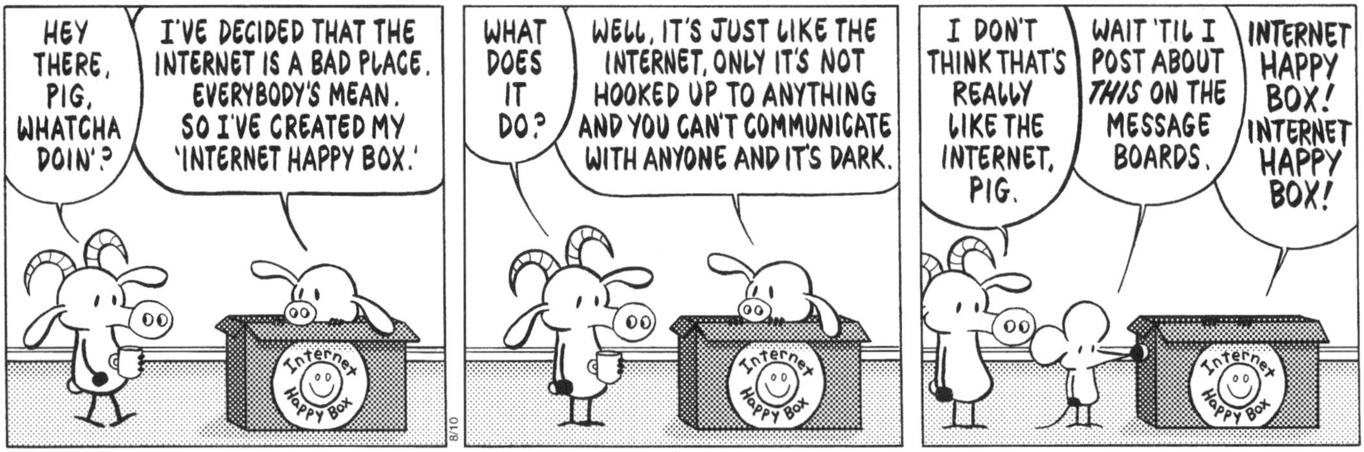
HEY THERE, PIG, WHATCHA DOIN'?
I'VE DECIDED THAT THE INTERNET IS A BAD PLACE. EVERYBODY'S MEAN. SO I'VE CREATED MY 'INTERNET HAPPY BOX.'
Internet Happy Box
8/10
WHAT DOES IT DO?
WELL, IT'S JUST LIKE THE INTERNET, ONLY IT'S NOT HOOKED UP TO ANYTHING AND YOU CAN'T COMMUNICATE WITH ANYONE AND IT'S DARK.
Internet Happy Box
I DON'T THINK THAT'S REALLY LIKE THE INTERNET, PIG.
WAIT 'TIL I POST ABOUT *THIS* ON THE MESSAGE BOARDS.
INTERNET HAPPY BOX! INTERNET HAPPY BOX!
Internet Happy Box

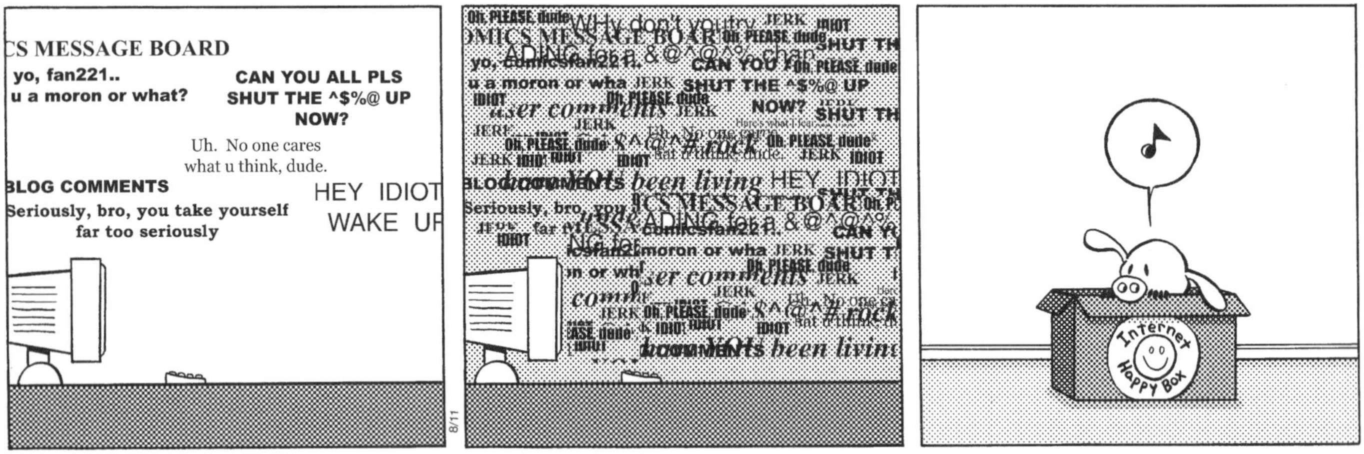
CS MESSAGE BOARD
yo, fan221..
u a moron or what?
CAN YOU ALL PLS SHUT THE ^$%@ UP NOW?
Uh. No one cares what u think, dude.
BLOG COMMENTS
Seriously, bro, you take yourself far too seriously
HEY IDIOT
WAKE UP
8/11
Internet Happy Box

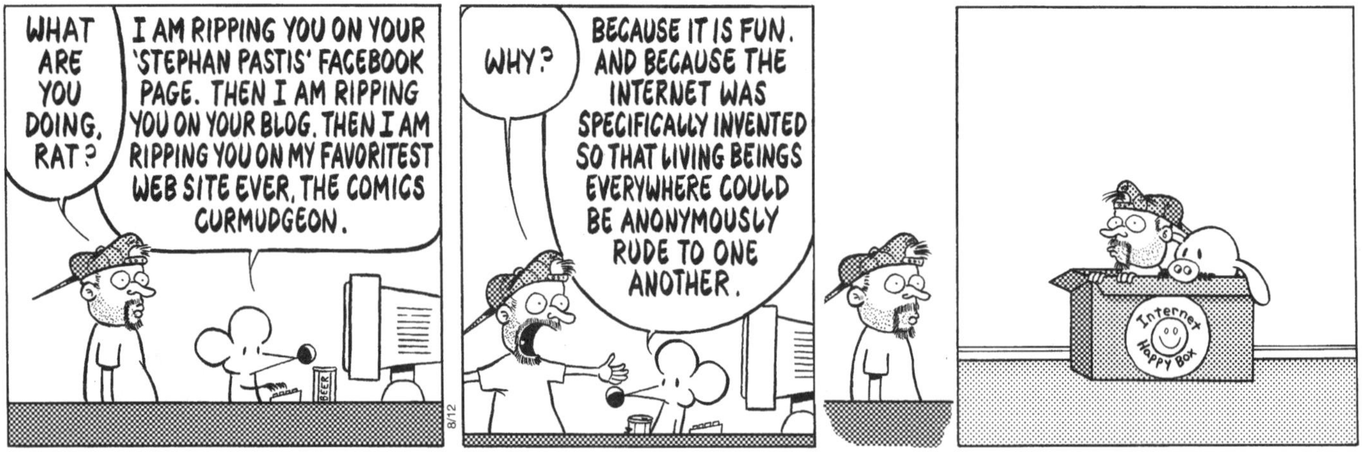
WHAT ARE YOU DOING, RAT?
I AM RIPPING YOU ON YOUR 'STEPHAN PASTIS' FACEBOOK PAGE. THEN I AM RIPPING YOU ON YOUR BLOG. THEN I AM RIPPING YOU ON MY FAVORITEST WEB SITE EVER, THE COMICS CURMUDGEON.
BEER
8/12
WHY?
BECAUSE IT IS FUN. AND BECAUSE THE INTERNET WAS SPECIFICALLY INVENTED SO THAT LIVING BEINGS EVERYWHERE COULD BE ANONYMOUSLY RUDE TO ONE ANOTHER.
Internet Happy Box

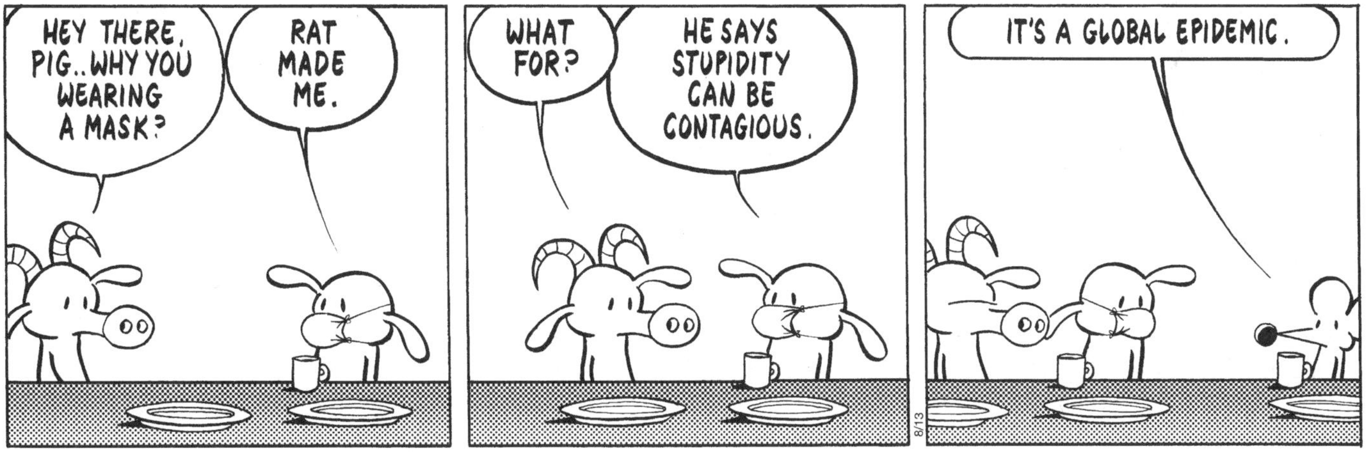
HEY THERE, PIG..WHY YOU WEARING A MASK?
RAT MADE ME.
WHAT FOR?
HE SAYS STUPIDITY CAN BE CONTAGIOUS.
IT'S A GLOBAL EPIDEMIC.
8/13

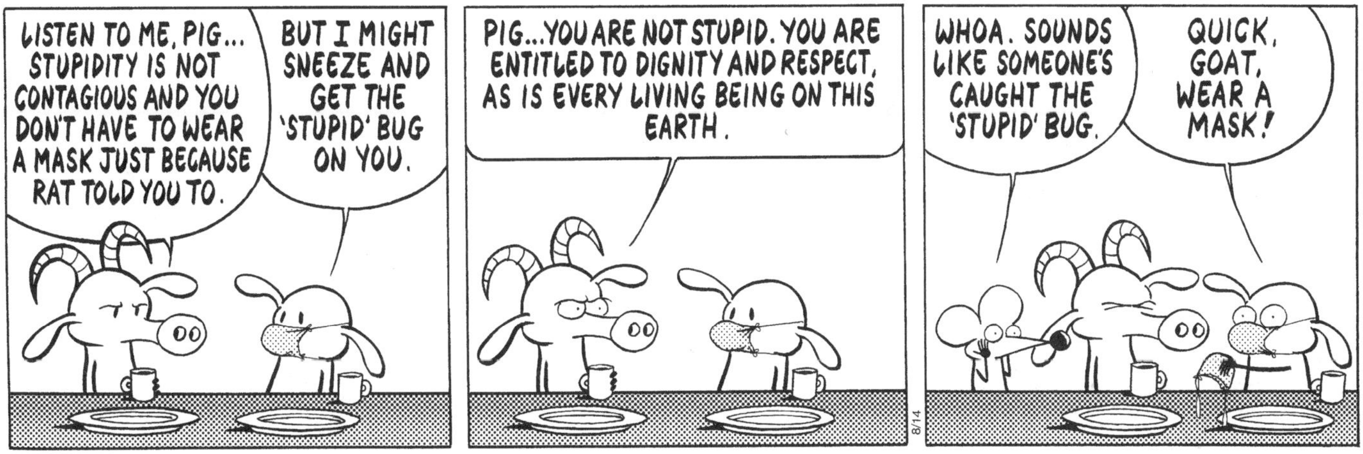
LISTEN TO ME, PIG... STUPIDITY IS NOT CONTAGIOUS AND YOU DON'T HAVE TO WEAR A MASK JUST BECAUSE RAT TOLD YOU TO.
BUT I MIGHT SNEEZE AND GET THE 'STUPID' BUG ON YOU.
PIG...YOU ARE NOT STUPID. YOU ARE ENTITLED TO DIGNITY AND RESPECT, AS IS EVERY LIVING BEING ON THIS EARTH.
WHOA. SOUNDS LIKE SOMEONE'S CAUGHT THE 'STUPID' BUG.
QUICK, GOAT, WEAR A MASK!
8/14

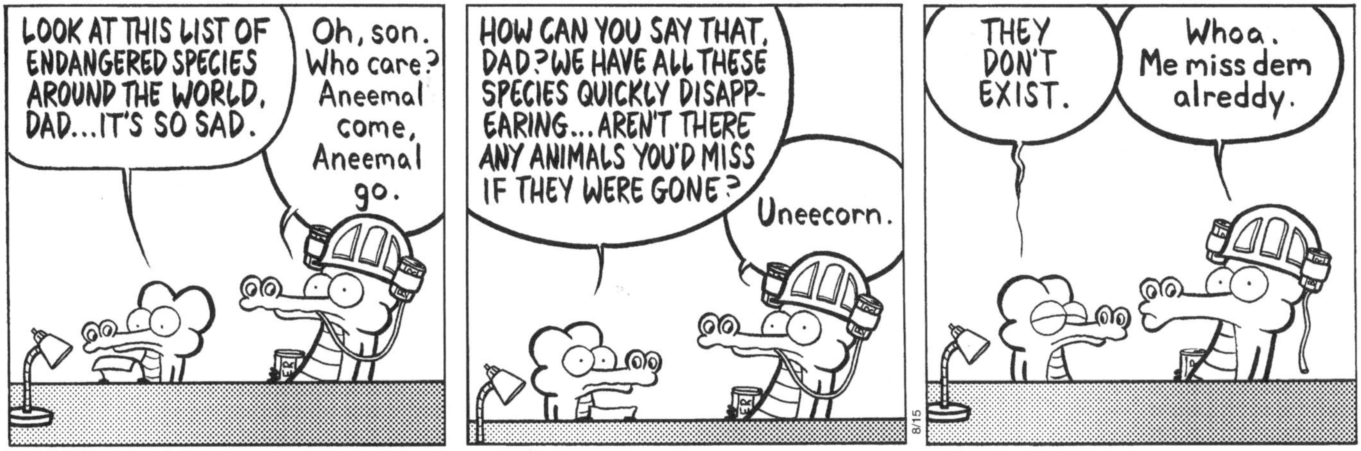
LOOK AT THIS LIST OF ENDANGERED SPECIES AROUND THE WORLD, DAD...IT'S SO SAD.
Oh, son. Who care? Aneemal come, Aneemal go.
HOW CAN YOU SAY THAT, DAD? WE HAVE ALL THESE SPECIES QUICKLY DISAPP-EARING... AREN'T THERE ANY ANIMALS YOU'D MISS IF THEY WERE GONE?
Uneecorn.
THEY DON'T EXIST.
Whoa. Me miss dem alreddy.
8/15

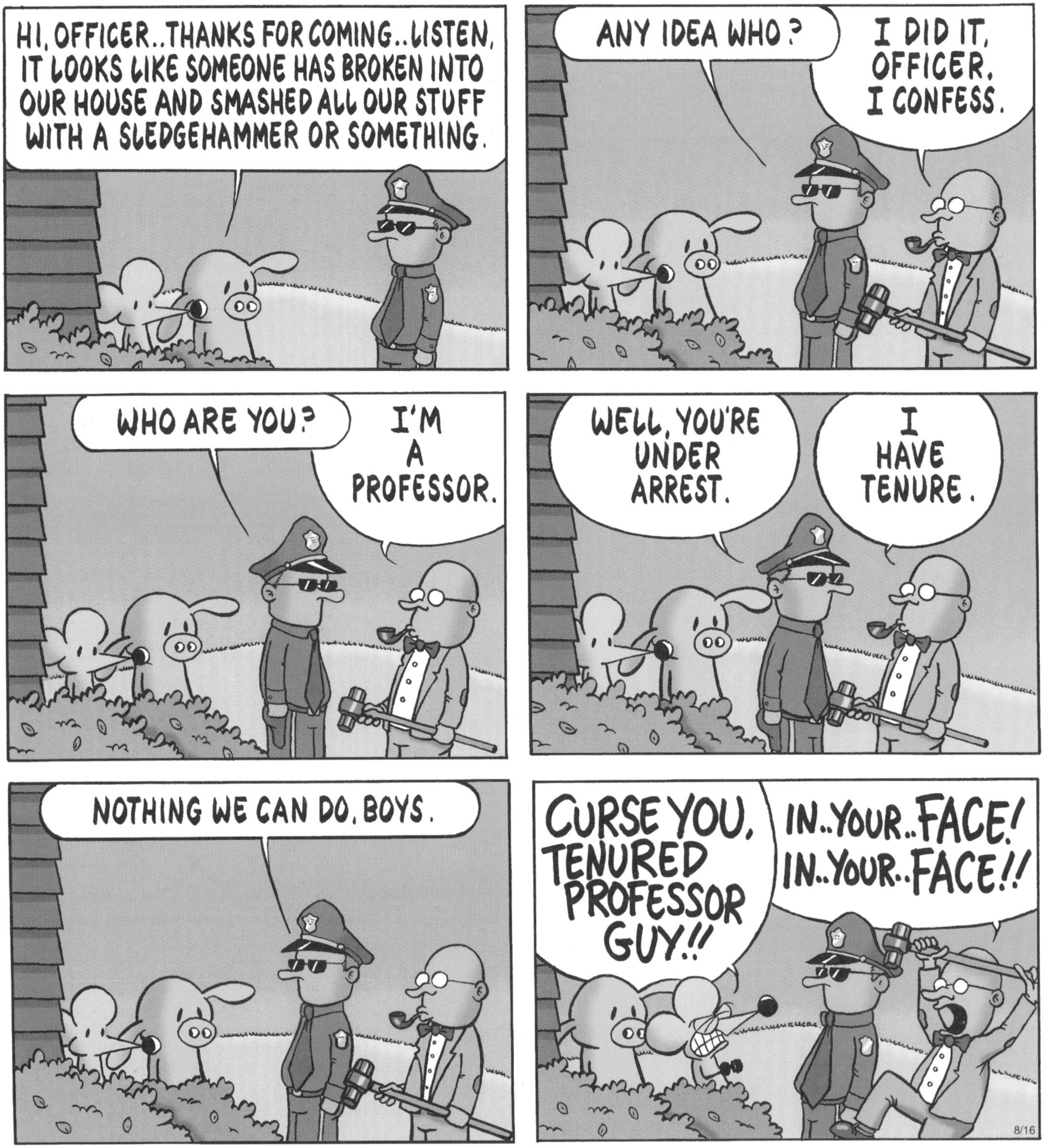
HI, OFFICER..THANKS FOR COMING..LISTEN, IT LOOKS LIKE SOMEONE HAS BROKEN INTO OUR HOUSE AND SMASHED ALL OUR STUFF WITH A SLEDGEHAMMER OR SOMETHING.
ANY IDEA WHO?
I DID IT, OFFICER. I CONFESS.
WHO ARE YOU?
I'M A PROFESSOR.
WELL, YOU'RE UNDER ARREST.
I HAVE TENURE.
NOTHING WE CAN DO, BOYS.
CURSE YOU, TENURED PROFESSOR GUY!!
IN..YOUR..FACE! IN..YOUR..FACE!!
8/16

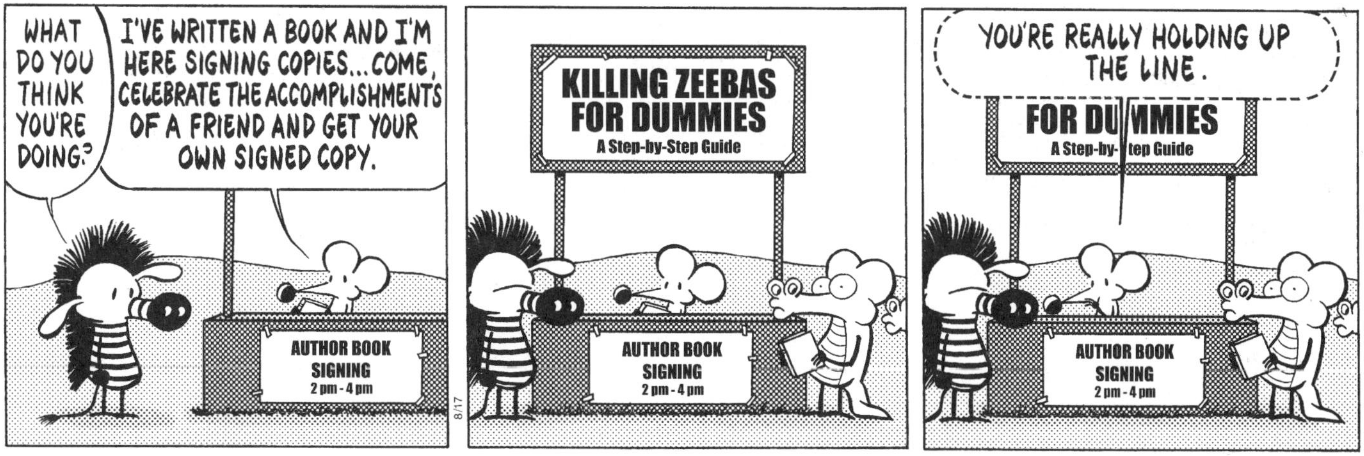
WHAT DO YOU THINK YOU'RE DOING?
I'VE WRITTEN A BOOK AND I'M HERE SIGNING COPIES... COME, CELEBRATE THE ACCOMPLISHMENTS OF A FRIEND AND GET YOUR OWN SIGNED COPY.
AUTHOR BOOK SIGNING 2 pm - 4 pm
8/17
KILLING ZEEBAS FOR DUMMIES
A Step-by-Step Guide
AUTHOR BOOK SIGNING 2 pm - 4 pm
YOU'RE REALLY HOLDING UP THE LINE.
FOR DU MMIES
A Step-by- tep Guide
AUTHOR BOOK SIGNING 2 pm - 4 pm

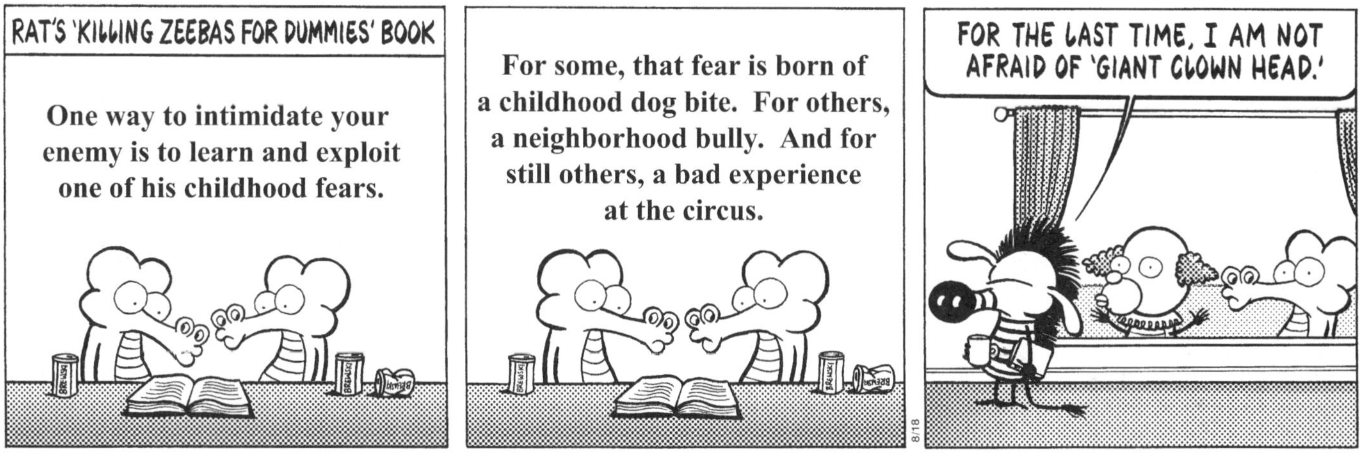
RAT'S 'KILLING ZEEBAS FOR DUMMIES' BOOK
One way to intimidate your enemy is to learn and exploit one of his childhood fears.
For some, that fear is born of a childhood dog bite. For others, a neighborhood bully. And for still others, a bad experience at the circus.
8/18
FOR THE LAST TIME, I AM NOT AFRAID OF 'GIANT CLOWN HEAD.'

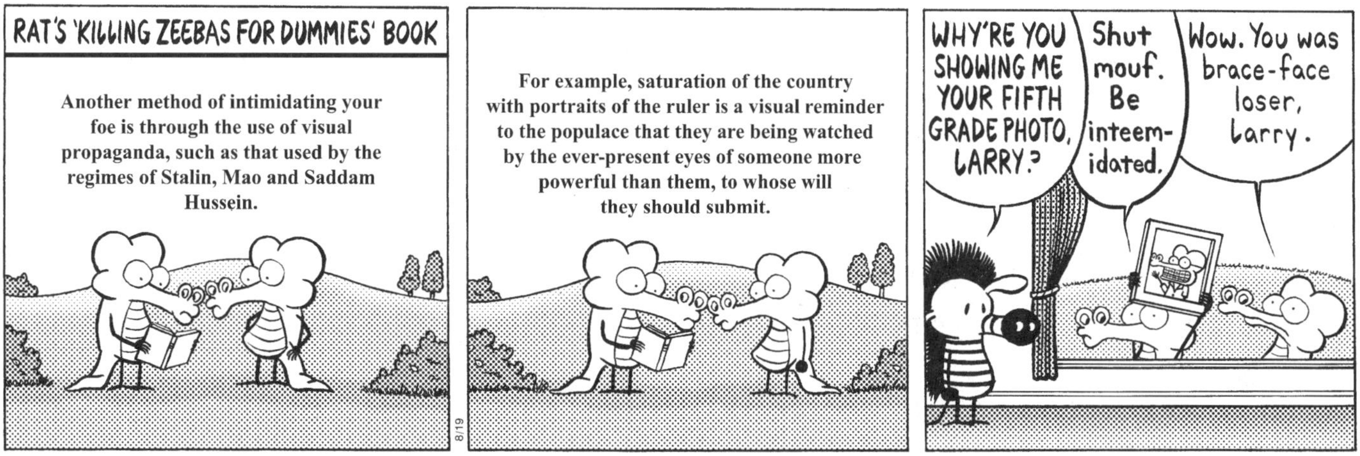
RAT'S 'KILLING ZEEBAS FOR DUMMIES' BOOK
Another method of intimidating your foe is through the use of visual propaganda, such as that used by the regimes of Stalin, Mao and Saddam Hussein.
8/19
For example, saturation of the country with portraits of the ruler is a visual reminder to the populace that they are being watched by the ever-present eyes of someone more powerful than them, to whose will they should submit.
WHY'RE YOU SHOWING ME YOUR FIFTH GRADE PHOTO, LARRY?
Shut mouf. Be inteem-idated.
Wow. You was brace-face loser, Larry.

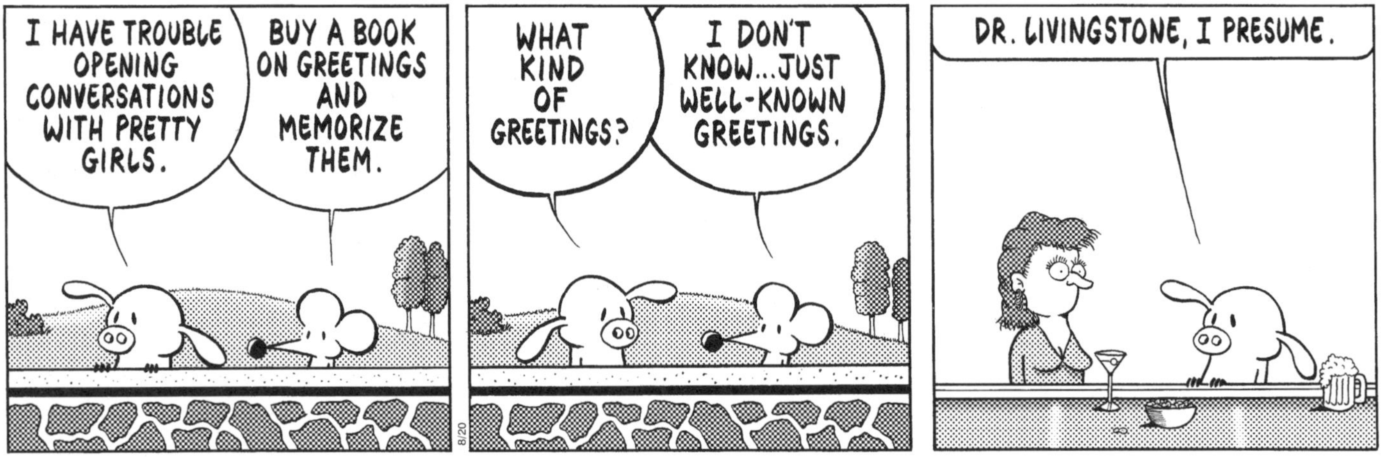
I HAVE TROUBLE OPENING CONVERSATIONS WITH PRETTY GIRLS.
BUY A BOOK ON GREETINGS AND MEMORIZE THEM.
WHAT KIND OF GREETINGS?
I DON'T KNOW...JUST WELL-KNOWN GREETINGS.
DR. LIVINGSTONE, I PRESUME.

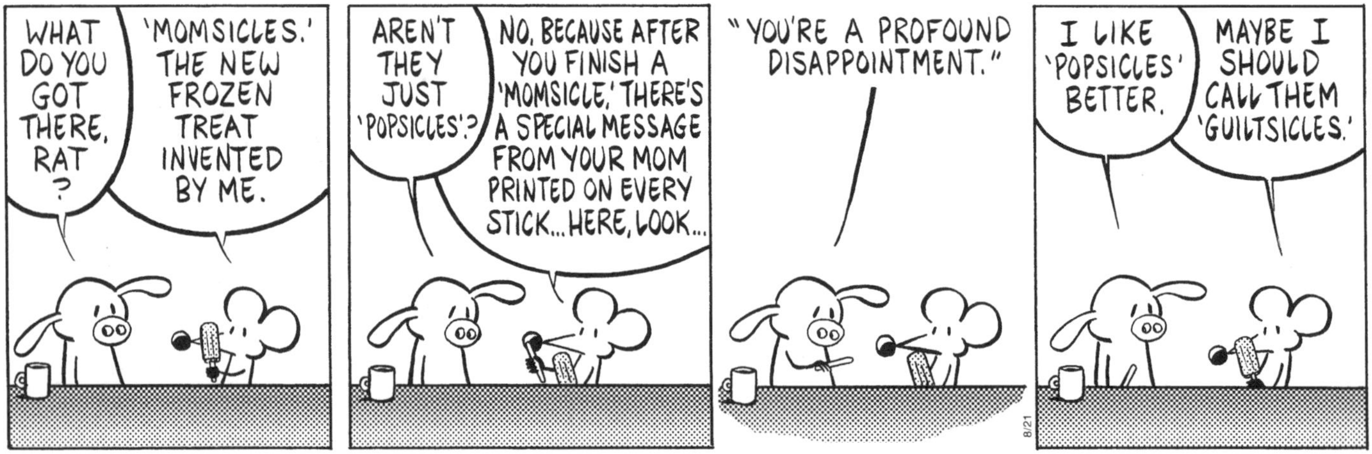
WHAT DO YOU GOT THERE, RAT?
'MOMSICLES.' THE NEW FROZEN TREAT INVENTED BY ME.
AREN'T THEY JUST 'POPSICLES'?
NO, BECAUSE AFTER YOU FINISH A 'MOMSICLE,' THERE'S A SPECIAL MESSAGE FROM YOUR MOM PRINTED ON EVERY STICK...HERE, LOOK...
"YOU'RE A PROFOUND DISAPPOINTMENT."
I LIKE 'POPSICLES' BETTER.
MAYBE I SHOULD CALL THEM 'GUILTSICLES.'

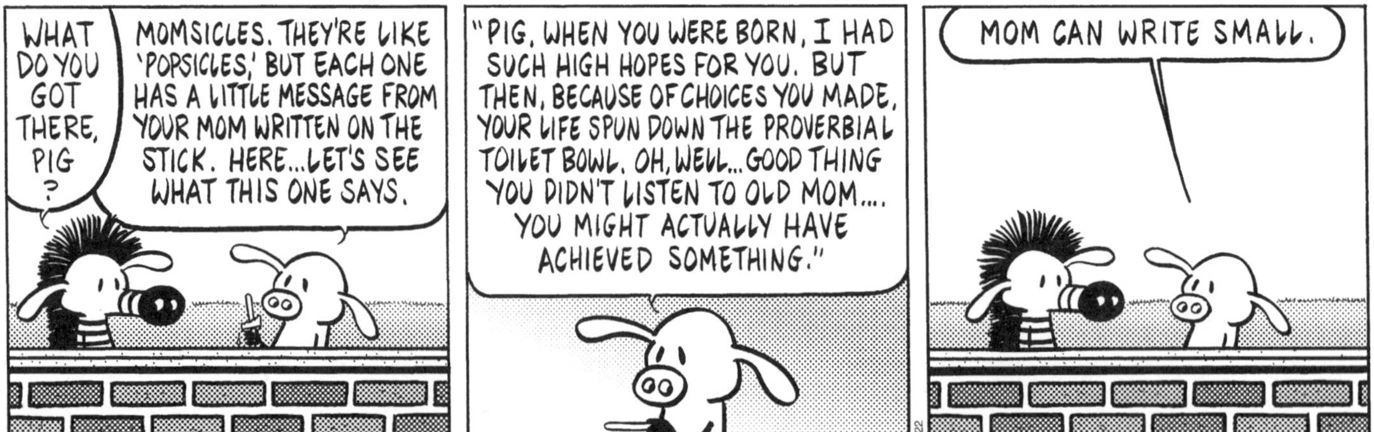
WHAT DO YOU GOT THERE, PIG?
MOMSICLES. THEY'RE LIKE 'POPSICLES,' BUT EACH ONE HAS A LITTLE MESSAGE FROM YOUR MOM WRITTEN ON THE STICK. HERE...LET'S SEE WHAT THIS ONE SAYS.
"PIG, WHEN YOU WERE BORN, I HAD SUCH HIGH HOPES FOR YOU. BUT THEN, BECAUSE OF CHOICES YOU MADE, YOUR LIFE SPUN DOWN THE PROVERBIAL TOILET BOWL. OH, WELL...GOOD THING YOU DIDN'T LISTEN TO OLD MOM.... YOU MIGHT ACTUALLY HAVE ACHIEVED SOMETHING."
MOM CAN WRITE SMALL.

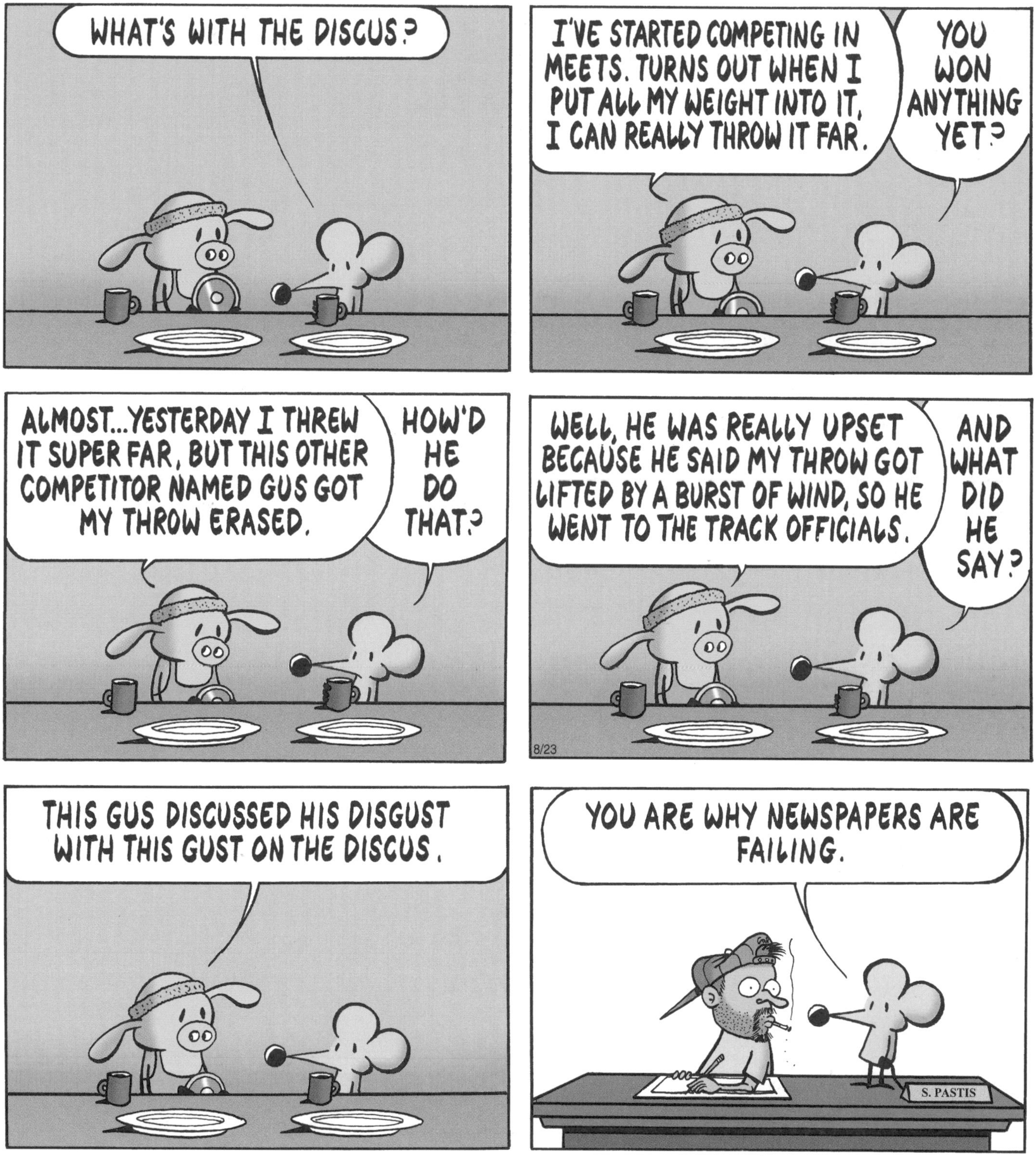
WHAT'S WITH THE DISCUS?
I'VE STARTED COMPETING IN MEETS. TURNS OUT WHEN I PUT ALL MY WEIGHT INTO IT, I CAN REALLY THROW IT FAR.
YOU WON ANYTHING YET?
ALMOST... YESTERDAY I THREW IT SUPER FAR, BUT THIS OTHER COMPETITOR NAMED GUS GOT MY THROW ERASED.
HOW'D HE DO THAT?
WELL, HE WAS REALLY UPSET BECAUSE HE SAID MY THROW GOT LIFTED BY A BURST OF WIND, SO HE WENT TO THE TRACK OFFICIALS.
AND WHAT DID HE SAY?
8/23
THIS GUS DISCUSSED HIS DISGUST WITH THIS GUST ON THE DISCUS.
YOU ARE WHY NEWSPAPERS ARE FAILING.
S. PASTIS

The Unseen *Pearls*

Pearls began running as an Internet-only strip on United Media's Web site comics.com in November 2000, and it remained as an Internet-only strip until it launched in newspapers in January 2002. I'm often asked by fans where these Internet-only strips can be seen, but the truth is you've already seen almost all of them.

The reason for this is that when *Pearls* started running in newspapers, I simply took the ones I had run online and reran them. However, I didn't rerun *all* of them. Why? Because some of them really, really sucked.

Really.

Recently, I found some of these unpublished strips in a filing cabinet in my house. Sadly, time has not improved them. The characters look terrible. Their personalities are inconsistent. And many of the jokes put the "U" in "unfunny."

However, in the interest of presenting the "Complete *Pearls*" (not to mention publicly humiliating myself), I've decided to run these strips in the books. If and when I find more, I'll publish them. But for now, here are eleven of them.

...AND SO THE PASTOR'S GETTING TO THE GOOD PART OF THE SERMON AND BEEP, BEEP, BEEP, HIS CELL PHONE RINGS.....
...SO HE ANSWERS IT AND YELLS, "I DON'T CARE WHAT BLEEPING ROAD YOU'RE STRANDED ON...I'M IN THE MIDDLE OF A BLEEPITY BLEEP SERMON!"
WHAT HAPPENED THEN?
HE FINISHED THE STORY OF THE GOOD SAMARITAN AND WE ALL WENT HOME.

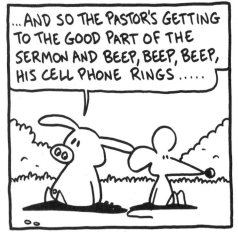

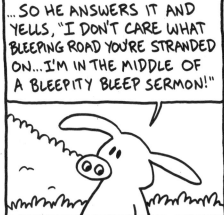

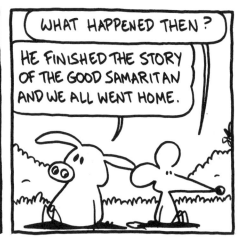

Wow, how different the characters once were. Pig seems too observant and wise. Rat is too placid. And man, they look so odd. Pig's ears are gigantic. Rat's nose is huuuuuuuge. In short, a total mess. I knew there was a reason I didn't run this.

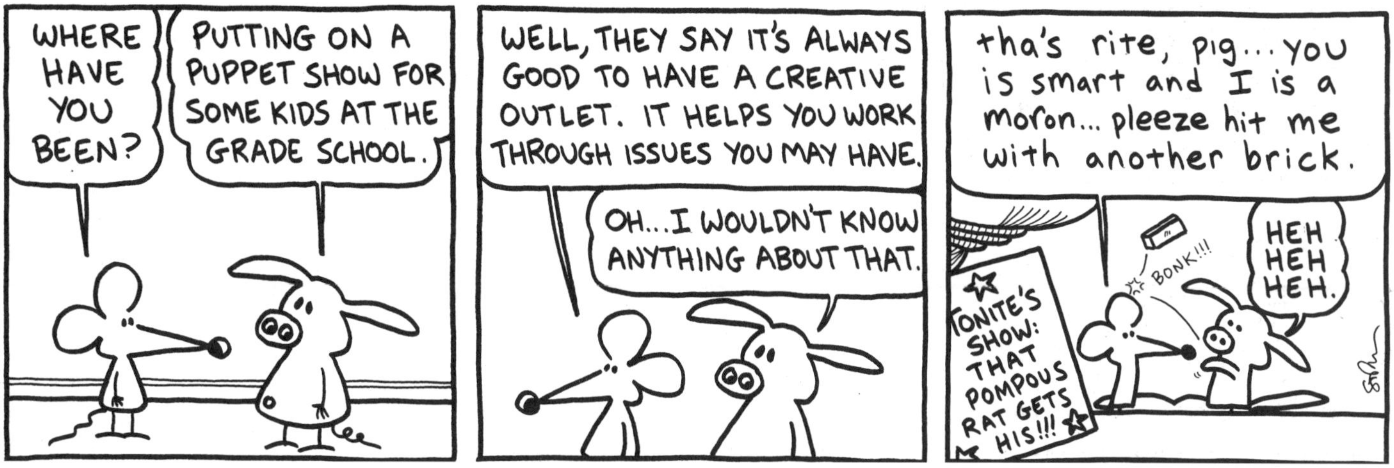
WHERE HAVE YOU BEEN?
PUTTING ON A PUPPET SHOW FOR SOME KIDS AT THE GRADE SCHOOL.
WELL, THEY SAY IT'S ALWAYS GOOD TO HAVE A CREATIVE OUTLET. IT HELPS YOU WORK THROUGH ISSUES YOU MAY HAVE.
OH...I WOULDN'T KNOW ANYTHING ABOUT THAT.
tha's rite, pig... you is smart and I is a moron... pleeze hit me with another brick.
TONITE'S SHOW: THAT POMPOUS RAT GETS HIS!!!
BONK!!!
HEH HEH HEH.

This would now be totally out of character for Pig because it shows him harboring a secret resentment toward Rat. It also shows him as deceitful (he lies to Rat in the second panel) and violent (hitting Rat with a brick in the last panel). It goes to show that in the beginning of a strip, you're still learning your own characters.

DO YOU HAVE ANY DINOSAURS?
THERE ARE NO MORE DINOSAURS.
ZOO
WHERE'D THEY GO?
THEY DIED.
ZOO
I GOTTA START READING THE PAPER.

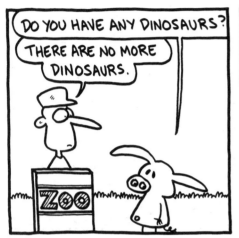

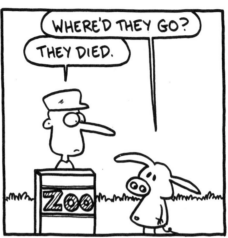

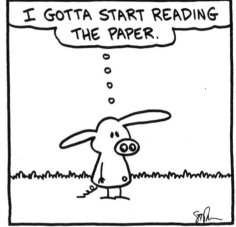

If you look at the third panel, you'll notice that I used to sign my strips. I stopped doing that early on in *Pearls*. The strip is already so sparse that anything extraneous (even a signature) looks unnecessarily obtrusive to me. Also, I never understood the point of signing a strip. In most newspapers, my name appears on the byline above the strip, so that would tell a person who created it. But if it doesn't, my signature is virtually unreadable, so it still wouldn't help.

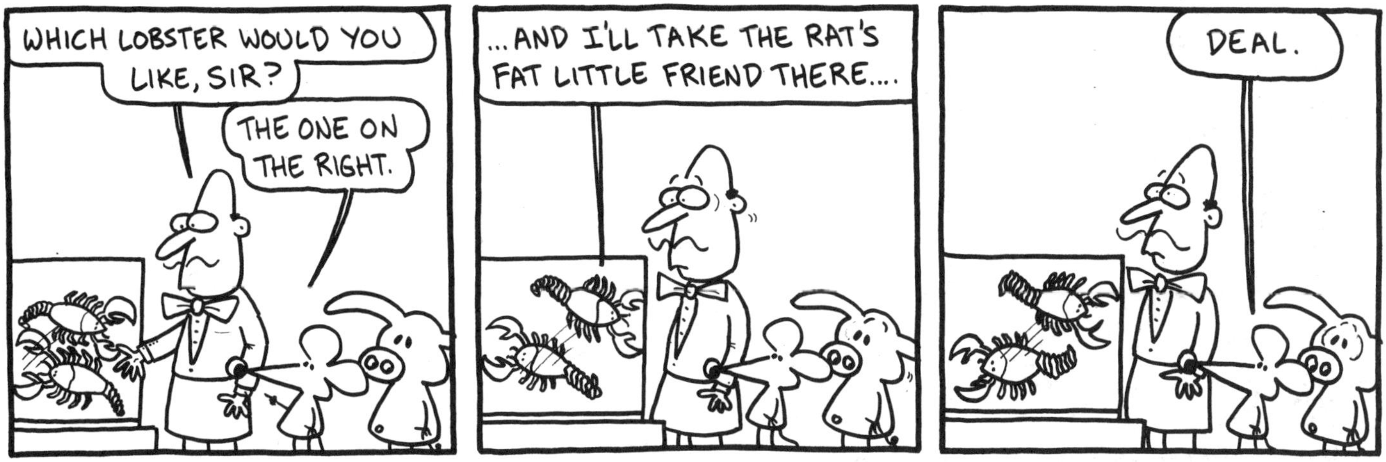
WHICH LOBSTER WOULD YOU LIKE, SIR?
THE ONE ON THE RIGHT.
...AND I'LL TAKE THE RAT'S FAT LITTLE FRIEND THERE....
DEAL.

I have to say, I kinda like this one. I'm not sure why I didn't run it in newspapers.

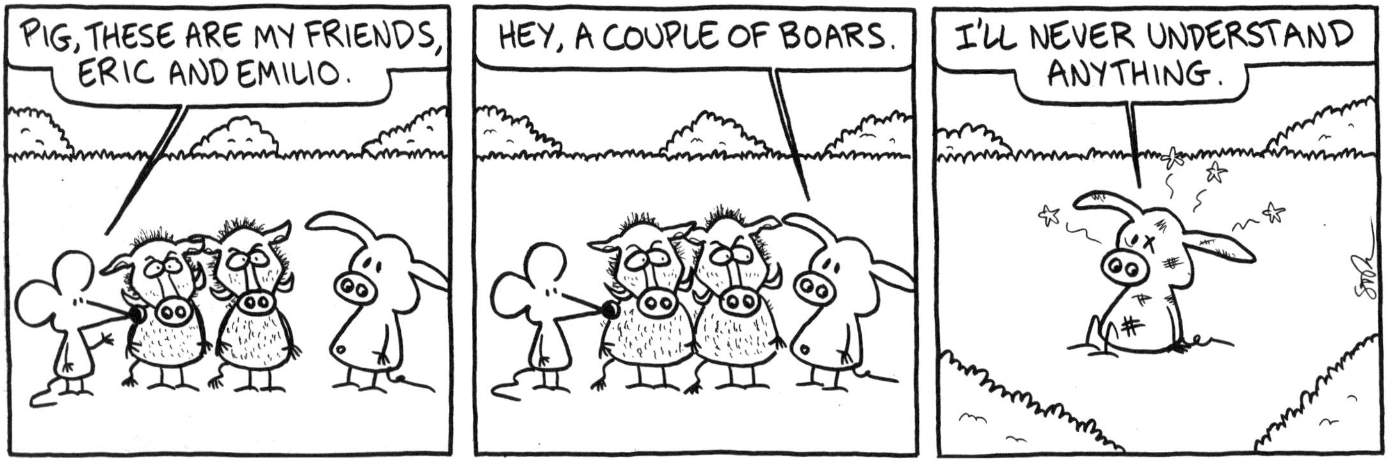
PIG, THESE ARE MY FRIENDS, ERIC AND EMILIO.
HEY, A COUPLE OF BOARS.
I'LL NEVER UNDERSTAND ANYTHING.

I named these guys after my friends Eric and Emilio, but holy smokes, the drawing is so ridiculously bad I feel like I should hide in a hole somewhere. Please don't share this strip with friends. Just glance at it once and walk away.

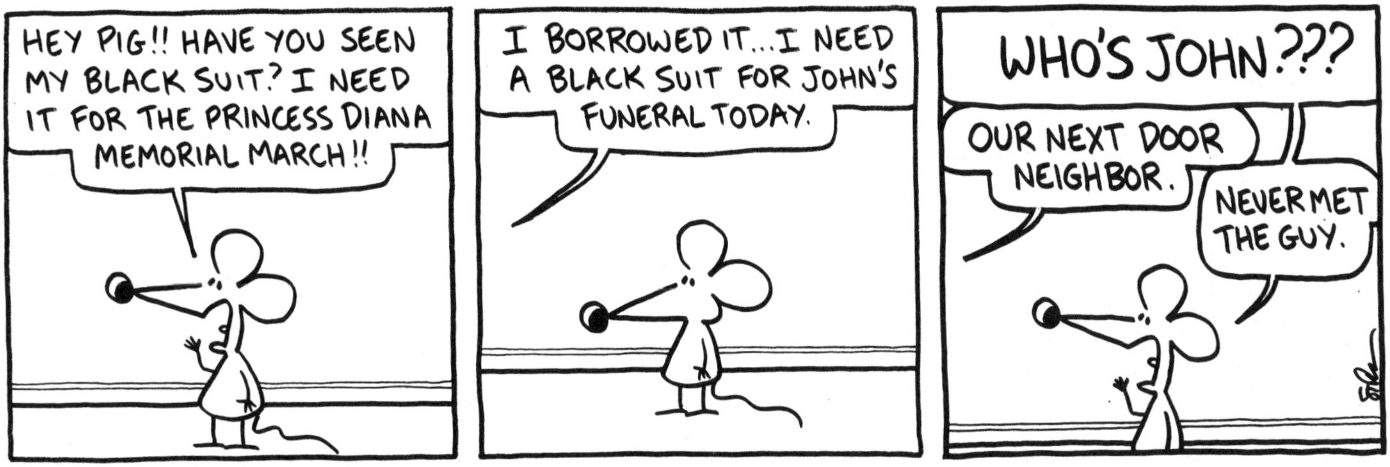
HEY PIG!! HAVE YOU SEEN MY BLACK SUIT? I NEED IT FOR THE PRINCESS DIANA MEMORIAL MARCH!!
I BORROWED IT... I NEED A BLACK SUIT FOR JOHN'S FUNERAL TODAY.
WHO'S JOHN???
OUR NEXT DOOR NEIGHBOR.
NEVER MET THE GUY.

It's hard to imagine a more out-of-character strip for Rat. If anything, he would now ridicule such a gathering. But again, in the beginning, you don't always know your own characters.

MY ZEBRA HERD IS DRESSING UP OTHER SPECIES AS ZEBRAS AND SEEING WHAT THE LIONS DO.
WHY?
WE WANT TO SEE IF THERE'S SOMETHING ABOUT A ZEBRA'S APPEARANCE THAT MAKES HIM MORE LIKELY TO BE EATEN.
WHO'D VOLUNTEER FOR THAT?
SO YOU'RE THE GUINEA PIG?
NO. JUST A PIG PIG.

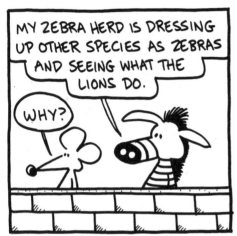

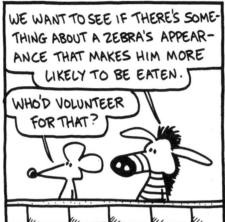

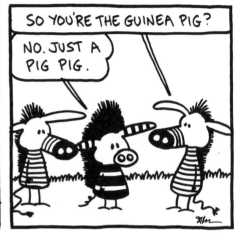

It's interesting for me to look back at strips like these and see how different the strip was in the beginning. The panel lines were crudely hand drawn (as opposed to lined with a ruler nowadays), the lettering had a notable slant, and the characters had a wildly different look. On the other hand, I suppose there is a little "garage band" charm to almost any cartoonist's early stuff.

RAT TOOK MY BROTHER BOB TO SEE THE KILLER WHALE SHOW AT "OCEAN WORLD" TODAY.
HOW'D IT GO?
NOT GOOD... BOB VOLUNTEERED TO BE THE GUY THAT KISSES THE WHALE ON THE NOSE.
WHAT'S WRONG WITH THAT?
IS HE SUPPOSED TO SWALLOW HIM WHOLE LIKE THAT?
BAD SHABOO.

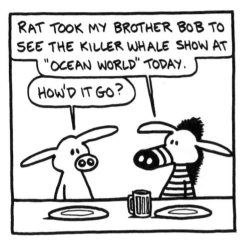

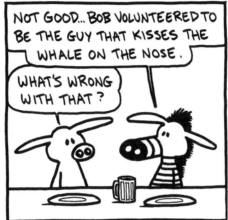

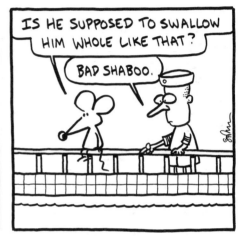

All right, this was a funny strip. Too bad Pig's head looks like an airplane propeller.

I'M SORRY ABOUT YOUR BROTHER.
YEAH...RAT INSISTED ON TAKING HIM TO "OCEAN WORLD"...AND THAT WHALE JUST SWALLOWED HIM WHOLE....
WELL, IF IT'S ANY CONSOLATION, I'M SURE RAT FEELS TERRIBLE ABOUT IT.....
YEAH, HE PROBABLY DOES, HUH?
WITNESS THE HORROR!
WHEN WHALES GO BAD!!! ACTUAL PHOTOS!
ONLY $50.00

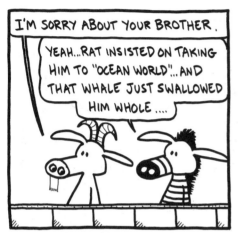

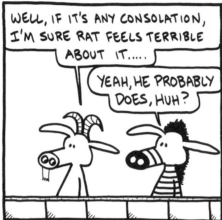

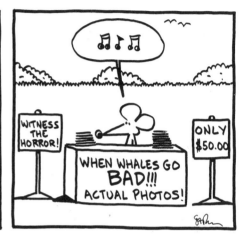

This one's pretty decent as well. Now that I look back on why I didn't run these, I think it was because there was some fear of doing too many series when the strip first started. The reason for the fear was that when a strip first starts out in newspapers, it's in a pretty precarious position (i.e., always on the verge of being cancelled by the newspaper). And a series represents a risk, because if the basic premise of the series isn't funny, that unfunniness lasts the entire duration of the series and could make a very bad first impression on new readers.

WHERE IS RAT?
HE WENT TO THE FUNERAL FOR ZEBRA'S BROTHER.
ISN'T THAT SORT OF HYPOCRITICAL?.. I MEAN, HE TRIED TO SELL PHOTOS OF THE WHALE EATING THE GUY.
MAYBE HE WANTS TO MAKE AMENDS...
WANNA BUY A PICTURE?

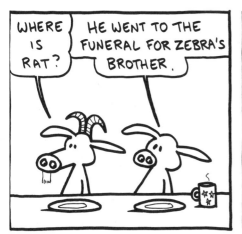

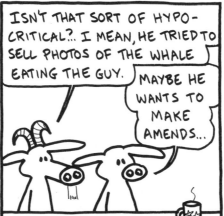

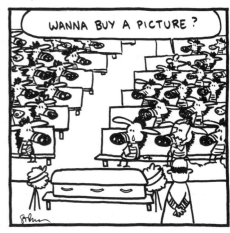

I forgot that in the very beginning of the strip, I used to put those little stars on the coffee mugs. That was gonna be my signature coffee mug. I soon abandoned that lame idea.

GOSH.... I'VE MADE TONS OF CASH SELLING PICTURES OF ZEBRA'S BROTHER GETTING EATEN BY THAT WHALE.
I'M THINKING ABOUT TOSSING ALL SORTS OF ANIMALS INTO THE WHALE TANK AND TAKING PICTURES.... Y'KNOW, SQUIRRELS AND MONKEYS AND SHEEP AND DUCKS...
I WONDER IF ANSEL ADAMS STARTED THIS WAY.

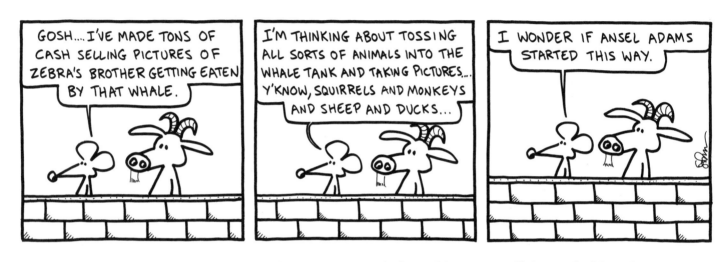

In the beginning of the strip, Goat used to have that little beard hanging off the end of his chin. Later, I got tired of the way it looked and abandoned it altogether.

That's it for the public humiliation for now. More bad strips as I find them.
(Unless I recover my good sense and burn them.)

Stephan Pastis
September 2010